COLLINS GEM DICTIONARY OF ENGLISH USAGE

Ronald G. Hardie M.A.(N.Z.), M.A.(Lond.)

HarperCollins*Publishers*

Previous Edition 1970
New Edition 1991
Latest Reprint 1992

© HarperCollins Publishers 1991
PO Box, Glasgow G4 0NB
All rights reserved.

ISBN 0 00 458772-3

British Library Cataloguing in Publication Data
Hardie, Ronald G.
  Collins gem dictionary of English usage. –2nd ed.
  1. English languages. Dictionaries
  English usage
  428.003

Editorial Staff
Managing Editor   Marian Makins
Editor   Catherine Lyons

Typeset by Ronald G. Hardie

Printed in Great Britain by
HarperCollins Manufacturing, Glasgow

Introduction

A dictionary tells us the meaning of words; a grammar tells us how words fit together in sentences; a usage helps us to choose the word or way of saying something that is most appropriate to the circumstances in which we are writing or speaking.

For example, do you say *bored of* or *bored with*? Should we use *their, there* or *they're* at this point in the sentence? Should it be *its* or *it's* just here? English is a very rich language, but this very richness is the cause of many problems. There are numbers of words that look the same, or sound the same, or are very close in their meanings. Is a particular activity *illegal* or *illicit*? Is it correct to say that you are feeling *ill* or *sick*? There are those who leap on small points of vocabulary and make much of their significance, real or imagined. Are they justified? This little book will help you find the answers to these and similar problems.

All the comments made and the judgments that are passed are supported by reference to the real sentences of skilled writers. There are hundreds of examples of correct usage drawn from modern authors. The sources of this information include citations from the Collins Birmingham University International Language Database (COBUILD), which is a computerized corpus of carefully chosen texts comprising some 20 million words of modern English from a whole range of writers. To this the author has added his own observations, collected over many years as a teacher of English language at all levels. This wealth of material is supported by the experience of the HarperCollins editorial staff and the authoritative HarperCollins English dictionaries and reference books.

What to look for when using this book

This book is arranged alphabetically. Some words have an entry to themselves, some are grouped with similar words that they are sometimes confused with. All the grammatical terms are the same as those used in the *Gem English Grammar*.

Cross references

You will notice that some entries have the sign ⇒ after them, followed by a word. This directs the reader to the main entry for a word, or, if it follows a discussion, to another entry that you might find it useful to read.

Examples and recommendations

The sentences and phrases in italic type are examples of correct educated British English usage and for the most part come from the COBUILD corpus. It has been a deliberate policy to exclude long samples of incorrect usage to avoid confusing the point. When an example of incorrect or nonstandard English is quoted, the entry is enclosed by [square brackets] to emphasize that it is unusual.

Pronunciation guide

When it is helpful to show how a word is pronounced, it is broken into syllables and a pronunciation guide based on simplified spelling is given. Slanted strokes like this /en-**cloze**/ the word, and the stressed syllable is given in bold type. The pronunciation guide may oversimplify some words and those who need a more detailed description will find one in *Collins English Dictionary* – CED.

The careful user and the purist

As language changes, the **purist** is often found attempting to stem the tide. A purist may attempt to uphold rules that in truth have no relationship to the real facts of language. It is purism, for example, to place weight on not splitting infinitives, or not ending a sentence with a preposition. A **careful user** of language is not a purist, but one who cares for nuances of expression.

Formal and informal styles

As we talk and write we consciously or unconsciously move between different styles. Aspects of usage that are acceptable in the informal speech style of everyday conversation may become less acceptable, or even totally inappropriate, in a formal situation.

Written and spoken styles

Written usage often differs from spoken usage and what may seem pompous or affected in speech may read more naturally and fluently when written down; what is easy to understand in the interrupted give and take of a conversation may be muddled and confusing when seen in writing. Many usages are labelled informal, formal, or literary, to show the style of language they are best suited to.

Slang and jargon, buzz words and vogue words

Slang is a very informal part of language. New words are invented or existing ones given new meanings in order to undermine solemn or pompous language and behaviour. *Slang* also serves as part of a private language within special groups, such as children or the army.

Buzz words are found in high profile interest groups, such as advertising, business, and computing. A *buzz word* is another type of slang; it is a word used partly as a technical term and partly as a way of saying, 'I use all the right language, I know the up-to-date way to describe this sort of situation, so I'm one of you.'

Jargon is the necessary technical language of a group of specialists. There is nothing wrong with jargon in its place among those who need to use it. It is less acceptable when specialists forget that it is not part of common language and use it in non technical situations. Because those who use *jargon* encounter it daily, it is sometimes not clear to them that it is difficult for others.

Certain human situations strike some people as 'too nasty for words'. A frequent response is to try to find a word or phrase to hide behind that does not express the full facts. This often gives rise to **genteelisms**; a *lavatory* becomes a *comfort station* and *dead* becomes *gone before*. At other times a *genteelism* may simply be a word that the user believes to be more elevated than its everyday counterpart. This is a matter of taste. To some *serviette* is a genteel word for *napkin*. We have drawn attention to those included in this book.

Language has its fashions and when words become fashionable accessories they become **vogue words**. But *vogue words* are usually soon overworked and go out of fashion. Since they are so short-lived, like almost all slang, we have not given them much attention.

R.G.H.

SUSSEX · 1991

A

a, an

A is the normal form of the indefinite article. The form
an is used before a vowel or a silent **h** (as in *an hour*). *An*
is also found before the letters of an abbreviation, since
these are usually pronounced with the sound of the letter names, e.g. *an MA* /an em eh/. In phrases like *sixty
miles an hour,* **a** or **an** means *per.*

abbreviations

There are no set rules for the way abbreviations are used.
Current practice when writing is to use a full stop after
any abbreviation that does not end with the final letter of
the word, e.g. *Co., Esq.,* and to omit the full stop when
the last letter of the abbreviation is the final letter of the
word, e.g. *Dr, Mr, Mrs, Revd,* have no full stop. The inser-
tion of a full stop in these cases is not incorrect, however,
and is still standard in American English. When an
abbreviation forms an acronym, e.g. NATO, UNO, there
is no full stop, since it is treated as a word.
⇒ **acronym** ⇒ **punctuation**

abetter, abettor

If you **abet** someone, you help them, usually to perform
a crime. That makes you an **abetter** or **abettor.** The second form is the one preferred in legal contexts.

ability, capability, capacity

The **ability** to do something is the possession of the necessary skills or means for its performance. To have the
capability for something is to have not only the necessary skills but perhaps also the will or power to do it. This

is certainly so when *capable* is used as a predicative adjective followed by *of: We sought a man capable of killing the President; Moths are capable of speeds of 50 m.p.h.*

Capacity is used, in a loose way, as a synonym for *capability*, often with the added sense of a potential ability to do something: *I've got the capacity to carry on with this for hours; Silting had reduced the capacity of the irrigation canals.* The meaning 'role' or 'position' as in *He welcomed them in his capacity as President,* is a well-established sense.

-ability, -ibility

The *-ible* and *-able* endings are used to form adjectives from transitive verbs, e.g. *love, lovable.* Many of the adjectives so formed can become abstract nouns by the addition of *-ity*, e.g. *adaptable: adaptability; credible: credibility.* The selection of the ending follows the guidelines given for *-able*.

-able, -eable, -ible

The most common ending for an adjective formed from a transitive verb and some nouns is *-able*. Normally, a word that ends in *-e*, such as *note* or *quote*, loses the *-e* before adding the suffix *-able*. If the word ends in *-ce*, *-ke*, or *-ge*, the *-e* is usually retained, e.g. *serviceable, likeable, manageable.* However, a few exist with both spellings. Unfortunately, there are no easy guidelines.

This is a list of words that commonly have an optional **-eable** spelling: *bridgeable, hateable, likeable, liveable, loveable, manageable, mistakeable, moveable, pronounceable, rateable, recycleable, saleable, saveable, sizeable, unmistakeable, useable.*

A number of words take the ending **-ible** because they

come from Latin stems. It is not easy to give simple guidance about which adjectives end in **-ible** and which in **-able**. The **-able** ending is the productive one. If you are making up a new usage of this type from a verb, as in: *It's quite hard to find size 13 shoes. No, they're not readily findable*, the ending will normally be the **-able** form. The **-ible** ending is used for about 75 words in all. However, these words include many very common ones, e.g. *admissible, audible, credible, edible, flexible, incredible, legible, possible, responsible, sensible*, and *visible*. In the end, the common ones need to be learnt.

abnormal, subnormal

Both words take normality as the reference point. Something **abnormal** is outside the usual run of things. Something **subnormal** does not reach the expected or normal state.

abolition, abolishment

The normal abstract noun form is **abolition**. A secondary form, **abolishment**, is found but is not as widely used.

aboriginal

Aboriginal means native to a country in the sense of 'being descended from the original inhabitants'. In Australia, the word *Aborigine* is the term for someone who is a member of one of the many tribes of original inhabitants. The plural is *Aborigines*, not *aboriginals*. The abbreviation *Abo* should be avoided because it is considered extremely insulting. ⇒ **native**

about ⇒ around

above, below

Several commentators criticize the use of **above** and **below** as a noun, adjective, or adverb, meaning 'as described earlier/later', e.g. *...the above indicates a loss*

*of confidence; the above reference; …the passage below…
See below.* They suggest that this particular use should be limited to captions where an illustration is literally above or below the text. However, although the usage can only apply in written contexts, it is not only well established but useful.

abrogate, arrogate

When you **abrogate** a law or a rule, it is formally repealed or cancelled. If you **arrogate** a right or a privilege, you take control over it without justification. This may be done on your own behalf or to benefit someone else.

absent

When **absent** is used as an adjective, it is pronounced /ab-sent/ …*absent friends; Seventy-five percent might be absent at any one time.* When *absent* is used as a verb, as in *He had absented himself for an entire day*, it is pronounced /ab-**sent**/.

absolutely

Absolutely has become common in casual speech as a substitute for *yes*. When it is used, as it can be, several times in the course of a few sentences, it becomes affected and is best avoided.

absorb, absorbent, absorption

The verb **absorb** has an adjective form with *b*, **absorbent**, but the noun form replaces the *b* with *p*, **absorption**. All refer to the capacity to soak up liquid or, by extension, to attract attention.

A much rarer verb *adsorb*, and its derived noun *adsorption*, has to do with the way in which a thin layer of gas may be held on the surface of solids or liquids.

academic

Note that there is a possible ambiguity in the use of the adjective **academic**. Apart from its meaning 'related to scholarship' or 'theoretical', it has a second informal sense of 'impractical' or 'remote' which is extended from the formal sense.

accede, exceed

This pair is often confused but there is no connection in meaning between them. If you **accede** to someone's request, you allow them to do what they have asked. It is a very formal word. An even more formal meaning of *accede* is linked to *succeed*, when it means 'take up a position or an office'. It is usually restricted to the taking up of high office: *Charles will then accede to the throne.*

If you **exceed** something in some respect, you go over a set amount or a limit.

accent

Accents and other diacritical marks are part of many foreign loan words. When the accent or diacritic forms part of a proper noun, it is best to retain it.

In the case of words that have long passed into the language, e.g. *...rather an old precis...*; *He is not sure of his role*, the accent is usually omitted. The rarity of such words generally causes no conflict of meaning. It may be helpful to retain an accent when it gives a clue to pronunciation, as in *blasé*. The omission of the circumflex accent is now permitted in French by the French Academy and the use of other accents is under review.

accept, except

When the verb **accept** is used to mean 'receive' or 'admit to', e.g. in the context of university, college, or club admissions, the preposition that follows it is *by* not *to*:

Madeleine was accepted by Cambridge. When it means 'offered employment' it is followed by *for: I was accepted for the post of secretary.* Take care with the pronunciation of *accept* which is often mispronounced /ek-sept/ but should be /ak-sept/. There is a verb **except** that means 'omit'. ⇒ **except**

access, accession, excess

The most common use of **access** is as a noun meaning 'ability or right to enter': *A long drive gave access to the property at the rear;* or 'permission to meet': *He was granted access to the children once a month.* **Access** may be used as a verb in the context of computing and databases. Do not confuse it with **excess**, which in some accents of English it resembles. **Accession** is a rather specialized word used by librarians when entering books into the stock of a library. It is also the noun form of the verb *accede* in its meaning of 'take up a position or an office', as in *…accession to the throne.* ⇒ **accede**

accessory, accessary

The usual spelling is **accessory**. A rarer form, **accessary**, is found only in legal contexts.

accommodate

This word is frequently misspelled. Note that it has a double *c* and a double *m*.

accompanist, accompanyist

The preferred term for someone who accompanies a singer on the piano is **accompanist**. The alternative spelling is sometimes found in American English.

accomplish

The normal pronunciation in British English is /a-**kum**-plish/. In American English the preferred form is

/a-**kom**-plish/ and this pronunciation is increasingly heard in British English.

accord, account
There are two idiomatic expressions: *to do something of one's own accord*, that is, without prompting, and *to do something on one's own account*, that is, to act in one's own interest. These are often confused.

The expression *in accordance with* means 'following', as in: *I acted in accordance with your instructions.*

accountable
The predicative adjective **accountable** applies only to people, and is usually found in the construction, *accountable to someone for something.*

accuse, charge
The construction is, *accuse* someone *of* something. This is sometimes confused with, someone *was charged with* a crime or something similar. Avoid using the preposition *with* after *accuse*.

accustom
There are two main constructions; you can use, *be, become* or *grow accustomed to something*, as in: *They grew accustomed to these mysteries*, or one can *accustom oneself to* something: *Could I accustom myself to being around them all the time?*

achieve
This is one of a group of words that does not follow the well-known spelling rule, *place i before e except after c*. Because *c* combines with *h*, it does not need an *e* sound directly after it to soften it. This is also true of *chief*. ⇒ -ie-

acid, acrid
Something **acid** has a characteristic sour taste. By

extension, a person who makes *acid remarks*, or has an *acid wit*, makes unkind or cruel remarks or has a sour nature.

The meaning of *acrid* is closely related to *acid*. The adjective **acrid** is usually found in collocation with *fumes* or *smoke*. An *acrid* substance has a sharp, cutting effect on the eyes, nostrils, and throat: *In the studio was the acrid smell of fast-drying paint and instant glues.* By extension, remarks can be *acrid*. A similar metaphor is *caustic*.

acknowledgment, acknowledgement

Acknowledgment and *acknowledgement*, with or without the *e* before *-ment*, are both recognized as acceptable spellings. ⇒ **judgment**

acquaint

The construction is, *acquaint someone with something.* As *acquaint* is a very formal word, use *tell someone something* unless style suggests otherwise.

acquiesce

The construction is, *acquiesce in something. Acquiesce* is rather formal and can often be replaced by *agree to* in plain styles.

acronym

An **acronym** is a word that is created from the initial letters of a phrase, often the name of an organization or a project, e.g. NATO, UNO. Many well-known names in industry are acronyms, as are some trade-names. In order to arrive at a memorable acronym, some projects manipulate their title or use additional letters, e.g. CLEAR: *Campaign for Lead Free Air.* An acronym is treated as a word and so there is no full stop after each letter.

acrophobia, agoraphobia, vertigo

Acrophobia is the fear or dread of being at a height. **Vertigo** is commonly used to mean *acrophobia*, but more properly means the dizziness this causes. **Agoraphobia** is the fear or dread of open or public spaces. This word is often misspelled. The prefix *agora-*, the ancient Greek word for a marketplace, should not be confused with the prefix *agri-* from the Latin for field.

action

Avoid the use of **action** as a verb: *Mrs Kennedy will action this for you.* Many people regard it as unacceptable jargon.

activate, actuate

When you **activate** something you cause it to start working: *...a device that sends pulses of electricity to activate the heart...* ; *Both systems are now fully activated.* *Activate* can also be applied to people, meaning broadly, 'make (someone) work more effectively': *My impression is that these people are only being activated by money.* The past participle is used as a modifier in: *activated charcoal; activated yeast.* Both phrases suggest something that has been made more effective.

Actuate has a more restricted meaning and is only used when you put a machine, or something of that kind, in motion or start it functioning: *He fastened the helmet of his suit, sealing himself in, and actuated the hatch of the space-pod; Push buttons instead of coins were required to actuate it.*

actual, actually

The excessive use of **actual** and **actually** should be avoided. They are unnecessary in sentences such as: *In actual fact, that is true,* and *I like going there actually.*

acute

Acute can mean sharp-witted and observant or powerful: *He was an acute observer; ...her acute analytical powers.*

When the event concerned is an illness, *acute* should be used to describe symptoms that rapidly become severe but can be short in duration: *...acute abdominal pain; ...an acute poison like arsenic. Acute* does not mean 'life-threatening' or 'fatal'. ⇒ **chronic**

AD

In strict usage, **AD** is only employed with specific years: *He died in 1621 AD*, but not with indications of the period: *He died in the 17th century* [not *the 17th century AD*]. Formerly the practice was to write AD preceding the date (*AD 1621*). The sense of *in* is contained in the meaning of the Latin *anno Domini* (*in the year of Our Lord*). It is therefore strictly correct to omit *in* when AD is used; *He died 1621 AD*, but this is no longer general practice.

BC is used with both specific dates and indications of the period: *Heraclitus was born about 540 BC; the battle took place in the 4th century BC.* Modern practice is to write these abbreviations without full stops. ⇒ **dates**

adapt, adaptation

The normal noun form is **adaptation**: *The windmill was designed for adaptation to different local conditions.* The form *adaption* is not standard. It is formed by analogy with **adoption**.

adaptor, adapter

The most frequently used spelling for a device to make electric plugs or hoses fit is **adaptor**: *You can get two-pin adaptors that plug into three-pin ones.* Some writers use **adapter** to mean someone who adapts something: *We* *have to lay differences between the book and the play at the door of the adapter.*

address

Note the spelling: double *d*, double *s*. As a synonym for *speech*, the word **address** is only used in very formal situations, e.g. *the loyal address; an address to Parliament or the nation.*

When *address* is used as a verb with the sense of 'facing up to or dealing with' something it may either be used with a direct object: *He did not address the issue of the alleged wrongdoing,* or in the construction *address* oneself *to* something: *He addressed himself to the critical question.*

addresses

In addresses on letters, the modern style has no comma after house numbers, e.g. *15 Balcombe Rd* nor any form of punctuation at the end of each line. ⇒ **punctuation**

adduce, deduce

If you **adduce** something you supply the reasons that lead you to a conclusion: *Darwin adduced the fossil record as support for his theory.*

When you **deduce** something, you reason it out from various clues or pieces of evidence: *If they were to concentrate on fossil bones, they might deduce something of what these creatures looked like.* ⇒ **induction**

adherence, adhesion

Both words come from the same stem, *adhere*. The distinction in meaning is that **adherence** usually has a figurative sense, especially to convey loyalty to something: *Traditionalism does not necessarily mean a slavish adherence to things of the past; ...the new society was* *able to absolve gentlemen from rigid adherence to the laws of honour.*

Adhesion is used when talking about the clinging property of a glue: *There was a resinous adhesion setting up between the plastic and the cellulose.*

adjacent, contiguous

Both words have similar meaning, 'next to' or 'beside'. Two things that are **contiguous** are generally touching or in contact: *...the Soviet areas contiguous to China...* (where the Soviet and Chinese borders meet). **Adjacent** things generally lie near or next to each other, they are not necessarily in contact: *Our rooms were on the same floor but not adjacent; ...The Medical School and the adjacent Queen Elizabeth Medical Centre.*

One difference is in the degree of formality; **contiguous** is very formal, and is sometimes used in technical contexts, while **adjacent** is quite formal. Less formal alternatives are *touching*, or *adjoining*.

administer, administrate

Both words have the same basic meaning. The longer word, **administrate**, is a back formation from *administration*. You should always prefer the shorter form, **administer**. The verb *administrate* only means 'control a business or enterprise'. It does not have the range of meanings that *administer* does.

admission, admittance

Admission is used in the normal sense of allowing someone to enter a building or an enclosure or to undertake a course of study: *No admissions are permitted in the hour before closing; ...the University Admissions Officer.*

Admission can also be used with the sense of 'owning up to something': *The admission of guilt is hard.*

Admittance is very formal and is usually found in the context of official notices: *He turned down a hallway, opened a door marked NO ADMITTANCE and spotted D—'s name on a door.* In the following clause, *admission* is preferable to *admittance: ...having been refused admittance to many hotels and restaurants.*

admit

Some careful users dislike the use of **admit** *to* followed by the present participle to mean 'say': *A voice admitted to knowing Celia.* However, the form is well established and the general overtones of *admitting* something make it more than just a replacement of *say*.

It is standard usage to use the construction **admit that** with the general sense of 'owned up': *A government minister has admitted that many of Britain's hospitals are underfunded.*

adolescent, teenager

The term **teenager** is a relatively recent coining to describe a loosely coherent age range, nominally between thirteen and nineteen. **Adolescent** is a more clinical term. It has to do with social and sexual maturity: *The coping techniques of the child often continue in the adolescent years.* Note the spelling of *adolescence.*

adopted, adoptive

These words describe two perspectives on the same fact and there is a fine distinction to be made between them. **Adopted** means simply 'who has been adopted'. It is used to give extra information: *The adopted child's feeling of difference.* **Adoptive** is used to mean 'related by adoption', as in *The attitude of adoptive parents towards their child.* Here, the specific relationship of *parenthood* exists only because of adoption. Your daughter cannot be called *an adoptive child* since she remains a *child*, regardless of adoption.

advance, advancement

One of the meanings of **advance** is 'progress in the understanding or development of a field of knowledge': *...advances in scientific knowledge...* This is especially a meaning of the plural form.

Advancement, on the other hand, means the process of helping something happen or succeed: *The third aim was the advancement of learning; Life continues to undermine economic advancement in many African countries.* Another use of *advancement* is to mean growth in one's personal status or in one's career: *Macbeth murders not only for ambitious advancement...* ; *...they are concerned with career maintenance and advancement.*

advantage, vantage, advantageous

An **advantage** is something that puts you in a favourable position compared to other people: *They threw away their advantage by their savagery to the black population.*

Vantage is an archaic form of the word *advantage*. It is still used in some idioms and especially in tennis. A *vantage point* is also a position that enables you to survey a scene with ease: *I had a vantage point of a height of about five hundred feet that enabled me to look into the next bay.* The pronunciation of **advantageous** is /advan-**tay**-giss/.

adventurism

This word is political jargon. It means 'political or financial recklessness': *He wanted to highlight the irresponsibility and adventurism of the Ultra-Left.*

adventurous, adventitious, venturesome

When you want to indicate that someone is daring or not afraid of taking risks, you can use the adjectives **adventurous** or **venturesome**: *Start telling yourself that you're really a brave and adventurous person and you'll deal with it easily; He stared at me with venturesome eyes and dagger brows.* Venturesome is a more formal and literary word than *adventurous*.

Adventitious refers to chance or accident: *These incidents superficially appear to be adventitious... ; ...the adventitious possession of private means.*

adverse, averse

Adverse means 'unfavourable'. You describe something as *adverse* when it interferes with your plans or wishes. It is usually used before the noun: *adverse comment; adverse conditions.*

When you are **averse** to something, you are against it. *Averse* is generally restricted to human subjects. The opposite is *not averse*: *My aunt was not averse to party-going on Sundays.*

The preposition *to* is normally used with *averse*: *He was deeply averse to unions and the policies of Franklin Roosevelt;* although *from* is often used with both *averse* and *aversion* and was at one time considered to be standard usage.

advertisement, advert, advertise, ad

The full form **advertisement** should be used in all formal speech and writing. **Advert** and **ad** are both very informal; the latter is newspaper jargon.

Advertise is pronounced /ad-ver-tise/ and *advertisement* is pronounced /ad-**ver**-tis-ment/, not [/ad-ver-tise-ment/]. Note that *advertise* is never spelled -*ize*.

There is a very formal verb, **advert**, pronounced /ad-**vert**/, which means 'refer to': *...an extremely important point that I will advert to again in a moment.*

advise

Advise is often used in the same sense as *inform*: *As we advised you in our last communication, the order is being dealt with.* This use is accepted and common in business correspondence. Careful users of English prefer *inform*, *notify*, or *tell* in general English: *When he returned home, the police informed him* [not *advised him*] *that his car had been stolen.* Note that *advise* is never spelled *-ize*. ⇒ **license**

æ-, œ-

Because they are not present as a single letter on most typewriters, the æ-, and œ-digraphs spelling are usually written *-ae-* and *-oe-*. These often cause spelling difficulties. In some words they have been superseded by a simpler spelling, e.g. *medieval* instead of *mediæval*. In medicine for example, the profession favours the use of *-e-* for *-oe-* hence *estrogen*, not *oestrogen*, *fetus* rather than *foetus*. Outside the medical profession the older forms survive. It is not quite as simple with æ. Most of the *æ/ae* forms that are found in initial positions, e.g. **aerobics, aerial, aeroplane, aerosol**, retain the digraph. In other positions they may be dropped for a single vowel. ⇒ **digraph**

aerial, aerosol

The initial syllable is naturally confused with *air* on account of the sound and the sense. Note the correct spelling. ⇒ **æ-**

aeroplane, aircraft, plane

Aircraft is the normal term in the airforce and in civil aviation, among aircrew, for an **aeroplane**. The form **plane**

is usual in all but the most formal usage. The form *'plane* with an apostrophe, is no longer used. The Canadian and American form of the word for *aeroplane* is **airplane**. This form is becoming more common in British English.
⇒ apostrophe

affect, effect

There are two separate verbs spelled **affect**. The first means 'act on something in such a way that it may change'. Usually it is a change for the worse: *The harsh economics of today affected the forest*. It may be an emotional disturbance: *His letters affected her profoundly*.

The second word spelled **affect** means 'make a pretence of': *'Hickey!' shriek the women on the settles in affected outrage*. Another sense is 'behave in a particular fashion': *On a personal level he affected to despise every Briton he met*.

When you **effect** something, you make it happen: *In a short time he had effected a political revolution; A breach was effected in the walls*. This is a rather formal word, and is most often found with a past participle.

affection, affectation

Affection is an emotional response involving tenderness or fondness: *Her affections were engaged elsewhere; She had little affection for him*.

Affectation is a false manner of behaving or dressing oneself: *It was, people thought, a harmless affectation*.

afflict

When something **afflicts** someone, they suffer some misfortune or disease: *The diseases that afflict people in poor countries are a vicious crowd; They may grant you power, honour, and riches but afflict you with servitude, infamy, and poverty*.

The verb *inflict* (often with *on*) is used when someone causes another person to suffer as a punishment and out of anger. ⇒ **inflict**

affront, effrontery

When you receive an **affront** you feel that you have been insulted, usually by means of someone's words or behaviour: *Though this was meant as a joke, Nell takes it as a personal affront, I'm afraid.*

Affront is frequently followed by *to*: *This frightened Harold Rothermere, and it was also an affront to the natural ruling class; Now that is a great affront to some traditional teachers.*

Effrontery is rude or cheeky behaviour: *For sheer brazen effrontery and gross idleness, Ernest takes some beating.*

after, afterwards, afterward

After is used mainly as a preposition, with a meaning related to time or position: *after April; after Gallipoli I went to France; the garage is three hundred yards after the shops.*

Afterwards is an adverb with the meaning 'later' or 'subsequently'. It is used to modify a whole clause: *She wrote to me afterwards that her day had been perfection; Afterwards, we all helped with the washing up; I was wretched afterwards, thinking what I'd done to you.* British English prefers *afterwards*. American English tends to prefer **afterward** but may use either form.

age, conventions in expressing ⇒ dates

aged, elderly

When **aged** means 'having a certain age' it is pronounced /aygd/: *She was aged thirty-two.* It also means 'old' or 'very old' and is then pronounced with two syllables /**ay**-jed/: *She simply glared at the sick and aged.*

When *aged* and *elderly* are adjectives and have this last meaning, they overlap in use: *caring for aged parents; problems with elderly parents.* Of the two words, **elderly** is much more usual.

When **aged** is used as a noun, it tends to be a loose way of referring to old people as a social and age group: *Houses occupied by the aged must be centrally heated; care of the aged.*

ageing, aging
Both spellings are accepted.

agenda
Agenda is a singular noun in English. The plural form is *agendas.* The use of *agendum* as a singular is pedantic.

aggravate
The established meaning of **aggravate** is 'make worse': *The Nationalist budget took £1100 million out of the economy, aggravating industry's cashflow problems.* It is the opposite of *alleviate.* It has taken a second sense of 'annoy' or 'irritate'. Purists object to this usage, and so careful writers usually avoid it in formal English, but it is current in informal usage.

aggressive
The typical meaning is 'hostile and contentious'. It has also become a fashionable substitute for *energetic* or *assertive: …aggressive marketing strategies.*

agnostic ⇒ atheist

ago
The use of **ago** with *since* is redundant: *It's ten years ago since he wrote the novel.* It is therefore avoided in careful

English. In such contexts, **ago** should be followed by *that*: *It was ten years ago that he wrote the novel.*

agree

The verb **agree** can be followed by one of three prepositions; *to, on,* or *with*. When two people are of the same opinion, usually because they think alike, use *agree with*: *I agree with Campbell's points.*

When someone has been brought to a point of agreement, use *agree to*: *The employer has to agree to the Scheme; They were asked to agree to a legally enforced delay of twenty-eight days.*

When someone has reached a point of reconciliation with another person, use *agree on*: *It was one of the few things that they were able to agree on in later years; 'I don't think we agree on that,' said Henry.* The use of **agree** with a direct object, as in *They agreed a strategy,* while increasingly common, is not fully accepted by users of British English.

agriculturist, agriculturalist

The longer form **agriculturalist** is preferred by most users. The shorter form is not incorrect, however.
⇒ **accompanist**

aim at, aim to

In general, **aim** is used with *at* when the objective is a target: *He took careful aim at the centre of the melon and fired; These are clearly marvellous goals for the world to aim at.* When the objective is an intention, use the *to* infinitive (the base form of the verb following the preposition *to*): *My aim is to use my full potential; The prime aim of our cause is to liberate France.*

ain't

Although the interrogative form *ain't I?* would be a

natural contraction of *am not I?*, it is generally avoided in spoken English and never used in formal English.

aircraft ⇒ **aeroplane**

aka

This is an Americanism taken from the abbreviation used in police reports, *also known as*. It is best avoided, except as a jocularity, in British English, which already has the well-established word **alias**. Otherwise, use *also known as* in full.

alias, alibi

An **alias** is an assumed name: *The law did not hold it criminal to adopt or use an alias.*

An **alibi** is someone or something that allows a person accused of a crime to prove that they were elsewhere at the time: *Waddell's alibi for the hour of 11.p.m to 2.a.m. should be checked.* The plural is *alibis*. The noun *alibi* is often used informally instead of *excuse*. ⇒ **aka**

alien, alienate, inalienable, alienist

These words are related through the meaning of the word that forms their base. Strictly an **alien** is someone who is not a citizen of a particular country: *You must produce your Alien's Registration Certificate.* As the word is regularly used to label someone living in a country in which they were not born, in informal use, *alien* has taken on overtones of an unwanted visitor to a country: *…illegal aliens; Those aliens already here pose a graver threat.*

When you **alienate** someone, you cause them to become unfriendly or like a stranger: *a tragic event occurred to alienate the Maccabees forever.*

Something **inalienable** can never be taken away and

given to another: ...*personal freedom, the inalienable right to do anything you want.* An **alienist** in American English is a psychiatrist who specializes in the legal side of mental illness.

alkali, alkaloid

An **alkali** is the opposite of an acid: *It had been boiled first in acid then in alkali (caustic solution) in the laboratory.* An **alkaloid** is a plant compound. Many of these are poisonous or used in drugs: *Broom contains minute proportions of certain alkaloids.*

all

In British English you can say either *all the time* or *all of the time.* Speakers differ in their preference for these constructions, each of which is well supported. *All of the time* is the preferred construction in American English. *All* can be followed by a plural or a singular verb: *All leave is cancelled; All (our students) are professionals.* The choice depends on whether the accompanying noun is countable (s*tudents*) or uncountable (*leave*).

When **all** is part of a compound, keep the double *l* when the word has a hyphen: *all-star, all-night.* When it is a single word there is only one *l*: *almost, already, always, altogether.* ⇒ **alright**

all-

Compounds formed with **all** are usually hyphenated. Common examples are: *all-American, all-girl, all-important, all-inclusive, all-purpose, all-star, all-round.*

allege, alleged

To **allege** something is to state it without or before being able to prove it; thus in law one must refer before a trial to a person's **alleged** crime. **Allege** takes an object which can be either a noun or a clause: *He produced in court an* *alleged copy of Amanda's birth certificate; Its authors allege that the figures were simply invented.* The use of **allege** in legal circumstances has given it overtones that can suggest the opposite of its meaning. To avoid this, use an alternative, for example, *declare, maintain,* or *uphold,* since if someone is *alleged innocent* hearers often assume their innocence is dubious.

allegory ⇒ parable

allergic

Allergic and **allergy** refer to a medical condition of over-sensitization to various substances: *In hay fever the nose is allergic to a pollen.* Purists object to its more general use as a synonym for *dislike,* or *aversion:* [*I happen to be allergic to Europe; I am allergic to poetry.*] This is a use that is best reserved for very informal contexts.

all-time

All-time is an imprecise superlative and is avoided by careful writers as being superfluous: *his high jump was a record* [not *an all-time record*].

allude, elude

When you make a passing reference to something, you **allude** to it. The noun form is **allusion**.

If you are pursued and cleverly manage to escape, you **elude** your pursuers: *I seriously doubt that it would be possible to elude the police without leaving the country.* The use of *elude* when something escapes your memory is informal: *She tried to recall his face but it eluded her.* ⇒ allusion

allure, lure

The **allure** of something is its attraction: *An actress can project an illusion of infinite allure.* The word is also a verb meaning 'attract' or 'entice'. The most frequent form is the present participle: ...*morbidly alluring*; ...*an alluring goddess.*

allusion

An **allusion** is a reference to something, often an indirect reference: *Without further allusion to this incident, Mrs Sacker went on.* ⇒ **illusion**

alone, lone

Alone and **lone** are distinguished by the place they take in a sentence and by their meaning. Compare: *A lone walker: He is alone.* The adjectives cannot be interchanged. In both phrases the person is on their own, but in the second (*he is alone*) the overtones of *alone* suggest that he may feel lonely. We can know nothing about how the walker felt. When **alone** is used directly after a noun or pronoun it means 'exclusively' or 'only': *It should be done for love alone...*; *She alone could be sure...*; *the Guardian, which alone had stood out against it.*

along ⇒ plus

alongside

When **alongside** is followed directly by an object it is not correct to insert *of*: *The log crashed into position alongside* [*of*] *the saws.* ⇒ **beside**

a lot

Note that **a lot** should always be written as two words. Writing *a lot* as a single word is a very common misspelling.

alright

The form **alright**, though very commonly encountered, is still considered by many careful users of English to be wrong, or less acceptable than **all right**.

also

Also generally introduces additional information in a sentence: *One of them was also a mountain climber; an interesting challenge for you and also a rather unusual situation*. The sequences *and also* and *but also* are entirely acceptable.

When a whole clause introduced by **also** is additional to the one before, *also* is normally separated by a comma from the remainder of the sentence: *Also, Jane didn't like him to stick around; Also, they had never done a historical survey before.*

alternative

In the Latin from which this word is derived, an *alternative* involves a choice between two items. In contemporary English, however, the use of **alternative** when a choice among more than two items is to be made, is very well established and objection on the grounds of derivation is pedantic. Some very careful writers may still wish to avoid this usage. The use of *other* with *alternative* is redundant.

The use of *alternative* to mean 'unconventional' or 'not in the mainstream', as in *an alternative comedian; alternative life-styles*, has become established as an informal use.

although, though

Although and **though** have much the same meaning but are not always used in the same position in a sentence. *Although* is rather more formal than *though* and is usually found at the beginning of a sentence. ⇒ **though**

altogether ⇒ all

a.m., p.m.

The abbreviations **a.m.** (ante meridiem) and **p.m.** (post meridiem) are normally written with full stops. It is unnecessary to add phrases such as *in the morning, in the evening* when a.m. and p.m. are used.

ameliorate, alleviate

Ameliorate and **alleviate** are both to do with making something better. In general you *alleviate* pain or an unpleasant situation. The result is a partial lifting of the burden: *He rubbed his chest hoping to alleviate the pain; It is a model exercise in the wrong way to alleviate rural poverty.*

You can **ameliorate** an unsatisfactory general situation and this results in a change for the better: *Expose injustice and ameliorate conditions through social reform. Ameliorate* is a formal word. ⇒ **mitigate**

amend, amendment, emend, emendation

Amend means to improve, or change for the better, and is used of a situation or a character: *We develop our ideas, dream our utopias, amend our lifestyles.* Amend can also be used for improvements to a text, especially to a piece of legislation, as in: *This Act amended the definition of 'Trade Unions'.* This meaning causes it to be confused with **emend**, which is restricted to meaning 'change a text or manuscript': *We attempted to emend the text and to remove all references to the product.*

An alteration in someone's behaviour can be called an **amendment**, so could an improvement in a text. This use is common with regard to the American Constitution, e.g. *The Fifth Amendment.* An **emendation** is a correction to a text, but it need not be for the better: *In the circumstances, it is a reasonable enough emendation.* It is a much more specialized term than *amendment* and much less common.

American

British speakers tend to use the word **American** as a synonym for 'belonging to the United States of America'. There is no practical alternative, but British users should be aware that it is as likely a source of annoyance as is the use of **English** to mean 'an inhabitant of the United Kingdom'.

American English

The USA has a large English-speaking population and rich literary resources. As in Britain, there are many dialects and accents of English current in the USA and, as in Britain, there is a generally agreed standard of usage. There is a misconception among many speakers of British English that all the perceived errors and faults of current English spring from corruption of the fountain of pure English by American patterns of usage. In fact, American commentators on English language tend towards a more, not less, prescriptive view of what is acceptable.

amiable, amicable

Someone **amiable** is kindly, likeable, and easy-going: *He was fairly amiable in these private meetings at first.* An **amicable** person is someone whom you perceive to be well intentioned towards you: *We can act in a hundred different ways to signal our amicable feelings towards our companions.* It is also used to describe a situation in which friendly relationships are maintained: *an amicable divorce.*

amid, amidst

Amid is a rather formal word. It overlaps to some extent with *among*. It is used when something is located somewhere in the middle of other things or takes place in the middle of other ill-defined events: *...tombstones stood amid the swaying grass; an innocent amid the strife.*

Amidst is an archaic and literary form of *amid:* do not employ it in general usage. ⇒ **among**

among, between, amongst, betwixt

In careful usage, **among** is used in cases where more than two possibilities or choices are concerned: *...doctrinal differences among Christianity, Islam, and Judaism; He looked for support among the working classes.* **Amongst** means the same as *among.*

Between is usually restricted to cases where only two possibilities or choices are concerned: *What goes on between you and your father is none of my business; Fill any gaps between window and frame.* An exception to this is made when *between* indicates a connecting relationship involving a group of people: *...an uneasy partnership between the Russians and the Poles; ...tension between Jenny and her family.* **Between** also indicates a combined effort: *The Secret Service and the FBI between them screen several hundred alarm calls monthly.* **Betwixt** is an archaic form of *between.*
⇒ **amid** ⇒ **between**

amoral, immoral

Amoral is frequently and incorrectly used where *immoral* is meant. In careful usage, however, **immoral** is applied to anything that infringes moral rules and **amoral** is only used of something to which considerations of morality are irrelevant or of people who lack any moral code: *In the amoral world of animals there are no murders.*

amorous, amatory

Feelings or behaviour that are **amorous** express or further sexual love: …*feelings of an amorous, hostile, or fearful kind.*

Anything **amatory** relates to or expresses sexual love. It is a formal and literary word: *Bronze figurines of amatory couples were his bookends;* …*the shift in sensitivity in the amatory epic.*

amount, number

Amount is used with mass nouns, that is those that refer to quantities of something: *There is a large amount of food left over from the party.* **Number** is used with nouns that take a plural: *A number of cars were parked on the footpath.* ⇒ **few**

ampersand

This is the name of the symbol &. Other than in notes, the use of the **ampersand** should be restricted to indicating a close union, such as linking the names of joint authors (usually of technical books): *Miller & Boyle,* in the titles of some books: *Writers' & Artists' Yearbook,* and in the names of commercial enterprises: *Romeike & Curtice Ltd.* An *ampersand* is a graphic device and not a substitute for *and* in formal writing. The plus sign + is not a substitute for an *ampersand.* ⇒ **and**

ample

When there is an **ample** amount of something there is usually more than is strictly necessary. *Ample* is sometimes used to replace and soften the plainer term *fat* or *overweight*. To describe someone as being *of ample proportions* is euphemistic. The phrase *ample sufficiency* used as part of a response when someone is asked if they would like more to eat, is an affected and tautologous substitute for a plain *yes* or *no*.

an

An replaces the indefinite article **a** when the following word begins with a vowel sound. **An** was at one time used before words beginning with *h* that are unstressed on the first syllable: *an hotel; an historic meeting*. The initial *h* was not pronounced. This usage is now obsolescent in British English.

anachronism, anomaly

If a book, play, or film contains an **anachronism** it refers to, or portrays, an event or custom that could not possibly have happened at the time that the work represents. It is also used very informally for anyone or anything that is out of touch with its own time, as in *This influential, if amorphous, aristocracy became an anachronism; The whole place is an anachronism – a relic of older times.*

An **anomaly** is something that is different from what is normal or usual: *It was illogical in its structure, riddled with anomalies, and possibly corrupt.*

analogue, analog

The British spelling is **analogue**. The spelling **analog** is an American variant and is also the generally preferred spelling in the computer industry.

ancillary

Ancillary, meaning 'additional' or 'supplementary', as in *…ancillary hospital workers*, should not be spelled with a second *i* so that it has an *-iary* ending. The spelling error arises from confusion with **auxiliary**, which has a similar meaning, but is used with a broader range of reference.

and

A comma is used before **and** when the two words so joined are part of a list, e.g. *He bought pencils, paints,* *some brushes, a drawing block, and a drawing board.* A comma is not used when the words joined are taken to be a unity, e.g. *He was bruised black and blue.*

and/or

And/or means 'one or the other or both'. It is not universally accepted as being appropriate in good usage outside legal and commercial contexts. It is never used by careful writers and speakers where a simple alternative **or** is meant: *He must bring his car and/or his bicycle* does not mean the same as: *He must bring his car or his bicycle.*

angle

Angle meaning 'point of view' or 'approach to a problem' as in *news angle* is well established in informal talk and writing, especially journalism, but should still be avoided in more formal contexts. It may imply an element of bias.

angler, fisherman

Angler is a specific term in British English for someone who fishes with a rod and line. This use of *angler* is not well known in American English. **Fisherman** is a general term for any one who fishes.

anglo-

The prefix **anglo-** is not normally hyphenated, e.g. *anglophile, anglophobe,* except for adjectives of nationality or allegiance, e.g. *Anglo-Italian; Anglo-Catholic.*

angry

You normally say that you are **angry** *with* someone, e.g. *I was angry with myself; he was angry with me,* but **angry** *at* something: *You will be angry at what I have done.* When the person who is to blame comes between the verb and the thing that is done, the construction is *be angry at* someone *for* something: *I was angry at the brothers for leaving their posts.*

annex, annexe

A distinction is sometimes made in British English between the verb **annex** /a-**nex**/ meaning 'unlawfully take charge of' and the noun form **annexe** /**an**-nex/ meaning a building used, for example, to house an overflow of guests: *...they were not in the main body of the hotel, but in the annexe.*

annual, perennial

An **annual** event happens once a year. Something **perennial** lasts over the years. When these words are used to describe plants, either as adjectives or nouns, *annual* is used for plants that complete their life cycle within a year, *perennial* for those that regenerate every year.

anon.

An abbreviation for **anonymous**. Note the spelling of the ending of the full form.

-ant, -ent

The **-ant** suffix is used to form nouns by adding it to the base form of a verb (after removing any final *e*): *defend, defendant; depend, dependant.* Nouns that have this ending have a similar meaning to those ending in *-ee* or *-er*, 'one who performs or causes'.

The **-ant** and **-ent** suffixes are also used to form adjectives by adding one of them to the base form of a verb (after removing any final *e*). There are also some **-ent** nouns. Unfortunately, there is no rule that will easily identify the nouns that have this ending. ⇒ **dependant**

antagonist ⇒ protagonist

ante-, anti-

It is important to note the different meanings of these very similar sounding prefixes. **Ante-** comes from the Latin word meaning 'before' in time or position. It is found in, for example: *antechamber, antedate, antediluvian.*

Anti- is from a Greek word meaning 'against' or 'opposite to'. It is found in, for example: *anticlerical, anticlimax, antihistamine, antipersonnel.*

antenna, antennas, antennae

The word that means 'an aerial' has an English plural form in *-s*. The scientific word that means an insect's feelers has a Latin plural in *-ae*.

anticipate

The use of **anticipate** to mean 'expect', while very common, is avoided by careful writers and speakers of English. It has the much wider sense of realizing that something may happen and being prepared to act suitably: *In this way we can anticipate and avoid collisions more efficiently.*

anticlimax ⇒ climax

antipathy ⇒ empathy

antique, antiquated, ancient, antiquity

The noun **antique** is generally understood to mean an artefact of some merit that is over 100 years old. *Antique* is also an adjective and is used loosely to mean *very old*. It often has overtones of derision: *Florence, a devoted and antique servant of the family.*

When you want to suggest that something is so old that it is past its usefulness, you can call it **antiquated**: *the periodic clatter of the antiquated air-conditioning machine...*

When you want to say that something is very old and maintain a neutral attitude to it, the correct adjective is **ancient**: *Anyone can study the ancient Greeks; ...ancient cultural divisions.*

Antiquity is the general noun that covers the early historical past. It is frequently linked with the adjective *classical*: *It is a widespread fallacy that people of antiquity were shorter than we are.* It also means an artefact from that time, as in *In a shelved alcove of classical antiquities I saw two Etruscan vases.*

antiseptic, aseptic

An **antiseptic** is a chemical substance that is capable of killing certain bacteria: *Bleach removes colour and acts as an antiseptic; An antiseptic is less important than careful washing.* When you exclude all sources of bacterial infection from an area you are rendering it **aseptic**: *Cells and tissues of plants may be cultivated under aseptic conditions.* The resultant state is called **asepsis**.

antonym, synonym

These terms are used to describe the meanings of words. An **antonym** is a word opposite in meaning to the particular word being discussed, for example, an antonym of *short* is *tall*, of *cold* is *hot*.

A **synonym** has a similar meaning to the word being discussed, for example, a synonym of *weak* is *feeble*, a synonym of *brave* is *courageous*.

any

You use **any** in negative statements, in questions, and some conditional clauses, when you want to mention something without suggesting that it definitely exists: *She hardly had any money; Haven't you bought any bread today?; He asked if I had any news.*

In positive statements you use **any** to suggest that something is of little account: *It isn't any trouble.* You also use it when you do not want to be specific about something: *Give me a cloth quickly, any cloth.* When *any* is used with a singular noun, as in *Any big tin container will do,* it implies any one container but if it is used with a plural noun or a mass noun, as in *Have you bought any bread today?,* it implies 'some'.

When a clause containing *any* is followed by a relative clause, the relative pronoun used is *that: I'll take any that you have.* ⇒ **use**

anyone, anyway, anywhere

There are many compounds that use *any.* **Anyone** means the same as **anybody.** Purists often dislike the use of a plural possessive after *anyone* or *anybody* in sentences like: *Has anyone lost their ticket?* Because English does not have a pronoun that is neutral for gender, the alternative would be to use the construction: *Has anyone lost his or her ticket?*

Modern English usage permits the use of *their* after *anyone* to avoid the clumsiness of *his or her* and the impossibility of knowing which of the singular forms is accurate. A similar situation arises over choosing which of the pronouns *he* or *she* should follow *anyone* and *anybody.* In very formal writing, however, the use of a singular pronoun and verb is still good practice.

Anyway means the same as **anyhow.** In British and American English **anywhere** is preferred to *anyplace* which is not accepted as standard educated usage. In British English **any more** is always written as two words, but it may be used as one word in American English, e.g. *I don't see her anymore.*

apogee, apex, zenith

All these words mean the high point of something. The **apogee** is technically the point at which a moon or satellite in its orbit is furthest from the parent body. The **apex** is the tip (usually pointed) of something, e.g. of a triangle. The **zenith** in astronomy is the point in the heavens vertically above the observer. When these words are used figuratively, there is little difference between them.

apostrophe

In English punctuation, an **apostrophe** (') stands for the omission of a letter and is consequently the sign of an *abbreviated* form, e.g. *aren't, isn't, it's, don't*. In these examples a vowel is missing. Some very familiar nouns are short forms of longer words, e.g. *fridge, plane, phone*. It was once customary to write these words *'fridge, 'plane, 'phone* to show that something was missing. This is no longer standard usage.

An apostrophe is used in the *possessive* form of nouns, e.g. *girl's, horse's, child's*. In these cases, the apostrophe is the relic of an omitted vowel from an earlier stage in the history of English. It is useful now to show the difference between the singular possessive *girl's* and the plural noun form *girls*. When the noun makes its plural in -*s*, the plural possessive has an apostrophe after the -*s*, e.g. *girls'*.

It is a serious error, and one that has become too frequently seen, to use an apostrophe before the -*s* of a plural noun or the -*s* of a 3rd person singular present verb.

The possessive pronouns *yours, his, hers, ours, theirs*, and particularly *its* when it means 'belonging to it', never have an apostrophe. With an apostrophe, *it's* is short for *it is*.

An **apostrophe** is not necessary after numbers given in the form of figures, or when words not normally plural are made so: *in the late 70s; I don't want any of your buts.* You usually have to use an apostrophe when the item quoted is a letter, in order to avoid confusion: *Will you look at the way she dots her i's; Mind your p's and q's.*

apparent
The adjective apparent means 'clear', or 'obvious': *It was immediately apparent that they hated it.* The adverb **apparently** is rather loosely used in informal writing to mean either *obviously* or *seemingly: Caroline apparently adored him; Someone's at the front door apparently.*

appendix, appendices, appendixes
If you mean an addition or extra section at the end of a book, the plural of **appendix** is **appendices**. If you mean part of the human bowel, then the plural is **appendixes**.

apposite
Something *apposite*, usually a remark, is useful in the context of a discussion: *The most apposite remark was one made recently by Victor.* The usual pronunciation is /app-o-zit/ not /app-o-**zite**/

appraise, apprise, apprize
When you **appraise** something you put a value on it: *The pearls must be worth fifteen thousand because they had been appraised by the insurance company at ten; Harris stood back and appraised his work.*

Apprise and **apprize** mean the same thing. The form *apprise* is preferred. You *apprise* someone *of* something; it means let them know about it: *I apprised him of the political situation at Washington.*

appreciate, appreciative, appreciation

Appreciate has three main meanings depending in part on whether it is followed by an object or not. When you *appreciate* something you value it: *I appreciate your kindness very much; You don't appreciate me.* This sense is extended to the liking of objects and experiences: *Even a thoughtless person can appreciate beauty.* The adjective **appreciative** is linked to this meaning only.

A*ppreciate*, used with an object, also means 'understand' or 'take in what is involved': *They don't appreciate the need to ask why a thing is done; no-one can appreciate their problems.*

When something *appreciates*, it increases in value: *The value of your investment appreciates slowly over a ten-year period.* This is a very formal use. The opposite of this meaning is *depreciate*. The adjective *appreciable* is linked to this meaning only: *This is still an appreciable quantity; there are no statistics showing any appreciable improvement.*

The noun **appreciation** can be used with all three senses of appreciate: *This little gift is to show our appreciation of your hard work; If we accept that my appreciation of the situation is right… ; The appreciation on the lump sum over three years.*

appropriate

The adjective and verb meanings of **appropriate** are quite distinct. The adjective means 'suitable' or 'fitting': *…this is a very appropriate choice.* The verb means 'take' or 'put something aside for a special purpose': *Few purchasers realized that the airport appropriated twenty-five cents in every premium dollar.*

apropos

Apropos does not need an accent and is written as one word, not as *à propos*. It is fairly formal and can usually be replaced as follows: *Apropos (by the way), a question from Oxford; And apropos of (talking of) space medicine… : That remark really wasn't very apropos (appropriate), was it?*

apt, liable

Apt and *liable* are frequently followed by *to* and the base form of a verb: *He is apt to disagree; It is liable to break.* *Liable* can also be followed by *to* and a noun, as in *He is liable to bad attacks of asthma.* They overlap to some extent in describing a general tendency. **Apt** conveys straightforward probability: *Their babies are apt to shift over to a pattern of frequent waking; …this is apt to be less successful.* **Liable** has overtones of risk or danger. It has also begun to take some of the uses of 'likely' and can suggest future possibility: *They were particularly liable to get stomach ulcers; their flimsy mud and straw houses were liable to collapse in a heavy storm; …kill him and you are liable to turn him into a hero.*

In other constructions **apt** means 'suitable': *a more apt description; an apt phrase; a very apt analogy.* **Liable** can mean 'held responsible for': *he will become liable for the debts.* ⇒ **likely**

Arab, Arabia, Arabian, Arabic

Arab is used as an adjective and a noun, especially to refer broadly to nationality: *the Arab people; the Arabs had thirteen votes.* **Arabian**, which is also an adjective, is no longer used as a nationality name, having been replaced by *Arab*. It is used as modifier before things and places: *the Arabian desert.*

The land of the Arabs is called **Arabia**. This refers to the geographic region, but when talking about this region as a political or social body (Egypt, Libya, the Sudan, Lebanon, Jordan, The Emirates, Saudi Arabia are all part of this), the usual form of reference is to *the Arab world*. The language is called **Arabic** and this word is also used as an adjective relating to language and culture: *Arabic writing*.

arch-, archi-

A common prefix meaning 'principal', or 'chief'. When spelled **arch-** it is pronounced /artch/ (*archduke*). When spelled **archi-**, as in *archipelago*, and in all other cases where *arch-* is followed by a vowel, it is pronounced /ark/, e.g. *archangel* is /ark-angel/.

Note that the *arch-* in *archaic, archaeology* does not have the same meaning.

arctic, antarctic

Both **arctic** and **antarctic** can be used as adjectives or (when preceded by the definite article) as nouns. The pronunciation /(ant)-**ark**-tik/ is the correct version. A very common error is to pronounce these words without the first *c* in either word. **The Arctic** is the northern polar region, **The Antarctic**, the southern region.

arduous, ardent

Arduous means difficult: *An arduous rock climb*. **Ardent** means 'burning with desire and passion' or 'possessed by enthusiasm': *an extremely ardent love-letter; He was an ardent patriot. Ardent* is similar in meaning to *fervent*.

aristocrat

The usual pronunciation is with the main stress on the first syllable, not the second: /a-ris-to-krat/.

around, round

In American English, **around** is usually used instead of **round** in adverbial and prepositional senses, except in a few fixed phrases such as *all year round*. Such uses of around are less common in British English.

arse, ass

The vulgar Anglo-Saxon word **arse**, meaning 'buttocks', has been gradually altered by prudery to **ass**. The situation is somewhat confused by the existence of two pronunciations of *ass*. One has a short *a*, the other a long *a*, as in *arse*. The expression *silly ass* is consequently ambiguous. The word *arsehole* is vigorous and vulgar, compared to which, the American use of *kick ass* or *kick some ass* and *asshole* seems rather effete.

artefact, artifact

Artefact is the British spelling, **artifact** the preferred American form.

artist, artiste

An **artist** is someone who paints, draws, or produces sculpture. The pronunciation has a short *i* sound like 'in'. An **artiste** is a professional entertainer of either sex. The pronunciation has a long *i* sound like 'peace'.

as

As has a number of uses and some can interfere with each other, giving rise to potential ambiguity.

The conjunction **as** means *because, since, when*, and *while*. A sentence like: *I saw her as I was walking home* can have any one of the meanings above. It may be clearer to replace **as** with one of these conjunctions.

In a sentence like: *She likes me as well as you*, the ambiguity can be removed by being more specific. For example, you can write: *She likes me as well as she likes you* or

She likes me as well as you do.
In a sentence like *'What do you think of Jane, as a woman?'* there is a chance of misunderstanding. Is your impression being sought because you are a woman, or are you being asked about the sort of woman that Jane is? Luckily, context usually resolves these ambiguities, but they are sometimes less easy to resolve when written down than when they are spoken.

When a comparison is being made, the construction used is **as…as**: *She's nearly as tall as her mother.* The convention in traditional grammar is to change this to **so…as** if the comparison is negative: *Although I'm not so tall as he was,* but this is often ignored and *as…as* is used for both: *It's not quite as short as the programme says.*

Many users object to the use of the phrase **as of** in groups like *as of now, as of yesterday,* and *as of today.* (*As of now/today I'm without a job*). The substitution of *now, at present, from today* is suggested.

An objection can also be made to the use of **as from** in references to a time in the future where *from* is sufficient: [*As*] *from March, he will be in New York.* It is acceptable to use *as from* with reference to a time in the past: *The increase in salary will be paid as from last April,* since it clarifies what the starting point in the past is to be. ⇒ **like**

ascend, ascent, assent

Ascend is a verb and **ascent** the related noun. Both have to do with climbing or mounting something: *…ascend a steep flight of steps; the path led up to an easy ascent.*

Assent is the act of agreeing to something (verb) or the agreement itself (noun): *'Yes,' assented Bishop Brain; The student had to gain the assent of the two tutors to this* *statement.* Both *ascend* and *assent* are formal words.

ascetic, acetic, acerbic

Someone who lives a life of strict self-denial is **ascetic**, pronounced /a-**set**-tik/. The adjective **acetic**, as in *acetic acid*, relates to vinegar. This word is pronounced with a long *e* sound, /a-**seet**-tik/. If something, or by extension someone's attitude, is **acerbic**, it is harsh or bitter. The pronunciation is /a-**ser**-bik/. ⇒ **acid**

Asian

Asian is the correct noun for indicating a person from Asia. The use of the word **Asiatic** in this sense is regarded as offensive.

assemblage, nouns of

Some, like *a flock of geese* or *hens*, *a shoal* or *school of fish*, *a yoke of oxen*, are traditional, but a large number are merely academic or sentimental whimsy, e.g. *an exaltation of larks*, *a leap of leopards*, *a skulk of foxes*. One or two that began as whimsy have become accepted, e.g. *a pride of lions.*

asset

In the singular an **asset** is an 'advantage': *His chief asset is his winning smile.* In the plural, **assets** are property that can be used to raise or repay a debt: *The liquidation of these capital assets is proceeding rapidly.*

assignation, assignment

An **assignation** is a secret meeting: *What can you tell us about the assignation you had yesterday morning?* An **assignment** is a task that has been specially set: *The four inside men carried out their special assignments.* It is often an academic task: *The students missed the early assignments.*

assume, presume

When you **assume** something or make an **assumption**, you act on a belief that something is so, often without evidence: *For some reason, I think he assumes most trade union leaders are as he was.* We frequently *assume* something as a basis for discussion: *Let's assume that it occurs.* When you **presume** or make a **presumption** you similarly take something for granted, usually by working from the facts that you already have: *If you do not come, I shall presume the deal is off.* In most of these uses either verb can be followed by *that*: *Everyone assumed (that) it could not be built; We presume (that) the writer of the article drew the wrong conclusions.*

Assume has a wider range of uses. It can also mean 'take on the appearance of', as in *Her eyes assumed a strange indifferent look,* and 'take over' power or control: *He at once assumed authority.* These uses are not followed by *that.*

assurance, insurance

The broad meaning of **assurance** is a pledge of support or freedom from doubt. As a technical and commercial word, **assurance** is a less frequent form of the word **insurance**. While some British users make the distinction that you may **assure** against a future certainty, e.g. death, and **insure** against chance eventualities, e.g. an accident, most employ the second spelling.

astrology, astronomy

Astrology is the study of star signs in the hope of discerning future events. **Astronomy** is the orthodox scientific study of the galaxy.

atheist, agnostic, heathen, pagan

An **atheist** maintains that no form of God exists. An

agnostic maintains that it is impossible to know anything about the nature or existence of God, should one exist: *She was neither religious nor agnostic.* A **heathen** is someone who believes in a different god or gods from the speaker. A **pagan**, similarly, does not believe in the speaker's god. The overtones of the words *heathen* and *pagan* suggest that a heathen is also barbaric, while many idealize the state of *paganism* as a representation of their ideal of natural mankind.

attempt
Attempt is very formal as a verb. It may sound pompous: *We have attempted* (use *tried*) *to provide enough resources.* As a noun, however, **attempt** has no particularly formal overtones.

aural, oral, audio-
The adjective **aural** relates to hearing, the adjective **oral** relates to speech. Both usually have the same pronunciation, /**awe**-ral/, except that in language teaching contexts, where it is often useful to distinguish one mode of presentation from another, *oral* is pronounced to rhyme with 'coral' and *aural* is pronounced as /**ow**-ral/. The prefix **audio-** meaning 'sound' is pronounced /**awe**-di-o/.

authentic, genuine
While both these words have the same basic meaning there are some differences in the contexts in which they are used. **Authentic** is associated with works of art. **Genuine** has the additional sense of 'sincere'.

author, authoress, co-author
The term **author** is used for both men and women writers today. **Authoress** has overtones of 'minor' or 'amateur' that make it unacceptable to authors of both sexes. A **co-author** or **coauthor** is someone who shares the task

of writing a book with another, but the term can also mean 'ghost-writer', that is, someone who undertakes the entire task of writing for someone without writing skills but with a good story to tell. Avoid the use of *author* as a verb.

authoritarian, authoritative

An **authoritarian** attitude is one that expects strict obedience: *An authoritarian leadership stifled internal debate…; They would not be crushed by egocentric and authoritarian adults.*

If someone or something is **authoritative**, they convey a sense of reliability or show that they have official support for their actions: *This was a figure not very different from the most authoritative current forecasts; This may well have been his last authoritative gesture.*

auto-

The **auto-** prefix means 'self' or 'independent'. It is a productive prefix used to form many words.

autocracy, autonomy

Government by an individual of unrestricted power is an **autocracy**: *The unions wanted to substitute power-sharing for managerial autocracy.* **Autonomy** exists when individuals or groups have the right of self-regulation: *The suggestion is that we surrender our autonomy and independence of action.*

avenge, revenge

Many users make no distinction between these two words. Others distinguish **revenge** as the action taken by the offended person on his or her own behalf. *Revenge* is a noun and is usually given verbal force by using *have, take, get,* or *exact* as main verbs: *He gave me a bloody nose. But no matter. I had my little revenge in time; Do*

not take revenge on someone who wrongs you.
Avenge is a verb. You usually *avenge* the crime done by someone to another party: *The motive was to avenge a murdered relative or friend.*

averse ⇒ **adverse**

awake ⇒ **wake**

award, reward, prize
In general you **award** (verb) someone something, usually a **prize** or a **reward** (noun). **Award** is typically used as a verb and as a noun the thing awarded is an honour or a recompense: *She was awarded her degree on Wednesday; He awarded her £104 000; …the premier British award for journalism.*

There is more than one construction for *reward* as a verb. You can *reward* someone *with* something *for* something: *She rewarded him with her deepest scowl; I will be rewarded for my acts of helpfulness.* In the passive, the agent that normally follows *by* can be replaced by an *-ing* clause: *They were rewarded by Jefferson; She had finally been rewarded by dancing with a prince.*

aweigh, under way
The nautical term **aweigh** used when an anchor is drawn up should be distinguished from **under way** meaning 'on the move'.

awful
Awful means 'very bad' or 'unpleasant': *It was awful. I couldn't get my breath.* The original sense of 'causing awe' is archaic and restricted to older religious writings: *…what Blake called 'the human awful wonder of God'.*

axe, ax
Axe is the British spelling, **ax** the American form.

aye, ay

Aye is an archaic form of *yes* that is now restricted (except in Scottish English) to use in formal debates. An *aye* is an affirmative vote: *The ayes have it.* In poetry **ay(e)** usually means *always: ...for ever and aye.*

B

back formation

Sometimes, a new word is created by removing a prefix or a suffix. An example is: the verb *administer* has the noun form *administration*, but by taking the noun as the starting point, we end up with a new verb *administrate* if we remove the *-tion* suffix. This is called a **back formation.** In this case it duplicates an existing verb.

Other examples are: *self-destruct* from *self-destruction; refrigerate* from *refrigerator; flammable* from *inflammable; process* from *procession.* Some back formations are not fully accepted into formal English, e.g. *self-destruct* is less acceptable than *self-destroy.*

backward, backwards

The first form, without *s*, is an adjective and is used before a noun. The second form, **backwards**, is an adverb and is used with a verb. The use of *backward* as an adverb is found in American English.

bacteria

The word **bacteria** is plural; its singular form is **bacterium.**

bail, bale

Bail is used to mean 'release a prisoner on security'. When you 'empty water from a boat or other container' or when you 'escape from a plane by parachute' either form may be used, though **bale**, followed by *out*, is more usual.

baleful, baneful

Something **baleful** is harmful or menacing. **Baneful** comes from an old word bane that meant poison, hence something *baneful* is capable of causing distress or death.

balmy, barmy

Pleasant, mild weather can be **balmy**, since it has a soothing effect like balm. When someone behaves in an eccentric or odd manner, they may be called **barmy**, a very informal word.

banisters, balustrade, baluster

Banisters may be spelled with one *n* or two. The word is always found in the plural form, never the singular. **Banisters** are part of a staircase. They consist of supporting columns, **balusters**, holding a railing. The *banisters* are also called the **balustrade**. The term *banisters* is usually found in the context of domestic architecture, and *balustrade* in the context of grand or public architecture.

bar

The preposition **bar** meaning 'except' is usually met in the set phrase *bar none* meaning 'without exception'. In other uses, e.g. *Everyone went, bar him,* bar is a rather formal word.

barely
Barely, meaning 'almost not', is one of a small group of words that give a negative meaning to a clause: *The water barely reached his knees.* It should not be used with another negative. ⇒ **hardly**

barrister, solicitor
In English and Welsh law, the pleading of a case before the higher courts is restricted to a **barrister**. All other legal work is undertaken by the **solicitor** who gives legal advice to clients and briefs the *barrister*.

base, basis, basic, basically
The usual pronunciation for all forms of **base** is with a long *a* sound, as in *face*, not a short *a* sound, as in *lass*.

bath, bathe
You have a **bath** in a bathroom or *bath* someone, for example a child. (In American English you *take* a bath.) If you wash something to clean it or if you swim in the sea, the word to use is **bathe**.

bathos, bathetic, anticlimax
Bathos is a sudden change in a story or in speech from an important or moving topic to one which, by contrast, is ridiculous. The adjective, a very rare word, is **bathetic**. *Bathos* is a literary term. The more common term is **anti-climax**. ⇒ **pathos** ⇒ **empathy**

BC ⇒ **AD**

beautiful, beauteous
Beautiful is the usual form. **Beauteous** is a poetic form and consequently not common.

befriend
This word has undergone an extension of meaning. Originally it meant 'act as a friend to someone by show-

ing kindness and sympathy'. It is now frequently used to mean 'make friends with someone'.

begin, start, commence

There is considerable overlap in the meaning of these words. It is generally preferable to use *begin* or *start*. Like many words derived from Latin, **commence** is very formal. **Start** has the additional sense of putting something mechanical to work.

beg the question

This expression is often understood to mean that someone is evading an answer or sidestepping an issue. It actually means to argue from a point of view that is unsound because you are assuming the truth of what you are discussing. For example, to argue that *the Prime Minister must be an excellent leader because he was elected Prime Minister* is **begging the question**. It must be noted, though, that if everyone misunderstands the meaning of an expression, it may end up with a new meaning. ⇒ **coin a phrase**

behalf, behest

The construction in British English is to act *on* **behalf** *of*. It means to take action as a representative in order to assist someone, as in *on behalf of his client*. **Behest** is a much more formal word. It is used in the constructions *at the behest of someone* or *act at someone's behest*, that is, to act because of a request.

beholder, beholden

A **beholder** is someone who observes a situation closely. It is a formal word and has archaic overtones. *Observer* or *watcher* is more current. Similarly, **beholden** is archaic. It means much the same as *obliged* or *indebted*, both of which are more current.

being as how

This phrase is not standard usage. It is generally used in contexts where *since* or *seeing that* would be more appropriate. ⇒ **how**

beloved

The pronunciation is either with three syllables /be-**luv**-ed/ or two as in / be-**luvd**/. It is the first that is more common in memorial services: *My beloved wife.* The second pronunciation must be used when *beloved* is used as a predicative: *...the honour of being beloved.*

below, beneath

These words overlap in meaning. The distinctions of meaning arise from the perspective of the onlooker. **Below** indicates something on a lower level than the observer. It contrasts with *above.* **Beneath** also has this meaning but with the added sense of 'directly under'. *Beneath* also has somewhat old-fashioned overtones. The distinctions are often blurred by use and by idiom. For example, we speak of someone being *beneath contempt*, and of something being *under control.* ⇒ **under**

beneficence, benevolence

The distinction is between doing good deeds, **beneficence**, and wishing an enterprise or person well, **benevolence**. A person who behaves in either way is a *benefactor*, so that, in practice, the lines are blurred; someone *benevolent* can also be a *benefactor*.

bereaved, bereft

Someone who is **bereaved** has had a member of their family die. *Bereaved* can be a noun: *We provide a counselling service for the newly bereaved*, or an adjective: *The bereaved parents... .*

Bereft is a very formal word that also means that someone has suffered a loss, although if someone is *bereft* it is not necessarily because of a death. It may be because they have lost something precious to them, or no longer have some quality that was theirs before. It is generally only used as a predicative adjective and is frequently followed by *of*: *Her cheeks were bereft of colour*; *He had imagined her as utterly bereft and friendless.*

beside, besides, alongside

The main use of **beside** is positional. It is a preposition meaning 'at the side of', or 'next to' something, and is appropriate for use with people. If the reference is to ships, trucks, and other mechanical objects, and if position is the main meaning, **alongside** is usually used. You would talk of ships lying *alongside* each other, but you would normally refer to two people lying *beside* each other. When *alongside* is used in connection with people, it means 'near' or 'in cooperation with': *They worked alongside him for six years.*

Besides is both a preposition meaning 'in addition to': *Besides Hebrew and English he mastered Arabic*, and an adverb meaning 'moreover': *Besides, I have a car and I can drop Daisy off.* Beside is sometimes also used to mean 'apart from': *There was little to do beside hunting.*

better, best

Better can be used with **have** to make a verb that expresses an element of necessity. The idiom is **had better** and, if you need to make it negative, **had better not.** This compound verb has no other tenses or parts, except for a short form *(you)'d better.* The form *you better*, without *had*, is very casual and used in informal speech.

However, since *better* has a superlative form, *best*, you will hear some speakers using the form *you had best.*

While this is unusual, there is no particular reason why it should not be an acceptable usage.

Much less acceptable is the use of *you better had*. This form can be heard when someone uses the construction *had better* as part of a short response: *I promise to bring it tomorrow. You better had.* The reason for its use would seem to be that placing *had* last gives the sentence a much more emphatic tone. It is best to avoid this last form as unidiomatic.

between, among, betwixt

In careful usage, **between** is restricted to cases where only two objects, possibilities, etc., are concerned: *This is just between the two of us.* Where three or more are involved, **among** is used: *I know I'm among friends here.* When there are more than two things, but only two are involved at any one time, *between* can be used instead of *among*, as in *Treaties were drawn up between the nations.*

Because a preposition like *between* should be followed by an object pronoun, *between you and I* is incorrect. The proper construction is *between you and me*. The mistake is usually the result of someone who has been warned against making errors like '*me and Bill went to town*', trying too hard to be correct. *And*, not *or*, should be used as the connector after *between*: *She had to choose between staying and* [not *or*] *leaving immediately.* **Betwixt** is archaic. Nowadays its use is appropriate only in the set phrase *betwixt and between*.

beware

The verb **beware** gives a warning and is used in the imperative followed by *of*. It is used either before a noun: *Beware of the dog*, or before a verbal noun: *Beware of* *working in cold winds*. *Beware* in other constructions is an archaism: *Beware the slings and arrows*.

biannual, biennial

A **biannual** event happens twice a year: *They kept a file on me for seven years and biannual reports*. **Biennial** can be used as an adjective for something that happens every two years: *The plant is biennial and produces quite large swollen roots every two years*, or as a noun for a two-yearly event. It is often used as a title for a regular arts festival or exhibition: *The other tendency at the Biennial was the so-called 'Image Painting'*.

Bible, biblical

A **bible** is a collection of texts. When the bible referred to is the Old and New Testaments, use a capital letter, as in *The Bible class meets at 2 pm*. Otherwise *bible*, meaning 'a standard reference work', and the adjective *biblical* have lower-case initial letters: *the computer user's bible; biblical studies*.

bibliography, biography, autobiography

A **bibliography** is a list of books used in the course of background reading when writing an academic work. A **biography** relates the life of a third party. In an **autobiography**, the author writes about himself or herself.

bicentenary, bicentennial

A **bicentenary** is the 200th anniversary of an event: *Next month, Asprey's of Bond Street celebrate their bicentenary with an exhibition*. **Bicentennial** is the adjective form: *…during the American Bicentennial year*.
⇒ biannual

bike

Bike is a colloquial abbreviation for *bicycle*. It should be restricted to informal use.

billion

In British English a **billion** used to be used for a million times a million. The influence of the American usage, where a billion is only a thousand million, means that there can be confusion between the two scales. The tendency now is to favour the American form.

birthing

This former dialect word has become popular in American English. It means 'the whole process surrounding giving birth'. The term appears to be becoming current in British English.

bit, thing

English contains a number of general-purpose words. Among them, for an unknown amount, are: *bit, piece, portion, scrap*. For unnamed items, we have: *bits, bits and pieces, thing(s), stuff, gear, kit*. All of these are imprecise and should be avoided in cases where it is important to suggest care and precision in a description.

black

The words that can be used when you want to make an unbiased reference to people belonging to a minority culture within a society undergo frequent changes of use. Currently, someone of West-Indian or African origin who wants to preserve an element of racial or cultural individuality, apart from their status as British, will accept the term **black** as an identifying label. When used as a noun, or with political overtones, *Black* is given a capital letter.

A person of Asian origin will accept the use of *Asian* as a neutral label identifying the group. Someone within that group who wants to make a point about wider political issues might use the phrase *we Blacks* while making a generalization intended to embrace both the Asian and the West-African communities. The use of *black* for *Asian* would otherwise be a solecism.

In American usage, terms that are acceptable to members of the different subcultures include *WASP* for a person of Protestant Anglo-European origin, *Black* for a person of Afro-American origin, and *Chicano* for a person of Mexican-American origin.

blame

Blame is used with a direct object or a reflexive pronoun: *Oh yes, always blame me; I blame myself for not paying attention.*

You *blame* someone *for* something: *I don't blame her for being attracted to this trampish fellow.* It is not standard usage to say that you *blame* something *on* someone or something. A careful writer would rephrase the informal sentence *Fires were blamed on criminals*, as *Criminals were blamed for the fires.*

The fault arises through confusion with the construction *put the blame for* something *on* someone: *In fact, many put the blame for the workers' riots on poor communication.*

blanch, blench

To **blanch** is to cause something to whiten: *Sun can blanch or fade a carpet; Fear or illness can blanch someone's appearance.* Vegetables are *blanched* in boiling water to whiten them and remove bitter elements. While this word has a variant spelling *blench*, that spelling is usually reserved for **blench** meaning 'show fear' which has a different origin: *Experienced solicitor though he was, he blenched when he realized what the letter said.*

blatant, flagrant, in flagrante

When something is **blatant** it is glaringly and shamelessly obvious: *a blatant lie; This is obviously a blatant and deliberate attempt to elicit quite improper information; Blatant boasting is the typical status display of the insecure male.*

The adjective **flagrant** is also used for an obvious display, but it has the overtones of something *outrageous*, and is often used for a breach of the law: *The examples mentioned were a flagrant interference in the traditional rights of trading countries; His forced confinement was a flagrant violation of medical and legal norms.*

In legal jargon, the Latin term *in flagrante delicto* describes the situation of someone caught in the act of committing a crime. It is often used about sexual misdemeanours: *He had been discovered by Mrs Parrot, the housekeeper, in flagrante delicto.*

blessed

The pronunciation /bless-ed/ is generally reserved for someone who has been beatified and for mild expostulations: *I can't get this blessed car to start.* Otherwise the pronunciation is /blest/.

bloc, block

The French word **bloc** is used as a technical term in the discussion of politics to mean a strategic, economic, or political grouping of nations, as in *the African bloc*. It is also used in the set phrase *en bloc* meaning 'as a group'. **Block** should be used for all other senses.

blond, blonde, brunette, redhead

Blond means pale or light-coloured. Applied to men, it is normally used as an adjective; it rarely stands on its own as a noun: *The blond man closed the door.* Some writers use *blond* as the hair colour whether the subject is male or female. *Blond* can be used to describe the colour of bleached timber, *blond oak*, or a racial feature, *a blond tribe*. The feminine form, **blonde**, can be used as an adjective or as a noun. While the adjective means fair, golden or flaxen haired, the noun is not neutral in its application. Because it so clearly specifies the sex and one physical characteristic of the person described, it has come to be regarded as having sexist overtones. As the difference in spelling is not evident in speech, most listeners would assume that the words ...*a tall blond from Michigan*... applied to a woman. The term should be used with forethought. Similar remarks apply to the terms **brunette** and **redhead**. ⇒ **sexism**

bona fide(s)

The Latin term **bona fides** means 'honest intention' when it is used as a noun: *He wanted to check on my bona fides.* When it is used as an adjective, it means 'genuine' and is spelled **bona fide**: *This is simply a certificate saying you are a bona fide amateur athlete.*

bored

The usual preposition following **bored** is *with*: *But by then he was bored with the project...*; *I quickly got bored with it.* The use of *by* is also acceptable. It is noticeable, though, that even educated speakers are increasingly using a dialect form that uses the preposition *of.* Careful speakers should avoid *bored of* because it is not fully accepted.

born, borne, bourne

The past participle of the verb *bear* has two forms, *born* and *borne.* In passive constructions and as an adjective, you use **born.** *If it hadn't have been for Carson, Sam* *would have been born in a prison; …his Swedish-born wife…; a born liar.* The concept 'birth' is foremost.

When the construction is active you use **borne** if the mother is the subject of the verb: *She had borne eleven children to her husband; I have borne him a son in his old age.* The concept 'carry' is foremost. As an active verb, *borne* also means 'withstand': *The infant state had borne the first shock of invasion.*

You can use *borne* in passive constructions using *by, on,* or any word that suggests movement such as *away,* as long as the main sense is 'carry': *The cost is borne by the federal government; The entire chorus was to be borne aloft on wires; It was borne away round the bend of the lane.*

Bourn(e) is an archaic word for a destination or a boundary: *That bourne from which no traveller returns.*

borrow, lend, loan

These three words are the source of some very common errors. **Borrow** and **lend** are opposite actions. When you *borrow* something, the other person *lends* it to you. As *borrow* and *lend* are both verbs, it is not correct to ask: '*Can I have a borrow?*' of something. The correct construction is *May I borrow,* or *Would you lend me* something. What the other person does when *lending* something is *make (you) a loan* or *lend you* something. **Loan** is a noun, so that, unless money is concerned, it is not correct to ask: *Will you loan me* something. Someone can *let you have a loan* of something, or something can be *on loan* or be *as a loan.*

However, if you borrow money from a bank, either *lend* or *loan* may be used as the verb and what you have is *a bank loan.* When the verb used is *loan,* it is usually restricted to important sums of money: *The bank has loaned the firm sufficient to cover our plans for expansion.*

both, both of, both … and

When **both** is used before a plural noun it does not need a following *the,* though it is not incorrect to use one. You can either say *both men…* or *both the men…* . Some speakers dislike this usage altogether and prefer a construction that uses *of.* In this case it is necessary to have a definite article *the,* or any other determiner: *both of the men; both of our parents.*

The choice of the construction with *of* or without *of* is based on the user's preference, although the usage with *of* can suggest that the noun that follows is not necessarily a possessive relationship. For example, in: *The sergeant held both of his arms / The sergeant held both his arms,* the first sentence strongly implies that they were someone else's arms. In the second sentence, they are more likely to be his own arms. There is no strong grammatical argument in favour of either construction.

Both is also used in a construction with **and**: *Both the camels and I were totally inexperienced.* In this case you do not need to have a plural noun after *both: Both the man and the woman instinctively dropped to the ground.* The use of *both* after the nouns that it modifies, as in *Myra and I both …,* is generally more formal.

Other terms of inclusion, such as, *as well as,* are redundant with *both,* so it should be: *…both Ron and Ruth,* not [*…both Ron as well as Ruth*]. ⇒ **each**

brackets, parentheses, braces

There is confusion about the names of these punctuation marks. In everyday reference the word *brackets* (or *round brackets*) applies to the punctuation marks ( ). In fact, these are strictly called **parentheses**. The variation that is usually called the *square bracket* [ ] is strictly just a **bracket**. The variety that is known as the curly bracket { } is properly called a **brace**. As almost everyone knows and uses the popular terms, it is sensible to continue with their use and to note the technical names, which are often used in mathematics. ⇒ **punctuation**

bravery, bravado, bravura

Bravery involves courage. **Bravado** is the deliberate and self-conscious display of bravery to attract attention. **Bravura** is usually the skilful display of an advanced musical technique, although it can just mean daring behaviour.

breach, breech

A **breach** (noun) is a break or separation. The verb *breach* means to make a break or opening in something, often the initial opening for later widening.

Breech is an old word for buttocks. In technical terms, a breech is the lower part of a gun behind the barrel. It is often where the charge is inserted. In the plural only, *breeches* are *trousers* that extend to just below the knee.

brethren ⇒ brothers

bring, brought

The verb **bring** and its Simple Past tense and past participle, both of which are **brought**, are frequently confused with the same parts in the verb **buy**. The following illustrates the correct usage: *I bring my dog to work some days. I brought him in last Wednesday, in fact. I suppose that I've brought him in on about seven occasions this year.* ⇒ **buy**

Brit, Britisher

The term **Brit** (or the plural *Brits*) has not normally been used by the British about themselves, as it carries overtones of dislike and scorn. It is interesting to note that recently, some popular newspapers have adopted it as a convenient shorthand for use in headlines. One would expect the overtones of disdain to fade with this use, but they often linger because of the contexts in which it is used.

The term **Britisher** seems to be an American coinage. It is never used by a native of Britain.

British, Briton

When **British** is used with a plural verb and preceded by a definite article, as in *The British*, this means the inhabitants of Great Britain. It is used when you want to make a generalization. *Briton*, meaning 'an inhabitant of Great Britain', is not current but is used as a historical term.

British Isles

The term **British Isles** refers to the United Kingdom and Ireland as a geographical region rather than as a political one. You are most likely to hear it used in weather forecasts. ⇒ **Great Britain**

broad, wide, width, breadth

Although the words **broad** and **wide** overlap in many of their uses, there are some differences. *Broad* is the more general term and is usually used when no measurements are available. *Wide* is used for an exact distance between two points. For example, we tend to talk about the **width** of a piece of furniture and the **breadth** of a river. Shoulders are *broad* because we do not expect a literal measurement. A doorway is *wide* because the precise dimensions may be necessary at some time.

broadcast

The Simple Past tense of **broadcast** is the same as the stem. It is incorrect to add *-ed*.

brotherly, fraternal, fraternity

Brotherly is the plainest and most common form. **Fraternal** comes from a Latin word meaning 'brother'. Like many Latin derivations, it is more formal and specialized. A **fraternity** is any gathering of people who share similar interests, as in *the yachting fraternity*, or an American student social club (the equivalent for women is a *sorority*). One talks of the *brotherhood of mankind* not the *fraternity of mankind*.

brothers, brethren

The normal plural of brother is **brothers**. This can be abbreviated to **Bros** in commercial contexts, as in *Moss Bros*. **Brethren** is an archaic plural (compare it with *child, children*) which is now normally restricted to the established names of religious groupings, as in *Plymouth Brethren*. Never add another *s* to the form *brethren*. Also in the context of the church, a **brother** is a member of a religious community, such as a monastery, but usually not a clergyman.

bulk

The idiom *bulk large* is used to indicate that something, usually a problem, occupies a large part of one's attention.

burglar, burgle, housebreaker, robbery

In English law, a **burglar** is someone who forces an entry into a building between the hours of 6 p.m. and 6 a.m. If the entry takes place in the remaining period it is **housebreaking**. This distinction is not known in Scottish law, where the term *burglary* is not used, and is rarely observed outside legal contexts. In American English the common term is *burglary*. The verb **burgle** began as a humorous derivation from *burglar* but has gained more formal acceptance in British English, unlike the non-standard *burglarize* which is mainly found in American English.

Robbery is stealing from someone by the threat or use of force.

burned, burnt

The Simple Past tense and the past participle can be either **burned** or **burnt**. *Burned* can be pronounced /burnd/ or /burnt/. When the verb is followed by an object British English tends to prefer *burnt*, with *burned* used intransitively. The adjective form is always *burnt*: *'Burnt toast again, I see,' she muttered.*

bus, coach, omnibus

In British English, a distinction has in the past been made between a **bus,** which operates within a town and a **coach,** which operates over long distances in country areas. This distinction seems to be disappearing. In American English *bus* and *coach* are interchangeable terms.

but

But as a clause connector or conjunction normally comes first in its clause: *Later we'll be discussing the films of Alfred Hitchcock, but, first, we have this week's releases.* The use of *but* implies a contrast between the two clauses. When *but* is used as a preposition meaning 'except', it is generally preceded by a negative. In this construction, *but* is normally followed by the object pronoun forms, *me, us, him, her,* and *them: There's nobody here but us.* Many writers prefer to use a subject pronoun (*but + I,* *we, he, she,* or *they*) if this construction is immediately followed by a verb of which one of them could be the subject: *Why was it that no one but she could see....* The reason for this is naturalness, not correctness. If the sentence were to be written differently: *Why was it that no one could see but her,* the object form would be necessary.

In some varieties of English, e.g. Australian and New Zealand English, *but* can be found at the end of a clause with the meaning 'however' or 'though'. This is always a nonstandard usage. ⇒ **help**

buy, bought

Be careful not to confuse the Simple Past tense and past participle form of **buy,** which is **bought,** with the past form of *bring,* which is *brought.* ⇒ **bring**

buzz word

A **buzz word** is a word that is used with a special meaning for a small group of people. Its special meaning is often incomprehensible to those outside the group. The use of a *buzz word* is intended to show that the speaker is a progressive member of the group and shares its values. ⇒ **synergy**

by, bye

There is no clear guide to those words compounded with **by** that take a hyphen and those that are fully linked. *By* either means 'near', as in *bystander, bypass,* 'secondary' or 'minor', as in *byroad, byway, by-election,* or 'incidental', as in *by-product.* Note that in *bylaw* the prefix comes from a word that meant 'village'. *Bye* is generally no longer used. All compounds using *bye-* can also be spelled *by-.*

byword, by-line

If something (or someone) has become a **byword** it has won a name for itself in some special area. It may be because of excellence or notoriety.

A **by-line** or **byline** is a journalistic term. It is a line of type that indicates who wrote an article, e.g. *By Frank Flood, Education Correspondent*.

C

c.

When the lower case abbreviation **c.** is used with dates, it is short for **circa** (about) and is placed before the date, e.g. *c.1750*. This abbreviation never starts a sentence and is normally used in parentheses (*c.1750*). When the abbreviation is the capital letter C, it means *century* and is placed before or after the date, e.g. *C17* or *17C.*, where it means *the 17th century*. ⇒ **century**

cadre

Cadre is mainly encountered as part of the jargon of Communism, but it also has a military sense. It means both a nucleus of trained individuals on which a larger unit can be built, such as a group of activists, and a member of such a group. The pronunciation rhymes with 'harder' /**car**-der/.

caesarean

A birth by surgical intervention is a *caesarean section*.

Note that the ending is spelled *-ean*. The pronunciation is /si-**zair**-ri-an/.

cafeteria, café

A **cafeteria** is an inexpensive self-service restaurant, often one provided for staff, as in *the works cafeteria*. This is abbreviated in speech to the very informal / kaff/. A **café** is a small restaurant. It has a much more up-market image than a *cafeteria*. ⇒ **restaurant**

can, may

The distinctions between these two verbs can provide a field day for purists. The traditional viewpoint is that it is important to distinguish between **can**, meaning 'have the ability' and **may**, meaning 'be permitted' or 'be possible'. Some would maintain that only *may* should be used for requesting and granting permission, as in *May I borrow your long ladder*.

In practical social interchange this distinction does not hold. Both these verbs are used for asking permission and **can** is the more common of the two in all but the most formal contexts. The choice of *may* in forming a request often indicates that the speaker has a subordinate relationship to the person addressed: *May I leave now?*

Misunderstanding, when it does arise, is usually over the 'be permitted'/'be possible' uses of *may* and the 'have the ability' use of *can*. For example, the ambiguous notice: *This door may be used in an emergency*, could mean either, *The door will possibly be used* ... or, *You are allowed to use this door*. It would be much clearer if it had the form: *This door can be used in an emergency*.

can, tin

In British English the metal packaging for foods etc. is a

tin, except when it contains beer, when **can** is used. In American English **can** is used for all purposes. Users of British English may well find the following headline from an American DIY magazine confusing at first reading: *Rubber band stops paint can drip*. Use of the phrase *a tin can* has recently become more common in British English in order to distinguish a metal from a plastic container.

cannot, can't, can not

The compound word **cannot** is the normal form for the negative of **can** in British English and in American English. Written British English normally uses the form *cannot* at all times, but in both familiar and formal spoken British English, *cannot* is shortened to **can't**. In American English *can't* is rarely used and the full form *cannot* is preferred, causing American speakers to often sound stilted to British listeners.

The form **can not** may be used when a strong negative emphasis is needed: *You certainly can not!*

canon, cannon

There are two words spelled **canon**. The first is used as a title for a priest who forms part of a cathedral chapter or a member of certain Roman Catholic religious orders: *Canon Johnston had lost his temper; An old canon had died and was cremated.*

The second noun spelled *canon* basically means 'the laws of the church' and from this derives the term *canon law: Canon law decreed that adultery was reprehensible*. A *canon* is also 'an established body of rules', and this sense has become extended to mean 'the established body of work that makes up an author's output': *As a lover of Jane Austen, he would work through the whole canon, one volume at a time.*

More recently, it has been used to refer to a group of writers whose work, according to the critics, has an established value: *Why do we exclude so many admirable writers from the English canon?* The term *canon* is also used for a musical composition of a particularly formal kind: *There are no strong beats in these canons.*

In the plural, **canons** are principles of taste or general rules: *These so-called canons of artistic realism are purely formal; This offends the properly developed canons of public finance.* The artillery weapon is a **cannon**.

cant

Cant, pronounced /kant/, is hypocritical speech or writing. It is also another word for jargon. It is a rare enough word not to be confused with *can't*.

canvas, canvass

Canvas is strong cloth that is often used for tents or chairs.

When you **canvass** people you actively seek support from them, as in elections. *Canvass* can also used as a noun: *It was the fullest canvass I've ever managed,* but the verbal noun *canvassing* is more common: *House-to-house canvassing is very tiring.*

capable ⇒ **ability** ⇒ **liable**

capital letters

The technical term for a **capital letter** is an *upper case letter* while a small letter is a *lower case letter*. These terms originally referred to the cases in which printers kept metal type letters ready for use. These were arranged one above the other. Capital letters were kept in the upper case and small letters in the lower case.

Nowadays, the term distinguishes two forms of the same letter. ⇒ **punctuation**

carat, karat, caret

Carat is a unit of weight used for the measure of precious stones. A diamond of *one carat* is 0.20 grams. In British English, a **carat** is also a measure of gold purity representing one 24th part of gold in an alloy, so 18 carat gold is 18/24ths pure gold. In American English the gold measure is spelled **karat**.

A **caret** is the special mark ⟨ used by writers to show that they are inserting a missing word or letter in a line.

carcass, carcase

The preferred spelling is **carcass**.

career, careen

If someone, or a vehicle in motion, **careers** along, they are moving at a headlong, breakneck speed: *He was in a car careering out of control down a slope.* In American English the word **careen** has taken on this meaning, probably by extension from the movement sideways that is involved when *careening* a ship. In British English however, **careen** is what you do when you take a boat out of water for repair: *The boats all had to be careened at the end of the season.*

caricature

This word has four syllables /**ka**-ri-ka-ture/. It is often given three only.

case

Nouns in modern English do not have a **case** in the way that nouns in, say, German or Russian do, but the legacy of Latin has left an old-fashioned grammatical terminology with many references to the *nominative* and the *accusative* 'cases' in English. *Cases* involve special changes in the form of a word which English does not have. It is usual to talk about *subject* and *object* in English, but these are the *functions* of words in a sentence, not their cases. The term *genitive* refers to a case; in English use the term *possessive*.

caste, class

Class is the division of society into groups depending on differing social and economic status: ...*English society is still a class society*. **Caste** is the traditional division of Hindu society into hereditary groupings: ...*the Brahmin caste*. Groupings in a *caste* system are generally static, but those in a *class* system are not necessarily so.

caster, castor

Finely ground sugar is **caster sugar** but the perforated bottle from which you can sprinkle it is either a **sugar caster** or a **sugar castor**. You can use either of these spellings for a wheeled foot on furniture. The unpleasant old-fashioned medicinal oil is always spelled **castor** oil.

catholic, Roman Catholic

In nonreligious contexts **catholic** means broad-minded or universal: ...*in art, my tastes are catholic*. In a religious context the meaning becomes more complex.

Catholic can refer to the whole body of the church or to divisions of the church. In particular, **Roman Catholic** is commonly used in British English to distinguish those who accept the authority of the Pope from others who regard themselves as equally Catholic, as in *Anglo-Catholic*. But because *Roman Catholicism* does not accept the catholicity of other denominations, it makes no use of the adjective 'Roman'.

cause, reason

Distinguishing between **cause** and **reason** is sometimes difficult in English since we can use *because* to introduce clauses that give the **reason** for something: *I don't like the design of this because little children could push their thumbs into it.*

A *cause* is something that produces an effect. Something can *cause* another thing or be *the cause of* it: *The sudden loss of pressure caused the speeding car to lurch; severe repression is the main cause of instability.* An event or situation can be the *cause for* something: *Your age and frailty are giving him cause for concern.*

When you are stating a **reason**, you can talk about the *reason for* something, or the *reason (that)* something happened: *That's an even better reason for learning statistics; They said the reason (that) mother has gone insane is probably the stress.* Avoid writing *the reason is because* since *the reason is* and *because* mean the same thing.

cement, concrete, mortar

A **cement** is a substance that bonds two things together. A cement can be made from many things, but, as a very common form is *Portland cement,* which is used widely for mixing *concrete,* there is a popular misconception that *cement* and *concrete* are identical.

Concrete is a mixture of *cement,* sand, ballast, and water.

Mortar is a weak mixture of *cement* or lime with sand and water.

censor, censure

If you read a book before its publication or watch a film before its distribution with the intention of removing sections that offend some code, you are acting as a **cen-**

sor. If you scold or rebuke someone in speech or writing for some aspect of their behaviour, you **censure** them.

centigrade

Although the term **centigrade** is still sometimes used in meteorology, it is now obsolete as the name of a scale of temperature. *Celsius* is used instead.

centre, middle

Centre is a precise term which indicates only one possible point within an enclosed area. **Middle** is not precise. To *centre round* is considered illogical by many writers and speakers, who prefer the more precise phrase *centre on*.

century

Dates involving centuries can be written as: *C17; 17C.* (with a full stop); *17th-century; the seventeenth century; a seventeenth-century author.* In formal writing the full forms are often preferable, but particular disciplines have their own conventions, which the writer should follow. ⇒ **c.** ⇒ **dates**

certain, certainty, certitude

The adjective **certain** means a particular but unnamed thing: *You couldn't buy cigarettes after a certain hour at night.* It can, on the other hand, be used to refer to something that you are sure about: *He is risking the certain irritation of his superiors.* The difference between *certainty* and *certitude* is small. **Certitude** is more an abstract state of mind, when you feel you have no doubts: *The placidity of her moral certitude is unruffled.* **Certainty** is the actual knowledge you have that something will be, or is, so: *Very quickly the possibility became a certainty.*

cervical

The usual pronunciation is /cer-**vai**-cal/ with an *i* sound as in *try*, but the pronunciation /**cer**-vi-cal/ with a short *i* as in *bit* is also acceptable.

chairman, chairperson, chair

The overtones of the word **chairman** are often felt to be too suggestive of the dominance of men in positions of authority. For this reason, some committees substitute the term **chairperson** in order to neutralize the gender bias.

However, this solution is not accepted by those who find **chairperson** an unwieldy title for practical use. The use of **chair** is an alternative, but this too is subject to objections on the grounds of semantics. Someone can *be in the chair* but they cannot *be the chair*. The choice of label is a matter less for usage than for the dynamics of the committee. Viable solutions include accepting the pair *chairman/chairwoman* or using **president**, which has no gender markers. ⇒ **sexism**

charge

When the verb **charge** is used in the context of crime, it is followed by *with*: *I'm charging you with embezzlement.* In a financial context, a **charge** (noun) is a cost normally borne by the purchaser. When someone *charges* another person, that person bears the cost: *They'll think we are millionaires and charge us double. Charge* can be used without an object: *We charged according to the size of the rick.* You *charge* someone *for* something when the context is a purchase: *He was charged for a bar of household soap.*

With the use of credit cards, the meaning of **charge** as a verb is altering, as the following examples show: *'Eighty* *cents. Charge or cash? 'I'll pay you for it.'; Norris went down to a sporting goods store and charged his equipment.* This is American English. In British English the construction is *charged* something *up: I bought £12 worth of petrol and charged it up.*

chastise

Chastise is one of a group of verbs ending in *-ise* that never has the alternative ending *-ize.* You *chastise* someone *for* something.

chauvinist, male chauvinist

A **chauvinist** is someone who supports a cause with an unthinking excess of zeal: *...social chauvinists clinging to the historic national patriotism; The Germans did not feel that they were expansionist chauvinists.* The word comes from the name of Nicolas Chauvin, one of Napoleon's soldiers, who was an unreflecting patriot.

The label **male chauvinist** was coined for men who have an unthinking belief in the superiority of the male sex: *...so many businessmen are unrepentant male chauvinists. They see most office work as women's work.* It is not correct to use the word *chauvinist* on its own to mean a man with sexist opinions. ⇒ **sexism**

cheque, check

In British English a **cheque** is a written order to a bank to pay a sum of money. The American English spelling of this word is **check**.

childish, childlike

These two words are distinguished by the speaker's attitude. If someone (or something they do) is **childish**, and they are not a child, the suggestion is that they are petty or superficial: *Her disappointments and childish enthusiasms grieved him.* If they are **childlike**, and they are not a child, the suggestion is that the speaker finds their behaviour charming or innocent: *...the almost childlike simplicity of John's nature.* A child can be described as *childish* but not *childlike*.

china, crockery

When you are referring to what is placed on the table, such as plates, dishes, and cups, the general term nowadays is **china**. *China* is also used as a modifier, as in *china cupboard, china candlestick.* An equivalent word is **crockery**, which includes items that are used in the kitchen, like mixing bowls: *We stacked the dirty crockery and cutlery.* *Crockery* is felt to be a somewhat old-fashioned term and is not used as a modifier. *Crockery* can be used for items not made from clay: *High quality Melamine crockery*, (although *tableware* is the more usual term in this case). You buy *crockery* in a *china shop.* The broad divisions of *china* are earthenware, stoneware, and *chinaware. Bone china* is a variety of porcelain.

China, Chinese, Chinaman

Reference to **China** means what is sometimes described as *mainland China* or, officially, *The People's Republic of China.* The word **Chinese** is used as a noun for an inhabitant of China, and, as an adjective, for anything related to China. The old term **Chinaman** is offensive nowadays because of the contexts in which it has been used.

choice

Choice can mean the act of choosing, the thing that is chosen, or the power to choose. Informally, if something is called *choice*, it is an ironic substitute for *vulgar* or *rude: There was some pretty choice behaviour last night, I can tell you.*

chord, cord

There are two words with the spelling **chord**. In music, a group of notes that are played simultaneously in a formal relationship constitute a *chord*. This word comes from *accord*. A **chord** in geometry is a straight line that joins two points on a curve. This word comes from the same Latin word as **cord** meaning a strong kind of string.

A common misconception concerns the spelling of **vocal cords**. These should not be spelled *chords* as their name has to do with their appearance, not their function in making sounds.

Christian name, forename, first name

If you are designing a form or questionnaire you need to remember that the term **Christian name** will not be applicable to people of other faiths. Offence will not be given by a request for a **first name** or the more formal term **forename**.

chronic

Chronic is a word that is frequently mentioned as an example of ignorant misuse. *Chronic* means 'lasting over a long time' or 'constantly recurring': *He was treated a number of times for chronic alcoholism.*

Because of its association in medical diagnosis with severe types of illness, the sense *bad* or *serious* became attached to *chronic*. Informally, *it was pretty chronic* means 'it was quite bad' and *Jack is chronic* can mean 'Jack is ill/Jack is very bad (at something)'. These senses of *chronic* are not standard; they are very informal in both speech and writing.

The loss of clarity involved in this extension of meaning is illustrated in this sentence: (*It*) *documented a saga of bad management, chronic industrial-relations problems, and restrictive practices*. Does *chronic* mean 'recurring' or 'awful' in this sentence? If we bear in mind the language of the rest of the sentence, the writer probably means *long-lasting*.

circumstances

You can say *under the circumstances* or *in the circumstances*. There is no difference. *Under no circumstances* means *never*. You have to follow this phrase with a reversed order of verb and subject: *Under no circumstances would he have interfered with evidence; Under no circumstances can Z ever betray us*.

city, town

A general distinction between a **city** and a **town** is one of size. A city is much larger than a town. The word *town* is taken as the converse of *country*. There are more technical differences, however. In Britain a *city* receives the title from the Crown and is usually the seat of a bishop (though many bishops have seats in towns). In the USA and elsewhere, a *city* is a centre of administration.

clad ⇒ clothed

claim

When used as a verb of saying, *claim*, along with several other verbs such as *maintain*, *assert*, and *contend*, can give an air of defensiveness or special pleading to a statement. In certain contexts this may not be desirable. Use *say* or *state* if this seems likely.

class, category

A **class** is a group of people or things that have certain characteristics in common: *We can identify several classes of fern; Gestures fall into six main classes*. A **category** is a more abstract, formal word for a group that has common characteristics, and is often used in scientific or philosophical writing: *There are many major categories of creatures. Software falls into two categories.* In most other contexts *class* is more suitable. ⇒ **caste**

classic, classical

The adjectives *classic* and *classical* can often be treated as synonyms, but there are two contexts in which they are used differently. **Classical** is used to refer to Greek and Roman culture. **Classic** is especially applied to art and literature of the first rank, as in *Lewis Carroll's classic works for children* or to something which is an outstanding example of its type: *A classic instance is Northern Nigeria.*

clean, cleanse

Clean is a general term. It is an adjective, a verb, an adverb, and can be used as a noun. **Cleanse** is a verb. It has overtones of a thorough cleaning, as in *cleanse a wound,* or of ritual cleaning: *All hearts could be opened and cleansed.*

cleanliness, cleanness

Cleanliness is the habit of keeping clean or of being clean: *Cleanliness costs you nothing, my mother used to say; Cleanliness is essential in all butchery operations.* **Cleanness** is the state of being clean: *I needed pure air and cleanness.*

clench ⇒ clinch

clergyman, minister, priest

In British English **clergyman** is a general term and simply means a male member of the clergy. A **minister** is usually a member of the clergy in a Nonconformist Church. A **priest** is generally a clergyman in the Roman Catholic church but the term is also used by some Anglicans.

cliché

A **cliché** is a saying or phrase that has been used so often that it has lost any power to surprise or inform the listener or reader. The expression 'to coin a phrase' (itself a *cliché*) should mean that the speaker is about to make, or 'coin', a new expression. Oddly, this is often used in error when someone is about to utter a *cliché*. ⇒ **jargon**

client, customer, trick, patron, punter

The word **customer** is a general term for someone who purchases goods or services. A more formal word for someone purchasing professional services (other than medical ones) is **client**. Some users feel that use of the word *client* enhances an otherwise prosaic relationship, so it is often used outside professional dealings.

In the effort to upgrade commercial relationships, hotels and restaurants often use the word **patron** to describe the customer. This casts him or her in the role of the person of influence distributing discerning favours.

In other professions the customer is deliberately downgraded. Prostitutes refer to their customers as **tricks** (among other terms). Use of this word has spread into more general use, particularly when the seller feels diminished by the transaction. A similar word is **punter**. Originally a name for the customer of a bookmaker, the word *punter* has been given a wider use as a general but somewhat scornful term for someone who, having paid their money, deserves a reasonable deal.

climatic, climactic, climacteric

Climatic is an adjective from climate: *...a climatic shift bringing increased rainfall*. A **climactic** incident is one in which an important event occurs or an important stage is reached: *He kept this secret from her until a climactic* *point in the story.* A **climacteric** is a critical or important stage. When talking of people, it is sometimes used, as an adjective or a noun, for the stage when sexual activity diminishes: *…a climacteric storm of hormonal activity.*

climax, anticlimax

The word **climax** comes from Greek. It is particularly used as a specialist term in discussion of plays and novels. The *climax* is the point where the most intense emotions occur. It is usually near the end. The word is extended to mean the most exciting point in any series of events: *This proved to be the climax of his political career.* Avoid the use of *climax* as a verb in formal English. The phrase *reach a climax* is preferred. An **anticlimax** is an event that disappoints you because it is not as exciting as you had hoped. In discussing events in literature, an *anticlimax* is the stage following a *climax.*

clinch, clench

These verbs have similar meanings. When you drive a nail in and flatten the protruding side to prevent it pulling back through, you are said to **clinch** the nail, hence other uses where the meaning is 'make firm', as in *clinch a deal; clinch an argument.* Carpenters often use the word *clench,* as in *clench nailed.* Otherwise the verb **clench** means to close or squeeze something together firmly, as in *a clenched fist; she clenched her teeth.*

clique

A **clique** is a small exclusive group. The usual pronunciation is /kleek/ but sometimes /klik/ is used. ⇒ **junta**

close, shut

Although **close** and **shut** overlap in most of their meanings, *close* has a range of additional senses and a greater degree of formality than *shut.* You can *close* or *close on a* business deal. When a business fails, it is usual to talk of it *closing: This branch is closed for business.* When *shut* is used, the same sense is conveyed by adding *down: The factory is shutting down.*

Close can be used as a noun, as in *bring something to a close; the close of day; the close of business. Shut* cannot be used as a noun.

clothed, clad

Clad is one of the alternative past forms of the verb *clothe*; the other is **clothed**. There is a distinction in their use. *Clad* is used when you want to talk about what someone was wearing: *clad in a brown uniform; clad in a pale grey lock-knit petticoat; soberly clad. Clad* can be used for a covering that is not cloth: *steel-clad; timber-clad.* It is a fairly literary word.

Clothed is used when you want to convey the opposite of *undressed: she was fully clothed.* It is used to express how a person is dressed not what they are dressed in: *They are better clothed; My idea was to see you warmly, presentably clothed.*

co-

Most words formed with the compound **co-** are spelled nowadays without a hyphen, e.g. *cooperative* rather than *co-operative*, but the latter form is not wrong.

c/o, Co.

The abbreviation for *care of* is **c/o**. It is used before names in addresses. **Co.** is the abbreviation for *Company*.

cohort

Cohort comes from the Latin for a division of ten soldiers in the Roman army and, later, a band of warriors: *A*

Roman cohort approaches - the natives flee terrified; The German cohorts ran into a hail of bullets. The word **cohort** has now entered sociological and educational jargon to mean the group of students born in, or admitted to a course in, a particular year: *...data on two loosely defined cohorts a generation apart; ...the examination results were taken for each cohort*. This recent usage has revived an old term. It may be somewhat pretentious but it is useful.

coin a phrase

The expression **to coin a phrase** means 'to invent a new way of putting something'. The word **coin** is an old synonym for *make* or *fabricate*, so that if you were to utter a novel comparison you might conclude by saying *to coin a phrase*.

However, the expression is misunderstood by many speakers who use it as if it meant *to quote a well-known phrase: To coin a phrase, this thing is bigger than both of us*. The following is another example of misuse by someone, who admits that what he is saying is not new at all: *And I think – to coin a well-worn word – it is 'relevant' today*. ⇒ **cliché**

collect

Although **collect** strictly means 'gather things together' it is acceptable to use it in the sense of 'call for' or 'pick up': *I'll collect you after school; Would you collect the dry-cleaning?*

collective noun

Collective nouns are usually used with singular verbs: *The family is on holiday; General Motors is mounting a big sales campaign*. In British usage, however, plural verbs are sometimes employed in this context, especially where reference is being made to a collection of individual objects or people rather than to the group as a unit: *The family are all on holiday*.

Care should be taken that the same collective noun is not treated as both singular and plural in the same sentence: *The family is well and sends its best wishes* or *The family are all well and send their best wishes*, but not: [*The family is well and send their best wishes*].

college, school

In British English a **school** is a place of initial or secondary education attended by young people up to the age of about 18. In American English, **school** generally means **university**, which is often the cause of confusion to British speakers. In higher education in Britain, specialist departments may be called a *school* when they have a very cohesive discipline: *School of Oriental and African Studies; School of Tropical Hygiene*.

College is a general term for an institution of higher education in Britain. It is also used for the building itself. A few secondary schools are called *colleges*. An American *college* is usually a place for undergraduate rather than advanced study.

collusion, collaboration

Collusion is the secret agreement of several people to work together for a deceitful purpose: *Brassau once wrote him a letter proposing collusion to double the profit margin on maize*.

Collaboration is working together with someone on a joint programme: *The Germans already have a scientific collaboration with the Japanese*. It is also helping and assisting the enemies of one's country: *…his grandfather had collaborated with the Nazis*.

colon ⇒ punctuation

coloured

The use of **coloured** as a description of racial difference is used only in South Africa. ⇒ **black**

comic, comical, farcical

The meanings of **comic** and **comical** overlap in that both refer to something that causes laughter. However, something **comic** is usually planned or contrived: *The effects of Wodehouse's comic approach,* while something **comical** is often not intentionally funny: *Adams was an imposing if somewhat comical figure; …something about the man, though in great physical distress, that was almost comical.*

A **farcical** situation goes beyond simple comedy to the absurd and almost implausible: *…garrulous, garlicky, with an almost farcical Provençal accent.*

comma ⇒ punctuation

commence ⇒ begin

commentate

The verb **commentate**, derived from *commentator* by back formation, is sometimes used as a synonym for *comment on* or *provide a commentary for.* It is not yet fully accepted as standard, though it is widespread in sports reporting and journalism.

committed, commitment, committal

Committed (adjective) and **commitment** (noun) are associated in meaning. Note the different spellings, which often cause a problem. Both words have to do with the extent to which someone has become involved in a cause or in a course of action: *His commitment and enthusiasm brought a dynamic impulse.* **Committal** has the special meaning of an order to send someone to prison or to confine someone in a mental hospital: *Ten days may elapse between committal and trial....*

common, mutual

When something is the property of a number of people, it is *common to* them. Extending this, if two or more people know another person well, they have this knowledge *in common* and the person is their *common acquaintance*. Because the overtones of **common** include *vulgar, ill-bred,* and *rude,* this last expression is generally avoided. Such a person is often called a *mutual acquaintance.* Purists dislike this use of **mutual**, pointing out that its meaning restricts it to reciprocal situations not shared ones. However, the use of *mutual* with this meaning is very well established, but it could be replaced by *joint.*
⇒ **mutual**

common sense, etc.

There is no firm rule for words compounded with *common.* Some, like **commonwealth**, are written as one word, others, like **common room**, are usually two words. **Common sense** is also written as **common-sense** with a hyphen. You need to look up each one in a dictionary.

comparatives

There are two ways of making an adjective comparative in English. You can preface it with *more* or you can add the suffix *-er* to it. However, not all adjectives can take an *-er* suffix, e.g. *small* can but *little* cannot. A very common error is to use the suffix incorrectly. Another is to duplicate the comparative by adding both *more* and *-er.* Both faults are regularly found in writing by children.

Basically, adjectives that take the *-er* suffix have one syllable: *sad/sadder; large/larger,* or end in an *ee* sound:

angry/angrier; happy/happier. All other adjectives of more than one syllable are prefaced by *more*.

compare

Careful users may wish to distinguish between two constructions that use **compare** while noting that these differences are rarely observed. You use *compare* followed by *to* when it means 'point out a similarity': *A dominant idea can be compared to a river that has cut deep into the landscape.* When you want to make a direct comparison or a contrast you use *with*: *The results are measured experimentally and compared with the theoretical predictions.*

Additionally, *compare* can be used with a plural object: *compare notes; …how do you compare these things?* You can also *compare* one thing *and* another: *Her report compares military and social expenditures.*

compass, compasses

Strictly speaking, a **compass** is a direction-finding device, and a two-legged instrument used in geometry, etc. is a **pair of compasses**. This is usually informally shortened to *compasses*.

compensate

If a person, a thing, or an action **compensates** *for* something, it makes up for it: *…nature seems to compensate for these losses. Compensate* is also used with a direct object and followed by *for*: *This is one of the ways a company can compensate a man for not paying him a higher salary.*

complacent, complacency, complaisant, compliant

Someone who is **complacent** is self-satisfied and smug, that is, in a state of **complacency** or **complacence**, (the last word is not often used): *There was something silly* *and complacent about her look; There's a totally unwarranted complacency in this country about the health of our democracy.*

The adjective *complaisant*, pronounced /cum-**play**-sint/, is often mistakenly used instead of *complacent*. A **complaisant** person willingly and cheerfully fits in with your wishes: *They fanned out over the green, their quarry three complaisant girls…* . A **compliant** person is unresistingly obliging rather than eager to help: *She was fed up with being eternally compliant; The other two were lazy, laughingly compliant.*

compliment, complement

The spelling **compliment** with an *i* can be a verb or a noun. It is used when someone receives praise and congratulations: *The Embassy man's compliments grew louder.*

The verb **complement**, spelled with an *e*, means 'provide whatever is needed to make up a whole': *Her interests and my interests complement each other.* The noun **complement** means a crew or a workforce: *A target tracker and a complement of four soldiers; …a full complement of laboratory technicians.*

In grammar a *complement* is, strictly, whatever completes the full verb phrase. In practice, the full descriptions, such as *direct object complement*, are shortened to *object* etc. and the term *complement* usually means whatever follows a linking verb like *be, seem, look, smell, taste* etc.: *Maddy is an illustrator; Anna seems happy.*

complimentary, complementary

A **complimentary** remark is one in which you are paid a compliment; a *complimentary ticket* is given free, often in recognition of a service. The adjective **complemen-**

tary is used for things that are themselves different, but in combination form a complete or better whole: *...a pattern of contrasting and complementary personalities.* Medicine that uses techniques from outside Western medical practice alongside Western medicine, is sometimes called **complementary** medicine. *Complementary* colours or angles are those that can combine with others. ⇒ **compliment**

compounds

Compounds are words that are created by combining two separate words. They are often created when two words are used frequently as a unit of description. Initially the words remain separate, then users tend to link them with a hyphen, until they are finally written as one word. Any dictionary contains examples of all three stages and some words waver between being hyphenated or a single word for many years. The preferences of users, taken collectively, in due course become reflected in the dictionaries. This is a productive feature in English, but not one that happens as readily as it does in German, for example. ⇒ **common sense**

compress

There are two pronunciations. The verb **compress**, meaning 'squeeze down' or 'pack tight', is pronounced /com-**press**/. The noun *compress* /**com**-press/ is used for a pad applied to an injury, as for example in first aid.

comprise, compose, constitute, consist

There is an overlap between the meanings of these words. Each has to do with the relationship between the parts and the whole, but each has a different type of construction.

Consist is the simplest verb to use. It is always followed by *of* and has the pattern A *consists of* B: *Mortar consists of sand and cement.* **Comprise** commonly causes problems. It already means 'consist of'. You do not follow *comprise* with *of*: *The first group comprises the world's developed nations.*

The verb **compose** means 'make up'. When it is used in the passive as *is/was composed*, it does have to be followed by *of*: *The rest of the delegation was composed of film-makers.* With all these verbs, the viewpoint is of 'a whole that consists of its parts'. When the parts are the subject, and the object is what they make up, the verb **constitute** is used: *Three tanks do not constitute a significant force.* More rarely the active form of *compose* is used: *Fret-sawyers and stamp collectors compose the backbone of society.* ⇒ **consist**

concern

There are a number of different constructions used with **concern**. If you are concerned *in* something, you are involved in it: *...all those concerned in the control chain.* If you are concerned *with* it, it is your responsibility: *The Public Appointments Unit is concerned with a whole range of appointments.* If you are concerned *about/at/for* something, you are worried: *You've got a Mum who is really concerned about you; He became increasingly concerned at our challenge; He was a little too concerned for his own image.* Concern followed by *that* also means 'worried': *He may be genuinely concerned that you are overworked.*

concise, succinct

There is a lot of overlap between these words. A speech that is brief and to the point could be either **concise** or **succinct**. The difference is that something *succinct* must be clear as well as brief.

conclude, end, stop

These words overlap in meaning. **Conclude** is a much more formal word than either **end** or **stop**. *Commence* and *conclude* form opposites as do *begin* and *end*, *start* and *stop*.

conducive

Conducive, meaning 'contributing', usually comes after the noun it modifies and is regularly followed by *to: surfaces conducive to comfort; an atmosphere conducive to quiet and to work.*

connote, denote, connotation, denotation

Something that is **connoted** is not the literal meaning but an implied one. The implied meaning is the word's **connotation** as in *…the word 'primitive' with all its subtle and nasty connotations.* Something that is **denoted** has a clear, literal reference: *My identity was denoted by a plastic label on my wrist; Coloured belts denote skill grades.* The noun **denotation** has the same relationship to its verb as *connotation* does to *connote.* All these words are used in the discussion of the way that words gain meanings. They are very formal. ⇒ **overtone**

consecutive, continual, continuous

Consecutive actions or events follow on without interruption and in order. When an action is **continual** it keeps happening: *His face was handsome though bloated by continual drinking; Obviously continual reprimands lead to a feeling of resentment.*

A **continuous** process has no foreseeable end: *Wear can be compensated by continuous growth throughout the animal's life; With big families there was a continuous supply of labour.* It may also be nonstop and so overlap with the meaning of the words above.

consensus

Avoid the very common mistake of spelling the end of this word -*census*. The word is related to *consent* and the correct spelling is **consensus**: *I don't know if there is a medical consensus about jogging.*

Since *consensus* refers to a collective opinion, the words *of opinion* in the phrase *consensus of opinion* are redundant and are therefore avoided in careful usage.

consequent, consequential

Although both **consequent** and **consequential** can refer to 'that which follows as a result', *consequent* is more frequently used in this sense in modern English: *The new measures were put into effect, and the consequent protest led to the dismissal of those responsible.* **Consequential** is often used in legal or commercial contexts.

conservative, Conservative

If someone is **conservative** they respect old values and resist change. A **Conservative** is a member of a political party.

consider ⇒ regard

consist

When **consist** is followed by *of* it means 'composed of various elements': *The thesis may consist of either published or unpublished work; Modern grasslands tend to consist of a small number of species.* When **consist** is followed by *in* (and sometimes by *of*) it can mean 'have its being in': *Her whole life consists in looking after her elderly parents.* ⇒ **comprise**

consult

You **consult** someone or something in British English: *I consulted several people; I consulted the menu.* The object can be followed by *about, on,* or *over* something: *I consulted him about my illness* or *on matters of policy* or *over everything.* The construction *consult with* is purely an Americanism.

consummate

The adjective **consummate**, pronounced /con-**sum**-mit/, means 'masterly' or 'supremely skilled': *She concealed herself under witchlike wigs and costumes of consummate eccentricity.* The verb **consummate** is pronounced /**con**-su-mate/. This means to bring something to completion. Be careful not to confuse the two pronunciations.

contagious, infectious

Certain diseases are passed on by contact of some sort. These are often called **contagious** diseases: *Ringworm is a fungal disease that is contagious.* An **infectious** disease is passed on without personal contact, e.g. by airborne viruses.

contemporary

Strictly, **contemporary** means 'of the same period', as in *It is useful to compare Shakespeare's plays with those of contemporary* (that is, other Elizabethan) *playwrights.* The word is, however, often used to mean 'modern' or 'up-to-date' in contexts such as: *The furniture was of a contemporary design.* The second use should be avoided where ambiguity is likely to arise, as in *a production of 'Othello' in contemporary dress.* In such contexts, *modern dress* or *Elizabethan dress* should be used to avoid ambiguity.

contemptible, contemptuous

These words represent different aspects of the same situation. When someone's behaviour falls below expected standards, they are regarded as being **contemptible**, or worthy of contempt. The person who feels contempt towards someone is **contemptuous**.

content

The noun **content** meaning 'substance' or 'subject matter', is pronounced /**con**-tent/, the verb, meaning 'willing', and the adjective meaning 'happy', are pronounced /con-**tent**/.

contiguous ⇒ adjacent

contraction

A **contraction** is any short spoken form such as *won't*, *can't*, *it's*, and so on. Many contractions that are common in speech are not used in written English unless it is very informal.

contrary, converse, opposite

The pronunciation of **contrary** can be either /**con**-trer-ie/ or /con-**trair**-ie/. When you use the first pronunciation you are stating an opposite point of view to one just uttered: '*You'll get tired of it.*' '*On the contrary. It'll save me beating you.*' You use the second pronunciation when you want to suggest that someone is stubborn: *A contrary race, the Liverpudlians.*

The **converse** of something is its direct opposite. It is a rather technical word: *…the converse is equally true.* **Opposite** is a much more general word and can be used in many contexts where the other words would not be appropriate.

controversy

There are two pronunciations for **controversy** depending on where stress is placed. The one used by RP speakers and in BBC news reports is /**con**-tro-versy/ but many

British speakers favour /con-tro-versy/. American speakers of English use the first form.

corn, maize

Corn is a general word for any grain crop in British English but in American English it means **maize**. *Sweetcorn (corn on the cob)*, *cornflakes*, and *cornflour* are three words where, exceptionally, *corn* specifically means *maize* in Britain.

corporal punishment, capital punishment

Punishing someone physically by beating them is **corporal punishment**, so called because it is inflicted on the body of the person. Punishment by execution is **capital punishment**.

corps, corpse

A **corps** is a group of soldiers. The word is pronounced /kaw/. A **corpse** is a dead body, and pronounced /kawps/.

correspond

When **correspond** is followed by *with* it means 'exchange letters with'. When it is followed by *to* it means 'match up with' or 'be similar to' something: *There are breaks in the sound but they do not correspond to the ends of the sentences.*

correspondent, co-respondent

A **correspondent** is someone who exchanges letters with you. A **co-respondent** is someone who, in terms of the divorce laws, has been cited as a third party in a divorce case.

corrigenda

Errors that have to be corrected in a text that has already been printed are called, **corrigenda**, a plural word. The singular is **corrigendum**.

corroborate, verify

If you **corroborate** a statement you agree that the facts it contains are correct: *He begged her to corroborate his story.* You usually only use *corroborate* about statements. When you **verify** something, such as an experiment, you investigate all the facts to make sure that they are true.

council, counsel

A **council** is a meeting of an official body, and those who meet there are the *councillors.* To give advice is to **counsel** someone: *Part of the staff's work is to counsel families,* and those who give the advice are *counsellors: Get the help of the school guidance counsellor.* In the legal profession, however, a barrister is not called a counsellor but a **counsel:** *Prosecuting counsel called him 'a thoroughly filthy fellow'.*

couple, several

A **couple** is two of something but it is not treated as exactly two in familiar speech: *Let me have a couple of nails* is a request for *a small number* of nails. **Several** is an indeterminate number of something. It is much the same as *a few.* It suggests 'not many'.

credible, credulous, creditable

These three words are sometimes confused. **Credible** means believable: *'Tim has got a mistress.' 'Oh, it's scarcely credible.'* A **credulous** person is someone who is too ready to believe what they are told: *Rumours were whispered round the town and believed by the credulous folk.* Something **creditable** is worthy of praise: *That's very creditable in a young man of his age.*

credit, credence

Credit is a general term and can be used as a verb or a noun. It has more than one meaning.

It can be used about the strength of belief that is placed in someone or something and has overtones of trust: *There must be many of you who find this case hard to credit.*

It can be used for the repute that will be given to something: *The Times credited itself with having nudged the change; ...an 11th-century monk credited with the invention of the musical stave.*

Credence is a very formal word for the believability of someone or something: *Can you place any credence in the tales of a vagabond boy? He deployed The Times to bestow credence and respectability upon the slanderers.*

creole, pidgin

A **creole** is a particular variety of a language (usually European) that is spoken by the second or later generation of certain social or linguistic groups. A *creole* arises through colonization or enslavement, when people who usually speak their own language are obliged to learn a limited amount of the language of those for whom they are working in order to communicate effectively. This intermediary language, a *pidgin*, typically contains words and constructions from more than one language. If this intermediary becomes the first language of the family group, *creolization* has taken place. Some varieties of Jamaican English and other Caribbean Englishes are creoles. ⇒ **pigeon**

criterion

Note that **criteria** is the plural of **criterion**, although it is sometimes mistakenly used as a singular noun. In careful written and spoken English you should have either: *This criterion is not valid,* or: *These criteria are not valid.*

critical

The use of **critically ill** to mean simply *very ill* devalues its real sense of 'at a crisis point' or 'at a turning point'.

cult, religion

The overall term is **religion**. The word **cult** is usually disparaging. This attitude is expressed by: *I have a religion; other people belong to cults.* The exception is when it is used as a term in the sociology of religion: *the cult of the Virgin; It is difficult to conceive how an active pagan cult could have survived.* When talking about society in general, a *cult* is any temporarily fashionable pursuit with a large and fervent following: *It's part of the 'back to nature' cult.*

cupful ⇒ **-ful** ⇒ **spoonful**

curb

As a noun, a **curb** is a means of controlling a horse or, by extension, controlling anything else: *High interest rates act as a curb on inflation.* As a verb, it means 'constrain': *He curbed her enthusiasm for spending.* ⇒ **kerb**

current, currant

Current is the word for the flow of water or electricity. When something is up-to-date it is **current**. The berries or the small dried fruit are **currants**, as in *red currants; a currant bun.* The name is a short form of the older term *raisin of Corinth.*

cypress, Cyprus

The dark green trees common in all Europe (*cupressus*) are spelled **cypress**. Do not confuse the spelling with that of the island of **Cyprus**.

D

damn

Damn has a final *n* as it is short for *damnation*.

dare

When **dare** is used negatively or interrogatively and not followed by an infinitive with *to*, it does not add *-s*: *He dare not; Dare she come?*

dashes ⇒ punctuation

data

Although **data** is regularly used as a singular noun, it is properly a plural, with a singular form *datum*. Very careful users, particularly in the sciences, write *the data are prepared*, not *is prepared*, but others feel uncomfortable with this usage.

dates

The written form of **dates** has a number of minor variants. The major conventions in expressing dates are the British style that follows the day, month, year format, and the American style that follows the month, day, year format. The major forms within the British style are the **long date** and the **short date**. The long date gives the name of the month and, optionally, the name of the day: *11 August 1990/ Saturday 11 August 1990*. The use of *st, nd, rd, th* is optional. The long date is sometimes written in the American or reverse order: *August 11th 1990*. An alternative is *August 11, 1990*. The *short date* is written *11.8.90* or *11/8/90*. An apostrophe is not necessary.

When dates are written in pairs it is only necessary to

give as much of the second one as is needed to prevent ambiguity: *1990-2; 1936-90; 1895-1990* but say, e.g. *from 1990 to 1992.* ⇒ **A.D.**

de, de la, du, van, von, zu

These and other particles are sometimes part of a foreign proper noun. It is customary not to use a capital letter for them: *the Marquis de Sade; Herbert von Karajan*.

deadly, deathly

Deadly means likely to cause death. It is also used very informally to mean 'boring': *deadly dull*. **Deathly** is a fairly informal word and means 'as if already dead' or 'like death': *deathly pale; a deathly silence*.

debar, disbar

When someone is **debarred** they are prevented *from* receiving a privilege, or kept from a place: *These men were debarred from employment by their background*. The word **disbar** is a special term, used when a barrister's right to appear before the Bench is taken away as a penalty for improper behaviour. Both words are formal.

debouch

Debouch meaning 'move into an open area' is pronounced /di-**bowch**/. The word entered English with the sound of the original French *bouche*, pronounced /boosh/, but this is not much used today.

debris

No accent is needed on **debris**. In British English the pronunciation is /**deb**-ree/ or /**day**-bree/ with the stress on the first syllable. In American English, the stress can be on either syllable.

debut

Debut is a noun, not a verb, and it is incorrect to speak of *debuting* something in the sense of initiating it. The usage appears to be a recent American one. The idiom in British English is *make a debut*.

deca-

The prefix **deca-** multiplies by ten the item that it is associated with: *decahedron; decalitre; decathlon*.

decade

When referring to a decade you use the form *the 1960s, the 1720s*. It is not necessary to place an apostrophe before the *s*. When the century is clear from the context, you can use the form *the 60s* or *the '20s* (with an optional apostrophe before the date) but it is preferable to write it in full: *the sixties; the twenties*. ⇒ **dates**

deceitful, deceptive

Both **deceitful** and **deceptive** are based on *deceit*. The difference is that *deceitful* is generally used of a person who is deliberately dishonest: *Their evidence varied from the inept to the downright deceitful*. **Deceptive** is generally used about a situation or thing that leads someone astray by giving a false air of truth: *But the silence was deceptive; behind the shuttered windows people waited; Such labelling is both deceptive and dishonest*.

deci-

The prefix **deci-** divides by ten the item that it is associated with: *decibel; decimetre; decimate*.

decided, decisive

Decided overlaps slightly with **decisive**. A *decided advantage* is one which cannot be questioned. *A decided manner* suggests that a person is acting with considerable self-assurance.

The meaning of **decisive** has become expanded. It basically implies that something has caused an issue to be resolved: *The decisive blow was struck.* We can now talk of someone having *a decisive manner*, that is, the manner of someone who is capable of making decisions, and acting decisively.

decidedly

The adverb **decidedly** is often used as an intensifier and means much the same as *extremely* or *very: A man in his late forties with decidedly humorous, twinkling eyes; Arthur was decidedly drunk.*

decimal point

Conventions relating to the use of the **decimal point** are confused. The IX General Conference on Weights and Measures resolved in 1948 that the decimal point should be a point on the line or a comma, but not a centre dot. It also resolved that figures could be grouped in threes about the decimal point, but that no point or comma should be used for this purpose.

However, the Decimal Currency Board recommended that for sums of money the centre dot should be used as the decimal point and that the comma should be used as the thousand marker. Moreover, in some countries the position is reversed, the comma being used as the decimal point and the dot as the thousand marker.

decimate

The original meaning of **decimate** related to a Roman form of military punishment in which every tenth man in a mutinous regiment was executed. There has been a shift in meaning and *decimate* is currently used to mean 'kill almost all or a large part': *Sometimes entire wards of birthing women were decimated by this infection.* Do not use *decimate* with a modifier like *totally*, or followed by a proportion, such as *half* or a percentage.

decor, decoration

The pronunciation of the initial vowel differs. **Decor** is /day-core/, **decoration** is /dek-or-a-tion/.

deduction, deduce, deduct

Deduction has two principal meanings. A **deduction** is 'an amount subtracted from a total' as in *tax deductions*. The verb that relates to this meaning is **deduct**. Secondly, a **deduction** is 'a conclusion that is formed on the basis of reasoning': *My main academic work was on natural deduction*. The verb that relates to the second meaning is **deduce**: *From the way she replied, I deduced that visits were not allowed*.

defective, deficient

When something is **defective** it is faulty or flawed in some way that makes it unfit for use: *The inspection showed that not one part was defective*. Something that is **deficient** in a quality either lacks something that is necessary or does not come up to the expectations that are held of it: *Hardly anyone's diet is deficient in B-vitamins; They were deficient in experience*.

defence, defense

These are the same word. **Defence** is the British spelling and **defense** is the American spelling.

defensive, defensible

Defensive is most often used as an adjective and as a noun in military contexts as the opposite of *offensive*. A common phrase is *on the defensive: A spirited defensive campaign; The military is everywhere on the defensive.* Someone acting in a **defensive** manner rejects criticism and tries to cover up for mistakes: *His reactions were all defensive and resisting*. To say to someone, *You are being very defensive*, is to suggest that they are behaving weakly. Something that is **defensible** can be defended and, by extension, excused or justified by the person responsible for it: *Was his insolence defensible, in theory, as candour?*

deficit

A **deficit** is a shortage, especially of money. The accepted pronunciation is /**def**-fi-cit/, with stress on the first syllable.

definite, definitive

Definite and *definitive* should be carefully distinguished. **Definite** indicates precision and firmness, as in *a definite decision*. **Definitive** includes these senses but also indicates conclusiveness. A *definite* answer indicates a clear and firm answer to a particular question; a *definitive* answer implies an authoritative resolution of a complex question.

definitely

Definitely is often used in place of *yes*. This is not advisable in careful speech as it can become a mannerism and it devalues the word for other uses. ⇒ **absolutely**

deity

The older accepted pronunciation of *deity* is /**dee**-i-ty/ but /**day**-i-ty/ is now in common use.

delimit

To **delimit** means to mark out the boundaries of something, for example, a responsibility. It is sometimes incorrectly used to mean 'remove the limits'.

delusion, illusion

A **delusion** is a mental state in which someone is convinced of the truth of something that is not so. An **illusion** is something unreal or untrue that deceives you into believing it.

de luxe, deluxe

The British form for this adjective is **de luxe** or **de-luxe**. Some users of American English write **deluxe** and use it as an adverb. The usual pronunciation is /de **lucks**/ not /de **lukes**/.

demand

The verb **demand** is frequently followed by *of: the qualities demanded of junior leaders*. With a direct object, the construction is *demand* something *from* or *of* someone: *…demand an explanation from you; …demands too much of his staff.*

When **demand** is used as a noun, it is often followed by *for: the demand for labour; a demand for education*. The noun is regularly used in the plural; you *make demands on* something or someone *for* something: *demands on the system for more wages; demands for power sharing; demands for control.*

demi-, semi-

The prefix **demi-** means 'half' or 'not completely'. It is no longer used to form new words. The prefix **semi-** also means 'half' or 'partially'. If you wish to form a word with the 'half' prefix, *semi-* is still productive. ⇒ **semi-**

denote ⇒ **connote**

denouement

Denouement does not need an accent in English, though it is not incorrect to use one (dénouement). It is pronounced /day-**noo**-mon/ and means the point where a mystery is resolved.

depend

Depend means either 'rely on', or 'be resultant on' and is normally followed by *on* or *upon: That decision would* *depend on several considerations; Chances of survival depend upon the degree of exposure.* In informal speech *upon* and *on* are often left out, as in *It does depend what you mean; That depends.*

dependent, dependant, dependency

In British English, the noun **dependant** means someone who requires or receives aid and support: *Extra pensions for dependants; We were going to raise the tax threshold for taxpayers with young dependants.* A person in such a situation is **dependent** (adjective) on someone or something: *They found themselves increasingly dependent on the support of the British.* In American English, sometimes no distinction is made between the *-ent* and the *-ant* spellings in the use of these words

Dependency was once used as a concrete noun only, as in *the Antarctic Dependency,* but it is now used abstractly, as in *drug dependency.*

deprecate, depreciate

To **deprecate** something is to have scruples about it: *He deprecated Bernstein's disparagement of my approach,* or to show your poor opinion of it: *You may underestimate his general ability, or you may even deprecate his efforts; Mrs Mawne smiled deprecatingly and spread her hands.* This overlaps with one of the meanings of **depreciate**, which is to criticize something so that it begins to seem worthless: *He was keeping quiet about the whole thing, trying to depreciate it, play it down.*

The usual meaning of *depreciate,* however, is 'steadily lose value': *The fixtures and fittings had all depreciated in value; He had offered them an investment that was certain to depreciate.*

derisive, derisory

These two adjectives reflect different aspects of the same general meaning, which comes from the noun *derision*. If someone takes an attitude towards something that ridicules it or mocks it, you would describe it as a **derisive** attitude: *His tone was menacingly derisive; The sniggering of the savages became a loud derisive jeer.*

When something is so ridiculous that you find it hard to take it seriously, then you could say that the object of your scorn is **derisory**: *The amount of research into low input and biological farming is quite derisory; He had to sell his cattle off at derisory prices.*

descendant, descendent

Descendant is a noun. It is generally used to mean someone or something come down from the parental stock or source: *It was a nocturnal animal the size of a shrew whose later descendants adopted the daytime life of a fruit-eater; I will give this land to you and to your descendants.* It is sometimes spelled *descendent*, though there is also a little-used adjective **descendent**, used to describe something that has descended.

desert, deserts, dessert

There are two words spelled **desert**. The noun (pronounced /**dez**-ert/) is an arid, infertile region: *the boring old Mojave desert.* The verb (pronounced /de-**zert**/) means 'abandon' or 'run away from': *His supporters did not desert him in his hour of need.*

The plural noun **deserts** means 'what you deserve': *It can't be too long before he has his deserts.* Your *just deserts* are what you deservedly have coming. A **dessert**, with a double *s*, is the sweet course in a meal, sometimes called the pudding.

deshabille, dishevelled

Deshabille or dishabille means 'in a half-dressed state'. The form *deshabille* is marginally more common and is pronounced /days-ha-**beel**/. It is normally used with *in*, or sometimes *en*, as in *He had appeared in a rather daring form of deshabille; They were photographed posing en deshabille.* (Some writers prefer to use the accented French spelling *déshabillé* with *en*, but this is not necessary.)

Dishevelled originally meant 'with untidy hair' but has expanded to mean 'in a state of disturbed dress or generally personally untidy': *He presented a very dishevelled appearance.*

despicable

A BBC guide to pronunciation recommends that **despicable** should be pronounced with the stress on the first syllable. A stress on the second syllable /di-**spic**-able/ is much more frequently heard, however, and this appears to be the normal British form.

destruct, destroy

The verb **destruct** is a back formation from *destruction*. It is usually found as a technical term in weaponry: *If the launch mechanism fails the rocket will self-destruct.* Otherwise it serves no real purpose that **destroy** cannot satisfy, and should be avoided.

desultory

The preferred pronunciation places the stress on the first syllable /**des**-sul-to-ry/.

detail

In British English the stress is on the first syllable /**dee**-tail/. A stress on the second syllable /de-**tail**/ is American.

deteriorate

To pronounce **deteriorate** acceptably, avoid missing out the second *r* sound, an error which many people dislike. The correct form has five syllables, /dee-**tier**-ee-or-ate/.

detour

Detour is pronounced /dee-tour/.

develop, development

Something that *develops* moves forward by degrees: *...by a quite fortuitous process he has developed certain skills.* Avoid using *develop* when there is no suggestion of a gradual occurrence.

device, devise

Device is a noun. It means 'a piece of equipment': *...simple mechanical devices.* Nowadays, it is also a euphemism for *bomb*. The meaning 'plot' or 'trick', as in *a grasping woman who would stoop to any device to lay hands on his money,* is now rare. *Devices* is always plural in the idiom *leave (someone) to (his) own devices,* which means 'leave someone to look after himself'. The verb is **devise.** It means 'use skill and ingenuity to plan something': *He has been ingenious in devising new taxes.* A less common use of *devise,* found in wills, means 'give'.

devil's advocate

To act as **the devil's advocate** is to raise all the possible objections to a course of action and to suggest reasons why it should not proceed. This is to allow the other case to be put in its strongest terms. The phrase is often misused as 'someone trying to put a bad case in a good light'.

devolve, devolution

Devolve, meaning 'pass on authority to a successor', is normally followed by *on, upon,* or *to: Authority can be devolved to local and regional communities.* The noun **devolution** has the same broad sense, as in *It is a clear demand for the devolution of power from the boardroom to the shopfloor.*

In the context of biological science, the use of *devolution* to mean *degeneration* began as an academic witticism for the converse of **evolution**, but the usage has now become well established.

devoted, devotee, devout

Devoted strictly describes a quasi-religious attachment to something or someone: *I'm passionately devoted to music,* but it is often overused for an everyday form of attachment: *'They were fond of each other?' 'Yes, they were devoted.'* The noun **devotee** (pronounced /dev-o-tee/) is normally used to refer to a fervent follower of some religious creed.

Devout, except as a metaphor (*devout two-handed drinkers*), describes a pious attachment: *a devout Christian.*

diabolic, diabolical, demonic, demoniac(al)

The adjectives **diabolic**, **demonic**, and **demoniac(al)** are used about the devil, as in *Her hysterics led to their suspicion of diabolic possession,* but **diabolical** is now used as a very informal way of saying that something is excruciatingly bad or outrageous: *He took a diabolical liberty.*

diagnose

When a doctor **diagnoses** something, he or she identifies a disease from its symptoms; he does not diagnose someone: *a provisional diagnosis of schizophrenia; You need a doctor to make the diagnosis.* You should not say [*Dr Smith diagnosed Bill*] but *He examined Bill and his diagnosis was* (or *he diagnosed*) *influenza.*

dialect, dialectic, dialectics

The grammar and the speech patterns used by a distinct group of speakers within a language constitute a **dialect**: *Standard Southern English is a prestigious dialect; the thick dialect of the Mississippi delta*. **Dialectic** involves the exercise of the powers of argument. It is sometimes used interchangeably with **dialectics**, which is a particular philosophical approach to human history: *…the imperatives of the dialectic of revolution*.

dialogue

Dialogue is increasingly used to mean formal or informal discussions between two or more parties: *dialogue between Hungary and the NATO Alliance*.

dice

While it is true that *die* is the singular of the word **dice** it is effectively obsolete and only survives in the phrase *the die is cast*. Use *dice* as the singular and the plural form.

dictionary, lexicon, glossary

A **dictionary** and a **lexicon** are much the same thing except that the term *lexicon* is often used for the dictionary of an ancient language or for an explanatory list of the meanings of a specialized subject. A **glossary** is a set of explanations of specialized terms that the author of a book thinks readers will find helpful.

different

The choice of the appropriate preposition to follow **different** causes problems. If we look back at the usage of past writers of British English who have established reputations, the constructions *different from, different to,* and *different than* can all be found. Nowadays, in British English, the choice has settled on the use of *from* as the most acceptable preposition: *The point is that the 'L'* *unit is not different from the 'T' unit; There was a cluster of wooden huts not much different from what we had just left.*

Different to is not uncommon in British English, but many people find it unacceptable. They would substitute *from* for the word *to* in: *I am a Celt and different to them.*

The standard construction in American English is *different than: A learned neurotic is not any different than an unlearned neurotic.* This usage is not regarded as acceptable in British English.

differentiate, distinguish

There is no significant difference between these words. Both mean 'tell the difference between'.

digest

The pronunciation of the noun and the verb differs. The noun, meaning 'a summary of information', is /**die**-jest/, and the verb, meaning 'assimilate', is /die-**jest**/. Some speakers also shorten the *i* sound in the verb.

digraph, diphthong

A **digraph** is either a special symbol, or *ligature*, where a combined letter-form is used: *æ, œ* (these are less used today) or where a double letter form represents a sound: *ph, kn, gh.*

A **diphthong** is a typical English vowel sound; a syllable begins with one vowel sound and glides to another. In the word *my*, the vowel is a *diphthong*, /**my-ee**/. ⇒ -æ-

dilemma

A **dilemma** is a choice between two courses of action, neither of which is fully acceptable: *At the church gates they were presented with a dilemma. Should they go in and take their places, or should they wait?* Careful writers avoid using *dilemma* loosely for 'problem' if it does not involve choice.

diminish, minimize

When something **diminishes** it becomes smaller: *The sale of relics to attract pilgrims had not diminished; rather it had reached an all-time peak*. If you **minimize** a situation, you attempt, for your own reasons, to make it less likely or seem less significant: *Our aim must be to minimize the risks of war in the European theatre; All this is aimed at minimizing the human damage wrought by rapid change*.

diminutives

Diminutives in English are noun forms that have a suffix that means 'small' attached to them. Sometimes the base noun is shortened. The suffixes *-kin, -let, -ie, -ling*, and *-ette* are used to form diminutives e.g. *manikin, starlet, mousie, duckling, maisonette*. Diminutives of people's names (*Susie, Jilly, Ronnie, Frankie*) can be regarded by adults as presumptuous or belittling, unless used by people who form part of a close circle of friendship. Avoid using the diminutive of someone's name until you are sure that it will be acceptable.

dint, dent

The idiom **by dint of** means 'by use of': *Such sites might be protected by dint of sympathetic planning*. **Dint** is also an alternative spelling of **dent**.

direct, directly

You use **direct** if you mean *straight*. When you mean *straight away* you use **directly**. *Directly* is also used when something is in a precise position relative to something else: *...directly under the bed*. *Directly* is also used to mean 'in person': *I shall be writing to you directly, within* *the next few days*. Be careful that the context makes this use distinguishable from *straight away*.

direct speech

Direct speech is another name for the record of a conversation that quotes the exact words spoken by the participants. The actual speech is surrounded by *speech marks* or *quotation marks*. By convention, each speaker's words are placed on a new line. It is optional for the lines of dialogue to be accompanied by an indication of who spoke the words, and possibly the manner in which they were spoken.

'You are armed already?', he asked abruptly.
'No.'
'Then what is the difficulty?'

Direct speech is regularly found in fiction.

dis-, dys-

Dis- is a prefix that is added to verbs, words derived from verbs, and adjectives. Like *de-*, it includes the sense of the reversal or the negation of the base meaning: *disappear, discover, disgrace, dissimilar*. *Dis-* becomes *dif-* before *f* and *di-* before certain consonants.

The prefix **dys-** means 'faulty' or 'bad' and is extended to mean 'diseased'. It is regularly found as a prefix to medical terms such as *dysentery; dysfunction; dyslexia*.

disappear

Disappear is a commonly misspelled word; it has one *s* and a double *p*. It is a combination of double *dis-* and *appear*. ⇒ **disappoint**

disappoint

Disappoint is a commonly misspelled word; it has one *s* and a double *p*. It originally meant 'remove from office' and is formed from *dis-* and *appoint.* ⇒ **disappear**

disastrous, disaster

Disastrous is a commonly misspelled word. When the noun **disaster** becomes an adjective it is shortened to *disast-* and *-rous* is added; there is no *e.* Compare it with *enter,* which drops an *e* when forming the noun *entry.*

disc, disk

In general, the spelling **disc** is British and **disk** is American except that the musical device, the *Compact Disc,* is so spelled in both British English and American English. Usage in computing differs. American sources prefer *disk* as in *disk drive.* Some computer manuals insist on the spelling *disc,* but within the trade, both spellings are used, though with a tendency to prefer *disk.* Small disks are called *diskettes.* The form *disk* is well established in English dictionaries.

discomfort, discomfit

Discomfort is the feeling of not being at ease: *Physical discomfort melted into embarrassment.* **Discomfit** is a very formal literary word and much stronger than *discomfort.* When you *discomfit* someone, you upset their plans as well as make them feel uneasy: *Mrs Maune, though a trifle discomfited, joined battle.* **Discomfiture** is the state of being *discomfited: Hilary, trying to overcome her discomfiture, emerged into the sunlight as they returned.* ⇒ **discompose**

discompose, disconcert

If you *discompose* someone, you upset the even process of their life: *The situation worried and discomposed me.* This word overlaps in meaning with **disconcert**, which has the additional sense of 'make someone feel ill at ease': *The cat's cold stare disconcerted Rudolph; He* *found Gwen's directness disconcerting.* ⇒ **discomfort**

discreet, discrete
These words can cause considerable confusion. If you are able to keep your own counsel and not spread abroad other people's plans, you are **discreet**: *They had always considered Jill to be ladylike and discreet.* When something is separate and not part of a continued series it is **discrete**: *They operate in a series of discrete steps.*

discretion, discreetness, discreteness
Discretion is the ability to keep one's own and other's affairs private or to exercise good judgment. Another name for this quality is **discreetness**: *They behaved with taste and discretion; Use your discretion.* **Discretion** has a further use. It can mean the exercise of control over a course of action: *…the grant was at the local authority's discretion; We do not come here at the discretion of Mr Speaker.*

Discreteness is derived from *discrete*. It is the quality of individuality that some people or things may possess: *She had retained something of that old discreteness, some aura of difference from everyone else.*

discriminate
Discriminate has two meanings that are somewhat at variance. When it has the first meaning, 'make a judicious choice', it should be followed by *between*: *…equipped with devices that can discriminate between light and dark.* When it has the second meaning, 'exercise a prejudice', it should be followed by *against*: *It would discriminate against those who could not afford it.*

disenfranchise, disfranchise
Both words mean 'deprive someone of the right to vote'.

The form in normal use is **disenfranchise**.

disinterested, uninterested

In spoken and sometimes in written English, *disinterested*, meaning 'impartial', is often used where *uninterested*, meaning 'showing or feeling lack of interest', is meant. Careful writers and speakers avoid this confusion.

The difference lies not in the prefixes *dis-* and *un-*, which both indicate a negative quality, but in the two meanings of **interest**.

One is 'have a financial or personal involvement in something', probably for one's personal gain. The word that uses this sense is **disinterested**: *I don't think you should remain ignorant of so generous and disinterested a gesture*. The second is 'have an intellectual involvement in something'. The word that uses this sense is **uninterested**: *He gave an uninterested nod and waved him away*. ⇒ **dispassionate**

dislike

Dislike can be either a noun or a verb. You can have a *dislike of* something or someone: *Fashion typifies the crowd's dislike of freedom*, or *take a dislike to* something or someone: *This caused him to take an instinctive dislike to the man*.

The verb **dislike** either has a noun as a direct object: *How I dislike that man*, or it is followed by the *-ing* verb construction: *He disliked being called 'Phil'; She dislikes having people for dinner*.

dispassionate, impassive, impassioned

A **dispassionate** reaction to an event is one in which reason rather than emotion is in control: *He studied the view from the window with the same dispassionate inter-*

est with which he had examined the room. If someone or something is **inpassive** they give no sign of any form of response to a situation: *Straight-backed, silent, impassive, unheeding men and women.* Something or someone **impassioned** is the opposite: *impassioned quarrels; an impassioned attack on conditions.*

dispatch, despatch
These are alternative spellings of the same word. **Dispatch** is the more common.

dispense, dispose
When **dispense** has the meaning of making up and giving out a remedy as a pharmacist does, the thing dispensed is the direct object: *We cannot dispense certain preparations in the pharmacist's absence.* When *dispense* means 'do without' it is followed by *with*: *In the summer heat she dispensed with stockings.* **Dispose** meaning 'get rid of' is followed by *of*: *He hanged himself and his body was secretly disposed of.* When *disposed* means 'prepared' it is followed by *to*: *No one will feel disposed to comment adversely on that.*

dispersal, dispersion
These words reflect different aspects of the same situation. When you cause the spreading of a thing or a group of people, you are effecting **dispersal**: *...measures to control the dispersal of asbestos.* What results from that is **dispersion**.

dissatisfied, unsatisfied
If someone is **dissatisfied**, they are not pleased by some service or product that they have met with: *Too many clients are dissatisfied with the level of aftersales service.* If someone is **unsatisfied** their needs and wishes have not been provided for: *Unsatisfied demand for consumer goods could lead to unrest.*

dissemble, disassemble

If someone **dissembles**, they are hiding their true feelings: *...a faith dissembling behind scepticism.* When you **disassemble** something, you take it to pieces.

dissension, dissent, assent

Dissent is the act of objecting to something and is the opposite of **assent**: *The plan had won approval without dissent.* It can also mean a radical position against conformity in one's religious or political beliefs: *The moral vision of dissent informs his notions of democracy.*

Dissension means taking part in a discussion or an activity that leads to a quarrel: *From the very beginning there was dissension and confusion.*

dissoluble

Despite appearances, **dissoluble** means the same as **soluble**, that is, able to be dissolved.

distinct, distinctive, distinguished

Something **distinct** can be seen or heard clearly. Something **distinctive** is clearly different from similar things: *Each clan has its distinctive pattern or patterns*, or typical of its kind: *Stem tall, yellowish brown, with a distinctive yellow ring.*

Generally, **distinguished** as an adjective means 'famous' or 'significant': *He had completed a distinguished career.* However, the verb *distinguish* means 'perceive' or 'differentiate' and is often followed by *between*: *The squid can distinguish polarized light; There is no reason to distinguish between the two.* The past participle **distinguished** is used in constructions like: *It can be distinguished by its brilliant red coloration*, where the sense is 'told apart from a similar one'.

distrust, mistrust

Distrust means a fundamental lack of belief in the sincerity of someone's motives: *Distrust, suspicion, jealousy, Dr Marlowe; …there is a profound abyss of mutual distrust and lack of understanding*. **Mistrust** is the lack of faith in someone or in one's own judgment, marked by hesitancy and indecision: *…the two are separated by silence, by awkwardness, by mistrust or exasperation; someone with a profound mistrust of words*. Someone you **distrust** could be treacherous; someone you **mistrust** might let you down.

divorcée, divorcé

A **divorcée** is a woman, and a **divorcé** a man, who has been divorced. Keep the original French accent on these spellings. A preferable alternative form, **divorcee**, has no accent and, like *employee*, can be used for both sexes.
⇒ **-ee**

dogged

Dogged pronounced with two distinct syllables /dog-ed/ means 'stubborn and persistent'. **Dogged** /dogd/ means 'followed closely': *Bad luck had dogged Vandervoort*.

do let's, don't let's, let's not

Sentences that include one of these clauses are a form of command. Some people dislike the use of *do* in combination with the abbreviated form of *let us*, which is **let's**. There is no sound reason for this dislike. **Do let's *go*** is a more pressing way of saying *let's go* and it is no different in this respect from the use of *do* in other emphatic statements, e.g. *Do come along! Do finish it tonight!*

When **let us** is made negative, **let's not** is a standard construction and, if it is used in conjunction with the emphatic *do*, the negative form is **don't let's**. Speakers of

British English find the American form *Let's don't...* very unusual. These abbreviated forms are all informal. ⇒ **let**

dominate, domineer

Both words mean 'control firmly': *The United States no longer dominates the world as it did 30 years ago.* **Dominate** is neutral but **domineer** means 'control in an overpowering way': *He becomes more domineering, she more cringing.*

don

Don is used in newspapers as a general term for a university teacher. The term is traditionally used for members of the teaching staff at Oxford and Cambridge and it is applied by extension to lecturers at other universities. Very few lecturers would actually use *don* as a description of their job.

double negatives

Double negatives are condemned by purists who regard them as one of the touchstones of uneducated speech. In fact, double negatives have a long history of acceptability and were common in earlier forms of English. The dislike of double negatives arose from the incorrect belief that two negatives always make a positive. This concept was taken from formal logic which is not relevant to the way language is used.

The use of what is technically a **double negative** is acceptable in several contexts. An adjective with negative force is often used with a negative in order to express a nuance of meaning somewhere between the positive and the negative: *He was a not infrequent visitor; It is not an uncommon sight.* Two negatives are also found together where they reinforce each other rather than conflict: *He never went back, not even to collect his* *belongings*. A third case, illustrated by *I shouldn't won-der if it didn't rain today*, has the force of a weak positive statement (*I expect it to rain today*) and is common in informal English.

Double negatives are also used acceptably in sentences where they are deliberately intended to cancel each other out. These are special cases. For example: *Don't not do it for my sake* is really a comment on a previous negative statement: *I won't do it (as you're here)*. The speaker uses a negative to 'undo' a previous negative.

While double negatives, apart from those illustrated, are generally not part of standard usage, they are usually part of regional dialect. In language terms, two or more negatives are often more emphatic than one, as in *I ain't never gonna do it no more*. Their use does not cancel out the meaning of a sentence as was once taught, whatever else such a sentence suggests.

doubt, doubtful

Where a clause follows the verb **doubt** in a positive state-ment, the conjunction may be *whether, that,* or *if*. *Whether* is universally accepted: *I doubt whether he is there*. *That* is less widely accepted: *I doubt that he is there,* and *if* is usually restricted to informal contexts: *I doubt if he is there*. Very informal contexts also allow you to leave out the conjunction entirely: *I doubt he's there*.

In negative statements, *doubt* is followed by *that*. In such sentences, you do not need *but*: *I do not doubt (but) that he is telling the truth*.

doubtless, no doubt

Both are usually found in sentences that have an ironic intention. In this they resemble *of course*. When you want to express a genuine lack of doubt the following constructions will not be misunderstood: *There is no doubt that, It is beyond doubt that, There can be no doubt that.* ⇒ **irony**

Down's syndrome, mongolism

The term **mongolism** was based on the supposed facial resemblance of children with **Down's syndrome** to Mongolians. Use of the terms *mongol* and *mongolism* is now regarded as negative and unacceptable.

Dr, Dr.

The abbreviation **Dr** meaning 'doctor' does not need a full stop. If the person is a *doctor of philosophy* or a *doctor of science* etc., the title is not used in conjunction with any other academic title, such as *Professor* (although this may be correct for some foreign academics). By custom, a doctor of medicine who is admitted to the Fellowship of the Royal College of Surgeons reverts to the title of *Mr.* **Dr.** followed by a full stop is used for *debtor to*.

draught, draft

These words can easily be confused. Beer drawn from the barrel is *draught beer*, heavy horses used to draw loads are called *draught horses*. A *draught* is a current of air coming through a crack. British **draught** is usually spelled **draft** in American English.

The first version of a piece of writing, or an initial drawing, is a **draft**. In British English, however, someone who draws plans is a *draughtsman*. This word is spelled *draftsman* in American English. The spelling *draughtsman* is also used for a piece in the game of *draughts* (which in America is called *checkers*). Bankers transfer money in the form of a *bank draft*. In America, *conscription* into the Armed Forces is called the *draft*.

draw, drawer

Although one of the meanings of **draw** is 'pull towards', this spelling is incorrect when used about furniture, which has **drawers**: *I'm sure I put them in the drawer last night.*

drier, dryer

We use **drier** as the comparative form of **dry**. A rack for drying clothes, or a machine for drying hair, is a **dryer**.

drily, dryly

These are alternative spellings for the adverb formed from *dry*. They are equally acceptable.

drink, drank, drunk, drunkard, drunken

Drink has **drank** as the Simple Past tense form: *I drank it quickly.* (Some dialects use *drunk* as the past, but this is not standard British English.) The past participle is **drunk**: *He has drunk four pints.*

Drunk is also used as a noun and *a drunk* is the normal term for someone who has casually had too much to drink: *I hope I've convinced you what a drunk's promise is.* Someone who is habitually inebriated is a **drunkard**: *The father, a heavy drinker, had become a hopeless drunkard.* This term is not often used nowadays and sounds old-fashioned and negative. Use of the word *alcoholic* recognizes that the condition is a complex one.

The past participle form *drunk* can be used as an adjective. It is always used after the verb as a predicative adjective: *Myra was very drunk; blind drunk; I'm pretty drunk.* It can also be used in front of the noun, but usually only when accompanied by a following adjective: *a drunk master sergeant; a drunk Black man; an extremely drunk young man.* Otherwise the adjective **drunken** is used before a noun: *drunken driving; drunken parties.*

dual, duel

Dual is an adjective meaning 'twinned' or 'made up of two matched parts'. The noun **duel** means a ritual fight between offended parties and the verb means to take part in a duel: *Duelling is forbidden by law.*

due, due to

The proper use of *due to* causes considerable discussion among those who take a conservative position, and those who allow a well-established extension to its use.

According to the traditional point of view, because *due* is an adjective, there must be a noun present to which **due to** can relate. It may be used after a linking verb such as *is/ was/ seems* or it may be used directly after the noun which it modifies. Thus, it is correct to say: *Death was due to an accident* (*due to* relates to *death* linked by *was*) or *This is obsolescence due to technical advance* (*due to* relates to *obsolescence*). These uses are not controversial.

It is controversial to say: *Due to riots, the traffic was snarled up*, as the phrase *due to riots* does not relate to a noun and is behaving like an adverb of reason, even though there is no introductory preposition.

The alternative point of view is to maintain that *due to* has already become a compound preposition like *owing to* or *because of*. It is just as correct to say: *Due to riots, the traffic was snarled up*, as it is to say: *Owing to/because of riots, the traffic was snarled up.*

The use of *due to* as a compound preposition is held to be acceptable by over 70% of writers on modern usage. The reader who is not concerned by the controversy can rely on the use of *due to* as a preposition being approved of by many educated speakers. The reader who wishes to be cautious may test the use of *due to*. If it can be replaced by *attributable to*, it is correctly used. If not, avoid *due to* altogether by using *owing to*, *because of*, or *on account of* as the text permits. ⇒ **owing to**

dues, subscription
Dues are usually payable to a club or society for membership. The term **subscription** is usually used for payments to journals and magazines. There is an overlap in meaning and use.

dwarf, dwarves, dwarfs
Dwarf has two possible plurals. The usual one is **dwarfs** but **dwarves** is often used in folk tales. Use of the word *dwarf* to refer to a small person who suffers from the condition called *dwarfism* will undoubtedly give offence.

dys- ⇒ dis-

dyslexia, dyslexic
Dyslexia is an impaired ability to deal with written symbols, giving rise to reading difficulties. The normal adjective form is **dyslexic**, derived from the Greek word *lexis*, meaning 'speech'. The American form of the adjective, *dyslectic*, can be found in some literature on the subject.

E

-eable ⇒ **-able**

each, every, each other, one another

You use **each** to refer to the people in a group as individuals rather than as a collection: *You could count thirty mowers in the same field, each followed by his partner; Before being locked into her cell, each prisoner was checked.* Notice that *each* can be used as a determiner or a pronoun.

You use **every** to refer to individuals as a collection: *Every parish had its own thatcher in the 1920s; Every musician in the whole world is going to want one.* Because *every* forms a group from a set of individuals, it is similar to *all*, and *every one* and *every single one* can be emphatic substitutes for *all*: *He had a word for every one of them; Every one of them was emaciated.* Both *each* and *every* are used with reference to people or things.

In modern British usage, the expressions **each other** and **one another** are interchangeable: *The rogues had little in common with each other.* It should be noted, however, that some earlier authorities used to recommend that the meaning of the former should be restricted to *each of two* and the latter to *each of three or more*.

east, eastern, easterly

You use the adjective **eastern** to indicate that the thing referred to is situated more or less in a region that is in the east: *the eastern shores of Tanganyika; the eastern half of the country.* Certain phrases such as *an Eastern* *state* mean, of course, the **East** politically, which is the East as viewed from Europe.

Easterly means towards the east: *...one of the most easterly Greek islands,* or from the east: *the bitter easterly wind.*

eastward, eastwards

Eastward is an adjective and is used to modify a noun: *the eastward facing entrance to a tiny harbour.* **Eastwards** is an adverb and is used to modify a verb or an adjective: *Others travelled eastwards round the Mediterranean; ...units had to be sent eastwards.* It can be confusing that the adverb sometimes drops the *s* and is spelled *eastward*. This is also the normal American spelling. ⇒ **indoor**

easy, easily

Easy (or the comparative form *easier*) is not used as an adverb by careful speakers and writers except in certain set phrases: *take it easy; easy does it.* Where a fixed expression is not involved, the adverbial form **easily** is preferred: *This polish goes on more easily* [not *easier*] *than the other.*

eatable, edible ⇒ inedible

eclecticism, eclectic

The process of **eclecticism** (adjectival form **eclectic**) means 'selecting or composing something from a variety of sources'. Careful speakers and writers avoid using it with the restricted sense of 'selecting only the best elements', as if it meant *fastidiousness.*

economic, economical

The adjective **economic** is used when talking about the management of money within national expenditure or industry: ...*the first stage of economic development*.

The adjective **economical** is used when someone saves on costs or when they cut back or watch over expenditure: *Use the high fifth gear for economical cruising*. The expression *economical with the truth* has become a synonym for 'deceiving by omission'.

ecstasy

Note the spelling. It has *ecs*- not *exs*-.

-ection, -exion

The suffix -*tion* is used to turn a verb into a noun. Words ending in -*ct* or -*x* often have two spellings when -*tion* is added, -*ection* or -*exion*, e.g. *connect: connection, connexion; flex: flexion, flection*. The -*exion* spelling is now rare.

editorial we

It is sometimes necessary for someone to act as the mouthpiece of a public institution and not as an individual member of society. Examples are the monarch, who speaks for the monarchy, an editor, who speaks for the policy of a paper, or a minister or director, who speaks for a government or an industry. In all these cases the so-called **editorial we** or *royal we* is acceptable: *The alliance says: 'We are not opposed in principle to this reform.'* The use of *we* is sometimes also acceptable in a free style of writing which attempts to involve the reader more directly with the writer.

When used outside these contexts, the use of the editorial plural is absurd and should be avoided.

educational, educative

The adjective **educational** is used for anything that has to do with education: *educational and social benefits; educational development*. We use the adjective

educative for experiences that develop the moral, mental, or physical side of a person and teach them something: ...*well informed, sage, educative, highly ethical yet drily humorous. Educational* can be used instead of *educative*, but *educative* cannot replace *educational*.

educationalist, educator

An **educationalist** is someone concerned with *education*, but the term has overtones of someone who is a theorizer rather than a practitioner. An **educator** is a teacher, although not necessarily a classroom teacher: *Industrial educators must not attempt to impose a rigid system of values.*

-ee

The **-ee** suffix is a source of some confusion because of the erratic way in which it has been used. The suffix is applied to words to indicate that the person denoted has been the subject of an action or state, *one who is being...*, or *has done...*, something: *employee, divorcee, internee, trainee.* In this use **-ee** often contrasts directly with **-er**: *employer: employee; trainer: trainee.*

There are *-ee* words that indicate that the person actually performs the action. An *absentee* is actively involved in his or her absence. In this use *-ee* becomes confused with *-er, -or.* Some are marginal between the two; *devotee, refugee.* These are neither fully subject to something nor performers of something. ⇒ **-er**

-eer

An **-eer** ending usually indicates 'someone who does something'. Typical are the occupations: *engineer, mountaineer, auctioneer.* This ending is frequently used for those who carry on a socially undesirable activity: *buccaneer, mutineer, privateer, profiteer, pamphleteer.*

effect, affect

When you **effect** a change, or something of a similar nature, you make it come into being or bring it to a successful conclusion: *A technological revolution had been effected within twenty years.*

If you **affect** someone or something, you influence them or it in some way. When *effect* is used as a noun, it is the result of something that *affects* a situation: *It is claimed that global warming has affected our weather patterns and that we shall suffer the effects for many years.*

effective, effectual, efficient, efficacious

All these words have to do with the type or nature of *effect* that something has. If something is **effective** it does just what it is intended to do: *People have been trying to find an effective shark repellent for over two thousand years. Effective* is used when the process is foremost.

If something has been **effectual** it has produced the effect that was desired: *These changes would have had to be very tough to be effectual. Effectual* is used when the result is foremost.

Someone or something that is **efficient** is of the right type to do what is needed in the most economical or speedy manner: *This tractor is efficient.* An **efficacious** remedy is one that acts as it is supposed to and achieves a beneficial result: *Scylla covered her with lotions usually efficacious in cases of prickly heat.*

effete, effeminate

Someone or something is described as **effete** when they or it seem weak-willed or decadent: *...an experiment in living which could be called utterly effete and pointless.* A man may be called **effeminate** if he affects feminine mannerisms or displays an unusually feminine appearance: *'I do like it', he said, in an effeminate mincing voice; It is only obviously effeminate men who are ostracized.*

efficacy, efficiency

These are the noun forms relating to *efficacious* and *efficient*. We can talk about the **efficacy** of a remedy or the **efficiency** of an organization. ⇒ **effective**

egotist, egoist

An **egotist** talks and writes about himself or herself too much, e.g. by boasting. When someone is called an *egotist* the speaker is usually passing a personal judgment: *She was so much the egotist her eyes were blind to anyone else.*

An **egoist** has an overwhelming concern, called *egoism*, for their own interests and welfare. Such a person is often called *egocentric* or *self-centred* but is not necessarily loud in their own praises: *The awful egoism of the dying; There was little if any egoism in his motives.*

egregious

The term **egregious** is used to indicate contempt. It is used of someone or something so conspicuously awful that they stand out: *He sat down and considered the iniquities of his more egregious colleagues.*

-ei- ⇒ **-ie-**

either, neither

Either is followed by a singular verb in good usage: *Either is good; Either of these books is useful.* **Neither** follows the pattern of *either* but when a plural noun comes after *neither* it is not unusual to make the following verb plural as well, as in the example: *Neither of these books are useful.* This is more acceptable in speech than in writing. Strictly, *either* is used for a choice between two items only and *any* should be used for more than two: *Any of these books would be useful.* In informal speech and writing, this restriction is frequently not observed.

By placing **either** and **neither** close to the part of the sentence that they refer to, you can give different types of contrast. In: *Either of these books will do*, the choice is between 'this book or that book'. In: *He would just say 'How much?' followed either by 'I'll have it' or by 'Too much'*, the choice is between two phrases. Careful writers and speakers are cautious of using *either* to mean *both* or *each* because of the possible ambiguity, as in the following sentence: *A ship could be moored on either side of the channel.*

There are two possible pronunciations of *either*, /ai-ther/ and /ee-ther/. In British English both are acceptable. The same is true of *neither*, /nai-ther/ or /nee-ther/. American English prefers the latter pronunciation.

either...or, neither...nor

When you use *either ... or* or *neither ... nor*, agreement between the verb and its subject is straightforward if the subjects are both in the same person and number: *Either Becky or Loretta has to go; Neither teachers nor parents are happy with this new syllabus.* If one of the subjects is plural and the other singular, the agreement is usually with that last mentioned. If the subject has two different persons, e.g. *Either he or I ...* , it may be necessary to rephrase the sentence to avoid awkward results. *Either he goes or I do* is preferable to [*Either he or I go(es)*].

eke out

Strictly, to *eke* means 'add to' something. If you **eke out** something, you are making up in some manner for its short supply. *Eke* has as its object the item that is being added to, so you can *eke out* food or *eke out* an income with something: *They live on pensions eked out by gifts from former employers.*

This basic meaning of *eke* has become extended and modified by use, so that it has gained the additional sense of either 'make something last as long as possible': *The loan had to be eked out very carefully,* or of 'manage (to do something) with difficulty': *eke out a poor existence; eke out a living in forest areas.* Both these senses have now become thoroughly established, although purists dislike them.

There is another word spelled **eke** but this is an archaic word for *also* and is rarely met with.

elder, older

The comparative and superlative forms **elder** and **eldest** are reserved for talking about relative ages within families or close groups: *Aunt Belle, my mother's elder sister; our elder colleagues.* **Older** and **oldest** can be used when making comparisons about the age of anything. There are some restrictions on when **elder** and **eldest** can be used. *Elder* must be part of a noun phrase, as in *Peter was the elder of the two (children),* otherwise you have to say *Peter is older than Ron.*

Elder can stand on its own as a noun, meaning 'a respected or influential member of a group' and is often written with a capital letter: *Council of Elders; ...urged artists to rebel against their elders.* The adjective also has this sense in one or two idioms such as *an elder statesman.*

electronic

Electronic is used to refer to equipment, such as television sets, computers, etc., in which the current is controlled by transistors, valves, and similar components, and also to the components themselves. **Electrical** is used in a more general sense, often to refer to the use of electricity as opposed to other forms of energy: *electrical engineering; an electrical appliance.* **Electric**, in many cases used interchangeably with **electrical**, is often restricted to the description of particular devices or to concepts relating to the flow of current: *electric fire; electric charge.*

elicit, illicit

Elicit is a verb meaning 'gain information' from someone. If you *elicit the truth* you imply that it has been a difficult process. **Illicit** is an adjective, related to *unlawful.* ⇒ illicit

ellipsis, ellipse, elliptical

In the grammar of English there are certain places where a sentence is normally shortened by leaving out repeated information. This is called **ellipsis** and it is very common in responses: *Are you coming? Yes, I am (coming).* Further examples of *ellipsis* are: *elderly men and (elderly) women; I'll either buy this book or (buy) a gift token.* In 'reporting sentences' the linking *that* is often subject to *ellipsis: He understood (that) she would be ready by twelve.* An *ellipsis* in punctuation is the deliberate omission of a number of words in order to abbreviate a long quotation. It is shown by a standard dotted symbol … also called *suspension points.* An **elliptical** shape (or **ellipse**) is an oval: *It was an elliptical grey stone, a little chipped at one end.* The adjective **elliptical** also means 'guarded or cautious', as in *He made a number of elliptical references to the recent trial.* Avoid the error of using it with the opposite sense as if it meant 'long-winded'.

else

The possessive of the expressions **anybody else, everybody else, nobody else,** etc., is formed by adding *'s* to else: *This must be somebody else's letter.*

Who else is an exception, in that **whose else** is an acceptable alternative to *who else's.* You may use either: *Whose else can it be?* or *Who else's can it be?* Careful writers and speakers should avoid *whose else's* since it contains two possessives, and also avoid the construction *Who else than...?* as there is an established preference for *Who else but...?* or *Who other than...?*: *Who else but Harriet could have invented such a story?*

elusive, elusory, illusory

Something which is **elusive** is difficult to catch or, in the case of abstract notions, hard to fully understand or grasp. The alternative adjective form **elusory** is now very rarely used: *The quarry proved very elusive; ...a collection of elusive, flabby sentiments; ...a certain elusive quality of detachment and beyondness; He possessed a vague, imprecise, elusive, malleable character; Once again the Grail showed its elusiveness.*

Illusory, or more rarely, *illusive,* means unreal, the product of an illusion: *The scene had a pearly stillness so that what was real seemed illusive and without definition; It was an idealistic and illusory dream, a lost ideal.*

emend, amend

The verb **emend** is used only with the sense of 'correct a written page': *Several sentences on page five need to be emended.* The meaning 'put right' or 'alter something, especially a law' is expressed by the verb **amend**: *We can no more amend this bill than we can reform the Government; The Act was amended in 1825.* An associated phrase is *make amends*, where the noun has a plural form but is regarded as singular: *It made him wish to make amends for his former unkindness.*

emigrant, immigrant, migrant, refugee

The distinction between an **emigrant** and an **immigrant** is one of viewpoint. When you leave your country of birth to settle in another, you are an *emigrant*. When you arrive at the country that you are going to live in, you are an *immigrant*. A **migrant** is anyone whose country of residence is not fixed and is generally voluntarily rootless. A **refugee** is someone whom circumstances force to be a migrant. Animals that voyage from country to country for breeding are called *migrant species*.

emotive, emotional

An **emotive** situation is one which causes someone to feel **emotional** and to display anger, sorrow, or some other feeling: *Pollock's earlier works are emotive but nostalgic evocations of rural America; ...the emotive issue of animal experimentation.*

empathy, sympathy, antipathy

Sympathy involves feeling for someone, usually someone in difficult or unhappy circumstances. **Empathy** is entering into and partaking in their feelings. It could be a participation in joy as well as in sorrow: *The tenderness, care, and empathy which we seek from the family.*

Antipathy is a strong feeling of dislike for someone or something: *An instant antipathy had sprung up between the two men.*

empirical, empiricism, pragmatic

A procedure that is **empirical** is based on direct practice and experience rather than on theory: *The empirical lessons of the past didn't work in the present situation.* **Empiricism** is based on the belief that knowledge comes from experience, not theorizing: *Philosophers discuss... empiricism and rationalism.* A **pragmatic** approach to something is based on what it is possible to do given the circumstances: *...a pragmatic, problem-solving attitude.*

employee, employé

The British spelling is **employee**, pronounced /em-**ploy**-ee/. The form **employé**, with or without an accent, pronounced /em-ploy-**ay**/, can be found in American English.

en-, em-

The prefix **en-** or its alternative spelling **em-** means *put in or on*, *go in or on*, *cover*, or *provide*. The **em-** form is normally used before any base word that begins with *b*, *m*, or *p*, as in *embalm*. An exception is sometimes made when the prefix **en-** means *go into*, as in *enplane*.

-en

The suffix **-en** is applied to adjectives (*blacken, dampen*) and to nouns (*heighten, threaten*) to form verbs. It has the broad meaning 'cause something to become'.

The **-en** suffix is also applied to nouns to turn them into adjectives. It means 'made of' (*earthen, wooden*), or 'similar to' (*golden*).

endorse, indorse

To **endorse** something is literally to write on the back of it. In banking this is sometimes done with cheques to verify them. It means, by extension, to give something your approval. *Indorse* is an alternative and uncommon spelling of *endorse*.

enormity, immensity, enormousness

In careful usage, the noun **enormity** should not be employed to convey the idea of great size, but that of something outrageous or horrifying. *Enormity* has strong overtones of a human cause: *It is to be doubted if, at the outset, he recognized the enormity of his wickedness.*

If you want to talk about physical scale, the word that should be used is **immensity**: *The immensity [rather than enormity] of the area covered by the lake is astonishing.* An alternative word is **enormousness**: *It is hard to describe the enormousness [not enormity] of the gale damage,* but some people feel that this is less formal.

enough, sufficient

Enough is to be preferred to **sufficient** in most cases. *Sufficient* is rather formal and is restricted in its use. It can suggest that something is just adequate; compare: *I'm warm enough now / I'm sufficiently warm now.* Notice that the usage is for *enough* to follow the adjective. The usual construction is for **enough** to be followed by *to* in comparisons: *...fortunate enough to get a job; ...not important enough to merit a discussion.*

Note the construction *enough for ... to* that is used in: *The bullets passed close enough for us to hear.* The construction *enough ... that* is an Americanism: *Each big enough that its insides might hold (big enough for its insides to hold) all the people.*

enquire ⇒ inquire

ensure, insure, assure

If you **ensure** something, you make sure of it by some means or other: *Those who criticized me did the least to ensure the success of the rally,* or you make sure that it takes place: *How was the device to ensure an even coating over an irregular surface?* It is frequently followed by a clause (*ensure that* something happens): *He felt it his duty to ensure that the constituency was not disenfranchised.* The American spelling for *ensure* is *insure*.

In British English **insure** means take out insurance cover against loss. You *insure* something *against* loss or damage. Confusingly, the word with this meaning is often spelled *ensure* in American English (see above).

If you **assure** someone of something you promise them something or make them confident in the correctness of their belief: *All the experts assure me that it is going to help.* A more restricted use of **assure** means 'guarantee', as in *He could resign and assure himself £126,000 a year in pension and other payments,* and is much closer in its meaning to *ensure*.

enthuse

This is a relatively new verb which is a back formation from *enthusiasm*. It is often objected to as an Americanism and is probably best avoided in formal contexts. There are many established alternatives and it can be avoided: *Thus enthused he went on;* use *inspired*. '*What an interesting man*', *enthused Miss Jackson;* use *said with enthusiasm* or *raved*.

envelop, envelope

The pronunciation of **envelop** is /in-**vel**-op/ and the usual pronunciation of **envelope** is /**en**-vel-ope/. A small number of speakers prefer /**on**-vel-ope/.

environment, environmentalist

The **environment** is our surroundings, the conditions in which we live. To the scientist it is the habitat of a plant or an animal and all that influences its behaviour or development. An **environmentalist** makes a specialist study of particular environments. Care is needed with the pronunciation of /en-**vire**-en-ment/, noting especially the consonant in the third syllable.

envisage

Envisage, followed by *that* and a clause, has come to be used in place of such verbs as *expect* and *think*: *The board envisages that there will be a high profit.* American writers often prefer **envision** for this usage. In careful English, *envisage* is usually used with a direct object rather than a clause to refer to future possibilities: *He envisaged great success for his project.*

epidemic, endemic, pandemic

An **epidemic** (noun) is an outbreak of disease in a community. If a particular disease becomes an established feature of a community and is difficult to get rid of, e.g. malaria, or sleeping sickness, it is described as an **endemic** (adjective) disease. *Endemic* is followed by *in*: *In the 1940s malaria was endemic in Ceylon.* If an *epidemic* spreads over many communities it can be called **pandemic**: *The Black Death was pandemic.*

The use of *endemic* is often extended to things other than disease: *Violent class conflict is endemic in our society; intrigues were endemic right across the hierarchy.* *Epidemic* can also be used as a figure of speech, as in *Headlight flashing is unofficial … and the current epidemic is highly dangerous.*

epitaph, epigraph, epigram

An **epitaph** is a memorial inscription, usually on a tomb.

An **epigraph** is usually a quotation at the beginning of a book or chapter, but it can still be used in the older sense of an inscription on a public building.

An **epigram** is a brief witty comment, sometimes in verse form: *I am His Majesty's dog at Kew, pray tell me sir, whose dog are you? (A. Pope).*

epithet, expletive
An **epithet** is a descriptive word or phrase, usually one associated with a personal name, as in *Vlad the Impaler, 'Postie' Johnson, 'Blind' Lemon Jefferson, 'Fats' Domino.* It is sometimes loosely used to indicate that someone is swearing at another person: *...used the most vulgar kind of racial epithets; The name was coupled with a very gross epithet.* There is probably also a link being made in these examples with the word **expletive**, meaning 'oath or curse' and 'exclamation'.

epitome
Epitome does not mean the peak of excellence but the typical example of something: *Australia would seem at first to be the epitome of a house-owning society.*

equable, equitable
A person with an **equable** temperament is calm and well-balanced in almost every circumstance. An *equable* climate is one that does not vary very much throughout the year. When a division of goods or property is made in a fair manner, you can speak of an **equitable** division.

equally, as
Equally is not used with a following *as* to form constructions like: [*...she was equally as important*]. One form of comparison allows *equally,* and another allows *as.* The accepted usage with **equally** is: *On her return she was equally successful on the London stage.* The accepted usage with **as** is shown in: *I had mentioned this casually to Wilfred, and he, as casually, had replied that I had better get one.*

equity, equities

The noun **equity** means 'fairness' or 'a system based on natural justice': *...an agreement to ensure equity between private and public tenants.* Another meaning is that interest that shareholders have in a company, hence the plural form **equities** is often used for ordinary shares: *...the supply of equity capital; ...yields on gilt-edged and equities.*

-er, -or

The suffixes **-er** and **-or** are used with verbs to create nouns. These *one who...* suffixes are a productive feature in English. *One who teaches: teacher; one who drives: driver; one who acts: actor,* etc. Any verb can take this ending, though in older formations the verb is not always clear, e.g. an *author* is not *one who auths.*

In many cases words in **-er** / **-or** have a paired word that ends in **-ee**: *employer, employee; donor, donee.* There are also a number of semiserious formations that use this pairing feature, e.g. *murderer, murderee.* ⇒ **-ee**

erotic, pornographic, erogenous

Something that stirs and provokes a sexual response is called **erotic**. It may be some form of writing, images, or sensations. Material that provokes an *erotic* reaction is not necessarily intended to do so. Use of the word **pornographic** suggests images or writing that are solely intended to excite a sexual response and in so doing usually overstep the boundary of social tolerance. Avoid using *erotic* as a euphemism for *pornographic.* The adjective **erogenous** is usually applied to parts of the body that are sensitive to stimulation.

errant, arrant

The word **errant** is somewhat old-fashioned. It means

straying from the set path of acceptable behaviour: *like an errant schoolboy summoned to the headmaster's presence.* **Arrant** was once an alternative spelling, but now it means 'complete, utter': *Stealing that baby was probably the most arrant piece of folly you have ever committed. Arrant* has nothing to with being arrogant or excessively self-important.

errata

The word **errata** is generally used to mean 'a list of errors or misprints in a book'. Careful writers and speakers treat the word as plural: *The errata for this book are* [not *is*] *complete.* The singular form, *erratum*, is uncommon. ⇒ **data**

eruption, irruption

These two words are generally treated as having the same meaning. There is a difference, however. An **eruption** is strictly something that bursts out, while an **irruption** bursts in on something, for example a sudden invasion of territory could be called an *irruption: They feared the sudden irruption of the inhabitants of the house.*

escalate

Escalate, as in *after the arrival of the troops the violence escalated,* is very commonly used in journalistic contexts in the sense of 'gradually increase the intensity or scope of' something (usually involving violence). The word is not completely accepted as appropriate in formal English.

especially, specially

Especial and **especially** have a more limited use than **special** and **specially**. *Special* is always used in preference to *especial* when the sense is one of being out of the ordinary: *...a special lesson. Special* is also used when something is referred to as being for a particular purpose: *The word was specially underlined for you.* Where an idea of pre-eminence or individuality is involved, either *especial* or *special* may be used: *He is my especial* (or *special*) *friend; He is especially* (or *specially*) *good at his job.* In informal English, however, *special* is usually preferred in all contexts.

espresso

The Italian coffee-making machine and the sort of coffee that it produces are called **espresso**. Because of the speed and the sound of the process, the mistaken spelling *expresso* has also come into use.

Esq.

As a form of written address, **Esq.** is becoming less frequently used. It is an abbreviation for **esquire** and meant that the addressee was a landowner. You place *Esq.* after the surname, not before it, and consequently it upsets computerized sorting programs. Do not use it together with *Mr.* Either use *Mr J. Lane* or *J. Lane Esq.*

-ess

The suffix -ess in such words as *poetess, actress,* and *authoress* is now often regarded as disparaging because of the overtones that these words have acquired, e.g. *authoress* can imply a minor writer. A gender-neutral term, *poet, actor,* or *author,* is to be preferred.

Manageress is difficult. At the professional end of management the term is inappropriate and *manager* should be used, but at certain levels in retailing the job description *manageress* is generally found acceptable. A number of words with the -ess ending have neutral overtones: *empress, princess, duchess, seamstress.*

estimate, estimation, esteem

If you give an **estimate**, you calculate a price for a job or form a rough idea of something: *I asked for a rough estimate of the price.* The verb *estimate* is often used to mean 'guess': *I estimate I spent 30% of the time making speeches.* The pronunciation is /**est**-im-it/.

An **estimation** is a considered judgment: *Sutherland, in his estimation, was being unreasonably soft.* If someone holds a high or low place in your *estimation* it is an indication of your respect for them: *At this stage White shared Luce's high estimation of Chiang.* When you **esteem** someone, they stand very high in your estimation. The pronunciation of *estimation* is /est-i-**may**-shun/.

etc., &c.

The abbreviated form of *et cetera* is the source of a common mistake, writing [*ect.*] instead of **etc.** The other abbreviation **&c.**, formed with an ampersand, is found in commercial contexts. Avoid using it in formal writing, though it is acceptable to use **etc.** in a formal context. Note that the word is pronounced /et-**set**-er-a/. Avoid using the pronunciation /ek-**set**-er-a/.

Since **et cetera** (or **etc.**) means 'and other things', careful writers do not use the expression *and etc.* because *and* is redundant. The overuse of *etc.* is to be avoided, especially as a weak ending to a sentence. The repetition of *etc.*, as in, *He brought paper, ink, notebooks, etc., etc.*, is also to be avoided, except in informal contexts.

ethics, ethical, moral

Ethics is treated as a singular noun not a plural. A professional group usually conducts its business guided by *a code of ethics*. **Ethical** behaviour is the code in operation. A different meaning of *ethical*, as in *an ethical preparation*, is used in pharmacy to mean a drug that can only be dispensed on a doctor's prescription.

Moral has a wider sense. *Moral* behaviour or attitudes are based on an understanding of right and wrong; *ethical* behaviour relies on someone following a code of practice.

-ette, -et

The suffix **-ette** is a diminutive form and usually feminine, although there is a masculine alternative ending **-et**. Though some *-et(te)* words have neutral overtones, e.g. *piglet, flatlet, maisonette, usherette*, use of this suffix often displays an element of condescension that is not present in the *-ie* diminutive suffix: *starlet, bimbette, hackette*.

euphemism, euphony, euphuism

A **euphemism** is an alternative word that is used in place of one less acceptable in sensitive society. There are many euphemisms, ranging from expressions like *pass away, go before* for *die; bottom* or *sit-upon* for *arse* and a range of other words for many parts of the body; *Oh, sugar, cripes* and other such innocuous words used as oaths; the many terms for lavatory; the different words used to disguise various forms of sexual activity; and so on. These words are all used to make what are felt to be socially embarrassing words 'safe'.

Euphony is the creation of pleasant and harmonious sound in the spoken word. It is often a mark of verse.
Euphuism is an old-fashioned literary style that involved much 'fine writing': *What joy in this common joy can I count joy, and not him enjoy who was my only joy?*

Euro-

The use of **Euro-** as a prefix is relatively new. The prefix is added without a hyphen, e.g. *Eurocurrency, Eurobond*.

evasion, invasion

Evasion is escape from something. It usually involves cunning and may be against the law, as in *tax evasion*. Invasion is an intrusion.

evasiveness, evasive, invasive

You use **evasiveness** to describe the type of behaviour that tries to avoid coming to the point about important matters: *What disturbed him was a certain evasiveness in the Swami's replies.* Such behaviour, or a person behaving thus, is **evasive**. In medicine a type of examination that involves surgery is described as **invasive**. It is also used to describe a disease that is harmful: *The third stage of the disease is called invasive cancer.*

even

When you are writing in a very formal style it is usual for **even** to be placed as near as possible to the word that it modifies: *He liked even Diana.* This can seem very stilted in a spoken context, so *even* often moves before the verb: *He even liked Diana.* Normally this is not ambiguous but it should be noted that in *He admired, even liked, Diana* the place of **even** would have a special meaning.

These sentences show different uses of *even: It is even possible that there will be an award for the best entry; It is possible that there will even be an award for the second-best entry; It is possible that there will be an award even for the worst entry.*

ever

Ever can be used to make an expression more dramatic. It is then called an intensifier. This use is common with wh- words, e.g. *Who can it be? / Who ever can it be?* Note that this is quite different from *whoever* meaning 'no matter who', which is one word.

Similar remarks apply to other combinations. *What ever did you do that for?* is like *What on earth...?* Compare this with: *Whatever it was, he disliked it. How ever did it happen?*, is like *How on earth...?* Compare this with: *However, it had happened and there was no changing things.*

Ever is also used as an intensifier followed by *such* or *so* in expressions like: *ever such a nice chap; ...ever so happy.* Like the use of *ever* after some superlatives, as in *her first ever boyfriend; my worst ever experience*, these are very informal constructions which should be avoided in writing.

every, everyone, everybody

Everyone and **everybody** are interchangeable, as are *no one* and *nobody*, and *someone* and *somebody*. *Everybody, everyone, none, no one, nobody, somebody, someone,* and *each* function as singular in careful English: *Everyone nodded his head.* However, the use of *their* in such constructions is common in English but note that the appropriate form is: *Everyone nodded their head.*

Careful writers distinguish between *everyone* and *someone* as single words and *every one* and *some one* as two words, using the latter form to refer to each individual person or thing in a particular group: *Every one of them is wrong; some one among us should be delegated.*

exceedingly, excessively

When something is **exceedingly** good (or bad), it is greater than is usual: *Schooldays can be exceedingly unhappy; How exceedingly thoughtful of you.* When something is **excessively** good or bad it goes beyond the acceptable or normal limits: *It was excessively hot; In time it causes eggshells to be excessively thin and break in the nest.*

except, excepting, excepted

When you use **except** as a preposition, any following pronoun must be one of the object pronouns *me, us, him, her, them*: *Everybody except her.* **Excepting** meaning 'not including' is rarely used nowadays. It is only found after *not, without,* or *always*: *These efforts might raise the IQ level, always excepting true morons.* In other cases *except for* is used with the same meaning: *They were not armed except for long knives; The desert was empty except for a heap of stones.*

An alternative for *except* is the use of **excepted** which must follow the noun it refers to: *However peacefully most of us – Margaret Thatcher excepted – want to live our lives… ; …the greatest of God's creatures, ourselves not excepted.* This is a formal usage.

exception

The expression *the exception proves the rule* is often used when something happens contrary to expectation, with the general sense of, *exceptions abound, no matter if they should not.* Looked at logically, this is a rather trite remark and not very helpful. The actual sense of the saying is that *exceptions put a rule to the test*, which is a reasonable point to make.

The confusion arises because of the two meanings of *prove*, the frequent one, 'show to be right', and the less frequent one, 'test', as is shown in two uses of its related noun, *proof*: *The proof of the pudding is in the eating; 40% proof whisky.* The misconception is very firmly established. ⇒ **coin a phrase**

exceptional, exceptionable

Something that is **exceptional** is outstandingly excellent. When someone says or does something **exceptionable**, it is rude, insulting, or offensive: *I find that point in your argument really quite exceptionable.*

excess ⇒ access

exclamation mark ⇒ punctuation

exhaustive, exhausting
Exhaustive means 'thoroughgoing and painstaking'. An *exhaustive* search for something could be **exhausting** and tire you out.

exotic, esoteric
When you use **exotic** about a plant, it indicates that it comes from outside the country and is different in some ways from the native species. It may need special culture. Less correctly, but in an extension of meaning that is now well established, it means 'colourful', 'glamorous', and 'strange': *The film takes in a number of exotic locations.* Something **esoteric** requires knowledge that is beyond the power of an uninitiated person to understand or involves special subtlety of perception: *Many of the discoveries of astronomy are very esoteric; an esoteric mythology well-stocked with heroes.*

explicit
Something **explicit** is clearly stated and contains no hidden details or information: *I have tried so hard to be clear and explicit.* ⇒ implicit

extant, existent
Careful writers distinguish between *extant* and *existent*. Both are used of something that exists at the present time, but *extant* has a further connotation of survival. **Extant** is therefore used of that which still exists, although there would be reason for believing that it might have disappeared: *The species was believed extinct,*

but a small population was found to be still extant in Africa; …according to a still extant document. Something that is **existent** is simply in existence at this moment: *This is no more than an attempt to refine the existent machinery of government.*

extempore, impromptu, improvised

There is a lot of overlap between the uses of these words. An **extempore** (or *extempory*) performance is one which is undertaken spontaneously: *Extempore translation from and to Modern Greek is an important part of the course.* Something **impromptu** is also done without being planned beforehand and is usually quite unexpected: *…fit for impromptu murders in fits of domestic passion.* Taking the first example, the difference in use is that you expect to be asked to make an *extempore* translation. An *impromptu* translation would come as a surprise to everyone.

Something **improvised** is often done without rehearsal: *He did a little improvised dance step.* More often it means adapting the existing situation, or describes something created from materials at hand: *A hastily improvised hospital was established at the hotel; She held the sheet by the corners, an improvised bag.*

extenuate, condone

If something **extenuates** the actions of someone who has done wrong, it provides a reason or an argument why they might be understood and less harshly judged: *It was essential to have a dossier with every extenuating circumstance, before issuing a verdict.* When an offence is **condoned**, there is an agreement to overlook or discount it: *A marginal failure in one paper out of the seven in the examination may be condoned.* ⇒ **mitigate**

exterior, external, interior, internal

These are matching terms. **Exterior** refers to the outside of something and **interior** to the inside. The presence of something concrete, rather than abstract, is usually implied. Both can be used either as an adjective: *exterior wrapping; interior decorations*, or as a noun: *the exterior of the house; a voyage to the interior.*

The pair **internal** and **external** usually refer to what happens, acts, or exists inside or outside something. They are adjectives only: *our internal human system; You should lag internal pipes; external forces constrain him; feathery external gills; thin, external walls. Internal* and *external* are used to mean *domestic* and *foreign* respectively in phrases such as as: *the internal politics of France; internal disorder and external threats.*

extract

The verb **extract** has two main senses. The first implies the use of force or skill, as in *extract a tooth*. This sense is extended to any situation where the advantage has been gained with difficulty: *…extracted the information; …extracted a pledge of secrecy*. The second use of *extract* is in connection with industrial processes: *…fuels which can be extracted from coal*. ⇒ **extricate**

extreme, extremely

An **extreme** situation is very great in its intensity or significant in its likely result. Avoid using **extremely** as a substitute for *very* in formal writing and speech. ⇒ **very**

extricate

When you **extricate** someone or something, you set them or it free from an entanglement or a difficult situation: *Rescue teams try to extricate those buried beneath rubble.* Avoid using *extricate* to mean 'take out'. You *extract* [not *extricate*] *a key from a lock.* ⇒ **extract**

extrinsic, intrinsic
Something that is **extrinsic** is not a necessary part of something. Something **intrinsic** is necessary and is part of what we understand the whole object to be: *Dependency is an intrinsic part of love.*

F

faction
In politics a **faction** normally means a small group of people who have broken away from the main group. It implies the presence of conflict: *Various battling factions arose.* Another word spelled **faction** is a blend of *fact* and *fiction.* It describes a literary work based on a true incident but containing invented details.

factitious, fictitious
When we describe something as **factitious**, we mean it is a sham; made up, but making a pretence of being the real thing: *He displayed the factitious enthusiasm of a games-show host.* You could describe a forgery as *factitious.* Something **fictitious** differs from this because there is often no attempt to disguise that is a product of the imagination.

fag
The word **fag** is an informal term in British English for a cigarette and, in references to previous public school

customs, for a junior pupil who acted as an unpaid servant to a senior pupil. In American English, this usage can cause surprise, because *fag*, or the longer form, *faggot*, is an offensive term for a homosexual. The Northern English word for savoury meat balls, *faggots*, can be a source of similar confusion. ⇒ **fanny**

fail, failing

It is common to find **fail** used when something expected has not taken place: *It seems the Republicans failed to report $114,000 in campaign funds.* Careful speakers and writers may prefer to restrict the use of *fail* to situations where someone tried to do something and did not succeed: *Exploratory gropings failed to locate a life jacket where it should have been; Not surprisingly, he failed to convert Reagan.*

Failing is now accepted as a preposition meaning 'in the absence of' or 'lacking': *Failing a solution, this problem has to wait until Monday; Wear evening dress or, failing that, a suit.*

fair, fare, fayre

It is often confusing remembering which spelling of *fair/fare* is required. The following are examples of *fair*. All but the last are adjectives: *a fair wind for France; a fair skin; a fair-haired child; a fair decision; a fair-sized piece; a local fund-raising fair*. The spelling *fare* is for these nouns: *a bus fare; country fare* as in *country food; a fond farewell*, and the increasingly archaic verb *fare* meaning 'get on': *How would an 8-stone boxer fare?*

The use of the archaic spelling **fayre** for the noun *fair* is not recommended. It is very affected and puts many people off.

fairly

Fairly can cause a problem because it may be used to give emphasis: *Oh, I'm fairly worn out; I'm fair(ly) pooped*, or as a mark of reservation: *I'm fairly pleased with his work but I'll have to ask him to repaint the garage door* means 'I'm not totally pleased'.

fallacy, fallacious, falsehood

A **fallacy** is something believed to be true that is not: *Hunting down logical fallacies can be enjoyable.* A **falsehood** is a deliberately concocted untruth, a lie, that springs from a need to deceive. Usually, *fallacies* are what people believe in, lies or *falsehoods* what they tell. The adjective **fallacious** can be used about *fallacies* or *falsehoods*.

falseness, falsity, falsify

These words are all concerned with untruth but the overtones are rather different. **Falseness** implies either a deliberate avoidance of the truth, or treachery.

The verb **falsify** means 'alter something in the hope of deceiving someone': *The facts concerning my birth have been falsified.*

Falsity is the state that exists when something is untrue but is not necessarily deliberate untruth: *He is not troubled by the truth or falsity of the author's account.*

false titles

In British English, a person's occupational status or profession is not used as a title, other than academic titles such as *Professor.* Mr Major is currently the Prime Minister but he is not *Prime Minister Major*, nor would we say *Chancellor of the Exchequer Smith.* The use of false titles comes from wrongly following the American example where President, Senator, etc. are titles.

familiar

Places, people, or emotions can be **familiar** *to* you. They are well known to you: *The neighbourhood was familiar to me; My name was familiar to millions of people.* Avoid saying that someone or something is *familiar to* a thing or a place. The preposition *to* must be followed by a person such as *me* or *Chris* as its object in this construction. You can be *familiar with* a thing or a place: *You will be familiar with this concept.* You know or understand it well.

Using another idiom, if someone is *familiar with* or *towards* another person, they act in an informal manner that may become offensive.

famous, notorious, infamous

The distinction between *famous* and *notorious* is in the nature of the reputation that is achieved. Someone or something **notorious** is well known, usually for a bad quality: *In 1987 came the notorious bid from Equiticorp; a notorious slum district.* Someone or something **famous** is well known, but the word does not have overtones of any particular moral value. In contrast, the adjective **infamous** is used as a strongly critical reference to a person or thing with the worst kind of reputation. Someone could be a *notorious swindler* yet never be *infamous.*

fanny

If a speaker of American English casually uses the informal word **fanny** when in British society, it can cause embarrassment. In American English your *fanny* is what you sit on: *Let's put a cushion under your fanny* (in British English your *backside* or *bottom*). In British, Australian, and New Zealand English *fanny* is a rude word for the female genitals. ⇒ **fag**

fantasy, phantasy

The spelling **phantasy** is now regarded as archaic. Note, however, the spellings of *phantasm* and *phantom*.

farther, further

In careful usage, **farther** and **farthest** are preferred when referring to literal distance: *They found a taxi two blocks farther on; Start painting at the wall farthest from the door.*

Further and **furthest** are used when there is really no underlying sense of *far* involved, for example when you are speaking of a greater or an additional amount of something, or about time: *No further negotiations are taking place; A further delay is likely.* These words are also preferred for figurative distance: *Dealers will try to avoid a further fall in the stock market.*

fatal, fateful

When something is **fatal** it brings about death: *They inflict nasty and usually fatal wounds.* Something **fateful** is full of significance for the future: *There are two fateful years in postwar history.*

fauna, flora

These are collective nouns so that they are followed by a singular verb. The **fauna** is the animal life, the **flora** the plant life, of a specific region. ⇒ **collective nouns**

fawn, faun

If someone acts in a cringing manner they are **fawning**: *...fawning profiles of the President.* A young deer is a **fawn**: *A small fawn, still spotted white....* The greyish-brown colour, like that of the animal, is **fawn**: *a fawn raincoat.* A **faun** was a Roman woodland deity with the body of a man and the horns, ears, tail, and hind legs of a goat. *Fauns* were identified with the goat-god Pan.

fax

Fax is an abbreviation for **facsimile** and refers to a machine capable of transmitting a facsimile of a document: *The fax is out of order;* also an actual document received through a fax machine: *He brought in a fax that had just arrived.* The verb *fax* means 'transmit a document by this means': *Why write when you can fax or transmit a message on to a computer screen?* ⇒ **Xerox**™

faze, phase

The informal word **faze** means 'disconcert' or 'bother': *Nothing seemed to faze them.* A **phase** is a particular state in a cycle of development.

feasible, plausible

If something is **feasible** it is possible; it could be done: *The electric car is technically feasible; Projects which are today barely feasible will become relatively easy.* A **plausible** person or suggestion is one that seems to be worthy of belief: *No one could suggest any plausible explanation for this; Uncle Nick's theories were very plausible.* The word bears a strong overtone that any belief might be misplaced.

February

Note the spelling, which has *-bru-*. Many people object to hearing this word pronounced without the central *r* sound: /feb-roo-a-ry/ not /feb-yoo-a-ry/.

feel

The verbs **feel**, **look**, and **smell** can be followed by an adverb or an adjective according to the sense in which they are used.

When you want to refer to some quality, or characteristic of the subject, an adjective is used: *I feel sick; he looks strong; this medicine smells bad.* For other senses an adverb is used: *She feels strongly about that; I must look closely at his record; This animal smells inefficiently although its sight is well developed.*

female, feminine

The word **female** is neutrally descriptive, the genetic opposite to *male,* and denotes a *woman* or a *girl* in human terms, or the 'egg-bearing member of a species' biologically. When the word *female* is used of a woman as a descriptive label (or *male* is used of a man), the intention is normally to denote the impersonal sexual aspect. Consequently, to speak casually of someone as *a female* as in: *That female at the garage…* is to disparage them by depersonalizing them. This is absent in *That woman at the garage….*

Feminine means 'displaying the qualities of a woman' in whatever way society usually codifies these qualities. The antonym is *masculine.* We can say: *He had a feminine handwriting* because the description is of handwriting like a woman's not of a woman. ⇒ **lady**

feminine forms

Many languages have separate forms of the same word associated with a grammatical class (such as adjectives in French). The term *feminine* is used for certain forms, *masculine* and *neuter* for others. The *feminine* is not necessarily directly linked with any *female* element of meaning. English only has separate **feminine forms** for the possessive and personal pronouns: *her, hers, she.* Certain nouns have *feminine forms* that are created from suffixes such as *-ess* or *-ette.* ⇒ **-ess** ⇒ **-ette**

ferment, foment

The verb **ferment** is used to describe the process of fermentation. There is also a noun *ferment* meaning the substance that produces fermentation. By extension, the noun is used to mean 'trouble' or 'excitement': … *a time of theological ferment.* When you **foment** something, you stir it up. It is often used with *trouble* but can also be used with *dissension, patriotism* or anything else that can be aroused: *He fomented quarrels and instigated strikes.*

fervent, fervid, perfervid

Both **fervent** and **fervid** mean 'glowingly, intensely passionate': …*a fervent desire for liberation;* …*full of fervid and misplaced loyalties.* The overtones of the contexts in which *fervid* is used suggest a rather unhealthy degree of passion. A **perfervid** passion is even more intense; *per-* is an intensifier.

fetus, foetus

Most written references use the spelling **foetus**. This is the general form. The spelling **fetus** is preferred by *The Lancet* and is the normal form in medical literature. It is also the American form.

few, fewer, less, a few

There is a useful difference between *few* and *less*. Both words refer to a reduction but they are not interchangeable. This difference is a point of usage that is nowadays under pressure and the distinction is on the point of being lost. The word *less* has taken over many of the functions of *few* and *fewer*, and even educated speakers use it inappropriately .

Few (and the comparative form **fewer**) is used of things that can be counted: *There are fewer cars down this road now the bypass has opened; There were very few women out shopping last Tuesday; We lost far fewer plants in last year's dry spell than in this.* **Less** is used for a quantity of the sort of thing that is normally not counted, like *butter* or *food*: *I use less electricity in the summer; You notice less noise from the traffic on this side of the house.*

There are now many examples of *less* being used where *few* would normally be used, that is, with count nouns like *car* and *book*, e.g. [*there are less cars…*]. It remains a nonstandard usage and should be avoided by careful writers and speakers.

Note that you do not use *few* if the phrase contains the word *number*: *The number of books sold was less than expected*, or if it contains a number that gives you the size of an amount. It is correct to use *less than four months* (the amount of *time* is not countable); it is correct to use *fewer than ten parents* (*parents* is a noun that can be counted).

Few usually signifies a negative element, as in 'not many': *Few writers are persuaded of the benefits.* On the other hand, **a few** has the opposite sense. When we select *a few things* we select *some* of them: *…a few pence; …a few people knelt and a few prayed.*

fictitious ⇒ factitious

fiddle, violin

A **fiddle** is a familiar term for a **violin**. Even classically trained musicians often call their instrument *a fiddle* in all but very formal situations. Folk musicians seem to prefer the term *fiddle* to *violin* at all times.

finalize

Although **finalize** has been in widespread use for some time, it carries strong associations of bureaucratic or commercial jargon for many careful speakers and writers, who usually prefer *finish*, *complete*, *conclude*, or *make final*, especially in formal contexts. However, many of those who object to *finalize* are quite happy to accept other *-ize* formations. The addition of *-ize* to an adjective is a productive device in the repertoire of English.

fine

Fine can be used as an adverb only in informal speech, and only to mean either 'well', as in *It's going fine*, or to mean 'to a well-judged degree', as in *You're cutting it rather fine, aren't you?*

first, firstly

Criticism of the use of **firstly** in lists is an invented problem, like the 'split infinitive'. There is no good reason why a list should not begin *Firstly... , secondly... , thirdly ...*. There is also no reason why one should not use the more traditional formula, *First..., secondly..., thirdly...*.

Both styles have a long history of use in educated English and have been added to by those who, not recognizing the use of *first* as an adverb, have introduced a third style: *First..., second..., third...*. Avoid mixing the styles after listing the first item.

first floor

This usage causes problems for visitors to Britain. In the United States and in New Zealand, the **first floor** is the one at street level, not the one above the ground floor.

first name ⇒ Christian name

fish, fishes

The traditional plural form of *fish* is *fish*, an invariable noun like *sheep* and *deer*. The alternative form, **fishes**, is increasingly used because of the pressures towards normalizing irregular forms that every language is subject to.

flagrant, blatant

If you do something **flagrant**, you behave outrageously: *Tourists feed peanuts to the monkeys in direct and flagrant contravention of the notices*. If you are **blatant** in your behaviour, then you act in an offensive or in a glaringly conspicuous fashion: *It turned out in 1955 that the Piltdown skull was a blatant forgery*. *Flagrant* emphasizes the seriousness of an action, *blatant* emphasizes the attitude of the person.

flair, flare

If you have **flair** you have ability, talent, and perceptiveness. It is usually followed by *for*: *She had a flair for this branch of law*.

A **flare** is a special device that burns brightly. By extension, it is used for any activity that starts suddenly: *Panic flared up in her*. The word is also used for a shape that spreads out at one end.

flammable, inflammable

Both words **flammable** and **inflammable** mean 'liable to catch fire' and are interchangeable when used of the properties of materials. *Flammable* is often preferred for warning labels as there is less likelihood of misunderstanding (*inflammable* being sometimes wrongly taken to mean 'not flammable'). **Inflammable** is preferred in figurative contexts: *His temperament could be described as inflammable*. ⇒ **inflammable**

flaunt, flout

Although these two words have quite different meanings they are often confused. If you **flaunt** a possession or an ability, you display it in a boldly ostentatious manner: *There was no need to flaunt the fact in public; Sabine flaunts her sexuality*. When someone **flouts** the law or someone's authority, they deliberately disregard it and often take pleasure in doing so: *The Organization flouted the law too brazenly; Poachers are willing to flout the Endangered Species Act.*

fleshly, carnal, fleshy

The adjectives **fleshly** and **carnal** are similar in meaning. Both are used in relation to the body and to sensual and sexual feelings. The word *fleshly* is literary and rather formal, while the word *carnal* is also used in technical and legal senses: *The soul has its fleshly envelope; It was love of the coarsest nature, a fleshly love; Spiritual and carnal love are inseparable.* Something **fleshy** is solid and well-covered with flesh. It has no sensual overtones: *…broad, fleshy jowls.*

flounder, founder

To **flounder** means to be in a situation of difficulty where progress is hard: *Lacking guidelines or precedents, we flounder over the moral and legal questions. Flounder* often has the sense of acting or moving in an uncoordinated manner: *He floundered into bed.*

When a boat takes in water and sinks, it **founders**. By extension, if a project is in difficulties and about to come to a premature end, we may say that it is about to *founder: His argument foundered on the Norfolk case of 1302.*

flu, influenza

The spelling *'flu*, with an apostrophe, used to be regarded as just the informal short form of **influenza**, but the form **flu**, without the apostrophe, seems now to have become the more common popular term for this illness.

flute, flautist

Someone who plays the **flute** is a **flautist**. The American variant of this word is **flutist**. This form has also been noted as an occasional BBC usage.

fly, flee, fled, flown

Two rather similar verbs in terms of spelling and sound are frequently confused in meaning and use.

The first is the verb **fly** which has the past tense **flew** and the past participle **flown**: *All bats fly at night; Moths flew about them while they talked; The weedy estuary out of which the kingfisher had flown.* The usual meaning of *fly* is 'travel through the air' but, partly by extension and partly through confusion with *flee*, it is also used to mean 'run away': *She flew from the noise and confusion.*

The second is the verb **flee** which has the past tense and past participle **fled**. This verb means 'run away from' somewhere, usually a place of danger: *Ben had only three hours warning to flee Palestine; I leaped away and fled down the drive without looking back; He was a Cuban revolutionary who had fled Palestine.*

focus

Focus has alternative spellings in current use for the plural of the noun; the English style, *focuses,* and the Latin form, *foci.* The verb forms can be spelled with either a single or a double *s: focusing; focussing,* and *focused; focussed.*

folk, folks

Folk is already plural, but some people use an informal plural **folks**, with the addition of an *s,* to refer to their family: *My folks had a wonderful Christmas.* The use of *folk* in *old folk's home; poor folk,* and similar expressions is a form of euphemism, and somewhat patronizing.

foment ⇒ **ferment**

foot, feet

In carpentry you use a **foot** rule and measurements are also given in the singular form *foot*, as for example, *5 foot 3*. In speaking of someone's height, use either **foot** or **feet**: *I am over 6 feet / 6 foot tall.* ⇒ **pound**

for-, fore-

The difference in meaning between the prefixes *for-* and *fore-* helps to distinguish between pairs of similar words like *forbear* and *forebear*, *forgo* and *forego*.

For- implies negation or prohibition while *fore-* has the sense 'before' or 'earlier'. An additional use of *for-* is to add to the intensity of a word, e.g. *forlorn*.

In practice, many writers do not observe the distinction between the *for-* and *fore-* spellings, but careful writers may wish to do so.

forbear, forebear

The verb **forbear** means 'hold back from' or 'deny yourself something'. It has the past tense **forbore** and the past participle **forborne**. The noun **forebear** (American *forbear*) is often used in the plural and means ancestors.

forbid, forbidding, foreboding

The verb **forbid** means 'prohibit someone in direct or forceful terms from doing something'. The past tense is either *forbad* or *forbade* and the past participle is *forbidden*. The present participle **forbidding** can be used as an adjective. This means 'threatening', 'hostile', or 'dangerous': *I can imagine no food more forbidding in appearance than certain fungi; He could arrange his eyebrows in a very forbidding fashion.*

Foreboding is a noun. It means a sense of impending

disaster or misfortune: *He was overcome by gloomy fore-boding and malignant fear; She found, almost with fore-boding, that the window was not latched.*

forceful, forcible

When talking of someone's character you might call them **forceful** which means to say that they have a strong dominant personality and are used to getting the better of situations.

The adjective **forcible** cannot be used of people. It is used in connection with incidents involving the use of force, e.g. rioters can suffer *a forcible dispersal*; where a house has been entered by breaking a window, the term used is *forcible entry*. It is also used for incidents that convey a strong effect, e.g. an exclamation can be *forcible;* something can *serve as a forcible reminder*.

forehead

The pronunciation of **forehead** as /faw-hed/ is increasingly used in preference to the older pronunciation of /fo-rid/ (thus spoiling the nursery rhyme about the moody little girl). Those who regard the pronunciation /fo-rid/ as 'correct', should note that it replaces an even earlier pronunciation that was much closer to /faw-hed/.

This change and others (e.g. *forecastle* and *waistcoat*) are brought about by using spelling as a guide to pronunciation.

forename ⇒ Christian name

for ever, forever

Both the one-word and the two-word form are used, although there are some shades of difference. *Forever* is used to mean 'constantly' and *for ever* to mean 'for all time': *You are forever pestering me; This is goodbye for ever.*

foreword, preface, introduction, frontispiece

The words *foreword, preface,* and *introduction* overlap in meaning and are not used in a systematic way in books. A **foreword** is a short introductory statement at the beginning of a book, usually explaining its scope and purpose. It is just as likely, however, to consist only of a note of thanks to those who have helped the writer. A **preface** is usually written by the author while a *foreword* can be a comment by an invited expert. The word *preface* is the more common and is used for both purposes. An **introduction** is a short preliminary chapter that outlines the background to a book. It is generally more a part of the main book than a *foreword* or *preface.*

A **frontispiece** is an illustration facing the title page of a book.

forgo, forego

The verb **forgo** means 'give up' or 'do without' something: *...exhorting the people to work harder, to forgo present pleasures.*

There is an archaic verb **forego** (with an *e* that means 'go before'. This is used in its participial form as an adjective, as in *the foregoing facts.* It also occurs in the phrases *a foregone conclusion* and *a foregone decision.* When something is **foregone** it is already decided.

Unfortunately, the spelling difference between these two verbs is not always maintained, so that each can be found used with the other's spelling.

former, latter, formerly, formally

The words **former** and **latter** are much more common in written forms of English than in spoken ones because a reader can always look back over the text. *Former* and *latter* establish a point of reference with regard to what has gone before or comes after: *There are two arcades, Piccadilly and Prince's. The former is very pretty doll's house taste. The latter contains two good coffee shops.*

Both words only allow two points of reference. If there are more than two places or persons involved, as there are in a sentence like: *Ron, Kate, and Mike were elected to the committee*, you have to say *the first-named* or *the first-mentioned was appointed Treasurer*, not 'the former'. Similarly it would be *Mike* or *the last-named became Secretary*, not 'the latter'.

Avoid confusing *formerly* and **formally**, which means 'in a formal manner': *We were formally introduced to the new manager.*

formula

The usual plural of **formula** is **formulas**. The Latin form **formulae** is found in scientific writing.

for the sake of argument

The expression **for the sake of argument** does not mean 'for the sake of an illustration' but 'to put the opposite point of view': *Let us assume, for the sake of argument, that his strategy is feasible.*

fortuitous, accidental

Fortuitous is a formal word referring to something that happens by chance. A *fortuitous* event is often linked to natural causes. It does not necessarily have any overtones of 'a fortunate chance': *...some not entirely fortuitous disaster; ...a fortuitous discovery.*

The adjective **accidental** often refers to a chance event that is unfortunate: *...accidental loss or damage.* Something *accidental* frequently involves human beings: *The evidence doesn't suggest accidental death.*

forward, forwards

Forward is an adjective: *forward-looking; the forward edge*. **Forwards** is an adverb: *run forwards; lunged forwards*. American English uses *forward* for the adjective and the adverb.

four, fourth, forty, forth

Note the different spellings of **four**, **fourth**, and **forty** (where the *u* is dropped). There is no connection between the numbers and **forth**, which is an adverb that means 'forwards in time or space'. Common idioms in which it is used are *so forth* and *back and forth*.

fractious

Despite a similarity to *fracture*, **fractious** has no connection with breaking something. It means 'irritable': *Melanie was always a fractious child.*

fragile, frail

We use the adjective **fragile** to describe any easily breakable item: *...fragile ivory figurines; ...fragile, birdlike bones. Fragile* is extended and used about people to mean 'physically weak': *a fragile and pitiful old lady*, sometimes with the sense of 'unwell': *Depleted and fragile, she crept back into the car, cold sweat on her forehead.* **Frail** is used of people who are not physically strong: *a frail old man; a frail young girl*. It is used less often to describe something that is easily broken.

fraught

The adjective **fraught** is usually placed after the noun it modifies, or after *be*, and is itself normally followed by *with*: *He and I exchange lingering stares fraught with meaning*. It means 'charged'. When *fraught* is used before the noun its meaning can change to 'showing tension': *...this fraught young woman.*

-free

The suffix *-free* can combine with a suitable noun to form an adjective in both single-word or hyphenated forms: *carefree; trouble-free*.

freely, free

The use of *free of* means 'not subject to': *free of charge; free of duty*, or 'not restricted or encumbered by': *All our vegetables are packed free of dirt*. This usage normally allows the formation of compounds, such as: *duty-free goods; dirt-free potatoes*.

The use of *free* followed by *from* has the sense of a change of circumstances, as in *He was at last free from arrest; The plates were now free from dirt and were softly gleaming*. In this sense, the formation of compounds is not normally possible.

The adverb **freely** can be replaced by **free** in very limited cases. These consist of set phrases where *free* follows the verb and means 'without restraint': *make free; run free*.

French words

Because of the history of English, it contains many words of French origin. Many are so well assimilated that it needs specialist knowledge to identify them. Words that have come into English from French in more recent times are often more easily recognizable because of unfamiliar spelling patterns. The current tendency is for a word that has been assimilated into English to lose any accent that it might have in French unless it is possible to confuse it with another word, e.g. *resume* (begin again) and *résumé* (a brief account). English speakers are advised to use an anglicized version of the pronunciation of assimilated French words. Attempts to copy the French pronunciation generally fail or prove somewhat pretentious in the context of an English sentence.

Certain French phrases in common use in English have to keep an approximate French pronunciation for reasons of sound only, e.g. *coup de théâtre; coup d'état.* British speakers should also be aware that there are some English phrases that appear to be French but are not recognized as such by French speakers. Examples are *cul-de-sac* and *nom de plume.*

from ⇒ off

fuchsia
This word is frequently misspelled because of its pronunciation, /**few**-sha/. The *s* follows the *-ch-*.

-ful
Where the amount held by a spoon or other container is used as a rough unit of measurement, the correct form is like **spoonful**: *Take a spoonful of this medicine every day. Spoon full* as two words is used to say what the spoon contains in a sentence such as, *He left a spoon full of treacle*, where *full of* describes the spoon. The plural of a word like *spoonful* is *spoonfuls* and not *spoonsful.*

full stops ⇒ punctuation

funereal, funeral
The adjective **funereal** means 'gloomy' or 'mournful'. Something may seem *funereal* without a funeral being in progress: *The dark walls and curtains, the funereal rubber plants unacquainted with sun....*

fungus, cactus
The plural of **fungus** can be either *funguses* or *fungi*. As with plant names in *-us*, e.g. **cactus**, the latter form is preferable in scientific or formal contexts.

funny

The informal use of **funny**, meaning *unwell*, *odd*, or *peculiar*, can be confused with its formal meaning, *amusing*. Suitable substitutes include *curious, peculiar, suspicious,* or *strange.* The phrases *funny-peculiar* and *funny ha-ha* are very informal.

furore, furor

The word **furore** means a large-scale outburst of enthusiasm for someone or something, or of mass indignation. In British English, the pronunciation of *furore* is /few-**raw**-ry/. In American English the word is spelled **furor.**

further ⇒ **farther**

G

-g-, -gg-

A word that ends in **-g** will always double the **-g** when it is followed by *-er, -ing,* or *-ed*. For example, *bag: We'll pick up the leaves. You be the bagger; jetlag: I feel jetlagged; nag: He keeps nagging me to get my typewriter repaired.*

gabbled, garbled

Both words have something to do with confusion. If you **gabble** you talk so fast that people have difficulty in understanding you: *The ceremony is too important to be gabbled through.* When a message or explanation is **garbled** it has been distorted or confused so that it does not make full sense: *I've only received a garbled message.*

gala

The usual pronunciation is /**gah**-la/ but some speakers prefer the older form, /**gay**-la/ which is also the one that is common in American English. Use the second form of pronunciation for the *Durham Miners' Gala*.

Gallic, Gaelic

The word **Gallic** is used in connection with something that belongs to or relates to France or the French people. It can be used in a formal way: *The proud roots of the Gallic nation*, or as part of a cliché such as, *She fell for his Gallic charm*. The usual pronunciation is /**gal**-lik/.

The adjective **Gaelic** refers to the Celtic people of Scotland, Ireland, and the Isle of Man: *Our prized Gaelic honesty is rather provincial*. As a noun, it means the Gaelic language: *My mother speaks Gaelic*, and in dialect it is sometimes preceded by *the*: *Do you have the Gaelic?* It is usually pronounced /**gay**-lik/, but those who speak it prefer /**gal**-lik/. Both words are connected by etymology to the Latin word for the *Gauls* or Celts. ⇒ **Welsh**

gambit

A **gambit** is an opening move in chess. In a *gambit*, a piece is sacrificed to gain an advantage. It is redundant to use the expression, *an opening gambit*. By extension, you can talk about *a conversational gambit* or some other manœuvre designed to secure an advantage in a discussion or a situation. This word is sometimes confused with *gamut*. ⇒ **gamut**

gamut

In music, the **gamut** is the entire range or scale of notes and, by extension, the range of emotions. It is often found in the expression, *run the gamut of* something. Do not confuse this with the expression, *to run the gauntlet*.

gaol, gaoler, jail, jailer

The forms **gaol** and **gaoler** (note the spelling and do not confuse *gaol* with *goal*) are no longer in regular use, except in legal references. The preference is for the forms **jail** and **jailer**: *Failure to support an ex-wife put him in jail.* It is equally correct to say that someone is *in prison*: *He spent most of those years in prison.*

gap

Most uses of **gap** involve some sort of defect: *a gap in the fence; a gap between his teeth.* However there is one use that treats a *gap* as something positive: *a gap in the market* allows a trader to establish a foothold. The word *gap* can also be used to mean a difference or divergence in some feature, e.g. *the generation gap; Most small businesses face a 'people gap'.* Although this is useful as a short reference, it is now a rather overworked expression and is best avoided.

garage

The word **garage** derives from French and has two possible pronunciations. The older one, /ga-**rahge**/, is an approximation to the French form. An alternative form is /**ga**-ridge/, although some listeners judge this to be less acceptable. When the word is used as a verb, the usual pronunciation is /**ga**-ridge/: *I'm going to garage the car.*

garbage, trash, rubbish, waste

The words **trash** and **garbage** are taken to be Americanisms by most British speakers, who prefer the words **rubbish**, **refuse**, or **waste**.

The word *trash*, meaning something worthless, can be found in Shakespeare. *Garbage*, an equally old word, is used informally in British English to refer to ideas that the speaker regards as worthless: *He talked a lot of garbage about peace and freedom.*

There is a difference between **rubbish**, **refuse**, and **waste.** The first two refer to any mixture of unwanted material: *She put it in the rubbish; The refuse collection is always a day late after a Bank Holiday.* **Waste** is surplus material: *wastepaper; waste sheet materials.*

garbled ⇒ **gabbled**

gas, gaseous
Gaseous is an adjective formed from **gas**. It has several possible pronunciations. The most usual one in British English has the same initial sound as **gas**, /**gas**-ee-us/, but /**gay**-see-us/ and, in American English, /**gash**-us/ are also used.

gauge
Note the spelling of this word. It is commonly misspelled.

gauntlet
A **gauntlet** is a protective glove that was worn by medieval soldiers. It is used in the expression *throw down the gauntlet,* meaning 'challenge someone'. Do not confuse this with another expression, *to run the gauntlet,* which refers to a form of punishment once used by the military in which an offender was made to run between ranks of soldiers armed with batons.
⇒ **gamut**

gay
Once a word has become established in a new usage, it is pointless bemoaning the fact that the original meaning has been hijacked. This is a fate that has overtaken many words about which not a second thought is given today e.g. *silly, cheer.* **Gay** is now a term for homosexual (noun

and adjective), and speakers of English need to be cautious of the context in which *gay,* meaning *happy* or *bright,* is used. You can no longer write, *She missed her gay parties,* without ambiguity, but literary phrases like, *Their ancient, glittering eyes are gay,* (W.B.Yeats) or those where a coupled adjective clarifies the reference, such as *At last they were peaceful and gay,* retain their meaning.

gender, sex

Gender is a term that is often used in grammar when a noun is placed formally in a particular category: *All second declension nouns in Latin are feminine gender.* In grammar it has nothing to do with the biological sex of the noun, even if it has one.

It is also, in formal English, the fact of being male, female, or neuter. When used in this sense, the word **gender** refers to all those of the same sex or to people grouped by sex: *Gender should not be important in offers of employment.*

Sex refers to the set of characteristics that distinguish the reproductive functions of an organism. *…both sexes take the next step into their gender identities; The triplets were of the same sex.*

gender-marked words

There are a number of words in English that are marked as specifically referring to male or female gender. Examples are: *cow, bull; ewe, ram; actress, actor; manageress, manager; mistress, master.* Some of these words are useful. The distinction between *cow* and *bull* enables important distinctions of meaning to be made.

The matter can be complicated. As the social roles of men and women alter, which they do in every generation, the use of words changes to match. In some areas today, the distinction, 'man's job' and 'woman's job', no longer exists, and what were *gender-marked* words have had to become *gender-neutral*.

For example, the difference between a *manageress* and a *manager*, an *actor* and an *actress*, is not one of function. Both may have the same type of responsibility in a job and the use of a *gender-marked* word can give needless offence because the form that marks the sex of the person often carries a message about the status of the job. We expect a *manager* to be high-powered and desk-based and a *manageress*, on the other hand, to be shop-floor management. In this case we should treat the simple form as unmarked and use it in all circumstances.

Sometimes an escape from the problem of gender-marked labelling can be avoided by changing the form of words. The words *headmaster* and *headmistress* are not neutral but the words *headteacher* or *head* are. Use of either of the two latter words makes neutral reference possible. This is not always a satisfactory solution. Sometimes the replacement words carry their own burden of reference, as in the case of the distinction: *master= private school; teacher=state school.*

A similar problem is raised by a group of words ending in *-man*. The ending is now perceived as gender marked, even though historically it was not. Some users may wish to substitute an ending that is perceived as neutral, such as *-person*. ⇒ **chairman** ⇒ **sexism**

generic, general

The adjective **generic** is ambiguous. In pharmacy it specifically denotes a drug or preparation that has no brand-name: *Generic preparations are sold under the heading of B.P. preparations.*

Otherwise, it refers to a whole group and means much the same as **general**: *The smaller boys were known by the generic title of 'littluns'; There have been many attempts to find a generic term for this group.*

Generic is used in biology as the adjectival form of *genus*.
⇒ **genus**

genetics, genetic

In common with the names of many sciences, e.g. *physics, mechanics*, the noun **genetics** looks plural but is always used with a singular verb: *As a science, genetics has only recently caught public attention.* The adjective form is **genetic**: *We can take genetic material from the mother.*

genius, genie

The word **genius** is used of a person with exceptional ability. The plural is **geniuses**: *Newton and Einstein were geniuses.*

In fairy stories there is often a magic servant, called, in *The Arabian Nights*, a **genie**. The plural of genie is **genies**. In other tales such a servant or guiding spirit may, instead, be called a **genius**: *Mr Hyde was Dr Jekyll's evil genius; The genius of the place led us to a small clearing in the woods.* This use of the word, which has the associated plural form **genii**, is rather rare.

gent, gentleman, gentry, gentlefolk

The abbreviation **gent** should be avoided in formal speech and writing. In its plural form it is acceptable on the door of a public lavatory. Used as part of an introduction, as in, *Ladies and Gents, we have with us tonight…*, it is regarded by most people as a vulgarism. Always prefer the full form of the word, **gentleman**, and its plural. Use of the word *gentleman* to describe a man is passing from regular use except in phrases such as: *Ladies and gentlemen of the jury...*; *Ask the gentleman in the far corner; a perfect gentleman.* In general use, the word can have overtones of irony or a reference to a past generation: *He found himself playing ball with commodity brokers and gentleman-hoodlums; ...by that time he had become merely a funny old gentleman.*

The word **gentry** can be ambiguous. In the conventions that govern very formal assemblies, the *gentry* are a high-born group ranking second to the nobility: *He came from a family of landed gentry; Gentry without money gradually cease to be gentry.* It has another informal and scornful use, and means 'one of a set of people': *These gentry often try their tricks on elderly people.*

The use of the word **gentlefolk** is a genteel affectation and should be avoided.

gentility, genteel, gentleness

These words should be distinguished. **Gentility** is used to mean polite good breeding: *...a young man with the marks of breeding, gentility, education, and good luck...*, or for affecting the pretence of possessing this quality: *He was an odd juxtaposition of gentility and 'bovver-boy' aggressiveness.*

The adjective **genteel** is related to this second meaning and is commonly used of speech or manners which are excessively proper or polite, often to the point of caricature: *She tended to fall back on quaintly genteel oaths in moments of great stress.*

Gentleness refers to behaviour that shows a mild or kindly nature.

gentry ⇒ **gent**

genus

A **genus** in biology is a group of one or more closely related species, which is regarded as a unit within a larger grouping. The name of the *genus* is always printed in italics, has a capital letter, and comes first: *The genus Hydnum is unique among fungi; It was a specimen of Trollius laxus.* The plural form is either **genera** or **genuses**. The word is pronounced with a soft 'g' sound, /**djee**-nus/. It has the adjective form *generic*.

gerund

This word is a grammatical term that is no longer used in modern descriptions of English. It was borrowed from the grammar of Latin. The present participle (-*ing* form) of a verb may be used as a noun. Modern grammars of English prefer to talk about *verbal nouns*. An example is: *She found his **thinking** positive and helpful.*

get

Use of the word **get** and its parts, **getting** and **got**, is sometimes criticized as a serious fault, either of style or grammar. There is no foundation for this prejudice except in so far as the overuse of any word may be a failure in style. The source of the prejudice against **get** and its forms is hard to trace, but goes back at least fifty years and probably stems from advice to writers to vary the choice of nouns and verbs in descriptive passages.

Get can be used in a wide range of sentences to express the verbal element. In a phrase such as *get a new tap*, the use of *get* is clearer and more direct than *procure a new tap*. *Have/has got* is often the simplest way of stating the fact of possession: *She has got a new car.* It can form a type of passive construction in place of *be*: *If you have things on the floor, they get trodden on.* It is often the most obvious choice of verb, although it is fairly informal. ⇒ **gotten**

geyser

In countries where the geothermal phenomena called *geysers* exist, such as the USA and New Zealand, the word is pronounced /**guy**-zer/ not /**gee**-zer/. On the grounds that those who have them ought to know best, this pronunciation is to be preferred: *Some geysers now have to be primed with soap before they will work.*

gibe, gybe, jibe, jib

A jeering or scoffing remark at someone's expense is a **gibe** or a **jibe**. Both forms are current: *He tended to be the easy butt of gibes about frivolity; There was more than a grain of truth in these jibes.*

The nautical verb **gybe**, used when a sail shifts suddenly from one side of a vessel to the other, has a number of other spellings. These are **gibe**, **jibe**, and **jib**. A **jib** is also a triangular sail or the arm of a crane. In all these words the 'g' or the 'j' is soft, as in *gem*.

gild, gilt, gilded, guild

Gild means to 'cover something with gold'. It has two past participles, **gilt** and **gilded**, both of which are used as premodifiers: *A fine pair of gilt candlesticks; the flimsy gilded panels.* When the meaning is literal, the usual form is **gilt** (but not exclusively, as the examples show), while the alternative form **gilded** is normally used for metaphorical expressions: *my gilded youth; gilded harshness.*

The sense of *gilded* is often closer to 'gave a gold colouring to' than to 'covered with gold'. However, *gilded* is the form used for the normal Simple Past: *Buttercups gilded the fields,* and for the past participle form in compound verbs, as in *The furniture was gilded and scrolled.*

Gilt is used as a noun to mean 'a gold covering', as in, *a baroque background of stucco and gilt.* The similar sounding noun **guild** means 'an association of craftsmen'.

gill

When the word **gill** is associated with the respiration of a fish, it is pronounced with a hard 'g' as in *go.* When it means an Imperial quarter pint measure, it has a soft 'g' as in *gem.*

gimmick, gizmo, McGuffin

A **gimmick** is something that is intended to draw attention to itself and to anything associated with it. The word carries the sense of something intrinsically worthless, so it should not be used as a synonym for 'a new idea': *It seemed too much of a trendy gimmick.*

A **gizmo** is a slang word that is used to replace the real name of something when you have forgotten it or when you do not know what it is: *You'll need to put a little gizmo in here to hold the door open.*

A **MacGuffin** is a term coined by the director Alfred Hitchcock to describe an apparently trivial incident in a film that turns out to be very important. It is a trick or device: *The author opts for a Hitchcockian ending in which the suitcases … turn out to be a MacGuffin.*

gipsy ⇒ gypsy

glance, glimpse

A **glance** (noun) is a hasty look. When you *glance* (verb) at something, you look at it hastily, sometimes without wanting to attract attention: *People flashed glances of* *recognition at me; I glanced round furtively from time to time.*

A **glimpse** of something gives you a brief or incomplete view: *She made the identification from fleeting glimpses of the two men.* Glimpse is also used as a verb: *He glimpsed the watcher in the black car.* By extension, a *glimpse* of something can be a brief experience of it: *a glimpse of happiness.*

go

Use of the word **go**, or any of its forms, as a substitute for *say* is not standard English. For example, in *And he goes, 'I really need to see you', so I went, 'You'll not be seeing me again for a while.',* the use of *goes* and *went* is not acceptable. This usage has become very common in casual speech, even among some educated users.

god, God

A capital letter is used for the word **god** when it refers to the notion of the existence of a single god. Thus it is usual to refer to **God** when speaking of the Christian, Jewish, and Muslim religions.

When talking of religions in which there are many gods, as for example ancient Greek or Roman religion, the form without a capital letter is normal.

gold, golden

Generally, when **gold** is used as an adjective it makes a literal reference to the metal gold. A *gold medal* is made from gold.

The adjective **golden** usually means 'as if it were gold' so that it is used of objects which are the colour of gold or, metaphorically, have the same value as gold: *She had golden skin and hair; The golden rule; A golden handshake.*

Exceptionally, the *golden calf* and the *Golden Fleece* contained the metal gold, while some bird names such as *goldcrest* and *goldfinch* are only 'as if gold'. ⇒ **gild**

golf

The usual pronunciation includes the *l* sound /golf/. An older form of pronunciation /goff/ is regarded as having 'higher status' by some speakers. Others regard this form as very old-fashioned. ⇒ **Ralph**

good

Careful speakers and writers of English do not use **good** and **bad** as adverbs: *She dances well* [not *good*]; *He sings really badly* [not *really bad*]. ⇒ **real**

goodbye, good-bye, good-by

All three forms are used by educated writers of British English. In British dictionaries, both **goodbye** and **good-bye** with a hyphen are given. The British preference is to write *goodbye* as one word. **Good-by** is preferred in American English.

good day, good night

Good day is usually two words, like **good evening**, not one: *'Good day to you,' he said, as he went into his office.* **Good night** can be either two words, as shown, two words linked by a hyphen, or one word. *'Goodnight love', said Flora.* ⇒ **thank you**

goodwill, good-will, good will

The form **goodwill** is normally used when referring to a kindly interest in something or to the commercial asset of a business that is generated by its relations with its customers: *The Government is buying large quantities of this butter as a goodwill gesture. Mr Jones has maintained the goodwill of the business.* **Good-will** is the alternative but less common form for both these meanings.

The form **good will** is used when referring to the more general sense. The adjective *good* can be exchanged for any suitable adjective in this meaning of the phrase: *He can always attribute it to the good will or malice of his employers; ...an explosion of good will and sympathy.*

gotta, gotter, hafta, wanna

All these forms are phonetic spellings The sound **gotta** is frequently heard in rapid, casual speech for *got to* but the word has no place in writing unless the writer is trying to give the flavour of very informal speech: *You gotta work fast; I gotta go out.*

The phonetic words **hafta**, used for *have to* and **wanna**, used for *want to*, similarly have no place in careful writing: *I hafta see him now; I wanna get out of here.*

gotten

The spelling **gotten** is not a normal past participle form for **get** in British English although it was once part of standard British English. It may be found in dialect and sometimes in the speech or writing of those who have been exposed to American English for lengthy periods. It is, of course, recognized as a common feature in much modern American usage: *His leg may have gotten tangled in a harpoon line; The business had gotten to be a frequent daydream of mine.* In British English the old past form survives in *ill-gotten*. The verbs *forget* and *beget* also preserve this form in *forgotten*, and *misbegotten*.

gourmand, gourmet

The distinction is between someone who is excessively fond of eating and drinking, a **gourmand**, and someone who has a fine appreciation of food, a **gourmet**. The latter word has currently been replaced in some journalism by the term *foodie*. The word *glutton* is similar in meaning to *gourmand*.

graffiti

Plural in the original Italian, the singular form is **graffito** but in English this sounds either pretentious or jocular. **Graffiti** has become well established as a collective noun and may be used with a singular or plural verb: *We saw a piece of graffiti reading, 'Free the Renault Five'; There was graffiti on the wall.*

-gram

This suffix means 'something written or inscribed', as in *telegram, hologram.*

gram, gramme

Either spelling is permissible. The *gram(me)* is an obsolete term no longer used in the scientific community as a standard unit of mass. Its equivalent is represented as $1/1000$ of a kilogram. ⇒ **kilogram**

grammar

The word **grammar** can be understood in several ways. To a linguist, **grammar** is the set of rules that govern word order, form, and meaning within sentences. Examples of these rules can be found in the *Collins Gem English Grammar.*

A less formal meaning of grammar is anything that has to do with speaking or writing correctly. This meaning includes everything in the present book called **usage** as well as the rules of spelling. People often say they have poor grammar when they mean that they are concerned about their spelling or their punctuation. The notion of 'using good grammar' is sometimes mistakenly thought to mean the same as 'using Received Pronunciation', as if having a regional accent ruled out the possibility of employing an acceptable grammar.

Another meaning is, a book containing exercises and rules for someone learning to write and speak a language: *I can't find my German grammar.*

grand-, great-

When **grand-** and **great-** are used in nouns that indicate family relationships, **grand-** is used for a close relationship that skips a generation, as in *grandfather, grandmother, grandson,* and **great-** (which can be duplicated) is used for a more distant relationship: *My father's sister is my aunt, but my grandfather's sister is my great-aunt; My grandmother's mother is your great-great-grandmother.*

gray ⇒ grey

Great Britain, United Kingdom

Great Britain is the name of the island that contains England, Wales, and Scotland. The **United Kingdom** is the political unit consisting of these three, together with Northern Ireland. ⇒ **British**

Greek, Grecian

The word **Greek** is the name for the language of Greece: *My wife speaks fluent modern Greek,* for the inhabitants of the country: *You will find it hard to believe the open-hearted generosity of the Greeks,* and for something that is Greek or relates to Greece: *She is a Greek model; This was the great age of Greek sport.* **Grecian** is used when talking of something relating to ancient Greece: *Ode to A Grecian Urn; the ruins of a Grecian amphitheatre.*

grey, gray

Grey is the normal British spelling. **Gray** is American.

groin, groyne

British English makes a distinction between these two words. Both have the same pronunciation. The **groin** is the area of the body where the legs meet. It usually follows *in*: *He was given a terrible kick in the groin.*

A **groyne** is a wall that is built out into a river or the sea as a defence against erosion: *Two children were washed off the groyne by a freak wave.* In American English this word is also spelled *groin*.

groom, bridegroom

A **groom** is a person employed to look after a horse. A *groom* may be of either sex, though most are young women. Men and women performing this task are also often called *lads* or *stable lads*.

The correct term for a man who is about to marry is a **bridegroom**. In this case, the word **groom** is only a shortened form, which is often found in the expression *the bride and groom*. If you want to be formal you should use the full form.

groyne ⇒ groin

guarantee, warranty, warrantee

Both a **guarantee** and a **warranty**, when associated with the sale of goods or services, give an assurance that these meet stated specifications. Historically, they are variant spellings of the same French word. A **warrantee** is someone to whom a *warranty* has been given.

guerrilla, guerilla

A **guerrilla** or **guerilla** is 'someone who is a member of an unofficial army'. Both spellings are acceptable. *Guerrilla* comes from the Spanish for 'a small war' and has no connection whatever with the meaning of the word *gorilla*, but both words have the same pronunciation.

gulf, bay

Both words refer to a part of the coastline where the sea is within a curve of the coastline. **Gulf** is used when the sea covers a very large area between the arms of the surrounding land: *Mission Bay; The Bay of Biscay; the Gulf of Mexico.*

gybe ⇒ gibe

gypsy, gipsy, traveller, tinker

The words **gypsy** and **gipsy** are alternative spellings. The usual form in British English is *gypsy*. When referring to someone of Romani origin, the form with a capital letter is used: *Many Gypsies were killed in Nazi concentration camps.* When talking about a way of life or behaviour, the word is used without capitals: *She's a proper tomboy, a little gipsy.*

The term **traveller** is often used to class together anyone of nomadic lifestyle, whether Romani or not. This gives rise to the sign, *No travellers,* seen outside some English pubs, which mystifies many English speakers from outside the U.K. The term **tinker**, meaning a gypsy, is now restricted to dialect. It was once common.

None of these words is entirely neutral and an element of prejudice is often indicated by their use. The use of the word *to gyp* meaning *to cheat* or *swindle* is an example of this prejudice. Gypsies themselves sometimes use the term 'travelling folk' as a neutral group label.

H

habitual

This adjective is always used with the indefinite article *a* not *an*: *He was a habitual criminal.*

had

Had we but world enough and time... ; *Had I received your education, I would have been more successful.* In phrases such as this, **had** invokes an unreal condition. It is equivalent to, *If we/I had...*. It is not a particularly common usage in modern English and can be regarded as a mainly literary form. ⇒ **was**

half

Half is used before a determiner in one of two ways. It may come directly before the determiner, as in *Half my share has been spent.* It may be used with *of* between the **half** and the determiner, as in *This accounts for half of the wheat sold.* This is an option that varies from speaker to speaker. When **half** is modified, it must be followed by *of*: *The northern, rich half of the world; the first half of the twentieth century.*

hamster

Note the spelling. There is no '*p*' in this word.

handful

The usual plural is *handfuls.* ⇒ **spoonful**

hang, hanged, hung

The normal Simple Past and past participle form of **hang** is **hung**: *The smoke hung over the city for days; The picture was hung from a nail.* Butcher's meat and game is

hung. When talking about capital punishment the form is **hanged**: *You may as well be hanged for a sheep as a lamb.*

hanger, hanger-on, hangar

A **hanger** is used to suspend something, such as a garment. A **hanger-on** is someone who trails about with a celebrity. The plural is *hangers-on*. A **hangar** is a large building used for garaging aircraft.

hara-kiri

Note the spelling of **hara-kiri**. However, the Japanese do not use this term and call ritual suicide *seppuku*.

harass, harassment

The traditional pronunciation of **harass** has the stress on the first syllable /ˈha-ris/. In recent years an alternative pronunciation, with the stress on the second syllable, has become very common. This form, /huh-ˈrass/, is unacceptable to many speakers of British English.

hardly, scarcely, barely

Since **hardly**, **scarcely**, and **barely** already have a negative sense, it is redundant to use another negative in the same clause: *he had hardly had* [not *he hadn't hardly had*] *time to think; there was scarcely any* [not *scarcely no*] *bread left*.

All these words should be paired with *before* or *when*: *They had hardly exchanged a word before Janet rushed in; He had barely stopped when the wail of sirens was heard.* The use of *till* or *than* in place of *before* or *when* is common but incorrect.

harmony, melody

The terms **harmony** and **melody** are complementary. Both words have to do with the combination of sounds.

Harmony is the vertical representation of musical structure, such as a chord; **melody** is the horizontally represented structure, such as a tune.

have

When you use **have** plus a main verb in an expression such as *I had my tooth filled*, there is the underlying sense that you intentionally caused the event that took place.

In American English, use of **have** plus a main verb commonly indicates the passive without intentionality. This use is becoming more common in British English. However, those who recognize it as expressing intention only, find it potentially ambiguous when used as a passive in sentences that relate a misfortune. We assume that the theft, etc. was not at the wish of the speaker in sentences such as *I had my car stolen last week*, or *I had my glasses broken in an accident*, nevertheless, many speakers of British English find the construction awkward if it involves an adverse event.

It is advisable to reserve this construction for sentences indicating intentionality and use the *be* auxiliary for other passives or use *get* as an alternative: *My glasses were broken; My glasses got broken.* ⇒ **get**

haven, harbour, port

A **haven** is a safe shelter, often one used in an emergency. A **harbour** is organized for shipping in a more formal way with jetties and docks. A **port** is a large commercial harbour with a considerable number of ancillary services: *We found haven from the squall in a sheltered bay; They ran into harbour to unload their catch; The port authority cannot allow unsupervised access to the docks.*

haver

Haver is a Northern and Scottish dialect word meaning to delay, to fuss about, or to talk nonsense. It is pronounced /**hay**-ver/: *For goodness sake, stop havering man!*

he/she, s/he

In some circumstances it is necessary to use a pronoun for a word that refers to either a man or a woman, such as *teacher, student, doctor*. If the sex of the person is unknown or irrelevant, the writer is often forced into using *'he'* as the general pronoun (which may be misinterpreted) or indicating the dual nature of the reference by using the form **he/she**: *If a student gets behind with work he/she should consult a tutor.* Since *he/she* is not a spoken form of English, avoid saying aloud 'he stroke she'.

As many people dislike the form *he/she*, despite its usefulness, it is not advisable in formal writing. The form **s/he** is a similar but less frequent substitute. It is not a standard abbreviation and is equally disliked.

One solution is to use *he or she*, but this can be clumsy. A better solution is to make use of *they*. The use of a neutral plural pronoun in this type of clause is well-established, although not yet universally accepted in formal contexts. ⇒ **their**

healthy, healthful

Healthy means enjoying good health or conducive to health: *We were healthy, strong children; I lost myself in the pungent, healthy heat.* **Healthful** is a less common word that is usually found with the meaning of 'conducive to health': *Watercress is delightful in flavour, healthful and antiscorbutic.*

hectic

Originally describing excited movement and over-activity, **hectic** was associated with feverish states. By extension it became associated with any hurried action: *They are used to the hectic action of one-day cricket.*

It has gained a further meaning, related to fever, of 'bright red, flushed': *Frederica stalked off under the hectic glare of the desert; …her cheeks were a hectic red.* Fowler disliked the use of **hectic**, noting it as a vogue word and as slang. It is now well established.

heinous

This word is frequently misspelled and mispronounced. Like *mischievous*, it does not end in *-ious*. There are two syllables and the first syllable has the sound 'hay'; thus, /**hay**-nuss/.

help

The normal British usage, when **help** is followed by another main verb, is to employ the *to* infinitive as the second verb, as in *…the situation he had helped to create; The news evidently helped to deepen his discouragement.* When the action of the second verb allows direct active participation by the person helping, it need not be followed by *to: Joanna helped them (to) gather their belongings.* Some writers on usage view this as an Americanism.

The usage **cannot help but** as in *Andy couldn't help but be touched* is controversial, being condemned by some writers, while others point out that its use is widespread. The usage is a mixture of two idioms, *cannot help being* and *cannot but be.* The objection is that it constitutes a classic 'double negative' but very few readers treat it as such, largely because double negatives often reinforce the negative element.

The use of **help** followed by a present participle to mean 'avoid' is well established: *One cannot help wondering what the minister would have said.* ⇒ **double negative**

herein, hereby, heretofore, hereunder

These words, and other similar compounds of *here*, are part of the formal and very particular language of legal documents. They are not common in any other form of modern English.

heritage, inheritance, heredity

A **heritage** is usually something handed down from the past to the present generation: *This building is an important part of our national and cultural heritage.* It has some elements in common with an **inheritance**, which is something that you are born to or to which you succeed as an heir: *It's just a device to avoid inheritance taxes.* **Heredity** means biological descent: *We have begun to discover how genes affect heredity.*

hero, heroine

The plural of **hero** is *heroes* and the plural form of **heroine** is *heroines*. The word *heroine* has the same pronunciation as *heroin*, the drug. In American English, a **hero** is also a kind of sandwich made from a loaf like a French stick.

hers

The possessive form is **hers**: *They gave me hers.* There is no such form as [*her's*]. The error is a common one. ⇒ **it's**

hesitation, hesitancy, hesitance

Hesitation is the act of hesitating, as in '*I'll wait for you here,*' he said after a moment's hesitation. **Hesitancy** is a personal characteristic: *A note of hesitancy in his secre-*

tary's voice made him look up. **Hesitance** is an obsolete word for *hesitancy.*

hiccup, hiccough

The usual spelling, as given in *Collins English Dictionary*, is **hiccup**. The use of **a hiccup** as a metaphor to describe a minor delay or holdup to work in progress is well established.

high, tall

People may be referred to as being **tall** but not **high**. Buildings and mountains may be either **high** or **tall**. *Tall* is frequently used in the figurative sense, as in *a tall story*, and when a comparison is implied between otherwise identical items, *Michael's a tall boy; Alison is tall for her age.* The element of comparison with similar objects is what distinguishes *tall* from *high*.

highly, hugely

Highly is used to mean 'in a high degree': *A highly valued member of the hierarchy*. **Highly** is frequently found in a compound form with a following past participle, e.g. *highly-charged, highly-skilled, highly-paid*.

Hugely is used with a similar meaning but, unlike *highly*, it does not form compounds. Many speakers regard it as informal: *He was hugely successful.*

hire, lease, let, rent

All of these words involve the exchange of money in return for the temporary use of property or goods. In the case of **hire**, a person can also offer a service in return for payment: *A Gun For Hire*. The overtones of *hire* in British English are of casual employment for a particular purpose based on a set fee, as in *...a hired assassin*. In American English it is the usual word for *employ*. Hire can also be used as a modifier, as in, *a hire car*. When you offer something *on hire* you can also say that you are *hiring it out*: *He hired himself out as a subcontractor.*

Lease is both a noun and a verb. A **lease** is a contract to allow someone to use property for a specified length of time, usually for a considerable period: *You can lease property for up to 999 years; I have my car on a five-year lease.*

Let is an alternative verb meaning *lease*. In British English **let** can also be used as a noun: *I've taken a long let on a little flat in Marylebone. Let* is usually used when a resident property owner allows someone to use part of their property: *Do not sublet the whole or part of the home or take a lodger.*

Rent is the money you normally pay regularly for a lease. It is both a noun and a verb. When you *rent* something other than property it is usually for a short time: *Car rentals by the day or week; Rent-a-Tool.* In British English a house will be *To Rent;* in American English it will be *For Rent.* ⇒ **lend**

his/her

This is a device to get round the fact that English does not have a gender-neutral possessive form. ⇒ **he/she**

historic, historical

Historic and *historical* have similar meanings but different uses. A distinction is made between what is **historic** because it is important or significant, such as a crucial meeting, a great battle, or a famous house, as in *a historic Conference; historic fighting; historic royal houses,* and what is **historical** because it is concerned with history, such as: *a historical novel; a historical perspective; historical tradition; historical photographs.*

hoard, horde

A **hoard** is any accumulation of objects that is significant to the person that has hoarded them. The word is also a verb: *The squirrel returned to its hoard of nuts; He found a Saxon hoard; She had hoarded away his childhood toys.*

A **horde** is a vast crowd, often an unruly band of people, and by extension, anything that throngs: *A horde of locusts reduced the maize crops to sticks.*

Hobson's choice

This is not a choice at all. It means much the same as *take it or leave it.*

hoi polloi

Purists point out that the Greek word **hoi** means *the* so the phrase *the hoi polloi* is tautologous. Like many other phrases of foreign origin, it is now regarded as a single word, so it follows the rules for English phrase formation.

homo-, hetero-

The prefix **homo-** means 'the same' or 'alike'. Some examples of words with this prefix are: *homonym; homogenize; homocentric.* The meaning of this prefix, which comes from Greek, is frequently confused with the Latin stem *homo* which means 'man'. The opposite meaning to *homo-* is provided by the prefix **hetero-** meaning 'other' or 'different', as in *heterocentric; heterosexual.* It is still possible to form new words with the prefixes *homo-* and *hetero-* but they are usually scientific terms.

homophone, homograph, homonym

Certain words in English look or sound the same as others. Examples of words that sound the same are: *write, right; bare, bear.* These are **homophones**. They have the same sound but different meanings.

Examples of words that look the same are: *bear* (noun), *bear* (verb); *left* (adjective), *left* (verb). These are **homographs**. They have the same spelling but different meanings.

The general word that means either looking or sounding alike is **homonym**. All the examples above are *homonyms*.

homosexual

The gender reference of **homosexual** is neutral. Both men and women can be called *homosexual*. The term *lesbian* is sometimes used for female homosexuals. The word is formed from the prefix *homo-*. ⇒ **homo-**

Hon.

The abbreviation **Hon.** stands for either *Honorary* or *Honourable*. Examples of both uses are: *Send all invoices to K. Jones, Hon. Sec., The Cleaver Society; The Hon. Peter Maybank.*

hoof, hooves, hoofs

The normal plural form is **hooves** but **hoofs** is an accepted alternative. *Horse and Hound* prefers **hooves**.

Hoover™

This word is a brand name but it has become widely used as a synonym for a *vacuum cleaner* or, as a verb, 'to use a vacuum cleaner' in British English. This use is not well known outside the UK. There are a number of brand names that have been given popular currency in this way. ⇒ **trade names**

hopefully

Certain usages cause a large outcry while quite similar forms find ready acceptance. The word **hopefully** used to modify a whole sentence has been the subject of much adverse comment, while *interestingly, surprisingly, presumably* and others have been accepted without comment. The use of *hopefully* in this way, meaning 'it is hoped', has been around for about 30 years. Interestingly, this usage attracted condemnation in Britain as an Americanism, but the outcry against its use was equally loud in the USA.

hospitable

The most favoured pronunciation puts the main stress on the first syllable. An alternative pronunciation puts the stress on the second syllable.

host

This word is used as a verb by some writers, for example: *Wogan is hosting a new show*, but many careful users of English dislike this usage and prefer: *Wogan is the host of a new show*. Many nouns can be used as verbs in English but the general acceptability of the new usage can be slow. It is often best to avoid such usages in formal speech or writing.

house, home

A **house** is a building in which people live. It a neutral word and indicates little more than the presence of a roof and four walls. It is also a word used in connection with commercial companies as both a noun and a modifier: *a publishing house; a house journal; house rules*. *House* has a more positive use as the specific term for the place where a religious community lives, as in *the mother house in Bruges*. **Home** is a more comfortable word that includes the idea of the family along with the place of residence. The word *home* is also used to give greater acceptability to an otherwise much less attractive notion, for example, an institution like *a rest home, a home for the disabled,* or *a funeral home.*

hove

Except in nautical situations, the word **hove** is an archaic past form of **heave.** The normal past of *heave* is *heaved.* Avoid worn comic phrases like *Mrs Smith hove into view.*

how

How means 'in what way?', 'by what means?' in sentences like, *How did you manage it?.* In reported statements it can also mean 'the way in which': *I know how he did it; I was just thinking how things have changed.*

How is sometimes used to replace *that* in reported speech: *He told them how he was missing them.* It is better to avoid this use when it can cause misunderstanding. It is not clear whether the writer means to make a simple statement or to express the extent of his missing them.

however, how ever

The adverb **however,** as one word, is used as the preliminary to a sentence to suggest that the information contained puts a different light on what has already been said: *However, the books never arrived.* When *however* is used in this way, it must be separated by a comma from the rest of the sentence. The usual position is as first word in the sentence, but it can come later, however.

Avoid using *but* and *however* together. *We took away two boxes of relics; however,* (or *but*) *the greater part remains for someone else to find. However* is also used to modify adjectives of quantity and degree, with the meaning 'no matter how': *However much we want to, there is no way we can help you.* When it is used like this, it is not separated by a comma.

You can include **ever** as a separate word to add a note of emphasis to a question beginning with **how**, such as: *How did you do it? How ever did you do it?* This is a different use of *how* and *ever*.

humane, humanity

The noun **humanity** has three main meanings. As a singular noun it generally means *compassion: Mother Teresa is noted for her humanity.* The adjective **humane** means displaying kindness and concern: *A humane killer* is one which, when used on animals, causes them the least degree of pain or distress. Also as a singular noun, *humanity* is a synonym for *mankind: Humanity has much to answer for in its treatment of the other animals.*

When the plural form of the noun is used, it means the 'liberal studies' (or 'liberal arts') of history, philosophy, languages, and music. *Humanities* is often preceded by *the* and written with a capital letter: *John has a degree in the Humanities*. The adjective *humane* used in connection with intellectual activity means 'concerned with the liberal arts'.

humanist, humanitarian

In the history of culture, a **Humanist**, during the Renaissance, was someone who was steeped in the literature and values of the classics. A **humanist** today is someone who holds the belief that people can formulate their own system of ethics and forms of civilized behaviour without the intervention of a religion.

A **humanitarian** is someone who has a deep concern for his or her fellow beings.

hummus, houmous, hoummos

Any of these three names may be used for the compound

of ground chickpeas. All these forms are correct because they represent attempts to represent the sound of a word taken from several foreign languages. It often takes a long time for a borrowed word to settle into an accepted English spelling or pronunciation. ⇒ **yoghurt**

humour, humorous, humorist
Note the change in spelling from -*our*- to -*or*- in the abstract noun, **humour**, the adjective **humorous**, and the noun **humorist**.

humus, compost
Humus is vegetable matter that has been broken down by soil bacteria and weathering. **Compost** is the product of deliberately inducing this process on garden and other waste for horticultural purposes.

hung ⇒ **hang**

hydro-
This prefix means having to do with *water*. Some examples of words with this prefix are: *hydrofoil, hydrophobia, hydroelectric*. It is still possible to form new words with this prefix.

hyper-
This prefix means *above, over,* or *in excess*. Some examples of words with this prefix are: *hypercritical, hyperactive, hyperinflation*. It is possible to use it to form new words. Words with this prefix are often confused with those beginning *hypo-*. ⇒ **hypo-**

hypercritical, hypocritical
If you are **hypercritical**, you find fault too readily. If you are **hypocritical** you pretend to be something which you are not, or behave in a way that is false, merely to deceive someone else.

hyphen

A **hyphen** is used to show that two parts of a word that has been split over a printed line belong together or that two words should be grouped. ⇒ **punctuation**

hypo-

This prefix means *beneath* or *below*. Some examples of its use are: *hypodermic, hypothermia, hypotonic*. New words can be formed with this prefix. Be careful not to confuse words with this prefix with those beginning *hyper-*. ⇒ **hyper-**

hypocrisy

Note the spelling. This word is frequently misspelled.

hypocritical ⇒ hypercritical

hysteria, histrionics

Although both **hysteria** and **histrionics** mark a display of excessive emotion they do not come from the same root and consequently have developed different overtones. *Hysteria* is uncontrollable emotional behaviour. The adjective *hysterical* is preceded by *a*, not *an*.

Histrionics functions as a singular noun. It is deliberate 'over the top' behaviour, playing up to the audience. It is derived from the Latin word for an actor.

I

I, me, myself

The appropriate use of these pronouns (and those in the same group) causes several problems. First let us distinguish them according to the role each has in a clause. **I** is a subject form, and **me** is an object form, of a personal pronoun. **Myself** is a reflexive pronoun.

The subject form **I** governs a verb. In simple terms that usually means that **I** goes before the verb. When the verb has a joint subject, typical in cases where two people do something, it is still **I** that is needed. The usual mistake is to use *me* here so that you find sentences such as *me and Dad went shopping…; me and my sister found a kitten…* These should be, *Dad and I went shopping…. My sister and I found a kitten….* Notice that it is not only the choice of pronoun but the word order that has to be altered.

The object form **me** needs to be used after a verb, as in *she likes me; they saw me,* and most people find no problem in this. The trouble comes when the pronoun follows one of the 50 or so prepositions, e.g. *between,* or *for.* Prepositions share with verbs the ability to take an object and must be followed by the object forms of pronouns. It is a mistake to use the subject form in this position, as in [*between you and I*]. Since *between* (and the other prepositions) must be followed by an object form, this phrase should be, *between you and me.*

Myself is a typical example of the group of reflexive pronouns. The reflexive has two uses. One is to provide an object for certain verbs expressing actions that people do to themselves, as in *He cut himself while he was sharpening a chisel; I hurt myself; She picked herself up.* The second use is to give an element of emphasis to a phrase, as in *She herself was to blame; I myself was fooled by him; I prefer French mustard, myself.* A similar use of *myself* is to make it clear that a thing has been or will be done without help: *I brewed it myself.*

One use of *myself* is only marginally acceptable, although it is common in some dialects of English and used by some educated speakers. *Myself* is not an alternative form of the subject or object pronoun. Sentences like *John and myself have just been to Greece; John and myself have a background in common* (instead of *John and I*) are not standard English usage. Neither is the use of *myself* as part of a compound object, as in *He said he had done it specially for Sue and myself* (for *Sue and me* is standard usage).

However, *I bought John and myself some chocolates* is quite all right since *myself* is used as the verb object, as it is in the sentence *I bought myself some chocolates.*

⇒ **it's me**

ibid., ibidem

In scholarly use, **ibidem**, or more usually, the abbreviation **ibid**. or **ib**., is used to indicate that a reference was to be found in the book already mentioned. *Ibid.* is always used with reference to the last book cited. It avoids the repetition of bibliographic detail on each citation. Because a translation of *ibid* is 'in the same place', never use 'in *ibid*.', which is tautological.

Today, *ibid.* is often misused by students wishing to impress and can seem rather affected, even in formal writing. Modern practice is to cite the author by name, date, and page, e.g. *Chomsky, 1968, p. 54*, and provide the full details in the bibliography.

-ible ⇒ **-able**

-ic, -ical

Both **-ic** and **-ical** are adjective endings although some *-ic* words are nouns. There is no regularity about their occurrence, however. Some words such as *comic*, *historic*, and *ironic* also have an **-ical** ending. Some, like *authentic* and *domestic*, never do. A few, like *critical*, *nautical*, and *lexical*, have no common **-ic** adjective ending. There is often a positive difference in the meaning of each form, but this is not consistently so. For example *electric* can mean 'exciting' and 'to do with electricity' but *electrical* usually only has the last meaning: *...dazzling me with her electric smile; ...lightbulbs, lightshades and electric plugs; Electrical storms raged in the clouds.* The meanings of the different forms need to be learnt.

-ic, -ics

The **-ics** ending is not only the plural form of the **-ic** ending (as in *a car mechanic*; *these grease-stained mechanics*) but a singular ending in its own right. It is particularly found as an ending for words that name a scientific discipline, e.g. *mathematics*, *physics*, *mechanics*, all of which are used with a singular form of the verb: *Mathematics is not a pompous activity; They can see the problems that physics tackles.*

ideal

Careful writers avoid using **ideal** with a superlative. By definition, something that is *ideal* cannot be surpassed: *This is by no means the blueprint for an ideal team.*
⇒ **unique**

identical to/with

The traditionally accepted preposition to be used after **identical** is *with*. However, the corpus shows that the preposition *to* is equally common in modern usage: *The living species seems to be identical with one whose remains are fossilized; It takes on a lustre identical to that which comes with very old brass.*

idiom, idiomatic

When discussing language, you use the term **idiom** to refer to an expression which native speakers of a language take, not as separate words, but as as a whole phrase, in order to correctly understand it. Consequently, expressions such as *a lame duck, a red herring, to talk your head off* are generally understood by native speakers to mean 'something which is inadequate'; 'a false trail'; 'to talk too much'.

Idiom and the adjective **idiomatic** are also used to refer to the way in which native speakers of a language would normally express themselves. For example, it is idiomatic to exclaim: *There's a spider in the bath,* rather than: *A spider is in the bath.* When a speaker of American English answers the phone, he or she may enquire *Who is this?* whereas in British English the idiomatic expression is *Who is that?*

idiosyncrasy

Note the spelling. This word ends in *-crasy,* not the more common suffix *-cracy* meaning 'control or rule by'.

i.e., e.g.

These abbreviations have quite distinct meanings. When you want to say something more specific just after talking about a subject generally, you use **i.e.,** which is an abbreviation of a Latin phrase meaning 'that is to say'

...modern (i.e. 19th and 20th century) sculpture; To keep a spaniel costs twice as much, i.e. £110 a year.

The abbreviation **e.g.** is used when you are giving one or more examples of what you are talking about. It comes from a Latin phrase meaning 'as an example'. Generally, when you use **e.g.** there are many examples that you could have given and you are choosing some typical ones: *This course contains sixteen topics offering considerable variety, e.g. Medieval Romance, Rabelais, Corneille, and Racine; Plastics can do some chores better than rubber (e.g. resist oil) and cost less.*

-ie-, -ei-

The general spelling rule is probably very well-known: *put i before e except after the letter c.* Unfortunately, there are exceptions to this general rule. The main ones, which can be explained by reference to pronunciation or derivation, are: *eight, efficient, height, inveigle, neighbour, plebeian, seize, sheik, sovereign, sufficient, surveillance, veil, weird.*

if I was, if I were ⇒ was

-ile

The **-ile** ending, as in *missile, juvenile,* and *sterile,* is normally pronounced to rhyme with 'while' in British English. The American pronunciation often rhymes with 'ill'.

ilk

In Scottish usage **of that ilk** means 'coming from a place with the same name'. Consequently it is used to show that someone is the laird of the district: *Moncrieff of that ilk.*

The use of **ilk** in the sense of 'type, class, or sort' is often condemned as being the result of a misunderstanding of

the original Scottish expression. It is nevertheless well established and generally accepted: *Blueberries and the many other small berries of that ilk....*

ill, sick, nauseous, nauseated

Some British speakers of English differentiate between the choice of *sick* or *ill* when discussing someone's health, on the grounds of being able to detect the social background of the speaker by their choice. By these lights, *sick* is approved and *ill* given the thumbs down.

However, it is not as clear cut as it might seem. The word *ill* is used for a long term bout of bad health: *She has been very ill with glandular fever.* *Ill* can be used before some nouns only to indicate that they are harmful, as in *ill effects; ill fortune; ill luck.* *Ill* is not used before a noun to describe someone's health, whereas *sick* is: *Howard is a sick man.* When you are **sick** it is often a short but very unpleasant episode: *Philly was sick in the car.* A blunter way of saying the same thing is: *She vomited*, or *She threw up*.

Something *nauseous* (or the participle form *nauseating*), causes feelings of revulsion or physical disgust: *It stirred up clouds of the sickly stench, so nauseous I found myself gagging; ...old cigarette stubs, a nauseating sight.* If you are *nauseated* by something, it has given you these feelings: *He was nauseated by the smears of egg and congealing fat.*

In British English, feeling *sick* is the same as feeling *nauseated*. Careful American usage treats *sick* and *ill* as interchangeable and *nauseated* is equivalent to either word. Speakers of American English who are less careful use *nauseous* as if it meant 'feeling sick', as in *I felt physically nauseous*, rather than 'causing nausea'. This error blurs a useful distinction. Note that if you are *sickened* by something, it makes you feel disgusted: *Anna was sickened by his callous attitude*. Something *sickening* can either disgust you or make you feel sick in your stomach.

illegal, illicit, unlawful, illegitimate

Illegal is a very broad term for activity that is forbidden: *These officials were alleged to be members of an illegal secret society; He was fined for illegal fishing*. Something **unlawful** is contrary to what the law says it should be: *This Act was declared unlawful by the Supreme Court*. *Unlawful* and *illegal* overlap a lot. These sentences could have *illegal* where *unlawful* occurs: *All unlawful business activities came to a standstill; It was unlawful for a German to possess foreign money*.

Something **illicit** contravenes the law or goes against custom. You can use the adjective *illicit* when you are talking about an illegal activity that is carried out secretly: *It was the place to sit and smoke our illicit cigarettes; ...the illicit gambling houses that ran poker games...*

Something **illegitimate** it is not necessarily *unlawful*. An *illegitimate* activity is one not recognized as acceptable according to natural justice, as in: *The illegitimate gain of a considerable empire*. Someone or something *illegitimate* is not recognized by officialdom as having any status in law. For example, '*illegitimate*' children born outside a marriage do not have quite the same legal status that children born in a marriage do.

illegible, unreadable, illiterate

When something is described as **illegible** it means that what is written has been, for example, scrawled, or is in very faint ink, or in some other form that makes it impossible to decipher the letters: *It was a blurred snap-*

shot of an old stone doorway showing an illegible date inscribed above the lintel; ...a worn card with illegible writing....

If something is **unreadable** it generally means that it is written in a style so difficult to understand, or so tedious, that it makes the reader unwilling to continue with the task of reading it: *He wrote much poetry – most of it unreadable – or so his family thought.*

Illiterate is an adjective used to refer to someone who has not learnt how to read: *...there was hardly a place for illiterate, ignorant peasants....*

illicit, elicit

These words have a similar pronunciation but very different meanings. Something **illicit** contravenes the law or goes against custom: *All the identity cards have coloured photos on the back, which makes their illicit use far more difficult.*

You can **elicit** a response or a reaction by something you say or do: *A rushed letter makes her bitterly despondent, a good one elicits a flood of gushing affection.* When you *elicit* information from someone, you obtain it from them, often by a process of questioning: *We assume that the courts work hard to elicit the truth.*

illusion, delusion

An **illusion** is an idea or situation which is presented as true and in which you believe, though in fact it is false, as in: *I speak in sorrow for I have lost my illusions about the medical profession,* or something which appears to be real but is a form of trick: *These were unreal figments, dreams, clouds, wisps, illusions in the face of an awful reality...; It was exactly like an optical illusion....*

A **delusion** is a situation that you believe to be true,

although it really is not, because you are suffering from some form of mental or physical disorientation: *A delusion is grounded in fear; ...the self-indulgence of the rich or the self-delusion of the mentally ill.* A delusion can also be a state of deliberate blindness to the truth: *I laboured under the nice middle-class delusion that everyone was a good guy at heart.* ⇒ **allusion**

illusory, elusive

Something **illusory** may appear to be true or possible but turns out not to be: *The idea of perfect compatibility is illusory; ...pictures that spread out a film of illusory reality.*

Something that is **elusive** is true but hard to pin down or capture: *Happiness is an elusive quality; Camouflage and nocturnal habits make long-eared owls elusive.*

imaginary, imaginative

Something **imaginary** is unreal: *We tied up our imaginary horses after playing the sheriff's posse.* Something **imaginative** makes use of the imagination to create a pleasing or different result: *He is still capable of imaginative and creative theories; Very often an imaginative person can find perfectly valid reasons.*

immature, juvenile

Immature is a general-purpose word meaning 'not fully developed' or 'unformed' either physically or mentally: *The first three months is a period of adjustment for the baby's immature nervous system and immature digestive system; He appealed to Kathleen in ways which I was too immature to understand twenty-five years ago.* It implies that a more advanced stage is to come.

The word **juvenile** is usually restricted to technical and legal contexts. ⇒ **juvenile**

immensity, immenseness
Immense has two possible noun forms but only **immensity** is used with any degree of regularity. **Immenseness** is found in several dictionaries but there are no corpus examples. ⇒ **enormity**

immigrant ⇒ **emigrant**

imminent, immanent
The spelling of **imminent** should not be confused with that of **immanent**, a word that is used chiefly in religious contexts to mean 'universally present': *…the universal law which is immanent in all things.*
Something **imminent** is 'likely to happen soon'. This word is usually used in the context of something unpleasant: *I felt oddly a sense of imminent doom; …like a crowd that knows that a baton charge is imminent.*

immoral ⇒ **amoral**

immune
You can be **immune** *to* a disease or to criticism. You are immune *from* punishment. You may be **immunized** *against* a particular disease. ⇒ **impunity**

impeach
The word **impeach** means 'bring a charge against' someone who holds a public office: *He could be impeached, convicted, and have an $18,000 pension annulled.* Because of Richard Nixon's resignation under threat of *impeachment*, the word is often misunderstood to mean 'to dismiss'.

impel, compel
When something such as an emotion **impels** you to do something, you do it as if you have been forced by some-

thing within you: *One or two carters, impelled by old instincts, still used the lane; Elaine strode forward, impelled by real relief and delight.*

When you are **compelled** to do something you are forced to do it, usually by someone who has power or authority over you: *The law cannot compel change; Indians were compelled to work the mines and estates of their new masters.*

imperial, imperious

Imperial is an adjective meaning 'relating to an emperor or an empire'. **Imperious** is an adjective used to describe someone's manner. If someone behaves *imperiously*, they may behave with an air of command but, more generally, tend to be overbearing and arrogant: *'Go away. All of you,' he imperiously commanded with a wave of the hand; She suddenly asked in a pure but imperious voice, 'In the back room?'*

implicit, explicit

When the meaning of a sentence or of an act can be understood, although it is not directly stated, it is **implicit**: *These underlying assumptions were implicit in the American educational scene.* You can also use *implicit* to mean that someone has no doubts or reservations about something: *...his implicit consent, his undivided dedication.*

When the meaning of a sentence or an act is quite clearly stated and does not need working out, it is **explicit**.

imply, infer, insinuate

The words *imply* and *infer* offer a way of expressing matching viewpoints on the same set of facts. If someone wants to hint or suggest that certain things are true, they can **imply** that things are so: *He wanted to present* *her in a favourable light so he implied that she had played a more important role in the business than was true.* The hearer is then in the position of having to **infer** from what is said that the speaker is telling the truth: *It was possible that they would infer that I knew something that they ought to know.* Careful users avoid the error of using *infer* in the sense of *imply*.

One sense of the word **insinuate** overlaps somewhat with *imply*. It means to imply something by hints and suggestions so that the hearer *infers* that the truth of a situation is different from what it seems to be. The difference is that an *insinuation* is usually to someone's discredit, whereas an *implication* can be favourable: *You are filled with spite and envy, coming around here and insinuating things.* The most common sense of *insinuate* is its basic one of twisting and twining: *A small flavour of true magic insinuated itself into the work; …soft tendrils insinuating through herbaceous borders.*
⇒ **induction**

importune
The usual pronunciation has the stress on the final syllable /im-por-**tune**/. Also accepted, but less common, is /im-**por**-tune/.

impotent ⇒ ineffective

impracticable, impractical, unpractical
When something is **impracticable**, it is difficult or impossible to carry it out: *It would be impracticable to ban all food additives; It is impracticable to store large volumes of biogas.* This word and **impractical** often overlap: *Vanbrugh is often thought of as an impractical architect,* but *impractical* is strictly used for something that could conceivably be done, but would be inadvis-

able or inefficient if done: *Low interest government loans became an impractical means of finance; The idea of a new centre party was rejected as impractical.* **Unpractical** is another word for *impractical.* Both words are also used for someone who has little manual ability or common sense: *They were quite impractical and didn't know the first thing about hygiene.*

impregnable

This word has two separate meanings and two separate word histories. The first meaning of the word is 'unshakable', as in *impregnable self-confidence,* or 'unable to be taken by attack' as in *an impregnable fortress.* It comes from the same base as the French *prendre,* meaning 'take'.

The other meaning is 'able to be impregnated'. This comes from the Latin word for 'fertile'. The first meaning is the more common.

impromptu ⇒ extempore

impunity, immunity, immune

Something can be done with **impunity**, when it is free from the fear of punishment or free from unpleasant consequences. Note that it is regularly preceded by *with: Show them they can't poach herring from our waters with impunity; Distinctions cannot be trampled on with impunity.*

The noun **immunity** is commonly used in connection with the ability of the body to resist disease, but the related adjective **immune** has a wider use. When followed by *from* it means 'not affected' by something: *immune from danger,* or 'exempt' from some duty: *He is immune from a court order.* When followed by *to* it means 'not responsive': *immune to temptation.*

in, within, into

The preposition **in** can be ambiguous when it refers to a period of time. *I'll meet you in five minutes* means 'I'll see you five minutes from now'. *I can do it in five minutes* might have a similar sense, but it could mean 'It will take me five minutes to complete the task'. In this case, if the context is not clear, the more formal **within** could be used instead or the sentence could be rephrased.

When **in** is used with a 'place' meaning there are also possible ambiguities. *He tripped and fell in the swimming pool* could mean that he tripped while he was in the pool or that the pool was what he fell into. Avoid using *in* whenever *into* is the meaning.

in-, il-, im-, ir-

The prefixes **il-**, **im-**, **in-**, and **ir-** have an alternative meaning to their common negative one. They also indicate the meaning 'able to be' or the meaning of 'motion towards'. Because of past changes in spelling, this *in*-prefix is also spelled *en-* in some words. Words typical of this meaning of *in-* are: *inaugurate; incandescent; incise; inflammable*. As a result of these two meanings for *in-*, the word *inflammable* (from *inflame*) became confused in some people's minds as signifying 'not flammable' so the safety authorities advised the use of the contrasting pair: *flammable* and *nonflammable*.

in-, un-, non-

All these prefixes involve an element of negation, but the meaning of each is not the same. The prefixes *in-* and *un-* are strongly negative. *Un-* is the preferred form when new compounds are made. The prefix **in-** (and its derivations *il-*, *im-*, *ir-*) is less often used in modern compounds, although, it is very common in older ones.

The prefixes **il-**, **im-**, **in-**, and **ir-** can all indicate that the word stem is to be understood with a negative sense, as in: *illegible, inflexible, impossible, irresponsible*. The shifts in spelling are because of blending with following consonants, thus *in+l* becomes *il-*; *in+m-* becomes *im-*; *in+b/p-* becomes *im-*; and *in+r-* becomes *ir-*. Most new negative formations use *un-* or *non-* in preference to any of these forms. Someone who is the opposite of dependable is described as *undependable*, not *independable*. (The risk of confusion with *independent* is too great.) Typical examples of recent negative compounds not using *in-* are: *unleaded* and *nonstick*.

Non- is a very productive prefix that allows adjectives and some nouns with a positive sense to form words with a negative sense. It usually involves a warning or advice. *Un-* and *non-* are sometimes used in contrast. For example, if you complain that someone's shirt smells as if it were *unwashed*, that means it has not recently seen soap and water. If a blouse were to be labelled *nonwashable*, that would warn that it should not be washed. We cannot label it *unwashable* and keep the same meaning. You can wash it but you will ruin it.

The current usage is for combinations formed with *non-* not to be hyphenated unless the second part is a proper noun, as in: *non-Euclidean*, or, optionally, when it begins with letter *n* as in: *non-native; non-natural*. ⇒ **un-**

inasmuch as

This linked form is correct. **Inasmuch as** means 'since' or 'because': *I was particularly glad to do so, inasmuch as you will now know that I am sincere; Censorship is feeble inasmuch as it does not protect anyone*. The meaning of this phrase often extends to take in 'to the extent or degree that': *The outcome of this is well known, and* *important inasmuch as it showed just what human beings could do.* Both uses of the phrase are fairly formal. ⇒ **in spite of** ⇒ **insofar**

incapable

There are two uses of **incapable**. The first is used to suggest that someone is unable to do something because it is not in their character. This sense must be followed by a statement of what they could not do, preceded by *of*: *He was incapable of breaking an arrangement; He was incapable of telling the truth.*

The second sense of *incapable* suggests that someone is either incompetent or stupid and not to be entrusted with an action: *He's both incapable and dishonest.* This is used without a following phrase.

incarnate, incarnation

In its literal use, **incarnate** is a theological term meaning 'made flesh': *He found a slim book called 'The Myth of God Incarnate'.* However, the extended sense 'personified' is the most usual sense of the word today and is used when something or someone is taken as the model of a particular quality: *'I must warn you, Colonel Burr. Hamilton is treachery incarnate.'*

The noun form is **incarnation**. The usual meaning of the noun is the literal one, which includes the theory that the soul is reborn in fresh incarnations. *…the doctrine of the incarnation…; what might he have been in an earlier incarnation, I wondered.* By extension, an earlier period in one's life can be described as an *incarnation*.

in case, incase

A common error is to write **in case** as a single word. It should be two words: *I'll just do another check in case I've left a window open.* There is a word **incase** but it is a very rare alternative spelling of *encase* which means 'surround something with a case-like structure'.

inchoate

The established sense of **inchoate** is 'just begun' or 'immature': *a dark, inchoate longing for the miracle of form*. Probably because of confusion with the word *chaos*, this word is sometimes used with the meaning 'confused or muddled': *Only he had the energy of spirit to pull together the vast inchoate mass of the building; They moulded the inchoate voices of dissent.*

Once a word becomes widely used and accepted with a new meaning, there is little chance of retrieving the older meaning exclusively and a loss in precision results.
⇒ **aggravate**

incredible, incredulous

If something is described as **incredible**, it is difficult to believe: *So, you have no basis for this incredible suggestion?* A person who is **incredulous** is unwilling or unable to believe what they are told: *The interviewer sounded incredulous, mainly because he couldn't conceive of someone wanting to do it.*

inculcate, indoctrinate

The word **inculcate** means to fix something, such as an idea, a habit, or a belief in someone's mind by constant repetition. The verb can be followed directly by the object: *…the Sisters knew how to inculcate strict habits of cleanliness.* The overtones of *inculcate* and the similar meaning word *imbue* are positive. When the sentence mentions the destination of the teaching, it is followed by *in*: *Many teachers tended to inculcate in us the official explanation for these policies; He imbued in us a respect for authority. Inculcate* is also followed by *into*: *A sense of* *service may be inculcated into the minds of many.*

When you **indoctrinate** someone they are taught to follow a single set of beliefs to the exclusion of others. Consequently, *indoctrinate* always has negative overtones: *He wasn't teaching anymore, he was indoctrinating.* **Indoctrinate** is followed by the direct object alone or the direct object followed by *with: It seems that he managed to indoctrinate us with his restricting philosophy.*
⇒ **instil**

incumbent

Incumbent, a rather formal adjective meaning 'needing to be done', or 'obligatory', is usually followed by *on* not *upon: It is more or less incumbent on him to let you win; No obligation is incumbent on the British people to make economic sacrifices.* **Incumbent** is used as a very formal noun to mean 'someone who is currently filling an official post or position'. It is redundant to speak of *the present incumbent.* The adjective has a similar formal use: *…an incumbent President of the United States.*

index, indexes, indices

The plural of the word **index** can be either **indices** or **indexes** but each plural form has a particular reference. The form **indices** is used when talking about economics or mathematics: *The CEA keeps its eye on economic indices; The data drawn from such crude indices cannot be said to be significant.* It is the correct form for referring to the superscript numbers that indicate the value of a variable: *In x^2 and y^3, 2 and 3 are indices.* All other plural uses have **indexes**: *You might just look through the subject indexes.*

indifferent

Indifferent has two main meanings, which are quite distinct. It can mean 'unresponsive' or 'unmoved': *The Colonel was uninterested in the house and indifferent to his financial affairs*. It also means 'of poor or mediocre quality': *He was elegant, handsome, a gifted painter but an indifferent actor.*

A third and older meaning of **indifferent**, 'impartial', is still used by some writers: *...selected by an indifferent Nature*. All these uses have literary overtones.

individual

In careful speech and writing, the noun **individual** is not used as a synonym of *person*, except when a single person is being considered in contrast to a group, as in *in mass democracy the rights of the individual must be protected*. In some contexts **individual** can carry overtones of scorn: *a bit of an odd individual*.

Individual is used in marketing jargon as a noun modifier meaning 'for one person only', as in *individual portions*, but this use often leads to its becoming synonymous with 'small', as in *individual bite-sized pieces*, and is disliked by careful writers.

indoctrinate ⇒ inculcate

indoor, indoors

The word **indoor** is an adjective and is used before the noun to which it applies: *a large, spiky indoor plant*. **Indoors** is an adverb: *Attempts to raise sheep indoors have been disappointing; Alexandra ran indoors.*

induction, deduction

Both are processes of reasoning. The difference is in the reliability of the conclusions. **Induction** is a process of reasoning from known facts to reach general principles. The solution may, however, go beyond the facts. For example, if someone has experience of two events that appear to occur together, he may *infer* that one event is responsible for the other, but the conclusion is only true if the observations on which it is based have been connected correctly: *If a motor cycle goes over a bump and the engine misfires, and then goes over another bump and the engine misfires, one can logically conclude that the misfiring is caused by the bumps. That is induction; Basing laws on accumulated observations is known as induction.*

If there are general principles that state that a certain process is possible, we can *deduce* that something based on these principles is also possible. Something arrived at by a process of **deduction** is normally true if the starting points are true. The writer does not need to rely on personal experience: *If the handbook says that the horn in your car is exclusively powered by electricity from the battery, then we can logically infer that if the battery is flat the horn will not work. That is deduction.*

There are also words of the same spelling with quite different meanings. *Induction* can be used in describing the behaviour of magnetic fields: *It uses a form of induction heating.* It also has a rare, formal meaning, 'install a person in high office': *I have been invited to the ceremony for his induction as rector.* Another meaning of *deduction*, and by far the most common in everyday use, is that of subtracting one sum from another. ⇒ **inference**

indulge, indulge in

When you **indulge** someone, you pander to their whims by doing as they wish: *Well, it pleased me really to indulge her wishes.* When you **indulge in** something, you allow yourself to enjoy a special weakness: *Wave away* *the sweets but indulge in cheese and biscuits; Let us indulge in a little daydreaming.*

inedible, uneatable

In careful speech and writing, **inedible** is not synonymous with **uneatable**. *Inedible* implies that something is of a sort not suitable for eating, while *uneatable* implies that it is so unpleasant (or so badly prepared) as to be beyond eating. ⇒ **illegible**

ineffective, ineffectual, impotent

When an action is described as **ineffective** it has not achieved its purpose: *The therapy was obviously ineffective*. *Ineffective* overlaps with **ineffectual** to some extent, but while a corkscrew could be *ineffective* or *ineffectual*, a person can only be *ineffectual*: *...a genial but ineffectual man; Our minds were in a constant state of ineffectual irritation.*

Besides meaning 'sexually powerless', **impotent** means powerless to act or unable to put a plan or other course of action into effect: *...parasites, impotent talkers, hypocrites...; The government seemed to be impotent.* Because of the sexual connotations this word should be used carefully for fear of ambiguity.

inept, inapt, inapposite

There is some similarity of meaning between these words. An action or statement can be described as **inept** if it causes social difficulty: *She even seemed inept at holding hands, for her long nails dug into my palms,* is incompetent, or is made at an unfortunate moment: *The first rift was caused by Baldwin's inept handling of the war debt.* When an idea or an action is not suited to the situation, it can be called **inapt**: *...this would not have been an inapt term for the phenomenon.*

Some writers prefer to use **inapposite** in the context of unsuitable behaviour: *He found a special delight in quoting at the Communards from their own sacred books in inapposite situations.*

in fact

There is a small group of expressions used by speakers as fillers while they organize the next section of their sentence, or as a mark of the end of a piece of information. This group includes *actually, you see, you know,* and **in fact**. Overuse of these expressions is a serious failure of control in one's speaking patterns and speakers who do find in themselves a tendency to this sort of overuse should try to avoid the word or phrase concerned. The problem for many is that the expression becomes an unconscious punctuation of each utterance. Note that writing **in fact** as one word is a common error. ⇒ **fillers**

inference, implication

If you reason from a set of given facts to arrive at a result, you draw an **inference**: *The first inference we can draw is Do Not Kill One Another.* When you connect one observation to another, you often see that there is a final result that has an element of additional meaning; you become aware of an **implication**: *He didn't want Tom to see that he had been lying down, with its implication of luxury and sloth.* ⇒ **induction**

infinitesimal, infinitely

A very small thing is **infinitesimal**. Avoid using the expression *infinitely small*. The two words *infinite*, with its sense of extending without limit, and *small* with its sense of limitation, contain meanings that conflict.

infinitive ⇒ split infinitive

inflammable, inflammatory

Inflammable substances are likely to burst into flame if they are overheated or near fire. In this case *in-* means the same as *en-* 'cause something to be'. It confuses some people because *in-* usually means *not*.

Inflammatory speech or behaviour is that which could cause tempers and ill-feelings to rise to the surface.
⇒ **flammable**

inflict, afflict

The difference between the two words is one of perspective. If you **inflict** something *on* someone or something you actively cause them to suffer: *The suffering inflicted on fish seems endless.* If something **afflicts** you, you are made to suffer and would speak of the suffering as an *affliction: Buddha had prophesied that such a disease would afflict mankind; She was afflicted in the night by a violent seizure.*

When *inflict* is used without *on* it means 'deal out' something unpleasant: *You cannot inflict a stab wound with a razor.*

-ing

There is a very common sentence structure that follows the pattern: *I hope your wife won't mind me saying this,* where an *-ing* form of the verb is preceded by a pronoun. The use of the object pronoun **me** in this construction (or any other suitable object pronoun) is now firmly established as part of educated usage, but it is still regarded as informal. In formal use, the possessive determiner **my** (or any other suitable possessive determiner) is advisable: *I hope your wife won't mind my saying this.* The reasons for this are rather involved. Briefly, we can either regard *saying* as a verbal noun or treat the whole clause as one that contains two verbs in a special relationship. If it is a verbal noun it can, like any noun, be preceded by the possessive determiner *my* (or its equivalent). If it is a complex clause, *me* (or its equivalent) is the object of the first verb and the virtual subject of the second, and consequently must be a pronoun.

ingenious, ingenuous

An **ingenious** person is skilful and clever, an ingenious device shows that skill has been used to make it work. If you call someone **ingenuous** you mean that they are naive and innocent by nature. By extension such a person will be honest and forthcoming: ...*the ingenuous English schoolboy look; His expression was bold, frank, ingenuous, and engaging.*

ingratiate

Ingratiate is not followed by a direct object. You ingratiate *yourself* with someone: *He'd done everything a man can do to ingratiate himself with a woman; They hastened to ingratiate themselves with the new power behind the throne.*

inherent, innate

An effect or a result that is built into a structure or a system is spoken of as **inherent**: *We have pointed to the dangers inherent in this kind of political system; This underlined the degree of fantasy inherent in the Party's dream of a New Britain.* When some aspect of behaviour is part of a living organism it is **innate**: *It made one wonder if the sense of competition was innate in human nature at all; Her innate stupidity makes her incapable of mature thought.*

inheritance ⇒ heritage

-in-law

The suffix **-in-law**, which is added to relationship names to indicate a relationship by marriage, is usually limited to the immediate family of *mother, father, brother,* and *sister.* Expressions such as *aunt-in-law* are not regular and are generally only used jocularly. *An aunt by marriage* is one way of expressing such a relationship.

innuendo

The plural form of **innuendo** is either **innuendos** or **innuendoes**.

in order that, so that

Careful writers use *may* or *might* after the phrase **in order that**: *He readily agreed to the examination in order that his name might be cleared; …in order that there may be no misunderstanding….* A very formal alternative is to use the subjunctive, which uses the same form as the base form of the verb: *So, in order that my daydreams not contradict my principles, I constructed a fantasy … ; This triggered the automatic response in order that the adult maintain control of the transaction.*

The use of **so that**, which can be used with a range of verbs, avoids the problem mentioned above. Instead of the nonstandard: *…it is necessary to disagree in order that there can be as many experts as needed,* you would write: *…it is necessary to disagree so that there can be as many experts as needed.*

inquire, enquire

The normal spelling uses the *in-* prefix for the verb, **inquire**, and the noun, **inquiry**. However, the *en-* spelling is not rare; indeed the latest stylebook for *The Times* insists on it, although the *en-* form of the word is not really justified in terms of its historical derivation. A few writers like to distinguish between **enquire** meaning 'ask about' and **inquire** meaning 'investigate': *'What are you going to do about a holiday then?' he would enquire, puffing on his pipe; This leads us to inquire into the nature of profit in private renting.* The 'investigate' sense is frequently followed by *about, after, into,* or *whether.*

in respect of, with respect to

The group of compound prepositions, **in respect of, with respect to, with regard to,** and **in relation to** have attracted a general dislike from a number of commentators, who suggest that the plainer words *about* or *concerning* are almost always preferable, as in *It's going to raise a lot of problems in respect of atmosphere pollution.* These phrases are not wrong, but they may seem pompous. However, sometimes a little pomposity is useful in a formal letter.

inside

Do not use the expression *inside of.* As both *inside* and *of* are being used as prepositions, *of* is superfluous.

insinuate ⇒ imply

insofar

Some purists regard the form **insofar** as incorrect and prefer **in so far**, but there is considerable evidence for the acceptability of the linked form. *Insofar* means 'to the extent' and is normally followed by *as: I turned round, insofar as it was appropriate to turn; Insofar as I can judge, that is the body of Mr Orton.* ⇒ **inasmuch as**

inspire

Inspire is followed by one of a number of constructions. You can inspire someone: *This seemed to inspire Edmund Wilkie to make speeches,* or *be* inspired *by* something: *He was first inspired by the drawings of*

Edmond Dulac. You can also inspire someone *with* an abstract quality: *He had succeeded in inspiring them with loyalty*, or inspire an abstract quality *in* someone: …*that meant a man able to inspire fear in his fellow men*.

in spite of, despite

In spite of must never be written with the first two words joined as [*inspite*]. This error probably arises through confusion with the word **despite** which has a similar meaning. Some authorities suggest that *despite* should be preferred to *in spite of*, but many users feel that *despite* is a part of a formal literary style: *In spite of the anxious moments, it was a stimulating journey; The film, despite its tough surface, is not without its sentimental moments*.

In spite of the fact that and *despite the fact that* are both over-wordy ways of saying *although*.

inst., prox., ult.

These abbreviations were once part of the formalities of commercial correspondence. **Inst.** means 'this month', **prox.** means 'next or coming month', **ult.** means 'last month'. It is generally felt that they are no longer current and should be avoided. Use the actual date or the full English form in correspondence.

install

The word **install** has an alternative spelling form **instal**.

instil, imbue, infuse

The verb **instil** means 'introduce something gradually' and, when it is used metaphorically about a quality, it is followed by *in* or *into*, never *with*: *His love of Homer, instilled in him by Ouwa; Mostly he instilled tremendous spirit into the spiritless refugees*. The American spelling is *instill*.

Imbue overlaps in meaning with *instil*. It differs in its construction. You *imbue* someone or something *with* a quality: *...individuals imbued with a strong sense of vocation; ...this imbues the water with even greater powers.*

Infuse has a technical sense; when you soak plants in a liquid to extract their flavour, you are *infusing* them. When *infuse* is used metaphorically, it overlaps with *instil* and *imbue*. You can *infuse* something *with* another thing: *He began to infuse his tones with a sarcastic, wounding bitterness,* or infuse a quality *into* someone: *That faith had to be infused into men; ...the discipline infused into workers by the factory.* ⇒ **inculcate**

instinct, intuition

Instinct is a subconscious set of reactions present in every animal from birth: *Babies have an instinct to turn towards anything that touches them.* **Intuition** is a subconscious mental reaction to a situation that provides you with knowledge or understanding: *A hint, no more; an intuition; the smell of greater trouble brewing.* Intuition might tell you that a situation was becoming dangerous; *instinct* would make you run away.

insure ⇒ ensure

integrate

Be careful with the spelling of this word. It is related to the word *integral* and does not start with the prefix *inter-*.

intense, intensive

Something **intense** is marked by an extreme quality: *intense heat; intense pain; intense pleasure.*

The adjective **intensive** is used to describe an activity that receives a great amount of input: *a fairly intensive* *and expensive teacher-training programme; …two years intensive study.*

inter-

The prefix **inter-** comes from Latin and means 'between' or 'among'. It can be added to adjectives, nouns, and verbs to create words which have those meanings as part of their sense, e.g. *interact, interbreed, interpersonal, international, interdependence*. This is a productive prefix. When you add **inter-** to another word, you do not normally use a hyphen unless the second word begins with a capital letter, e.g. *interdisciplinary, Inter-African News Agency.* ⇒ **intra-**

intermittent, interrupted

Something that is **intermittent** usually proceeds or happens at irregular intervals: *A major problem is caused by the intermittent nature of sunshine*. The opposite is *continuous*. If something is **interrupted** it is intended to be continuous but is prevented from being so.

interpolate, interpose

When you interrupt a discussion with some additional fact or when you add a passage to a manuscript, you **interpolate** this fact or passage: *'You are only exasperating him further,' interpolated Steven; The letter included this passage interpolated in the 14th Century.*

Interpose is used when you place something between two physical objects: *Amelia interposed herself as a screen between Luciana and the door*. It can, though, be used metaphorically about a verbal interruption: *'Let us save recriminations for later,' interposed the Minister.*

interval, intermission

In the cinema and the theatre, these words are synonymous for a break between parts of the performance. Of the two, **intermission** is less frequent and rather pompous.

into ⇒ **in**

intra-
The prefix **intra-** comes from Latin and means 'on the inside' or 'within'. It can be added to adjectives, nouns, and verbs to create words which have those meanings as part of their sense, e.g. *intrastate, intramural, intravenous*. This is a productive prefix. It is not normal to use a hyphen when you add **intra-** to another word. ⇒ **inter-**

intrinsic, extrinsic
Intrinsic is a rather formal word. It is used when talking about a characteristic that is part and parcel of something: *We know of no intrinsic limits to the life span.* If something has *intrinsic* value, it is valuable because of what it is, not because of what it is associated with: *He was caught up in the repetitious production of objects that had no intrinsic value.* The antonym of intrinsic is **extrinsic**. This is used to refer to a quality that is outside the thing, not part of it. It, too, is a formal word and not very common.

invalid
There are two distinct words **invalid** with the same spelling. A sick person is an /**in**-va-lid/, with stress on the first syllable. When something has no value or *validity*, it is /in-**val**-lid/.

inveigle
Note that the spelling is *-ei-* not *-ie-*. The consensus on pronunciation is /in-**vay**-gl/; the alternative, /in-**vee**-gl/ is dated.

inverted commas

Inverted commas are also called *speech marks* but they may be used for more than indicating that a written passage represents direct speech. In handwriting, they can have the function of italics in printed material and show that the words they surround are a title, as in "The Odeon", or "Far From The Madding Crowd". When they are used to enclose a word or words within a sentence, as in *We drank malt whisky, chasing it with "wee heavy" beers,* they serve to identify the expression as unusual in some way, and are usually equivalent to *so-called* or to *(sic)*. Double inverted commas are normal in handwriting. In printed books, publishers often favour single inverted commas, but there is no firm rule.

ir- ⇒ in-

irony

The word **irony** and its adjective and adverb forms *ironical* and *ironically*, describe humorous or mildly sarcastic comments that mean the opposite of what they say. The speaker intentionally says something that is contrary to the facts: *'You surprise me,' Tom said, though he knew all irony was wasted on Chas; 'That's very generous of you,' said Christopher, aiming at irony.* The aim is to make an implied criticism. The knowledge that we have of the speaker and the background to the situation allows us to perceive the *irony*. If we lack this information, what was intended as irony can be mistaken for a true indication of the speaker's thoughts. *Irony* is a stylistic device that must be used with care.

Irony also refers to a situation that reveals the difference between what is and what might or should be the case. This is a more formal literary use. ⇒ **sarcasm**

irrelevant

Note the spelling of this word, which is formed from *relevant*. It is not [*irrevelant*], a common error.

irreparable, irremediable, unrepairable

Something can become **irreparable** when it has been harmed or damaged to the point where no amount of effort will remedy it: *She may have done irreparable harm to her reputation*. The usual pronunciation is with stress on the second syllable /i-**rep**-re-bul/.

Irremediable is also used with the sense given above: *The trial of Dreyfuss shook the world and became an irremediable blotch on the cause of French Justice*.

Note that *irreparable* can be used for a broken object that cannot be repaired, but in this context some speakers prefer to use the negative formation from *repair*, **unrepairable**, which they feel is clearer and more direct.
⇒ **in-**

-ise, ize

Whether the ending *-ise* or *-ize* should be used for the spelling of certain verbs is a matter of some debate, because both these endings are favoured by different authorities. The spelling makes no difference to the pronunciation of the verb. In American English *-ize* is the preferred ending for many verbs. This form is followed by certain British newspapers, and by several leading dictionaries. This gives *-ize* an undoubted authority. The reason for this choice is based on word derivation. However, *-ise* is equally acceptable in British English and is the normal choice of many printers. A consistent use of the *-ise* ending is always acceptable.

Certain words (chiefly those not formed by adding the suffix to an existing word) are, however, always spelled with -*ise* in both Britain and the US, e.g. *advertise, advise, revise.*

Islam

Islam is the correct name for the religion of Muslims. It is pronounced /**iz**-lahm/ by most British speakers, but /is-**lahm**/ is closer to the Arabic form. The final syllable rhymes with 'charm'. Do not use the old term *Mohammedanism*, or any of its various spellings, as this causes offence to Muslims. ⇒ **Muslim**

Israeli ⇒ Jew

italic

Italic, the typeface *that looks like this*, is used in printed books in order to: call attention to a word or phrase (in this book *italics* call attention to examples); give special emphasis to a word, e.g. one that in speech might be especially stressed; indicate that a word in a sentence is from a foreign language; display the titles of books, newspapers, hotels, and theatres. In handwritten or typewritten documents it is the normal practice to use underlining instead of *italics.*

italicize

The *c* has an *s* sound; /i-**tal**-i-size/.

its, it's

There is an important and useful distinction between these two forms that, from the evidence of press advertising and public notices, is currently understood by fewer and fewer people and is consequently in danger of being lost.

When **its** is used without an apostrophe, it is the possessive pronoun meaning 'belonging to it'. It is part of the group that includes *hers, yours,* and *theirs: Can you* *describe its shape first of all?; Set the crockery back on its shelf.*

The apostrophe form **it's** is an abbreviation of *it is: It's your turn; Don't go in a strange car unless it's with someone you know well.* It is this form that is intruding on the domain of *its* and has even been seen incorrectly used in subtitles on the BBC.

it's me / her / him / us / them

There is no firm consensus on this aspect of usage. Most educated speakers, whether speaking formally or informally, would respond to the question *'Who's there?'* with *'It's me'* not *'It's I'*. The contrary purist view is that all the forms of *be* must be followed by a subject pronoun like *I, we, he, she, they*, not by an object pronoun like *me, us, him, her, them*, on the grounds that the pronoun is not the object of the verb but a complement. This view stems in part from basing English grammar on what happened in Latin.

Use of the form, *It is I* etc. as a sentence on its own is now regarded as so formal as to be pedantic. *It's me/It was me* etc. is the natural choice in most circumstances. However, when the phrase is part of a longer sentence, with a relative clause following the pronoun, the choice is more difficult. If in response to: *'Who organized all this?'* we say: *'It was (…) who cooked the dinner and Maddy who did the decorations'*, informal speech uses the pronoun *me* and more formal speech uses the pronoun *I*.

If the sentence is part of a comparison using *than* or *as*, a similar choice has to be made. Informal usage has: *You're as silly as him; She's stronger than me.* Formal usage prefers: *You are as prejudiced as he,* but we should note that formal usage is also more likely to continue the sentence: *You are as prejudiced as he is; John is much abler than I am.*

J

Jacobean, Jacobin, Jacobite

All the above are adjectives formed from the related names James and Jacques, both forms of Jacob. The adjective **Jacobean** means 'of the reign of James I' and is today mostly found in the context of a style of English furniture, architecture, or literature: *We were shown an elaborate Jacobean four-poster set up by James I for his mother.*

A **Jacobite** is a follower of James II: *renegade English Jacobites*, while **Jacobin** refers to a political group in the French Revolution, so called because they met near the church of St Jacques: *The Commune blended Jacobin patriotism with social radicalism.* Both are rare except to historians.

jail ⇒ gaol

jam, jelly, jello, conserve

The word *jelly* is a common source of misunderstanding between British and American speakers of English. The peculiarity of a *peanut butter and jelly sandwich* is not much modified when it is found that British **jelly** is American **jello** and American *jelly* is British **jam**.

Speakers of British English often distinguish **jam** from **conserve** by the presence of larger pieces of whole fruit in a *conserve*. When, in British English, *jelly* does mean a jamlike preparation, it has been strained to exclude seeds and consists of fruit pectin, e.g. *Blackberry Jelly, Crab apple Jelly*.

jargon

Jargon is a disparaging term used for language that is obscure or confusing. Terms that are well-known to people who work together in a trade or profession tend to be *jargon* to people outside the circle of users. It is good practice to avoid jargon or to provide an explanation of terms that cannot be avoided when you are writing for the general public. A more scathing, informal term for jargon is *gobbledegook*.

jejune

This is a word that has undergone a partial shift in meaning because of a misunderstanding by those speakers who believed that it was connected in meaning with the French word *jeune* meaning 'young', and the word is frequently misspelled as [*jejeune*]. In fact, it comes from the word for 'a fast' and, in its original English meaning, meant 'dull, barren, boring, insipid': *Their baggy flannels and jejune hacking jackets were mercifully left behind.*

Now **jejune** is often used with the new sense of 'ingenuous', based on the misunderstanding, as in *She had, or pretended that she had, a jejune notion that she'd seen it all.* Users of this word appear to be divided into those who know the original meaning and keep to it, and those who only know and use the second meaning and consequently annoy the first group. Either way, it is a very formal word. **Jejune** is pronounced /je-**joon**/.

Jew, Jewish, Israeli, Israelite

The noun **Jew** and the adjective **Jewish** refer to someone who follows the religion of Judaism. *Israel* is the ancient Jewish kingdom and the name of the modern republic. An **Israeli** strictly means any inhabitant of the modern republic of Israel but it is not a term generally used by the non-Jewish inhabitants of Israel. **Israelite** is an old-fashioned synonym for Jew.

jibe ⇒ gibe

job, situation, position, post

These words for work are ranged in an ascending scale of gentility. A **position** is a genteel term for a **job**. So is **situation**, which is not current except in a phrase like *Situations Vacant*, but was once often used when someone took a job as a servant. A **post** sometimes involves the holder in a transfer between places of work, so that it is often associated with the armed forces or the foreign service. The difference between being described as *jobless* or *unemployed* is also one of what seems to be the more 'official' or 'respectable' term. ⇒ **wage**

journal, magazine

The original meaning of *journal* involves the notion of something appearing daily. This is preserved in the use of *journal* in book-keeping, where it means the book in which transactions are entered on the day they occur.

In the context of the press, a regular academic publication is usually called a **journal**. A weekly or monthly publication that includes a mixture of regular features and specially commissioned articles is called a **magazine**. The term is often used by extension for more or less coherent broadcast material that comes under a topic heading, such as a motoring or children's programme. In practice, the information contained in a *magazine* has a short life, the back issues of a *journal* become a source of reference and scholarship.

journalese

This is a disparaging term for language that is either sensationalized or oddly compressed so that it ignores accepted standards of usage. In reality, most journalists are very careful about their writing and are often guided by detailed style books produced by the press that they work for. **Journalese** crops up most frequently in headlines and in ranting editorials. It is often caused by an attempt to compress a story to fit a space.

The following is an example of journalese: *Demands by the medical community to share in the Government's decision-making process on health issues.* It could be put more simply as *Doctors want to have a say in the reorganization of the NHS.*

judgment, judgement

Both spellings are permissible and both are very common in everyday writing. The spelling **judgment** is the one accepted by the legal profession when the word is used as a technical term: *The Divisional Court, in a 91-page judgment, dismissed an application for judicial review of the Secretary of State's decision. Judgment* is also the American spelling form.

judicial, judicious

Judicial is an adjective that refers to the dispensation of justice: *His case comes up for judicial review next month; …the British judicial system.* **Judicious** is an adjective that means 'exercising a fine judgment' in the choice of something: *The panel steered a judicious middle course.*

junta

Junta is both the singular and plural form: *The aircraft were in the hands of the unstable military junta; Dictatorships of junta serve only their own interests.* The usual pronunciation is /**jun**-ta/ but purists may insist on giving the word the pronunciation /**hun**-ta/ which approximates to the original Spanish. A rare alternative form, **junto**, is sometimes seen.

just

There are several ways in which **just** is used, some of them apparently contradictory.

You can use it to limit the action of a verb: *I just sat there staring; I was just joking,* have the sense 'that is all that I did'. It is also used to add special emphasis to the verb: *I just know it; I just like you; I just love your dress.* This means something like 'really' or 'certainly'. This use is informal and is often regarded as an Americanism. A similar very informal use is for *just* to replace 'very' or give emphasis before an adjective, as in *It's just marvellous; He's just so clever.* Avoid using all but the first in formal writing.

You can use **just** when you want to inform someone that an event or a situation relates to the immediate past: *I have just finished eating.* It is normally accompanied by the perfect auxiliary *have* with a past participle. American English permits the use of *just* in the simple past: *I just finished eating.* This use is gradually coming into British English. It should be avoided as there is the possibility of ambiguity between this use and the first one with the limiting sense.

You can also use *just* when you want to inform someone that an event or a situation relates to the immediate present or future: *I am just making some coffee; I am just going out.*

Just is used with *as* to indicate that something is an exact comparison, as in *I was just as good; They are just as ignorant of Africa as they are of Asia.*

just in case

One expression that uses *just* is potentially very confusing. In British English, **just in case** is used to mean 'on the off-chance that': *I'm going to let you have these now, just in case I forget later.* In American English the expression *just in case* can be used to mean 'only if': *An occurrence of the symbol V can be replaced by a complex symbol just in case it is in the environment –NP.*

juvenile, puerile, childish

Juvenile is a formal adjective meaning 'young or unformed'. It is common in legal writing, as in *juvenile crime has been going up; juvenile offenders.* It can also be used as a technical or scientific term, as in *juvenile, bottom-feeding fish.* An extended meaning of *juvenile,* as an adjective, is to describe someone who plays youthful roles on stage: *He was nearly forty, no longer a juvenile lead.*

All three words, **juvenile**, **puerile**, and **childish**, can be used as terms of scorn when referring to someone's immature behaviour. They have the meaning 'foolish or petty in behaviour', as in *juvenile little pranks; petty squabbles; childish petulance.*

Childish also means 'suitable for a child or in the manner of a child', as in *a childish fancy; childish tears.*

K

k

The use of **k** as an informal way of referring to the figure *thousand* has become more common recently, especially in relation to salaries, where *23K* stands for £23,000. This use is not advisable in any but very informal writing and speech, although in computing the use of **k** to mean *1024 bytes* is standard.

kerb, curb

Confusion between this pair gives rise to a common spelling error. A **curb** is a restraint: *...inevitable curbs on milk production; That horse has to have a curb bit, otherwise it's not safe.* Curb can be used as a verb, meaning 'restrain' or 'hold back'.

In British English a line of granite or concrete blocks edging a footpath is called a **kerb**. In American English both words are spelled **curb**.

kerosine, kerosene, paraffin

The spelling **kerosine** is now the preferred form in technical and industrial usage. In the USA, Canada, and New Zealand *kerosine* is the usual word for what is called **paraffin** in the UK, the term *paraffin* being reserved for *paraffin wax*.

kibbutz, kibbutzim

The plural form is **kibbutzim** but speakers with no knowledge of Hebrew often use *kibbutzes*. The choice of forms is a matter of personal preference.

kid, kids

Some older users still object to **kid** as a term for child: *How do they know it was my kid? This is an American kid who's been taught to spell phonetically.* However, it is now such a commonly found synonym that to carry an objection any further than noting its considerable informality is pointless.

Kid meaning 'deceive' is generally recognized as informal: *Don't kid yourself.*

kidnap, kidnapping, kidnapped

British English has a double 'p' in the present and past participle forms. There is only one 'p' in American English.

kilo-

The prefix **kilo-** is pronounced with vowels as in 'pillow'.

kilogram, kilogramme

The word is pronounced with a stress on the first syllable. The spelling **kilogram**, abbreviated to *kg*, is used in the scientific community as the standard term for a unit of mass. The alternative spelling **kilogramme** was until recently the accepted spelling of the SI (International System) unit but it is now obsolete. ⇒ **gram**

kilometre

The pronunciation of this word is controversial. The logical form would be to stress the first syllable, as /ki-lo-me-ter/, copying *centimetre* and *kilogram*. Many British speakers use this form, but a large number of British speakers and most American speakers place the stress on the second syllable, as in /ki-lo-me-ter/. The spelling in American English is **kilometer**.

kind

The use of **kind** and **sort** together with a demonstrative (*this/these* etc.) can cause problems. If the word *kind* or *sort* is singular, the demonstrative should be singular: *this kind, that sort*. If the word *kind* or *sort* is plural, the demonstrative should be plural: *these kinds, those sorts*.

A difficulty arises when *kind* or *sort* is followed by *of* and another noun, as in *That kind of dog…*. Where does the plural ending go, if there is more than one dog? The grammatically correct form is either: *Those kinds of dogs were used for hunting* or *Those kinds of flower have a long vase life*. That is, the noun that follows *of* can be singular or plural but *kinds* should be plural and so must the verb. This construction is often informally used with a singular after *what*: *What kind of cars?; What kind of things were they?* but formal usage expects a plural here too: *What kinds of cars?*

The use of *a* after *kind of* and *sort of* is generally regarded as unnecessary. *A cosy kind of play…* is usually preferable to *a cosy kind of a play…*, but there can be a small shift of meaning. For example, *What kind of man…* introduces a general query, but *What kind of a man…* questions whether someone deserves the name of man, as in *What kind of a man lets a six-year-old child play with a blowtorch?* A sentence of that kind is more an exclamation than a question.

kindly requested

This is outdated business jargon. Use instead, *ask* or *please*. *You are asked* [not *kindly requested*] *to settle this account in 30 days; Please settle this account…*.

kind of, sort of

Both phrases are overworked substitutes for 'more or less' and often become no more than meaningless fillers like *you know*. They should be avoided even in informal speech.

King's English ⇒ Queen's English

knife, knives

The plural form of the noun is **knives**. The 3rd-person Present singular of the verb is **knifes**.

knit, knitted

When talking of fabrics, as in *knitted woollens*, the Simple Past and past participle form of **knit** is **knitted**. If the use of the verb is figurative and means 'bind', as in *the ordeal knit them together*, use **knit**. A fixed expression is *with knitted brows*.

knock

Depending on the preposition that follows it, **knock** has a number of very informal uses in British English. These range from jargon to slang, as the following examples show.

Knock followed by *off* means 'leave a place of work for the day': *I knocked off at 5 o'clock.*

Knock followed by *off*, *down*, or *out* means 'reduce the price of something': *He knocked off £5.00 from the price; He knocked down the price by 10%. He knocked out the pine cupboards at £65 the pair.* This last expression is often used in auction rooms.

Knock followed by *off* or *up* means 'do something in haste': *He knocked off some more verses in the train that day; He knocked me up some new shelves in less than an hour. Knock up* also means 'waken by knocking', as in

We want to leave early, so I'll knock you up in the morning, To a speaker of American English this will have the meaning 'make pregnant': *He has knocked up a girl only once in his life.* In British English *knock* without a preposition or with *off* can mean 'have sexual relations with'.

It is clear that there can be more than one meaning for a particular combination of *knock* plus preposition and that the context is important in understanding the sense.

knot

A nautical **knot** is a unit of speed, approximately 1.85 km per hour. It is redundant to refer to *knots per hour* as this is equivalent to saying *1.85 km per hour per hour.*

know

Speakers involved in informal explanations often use the phrase *you know* as a filler while they are organizing their next utterance. The use of *you know* to end sentences can develop into a speech habit (as can *in fact*). This habit, if overused, will annoy and distract many listeners who see it as a mark of careless speech. Careful speakers usually monitor their talk for the overuse of such features.

The expression *don't know as how* is not regarded as standard English usage. Prefer *don't know that* or *don't know if: I don't know that* [not *as how*] *I can help you.*

know-how

This is also found spelled as one word, **knowhow. Knowhow** is an informal term meaning 'practical experience and knowledge learned on the job'. It is used for technical matters: *Third world countries need Western know-how.*

knowledge

Note the spelling of this word, which is commonly misspelled. It is pronounced /**nol**-idge/.

kraft paper

This is sometimes mistakenly spelled *craft paper*. It has nothing to do with handicrafts. The name comes from a German word meaning *strength*.

L

-l, -ll

Although the word *full* on its own ends in *-ll*, when it is used as a suffix it becomes *-ful*, as in *helpful, careful*.

laboratory, lab

The pronunciation of **laboratory** in British English places the main stress on the second syllable, /la-**bo**-ra-tri/, the American pronunciation stresses the first syllable, /**la**-bra-to-ri/. This was the original British form but speakers found it confusingly similar to the pronunciation of *lavatory*.

lack

The verb **lack** is sometimes found with a following *for*, as in *You will lack for nothing*. This construction is probably based on confusion with *You will want for nothing* ('want for' means 'need'). There is no need to use *for* after *lack*, which is followed by a direct object. It is more acceptable to write *You will lack nothing*.

When **lack** is used as a noun, it can be followed with the preposition *of*, as in *There was a lack of consideration in the way he responded to her.*

lad, girls

The expression the **lads** or the **girls** is often used to refer informally to friends of one's own age and sex, as in *I'm having an evening out with the girls; I went down to the pub with a few of the lads.* There is no age limit on who qualifies as a *lad* or a *girl* when the words have this meaning. Each is used in the plural with a preceding definite article.

A *lad* or *stable-lad* is someone who takes care of horses in a racing stable or similar establishment. *Stable lads* are often girls.

If a man is called *a bit of a lad* the implication is that he is given to drinking too much, perhaps to fighting or some other form of boisterous misbehaviour. The overtones are of general approval. There is no corresponding expression for a woman.

laden, loaded

The past participle of the verb *load* can be spelled either **laden**, as in *She was heavily laden with her timidity and shame*, or **loaded** as in *She was loaded with bread and buns.* Participles are often used as adjectives; the spelling *laden* is normally used as the adjective form, particularly when you have the weight of the load in mind: *Each of the heavily laden ships flew a barrage balloon.*

Loaded is also used as the Simple Past form: *I carefully loaded my pistol.* Several common phrases use *loaded* as an adjective, especially *a loaded gun*, and *a loaded question* (a question that hides a trap). *Loaded* meaning 'drunk' or 'ostentatiously rich' is a very informal use of the word.

lady, woman

There are two contexts in which **lady** can be used. One is formal or traditional, for example, in addressing a meeting, e.g. *Ladies and Gentlemen;* when referring to someone's title, e.g. *Lady Gregory;* in circumstances where it is used for a fairly formal oblique reference to an adult woman in circumstances where a man would be addressed as *a gentleman*, as in *This lady has lost her child somewhere in the store; Would you pass this to the lady at the checkout?* Most people, especially older ones, would feel that *woman* would be abrupt to the point of rudeness in the examples given, while *girl* would not be appropriate.

In other contexts, use of *lady* is condescending, as in *The little lady is upset; Come on lady, move down the bus; The cleaning lady came on Monday.* This can vary in the extent of its condescension. In the first, replacing *lady* with *woman* would not make it more acceptable, in the second, the very formal *Miss* or *Madam* is the traditional form of address. In the third example, using *cleaner* is neutral and more acceptable.

Less condescending is the use of *lady* in phrases like *a lady doctor* or *a lady pianist*, but since there is no equivalent phrase like *a man doctor* or *a man pianist*, it is not the most appropriate form. If it is important to know the sex of the doctor, the term *a female doctor* would be the most apt counterpart to *a male doctor*.

As a general form of neutral reference *lady* has been out of favour for some time and *woman* the preferred term: *She's a woman with real style; She's a strong capable*

woman. Recently there are signs that *lady* is coming back into favour in this type of neutral reference.
⇒ **sexism**

laid ⇒ lay

landward(s)
Landward without an *s* is an adjective. **Landwards** with an *s* is an adverb meaning 'towards the shore'.

languor
This word is often misspelled. It is related to the adjective *languid* and to the verb *languish*. Begin with the base *langu-* and then add *-or* to form the noun.

large
The phrase *a large number/proportion* is sometimes better or more simply written *many*. **Large** is often a euphemism for *fat* or *overweight*, as in *Clothes for tall and large men*.

largess(e)
Largesse is used to describe the generous bestowal of presents, money, or favour by someone important. It may also be spelled *largess*. The *g* in *largesse* keeps its French pronunciation and has a sound like the *s* in 'pleasure', not the harder sound of the *g* in *large*.

larva, lava
Larva is the term used to describe the intermediate form of many insects. It is commonly called a *grub* or a *maggot*. **Lava** is the molten outflow from a volcano. When it cools it forms a rock-like substance also called *lava*. One form of lava is known as *pumice*.

last, latest
The different use of **last** and **latest**, especially in the phrase *last/latest in a series*, is a source of confusion. The

last in a series is whatever concludes the series, e.g. the last match of the season. The phrase *latest in a series* implies that something is the most recent event of a series, and others may be expected. It is often used with negative overtones: *This was the latest in a series of attacks.*

late, ex-

Both **late** and **ex-** can be used to mean 'former'. However, a *late husband* or a *late wife* is one who has died. Because *late* is potentially ambiguous when it is used in in expressions such as *my late employer*, it may be simpler to use *last*, *previous* or *former* in similar contexts, to avoid the suggestion that your employer has died. An *ex-husband* or an *ex-wife* is one now divorced from the person in question.

lath, lathe

The word **lath** (plural *laths*), meaning a thin strip of wood such as those that support plaster or tiles, is pronounced to rhyme with 'bath'. The word **lathe**, (plural *lathes*), means a machine used for turning shapes in metal or wood. The first vowel sound rhymes with 'wave'.

lather

Lather, the foam produced when soap is worked in water, is pronounced to rhyme with 'rather'.

latter, last-named

In careful usage, **latter** is used when only two items are in question: *He gave the money to Christopher and not to John, the latter being less in need of it.* If there are three or more items, the phrase **last-named** can be used to refer to the last-mentioned item. ⇒ **former**

laudable, laudatory

Something **laudable** deserves to be praised: *The demolition programme was inspired by laudable motives of improving housing conditions.* A **laudatory** speech or newspaper article is one that gives praise: *...hundreds of press cuttings, no doubt carefully selected for the laudatory nature of their contents.*

lavatory, loo ⇒ **toilet**

lawful, legal, licit

Legal is a much more general adjective than **lawful**, which is restricted to meaning 'allowed by law': *He was acting in furtherance of a lawful trade dispute.* The adjective **legal** is also used for activities associated with the law: *the legal profession; legal advice.* **Licit** is an uncommon word with the same meaning as *lawful*.

lay, lie

The verb **lay** is used with an object: *The soldier laid down his arms,* and **lie** without one: *The book was lying on the table; I'm going to lie down.*

Some of the confusion arises from the spelling of the Simple Past tense of **lie**, which is spelled *lay*, as in *I lay down on the bed and went straight to sleep.* The past participle of **lie** is *lain: It has lain in that position for years.*

The Simple Past tense of **lay** is *laid: I laid the table for six but I left a space for Marnie.* This is also its past participle: *We had laid several sacks over the ground in an attempt to keep it dry.*

There is another verb **lie**, which means 'not tell the truth'. Do not confuse it with the one above. It has a different Simple Past tense and participle: *You lied to me; He has never lied to me about his habits.*

Lay has several specialized uses, of which the most common are associated with birds: *Hens lay eggs*, and, in a slang expression, with sexual activity: *Jack laid her after the party.*

In informal English, *lay* is frequently used instead of *lie*: *Ali was laying* (prefer *lying*) *on the grass enjoying the sunshine.* While many similar examples of this usage can be found, it is still not sufficiently established for it to be an acceptable alternative. The distinction should be observed even in informal contexts.

lay, set

One common idiom for 'preparing a table for a meal', is *laying the table.* An alternative idiom uses **set** instead of **lay.** There is no difference in meaning and a roughly equal number of users prefers each idiom.

lead

The verb **lead**, pronounced /leed/, has a variety of meanings including 'show the way' and 'control'. The Simple Past tense and the past participle have the same form, **led**, pronounced to rhyme with 'red'. The present participle **leading** has the same sound as the base form, /leeding/.

There are two nouns spelled **lead**. One that refers to the heavy, dull, silvery-grey metal is pronounced /led/. The other is related to the verb, as in *a new lead on the problem*, and has the same pronunciation as the verb, /leed/.

leading question

This idiom is often misunderstood. A **leading question** is not a particularly difficult one, but the sort of question that *leads* or *prompts* a witness to give the answer that is wanted: *A barrister in court must not ask leading questions.*

lean, leaned, leant

The verb **lean** has two possible spellings for its Simple Past tense and its past participle, **leaned** and **leant**, pronounced /lent/. Avoid confusing the spelling of this word with *lent*, the corresponding Simple Past and past participle forms of *lend*.

⇒ **loan**

learn, teach

Teaching and learning are complementary activities. They are sometimes confused, particularly when the sentence implies punishment or teaching someone a lesson. Expressions similar to: *That'll learn you to walk on the garden*, and: *I'll learn you to answer back*, are not acceptable in standard English.

The past tense is either *learnt* or *learned*. When *learned* is used as an adjective and is pronounced with two syllables /**ler**-ned/, as in *My learned friend*, it means 'having or showing fine judgment'.

least, at least

Least is used as both an adjective and an adverb. It is the superlative form of *little* when it means a small quantity, and as such is always preceded by *the*: *He used to quiver at the least noise*. The phrase **at least**, meaning 'as a minimum' is also correctly written **at the least**: *…this young man, who she knew was at the least 'off-colour', if not ill.*

leastways

Leastways, and its variant spelling *leastwise*, should be regarded as a very informal word. The phrase *at any rate* is another informal equivalent. Careful speech and writing uses *at least* or *anyway*.

leave

In general educated usage **leave** is not used in the sense of *let*. The expressions *Let go* and *Let me go* are preferred to the informal and dialect forms *Leave go* and *Leave hold of me*. However, the phrase **leave off** doing something, in the sense of stop doing it, is part of accepted usage: *He couldn't leave off looking at the violets.*

led ⇒ **lead**

leeward, leeway

The nautical pronunciation of the word **leeward** is /loo-ward/. The ordinary pronunciation is /lee-ward/. It is the point towards which the wind is blowing.

Leeway, pronounced /lee-way/ is the room that one has for manoeuvring in. It originated as a nautical term, but is now more familiar in contexts that have nothing to do with the sea: *If the party didn't allow Koornhof more leeway within the next few months, the opportunity would be missed on this issue.*

leftward(s)

When **leftward** is used as an adjective it does not have a final *s*: *The car veered off in a leftward direction.* For the adverb, either *leftwards* or *leftward* may be used.

legal ⇒ **lawful**

legible, readable

If something is **legible** it is clear and easy to read close up. The letters are not too faded or badly formed. If a novel or an account of something is **readable**, it is well written and holds the reader's interest. ⇒ **illegible**

leisure

The pronunciation of **leisure** in British English is /le-zjur/, the American pronunciation is /lee-zjur/. Note the *-ei-* order in the spelling.

lend

If you want to borrow something, you normally ask if the owner will **lend** it to you: *Could you lend me a pound? I've left my wallet at home; Would you lend me the dictionary for a while?* It is a common error to use *loan* instead of *lend* in these contexts. The Simple Past tense and past participle is *lent*. If you borrow money from a bank or building society, it is then correct to say that they *loaned* you the money. ⇒ **loan**

lengthways, lengthwise

Both forms are current and each can be used as an adjective or an adverb.

lengthy

In careful speech, **lengthy** is pronounced /**leng**-thy/ not [/**len**-thy/].

lens

The word **lens**, pronounced /lenz/, has the plural form *lenses*.

less ⇒ few

-less, -ness

The suffix **-less** means 'lacking in' something. When it is added to abstract nouns, for example *careless, helpless, timeless, thoughtless,* they become adjectives. If **-ness** is added to the adjective form, it becomes an abstract noun again: *carelessness, helplessness, timelessness, thoughtlessness.*

lest, in case

Lest is a very formal word that is becoming archaic. It is generally used in a clause that contains *should: I had to … lest he should hurt himself,* but the verb *should* can be left out: *I had to … lest he (should) hurt himself.*

In case is not as formal as *lest* and it is a current expression.

If you use **in case** instead of **lest** the sentence can be written in the same way: *I had to … in case he (should) hurt himself*. Neither of these words is used with *will* or *would* but you can use the ordinary Simple Present tense with *in case*: *…in case he hurts himself*.

let, let's

Let means 'permit' or 'allow' in modern English. It is used in commands and requests: *Let me go; Will you let us both have some?*

Let used once to have the meaning 'prevent' as a verb and 'obstruction' as a noun, which is quite the opposite sense of the modern meaning, but this old sense is now found only in certain set phrases, such as *without let or hindrance*.

Let followed by *us* is used to persuade someone. That is, in a sentence it forms the type of command that includes the speaker as well as the person who is being addressed: *Let us go out this evening*. The context and the tone of voice serves to distinguish this use of *let* from the meaning 'allow'. **Let's** is a contracted form of *let us* but it should only be used for persuasion: *Let's visit John; Let's have some coffee*. Most speakers use *let's not* as the negative form but a more informal form is *don't let's*.

If *let us* is a request, not a command, it should not be contracted to *let's*, so that: *Let's have one of your sweets* meaning 'let me have one', is not an acceptable usage in standard English, though it is common in informal speech.

letter writing

The most common conventions used in letter writing are as follows:

The **sender's address** is placed at the top of the letter. It is usually found at the top right corner but the conventions that used to apply to the setting out of this section have changed now that printed and typed headings have become more common. It is usual to include a postcode and to add the date. When the letter is being sent to a commercial organization it is advisable to write the **recipient's name** and position at the left-hand side of the page lower down than the address and before the opening salutation. If a **reference number** has been given, add it here.

The **salutation** varies according to the purpose of the letter and the relationship between the sender and the recipient. In a business letter to someone you do not know, begin with *Dear Sirs,...* if the recipient is the organization generally, e.g.

> *Computer Supplies Ltd*
> > *Dear Sirs,*

Use *Dear Sir,...* or *Dear Madam,...* when the person to whom the letter is addressed is known to the writer only by their position and not by name, e.g.

> *The Customer Services Manager,*
> *Computer Supplies Ltd*
> > *Dear Sir,*

Conclude the letter with *Yours faithfully,....*

When the letter is on business and to a person known to you, use their title and surname, e.g.

> *Miss J M Smith*
> *The Customer Services Manager,*
> *Computer Supplies Ltd*
> > *Dear Miss Smith,... /Mrs Smith* etc.

Conclude the letter with *Yours sincerely, ...*

This ending is usual in business letters. Long-established business correspondents also often use a first name and an informal salutation such as *Yours ever, ...* Concluding phrases such as *I remain your obedient servant, Yours truly,* and *Yours respectfully* are generally regarded as old-fashioned and very stiff and formal.

When the letter is not on business and to a person well known to you, the opening varies according to the warmth of the acquaintance and the circumstances, e.g. *Dear Tom, Darling Jane, My love, etc.* Conclude the letter with whatever seems suitable from *Yours ever, Best wishes,* and so on. The **signature** is usually written on the line below the conclusion. If you have a signature that is difficult to read, print or type your name underneath it. If the contents of the letter give no indication of your **status**, and if this information is relevant to the reply, give these details following the printed signature as in *Ms J. Smith* or *J. Smith (Managing Director)*.

Note that letter writers outside Britain have many different conventions. One which can cause problems to British recipients is the omission of a sender's address on the letter, placing it instead on the envelope. British recipients as a rule discard the envelope, making a response difficult.

liability, liabilities

When **liability** is used in the singular (apart from its meaning of something for which you are technically responsible, as in *a limited liability on each side; reduced liability for contributions*), it often means someone or something that causes embarrassment, as in *Colley was an asset in the drawing room, but a liability on the battlefield.*

Liabilities, always used in the plural, are the opposite of *assets* in a business. They are the financial obligations that show up on a balance sheet: *This booklet is designed to draw your attention to the opportunities and liabilities that may affect you.*

liable

Careful users of English take **liable** to mean 'responsible for' in sentences such as *He was liable for his employees' accidents* and 'subject to' in sentences such as *He was liable to accidents. Liable* is used in an informal construction with the sense of 'likely', as in *He was liable to have accidents*, but this should be avoided in formal situations.

libel, slander

Libel is the writing or printing of anything that will defame someone. **Slander** is defaming someone by what you say about them.

liberalism, liberal, liberality

The noun **liberalism** is used for the belief that social and political change can be brought about by consent and reform.

The noun *liberal* has meanings that the adjective *liberal* does not share. In Britain a *liberal* is someone who believes in *liberalism* as a political programme. However, in some political systems, for example, in the USA, the noun *liberal* has often been used to label people who are believed to be subversive or dissident politically. The adjective **liberal** has these meanings but can also be used to mean 'generous': *She uses liberal amounts of butter and wine in all her recipes for preparing meals.* When *liberal* is used about a course of studies, it means 'broadly based', often involving both the humanities and the sciences: *Chris is on a liberal arts course at university.*

The noun **liberality** has a meaning similar to *generosity: Above all, it was the liberality of their natures that was so marvellous.* ⇒ **humane**

libertarian, libertine

A **libertarian** believes that people should be free to act and believe in the way that best suits them. The word is also commonly found as an adjective: *...the renewed relevance of democratic and libertarian principles internally and in international affairs.* The overtones of the word are positive and suggest a supportive attitude.

A **libertine** is someone who lives in a way that is totally free of moral or sexual scruples. The overtones of the word are rather old-fashioned and strongly negative, suggesting a self-centred attitude: *...libertine playboys, unfrocked clergymen and the like.*

library

The careful, formal pronunciation of **library** has three syllables, /li-bra-ry/. The informal pronunciation has only two and is often disliked.

licence, license

British English makes a distinction between the spelling of the noun **licence** and that of the verb **license**. American English does not make this distinction. It uses *license* for both noun and verb. ⇒ **practice**

licit ⇒ **lawful**

lie ⇒ **lay**

lieutenant

In everyday usage, a **lieutenant** is someone who can take command in the absence of a superior: *Jane was his* *trusty lieutenant at these moments.*

In the British army, a **lieutenant** ranks between a second lieutenant and a captain. In the British navy, a *lieutenant* ranks between a sub-lieutenant and a lieutenant-commander, which is equivalent to the army rank of captain. The British pronunciation of **lieutenant** is usually /lef-**ten**-ant/, but in the navy it is /l't-nant/, and the American pronunciation is /loo-**ten**-ant/.

lifelong, livelong

Lifelong means 'long-lasting': *We shared a lifelong interest in zoology.* **Livelong** is now archaic and means 'whole' or 'long in passing'. It is rarely used outside the phrase *the livelong day*, meaning 'for the whole day'.

lighted, lit

The verb *light* has the alternative Simple Past tense and past participle forms, **lighted** and **lit**. The form *lighted* is the one normally used as an adjective: *a lighted match*.

lightening, lightning

The verb *lighten* has two meanings: become lighter in the sense of 'make less heavy', as in *You are lightening the load of the hospital doctors*, and become lighter in the sense of 'make less dark', as in *The stars hung faintly in the lightening sky*. **Lightening**, the present participle, is used with both meanings.

This verb is often confused with the noun **lightning** (note that it does not contain an *e*), the flash of electric discharge that creates the shock wave known as *thunder*.

like, as

Like can be a verb, as in *I really like her*, a noun (often used in the plural), as in *I'm fed up with your likes and dislikes*, and an adjective, as in *He soon found some supporters with like opinions.*

Like can also be used as a preposition. Prepositions can be followed by nouns (and noun phrases) or pronouns, as in the sentences: *Bear it it like a man; Be satisfied like me*. This accepted use of the preposition *like* gives rise to a common problem. *Like* is sometimes followed by a noun that is itself the subject of a following verb. This often has the effect of turning *like* into a linking word, as in *Cut it up it like I have*.

The accepted view is that *like* should not be used in this way, linking two clauses as if it were a conjunction. This is quite a common construction in American English, but in British English it is not regarded as educated usage and the preferred construction uses *as* or *the way* instead: *Cut it up as/the way I have*.

Although *like* and *as* are often interchangeable, there are some instances when they have a different meaning. For example: *He treated her as his mother*, means she became a mother to him, *He treated her like his mother* means he acted towards her as he did to his mother. *He played like a pro*, is not the same as *He played as a pro*.

Note that *feel like* means 'want' or 'fancy'. Be careful when using this expression. For example, *I feel like a cup of tea* is correct but *I feel like a fool* is not (it means 'I want a fool'). This should be: *I feel a fool*. ⇒ **preposition**

-like

The suffix **-like** can be used to form an adjective from a noun. The word does not need a hyphen: *ladylike; stalk-like; treelike*. ⇒ **-ly**

likely

When **likely** is used as an adverb in informal British English, it is normally preceded by an intensifying adverb, such as *very, highly, quite, most,* or *extremely,* as in *It will very likely rain*, or *It will most likely rain*. Its use without an intensifier, as in *It will likely rain*, is common in informal American English though it is regarded as unacceptable by most users of British English.

limit, delimit

If you **limit** something you restrict it in some way: *…measures to limit the effectiveness of their navy; Her enjoyment of life was limited*. If you **delimit** something like expenditure or the grounds for discussion, you make it clear beforehand what the boundaries are: *The case for sport cannot be properly made under the delimited heading of 'leisure studies'; We need to delimit the scope of our discussion*.

lingo

An informal synonym for *language*, it is rather disparaging and can also mean *jargon*.

lingua franca

A **lingua franca** is a language that is used as a medium of communication between people whose language of birth is not the same. Sometimes a *lingua franca* is a mixture of grammar and vocabulary from several languages, as for example in a pidgin. Sometimes it is a recognized world language. As an example, if a Swedish engineer communicates with a group of French and German engineers in English, English is acting as the *lingua franca*. ⇒ **pidgin**

linguist, linguistics, linguistician

A **linguist** is someone with a knowledge of foreign languages. It also means someone interested in the study of syntax, language use, and so on. This formal academic study of the way that language works is called **linguistics**. Avoid the awkward term **linguistician** for such a person.

liquor, liqueur

The word **liquor** is used as a general term for any alcoholic drink and particularly for spirits. It also has a less common use meaning the water that something has been cooked in. In American English the phrase *liquor store* is used for what in British English is variously an *off-licence,* an *off-sales,* an *outdoor,* and by other local terms. It is seen as a technical word, so that a British speaker would not ask for *liquor* but for *a drink,* or give the name of the drink.

A **liqueur** is a sweet infusion of herbs, spices, and alcohol. It is usually drunk after a meal. *Liqueur* is pronounced /li-**cure**/ in British English.

literally

The use of **literally** as an intensifier is common, especially in informal contexts. In some cases, it provides emphasis without adding to the meaning: *The house was literally only five minutes walk away.*

However, the basic meaning of *literally* is similar to the meaning of *actually,* and its use can result in unintended absurdity when it is used as part of a figure of speech. For example, *He literally swept me off my feet* suggests to hearers that the speaker 'actually took a broom and swept me off my feet'. *Literally* is therefore best used with care.

little, small

The word **little** is not regular in the way in which it forms its comparative and superlative parts. When *little* means 'not much', the comparative is *less: The smaller the computer, the less raw material it uses up,* and the superlative *the least: If they had been old enough to show the least hostility they would have been done to death.*

When **little** means 'small and young', it is sometimes given the comparative and superlative forms *littler* and *littlest* in imitation of the word *small*. In British English these forms are not regarded as standard usage, but one American writer on usage and two American English dictionaries give the words as standard. In British English, you have to use *smaller, not as big*, or *quite little*. Very *little* is used for quantities: *They have very little money.*
⇒ **few**

livid

The word **livid** refers to a colour but there is no agreement on the shade. It originally described the colour of a bruise but it has also come to mean 'pale and greyish': *a face livid with helpless rage.* Because of the frequent use of *livid* in phrases such as *He was livid* in describing an angry person, it has now additionally taken on the informal meaning 'angry and outraged': *Her whining and complaints got me so livid.*

Lloyd's, Lloyds

The London-based insurance-underwriters' association is spelled **Lloyd's**, with an apostrophe *s*. The British banking group **Lloyds** does not have an apostrophe.

loaded ⇒ laden

loan

Loan is normally used as a noun: *She gave me the loan of new car; He provided me with a camera on loan/as a loan.* Avoid nonstandard uses of *loan* such as: *Can you [loan] me a pen?* and prefer *Can you lend me a pen?*

Loan should only be used as a verb when referring to the formal lending of money: *The bank loaned him the money.* It is also perfectly acceptable to use *lend* in this context. ⇒ **lend**

loathe, loath, loth

When someone or something causes you to have feelings of disgust or hatred you can use the verb **loathe**: *Did these soldiers loathe or secretly desire warfare?*

The adjective **loath** has quite a different meaning from that of the verb above. Some writers prefer to use the alternative spelling **loth** in order to make this clear. As an adjective, it is usually followed by *to* and means 'reluctant': *This made them loath to cease their play.* Note that the set expression *nothing loath* is used to indicate willingness, not hostility, and means 'not at all reluctant': *Nothing loath, he set to work digging at once.*

locale, locality, scene

A **locale** is an area with which particular events are associated: *It must always be remembered that Joyce's locale is Celtic and his season is spring.* This is also one of the senses of the word **scene**, as in *the scene of the crime/accident.* A *scene* is a particular spot, but a *locale* is a rather broader notion, involving a particular atmosphere and associations.

Locality is also used with this sense but it is normally used in a vaguer way to mean 'the neighbourhood': *Angle Lane, Stratford, was a poor locality.*

locate, find

The verb **locate** is normally used when you are trying to find the precise position of a place on a map. In the passive voice it is used to indicate where a place is situated. Careful users avoid confusing *locate* with the more general sense of *find*: *I have managed to find* [not *locate*] *someone who will let us have the wine on sale or return.* The verb *relocate* is a recent piece of commercial jargon which is used when a factory or an office moves to a new site. It is useful but should not be overused.

-logy

The suffix **-logy** usually means 'the science or study of', as in *biology, geology, theology.* However, it has a second meaning, 'a work concerning' whatever the first part of the word indicates, so a *martyrology* is an account of the acts and lives of the Christian martyrs and a *hymnology* is a collection of hymns.

loose, loosen, lose

The verb **lose** (rhyming with 'fuse') and the adjective **loose** (rhyming with 'moose') are the cause of spelling problems in written English but are only rarely confused in spoken English because they have different pronunciations and are used in different places in a sentence: *This is one bet you are going to lose; Roof tiles and other pieces of loose masonry were propelled through the air.* It may help to remember that the spelling *loose* is normally followed by a noun or used after a link verb like *is/was.*

Loosen is a verb formed from *loose.* It means 'partly undo' or 'make something less tight': *He loosened his tie and rolled up his sleeves.*

There is also a verb *loose*, but this is not often used. It means 'let loose', as for example in *Loose the dogs!*

lord, lady ⇒ titles

lot

The informal expression **a lot** is always written as two words. A very common mistake is to join both words in writing because they seem to be said as a single word.

The use of **a lot**, or **lots of**, as in *A lot of farmers hid their horses; He put lots of hours in*, should be treated as very informal. In careful speech and writing use *plenty* for *a lot*, and *much, many*, or *a large number of* for *lots of.*
⇒ **in fact**

loud, loudly

Loud is generally used as an adjective; it may, with certain exceptions, be used as an adverb: *He had to speak loud as she was deaf; They turned it up very loud; It's not ringing loud enough to hear; She shouted long and loud.* **Loudly** may be used wherever *loud* is used as an adverb except in the set phrase *out loud*. When the meaning is 'in a very noticeable manner', the usual adverb is *loudly: In his sleep, he speaks often and loudly.*

lounge

In the home a **lounge** is another name for a *living room, sitting room,* or what was once called a *parlour.* In a public building such as a hotel or an airport, it is a public waiting room furnished with seats. The use of the name *lounge* for a room in a private house is treated by some speakers of English as a marker of social class.

low, high

Low and **high** can be used informally as nouns in phrases like *…a new low,* meaning a low point or *nadir,* and *He hit a high,* meaning a high point or *zenith.*

low, lowly

Low can be used as an adverb, as in *The hotel bill had left her funds pretty low,* and as an adjective: *Then he wheeled out a low racing bike.*

The form **lowly,** which looks like an adverb, is normally used as an adjective and means 'low in rank' or 'unimportant'.

lunch, luncheon, dinner

Luncheon is a formal word for the midday meal. The shortened form **lunch** is now commonly used, except in describing items from a delicatessen, such as *luncheon meat; luncheon sausage* and also in *luncheon voucher.* A *lunch* is often, though not necessarily, a meal consisting of cold food or snack food, such as salads, ham, or sandwiches.

A cooked midday meal is sometimes called **dinner**. A social distinction is involved in the use of these terms, as some social groups always associate *dinner* with a formal evening meal. ⇒ **supper**

lustful, lusty

Lustful is used to describe behaviour that is driven by *lust*, the desire for sexual gratification: *He gave a lustful glance at her plump figure.* **Lusty** is sometimes used for this but it is more often used to describe a vigorous robust attitude: *Below stairs was a lusty life, an underworld of warmth and plenty.* It describes activities that the speaker approves of and is commonly applied to healthy babies: *…a strong lusty boy of whom any father could be proud.*

luxuriant, luxurious, luxury

The adjective **luxuriant** is usually used to describe the growth of plants: *…the many-limbed shade of luxuriant trees.* It is similar in its use to *lush.* The adjective **luxurious** is usually used to describe rich or extravagant surroundings and possessions: *…a big desk with a luxurious leather blotting pad.* *Luxury* is often found modifying a noun and is frequently overused in commercial contexts where it often only means 'well-equipped', as in *luxury homes; luxury caravan.* The overtones of *luxury* in other contexts are of something pleasant but unnecessary: *These chocs are a luxury.*

-ly

The **-ly** suffix usually indicates that a word is an adverb. Most adjectives have a corresponding **-ly** adverb ending.

When an adjective ends in a silent *e*, as in *fine* or *immediate*, the adverb suffix **-ly** is simply added to it: *finely, immediately*. A very common spelling mistake makes a muddle of this simple process and puts the *e* between the *l* and the *y*. There are only 15 words ending in *-ley* and they are either nouns or adjectives.

Note that it is possible to add the **-ly** ending to a noun, as in *kingly, princely*. When these words are used, they are often followed by *manner, way*, or *fashion: He's always acting in a lordly manner. I really dislike him.* When the *-ly* ending is added to a noun, it is often very close in meaning to the *-like* ending: *queenly/queenlike*.

lyric, lyrical, lyrics

A *lyric poem* or **lyric** is one composed in a classical style that is distinct from an *epic, dramatic*, or *narrative* poem. A *lyric* has musical qualities of smoothness and flow, and uses simple, direct subject matter.

The adjective **lyrical** is used to describe an emotional or very exuberant response to something: *...lyrical descriptions of leafy walks and impassioned kissing.*

The words to a popular song are known as the **lyrics**. The plural form is always used.

M

macho, machismo

The adjective **macho** is a recent borrowing from Spanish that has become a vogue word. It means displaying the qualities and type of behaviour that is regarded as masculine, for example excessive drinking, or pride in physical prowess: *Young men often adopt a macho style to hide their insecurity in social situations.* A corresponding term is the noun **machismo**: *The culture of machismo, the only dignity a poor man has in the rural north-east.* **Macho** is pronounced /**ma**-tcho/, *machismo* is pronounced either /ma-**kiz**-mo/ or /ma-**tchiz**-mo/.

mad

Mad is not currently used as a formal term in psychology to mean 'insane'. It is often informally used with that meaning, as in *You must be mad,* but it most commonly has a range of meanings suggesting excitement or lack of control: *It was the usual mad panic.* It can also be used to mean 'absurd', as in *This is mad. You must get your sleep.* The expression *like mad* means 'excitedly': *They were arguing like mad.* The use of **mad** to mean 'angry' is an Americanism and is very informal: *My mother's really mad at me.*

Madam, Madame, Ma'am

Madam is the normal British form of polite address to a woman not personally known to the speaker. Use of the French form **Madame** in English conversation is affected. It is customary to address adult female members of the royal family as **Ma'am**.

magazine ⇒ journal

magic, magical

Magic is a noun. After a link verb, the adjective form **magical** should be used, as in *It was magical*. The expression, *It was magic*, is nonstandard and informal.

maitre d'

The use of **maitre d'** for *headwaiter*, or *restaurant manager* is an Americanism which has recently begun to gain hold in Britain. Short for *maitre d'hotel* it is a rather absurd usage, both in form and sound, as the French *d'*, unpronounceable on its own in French, has to become a most un-French /dee/. Either use the full French phrase *maitre d'hotel*, or use *headwaiter*, or *restaurant manager*. Otherwise you run the risk of sounding either ignorant or a poseur.

major, minor

The adjective **major** implies a comparison of parts, as in *A major section of the new motorway is open for use*. The word is now extended and rather overused as a synonym for 'substantial' or 'important', as in *the major reason; the major differences; a major event in theatrical history*, where a comparison is not implied. This weakens the sense of the word and is avoided by careful writers and speakers of English.

Similarly, **minor** is also a comparative and should be used with that sense, rather than 'small' or 'insignificant'. Phrases such as: *a minor accident; a minor novelist; a minor official*, are acceptable because they imply the existence of a more serious or greater counterpart.

majority

A **majority** is the greater part of a group of people. In technical terms, it is any proportion over 50%: *This Bill* *will pass if it has a majority in the House.* If someone is part of the larger group they are *in the majority.* In the context of an election, a candidate's *majority* is the number of votes by which their support exceeded that given to others: *Benn was returned by a majority of 15,479, receiving 20,373 votes.* There is a tendency to use *majority* as if it meant 'almost all'. If it is to have this sense it should be qualified, as in *a large majority.*

malapropism

When a speaker uses a word that is similar in sound but very different in meaning to the word that was intended, the mistake is called a **malapropism**, particularly if the result is ridiculous. Using *affluence* instead of *influence* or *stimulate* instead of *simulate* are examples of *malapropism.*

male, masculine

The word **male** is the opposite of *female* and means 'the member of a species that does not produce ova'. It is used very broadly as it describes both animals and plants. The word **masculine** is the opposite of *feminine* and is restricted to use with the human species. It means displaying the qualities and type of behaviour that a society or culture associates with men. Like the word *feminine*, it can be used to describe any behaviour by men or women that matches the expectations associated with the term: *Clarissa allowed herself to be checked by his masculine authority; The spoons were snapped up by a masculine-looking lady standing next to me.* Masculine (and *feminine*) can be applied to the atmosphere of a locality, as in *Another enclave more feminine perhaps than masculine; the opening into Burlington Arcade.*
⇒ **female** ⇒ **macho**

-man

The use of **-man** as a suffix occasionally gives offence to some users of English, who see in it an expression of male dominance. In deference to this, some words ending in *-man*, especially those referring to positions in public life, are often changed to a neutral form, usually by using the suffix *-person*, e.g. *chairman/chairperson*. This area of usage is still controversial for many users.

The use of words ending in *-man* is also avoided as implying 'male' in job advertisements, where sexual discrimination is illegal, and can be avoided in other contexts where a term that is not gender-specific is available, such as: *salesperson; barperson; camera operator*. ⇒ **sexism**

mandate, mandatory

The most common use of **mandate** today is in the political sense of 'consent by the electorate to certain actions on the part of an elected government': *The Rt. Honourable Gentleman does not have a mandate for this Bill.* There is a more formal legal use for a situation in which someone is given the power to act on behalf of another in legal or financial matters: *My brother has given me a mandate to operate his bank account for him while he is in America.*

When something is **mandatory** it is obligatory or compulsory: *If you get a place at University you will receive a mandatory grant.* In this sense, it is opposite to *discretionary: You may be eligible for a discretionary grant.*

margarine

The butter-substitute **margarine** (and the abbreviated form *marge*) is usually pronounced with a soft *g* sound as in 'margin'. Originally, it had a hard **g** sound like 'lager', but only a few speakers still use this form.

marginal, minimal

If something is **marginal** it is close to some lower limit. A *marginal constituency* is one where an MP has a bare majority of the votes. In itself, something *marginal* could be quite large, a politician could have 15,000 votes, but if his opponent had 14,980, the constituency would be *marginal*. The adjective **minimal** is used to describe something which is the least possible or smallest of its kind: *The recession has led to schemes with minimal support services and few staff.*

marital, martial

Marital is the adjective related to the noun *marriage*: *We asked about age, sex, and marital status.* The adjective **martial** means 'warlike' and is, for example, used with reference to shows of military power and to warfare: *the deadly martial music of the bombardment.*

marquess, marquis

A **marquess**, pronounced /mark-wess/, is a male member of the English nobility, in rank just below a duke. The feminine form is *marchioness*. The title **marquis** is the French equivalent. The French spelling *marquis* is sometimes used instead of *marquess*.

mastery, masterly, masterful

Mastery means full command: *He has gained mastery over his own actions*, or skill in a specialized area: *...his complete mastery of technique and timing.* **Masterly** is an adjective and means 'showing the skill expected of a master': *His presentation was so thorough and so masterly that the prosecution asked for a recess.* The adjective **masterful** also has this meaning: *This masterful presen-*

tation, but it has another, which is used of someone who likes to be master and to control situations or other people: *…a society dominated by ruthless masterful ambition.*

mat, matte

The adjective **mat** meaning 'not shiny', having a dull nonreflective surface, is sometimes spelled *matt*. The noun **mat** is used for a card insert, or mount, bordering a picture. The alternative spelling **matte** is often used when this idea is extended to a film technique in which a mask blacks out part of an image, allowing another picture to be superimposed.

mathematics, maths

In common with most words with an *-ics* ending that name a branch of study (*physics, economics, optics*) **mathematics** is a singular noun. The British abbreviation is **maths** but the normal abbreviated form in American English is *math.* ⇒ **-ics**

matrix, matrices, matrixes

Matrix has alternative plural forms *matrices* and *matrixes*. The spelling **matrices** is the form most commonly found. *Matrix* is a specialized word used in mathematics, the sciences, and certain crafts. It is often loosely used to mean 'framework' or 'setting'. The usual pronunciation is /**may**-tricks/ but /**mat**-tricks/ is used in printing.

may, might, mayn't

In careful written usage, **may** is used rather than *can* when reference is made to 'permission' and not to 'capability'. *He may do it,* is more appropriate than: *He can do it,* when the desired sense is: *He is allowed to do it.* In spoken English, however, *can* is often used where the correct use of *may* results in forms that are considered to be awkward. For this reason, *Can't I?* is preferred to *mayn't I?* in speech. The difference between *may* and *might* is one of emphasis. *He might be coming* usually indicates less certainty than *He may be coming.* Similarly, *Might I have it?* is felt to be more hesitant than *May I have it?*

When we speak of an event that could have happened but did not, often because something else prevented it, standard English uses **might** followed by *have: Do you realize that your name might have been added to the list?; If I had known him better, I might have come to like him.* It has become a common error to use *may* in place of *might* in this construction. Avoid doing so, as it is not standard English.

The abbreviated negative form **mayn't** is usually only found in speech and as a tag to *may: There may be some difficulty there, mayn't there?*

maybe, may be, perhaps

The use of **maybe** is generally felt to be informal and casual in tone: *Maybe I ought to grow a moustache; Maybe I'd like him better if he did.* The use of **perhaps** is rather more formal. *Maybe* should not be confused with the verb phrase *may be: She may be here tomorrow morning.*

me, myself ⇒ I ⇒ -ing

means

When the noun **means** is used with the sense of 'the method, process, or instrument' by which something is done, it is used with either a singular or plural verb depending on the construction: *The principal means of transport is the bicycle; We will pursue whatever means*

*are necessary to win. Means is frequently followed by of:
Advances in technological means of production.* When
the noun **means** is used with the sense of 'resources', it is
always used with a plural verb and is frequently followed
by *to: It is only this sector which has the means to gener-
ate growth; They are entitled to use whatever means are
necessary.*

media, medium

The word **media** is now used as a shorthand way of referring to the various forms of mass communication. As
media is, strictly, the plural form of **medium**, careful
writers and speakers do not use it as a singular noun,
although this use is common. For example, correct use
would be: *Television is a valuable medium* [not *media*]
*for advertising; It saddens me that the news media are
only interested in bad news from Northern Ireland.*

mediate

To **mediate** is to act as an intermediary in a dispute. The
verb is often followed by *in* or *between: As a twelve year-
old, he tried to mediate in a fight at school and was hit in
the eye.* Avoid its use as a piece of jargon, common in the
social sciences, meaning 'bring about' or 'provide', as in
Status does not seem to be mediated by education.

medicine

The usual pronunciation of **medicine** is /**med**-sin/. The
use of three syllables, /**med**-i-sin/, is a less frequent variant.

meet, meet with

In British English the verb **meet** is usually followed
directly by its object: *She had met his father.* **Meet with** is
used only when the object is an event, often something
unpleasant: *...a child who met with an accident.* The

idiom *meet with someone* is restricted to American English: *I'll meet with you at 10 am.* The idiom *meet up* (*with*) someone means 'join them at a later time' either by accident or on purpose: *We can all meet up again at about 10.30; We planned to meet up with them later.*

melody ⇒ harmony

melted, molten

The verb *melt* has two past participle forms, *melted* and *molten*. The normal form is **melted** and this is used whenever the participle is a modifier: *Water from melted ice swelled the rivers,* except when the substance is normally solid and has been reduced to a liquid by extreme heat: *molten glass; molten steel.*

ménage, manège

The French term **ménage**, meaning 'a household' or 'a group of close associates', pronounced /may-**narge**/, is often used with a faintly disparaging or sneering overtone in English: *a pretty uneasy ménage; that strange ménage; that unhappy ménage.* A term much used in riding, **manège**, pronounced /man-**aizh**/, and meaning the training of horse and rider, or the riding school itself, is often confused in pronunciation and in spelling with the former word: *Riders should assemble in the manège.*

Messrs

The plural form of *Mr*, **Messrs**, is now used only in commercial correspondence. Note that it is not spelled [*messers*].

meta-

The prefix **meta-** has three main uses. The first is to indicate 'change or alteration', as in *metabolism; metamorphosis.* The second is used before the name of a discipline to indicate the study of the principles that lie behind it: *metaphysics; metamathematics,* and the third indicates the sense 'following on', as in *metaphase; metastasis.*

metamorphosis

Metamorphosis has five syllables. The stress occurs on the third, /me-ta-**mor**-pho-sis/.

meticulous, scrupulous

If someone is **meticulous** they are particular about details to the point of being fussy: *He was unexpectedly meticulous in attending to unimportant details.* Someone who is **scrupulous** is also careful and precise, with a concern that everything done should be morally correct or fair: *He had a well-earned reputation for scrupulous scholarship; She was more sensitive and scrupulous than one might have supposed.*

metre, meter

The word **metre** is used for the standard unit of measurement common throughout Europe. British English also uses *metre* as a technical term when talking about poetry.

In British English a **meter** is a measuring device, as in *parking meter, gas meter.* American English uses the spelling *meter* for all these senses. ⇒ **gram**

micro-, macro-

The prefix **micro-** is used with a range of meanings that includes 'very small': *microclimate; microcircuit,* or 'underdeveloped': *microcephalous,* or as an indication that the base word is a precise measuring instrument, as in *micrometer; microbalance.* The prefix **macro-** is used with the sense of 'large' (in any dimension): *macronutrient; macromolecule,* or 'overdeveloped': *macrocyte.*

might ⇒ **may**

migraine

This word should not be used simply to mean 'a bad headache'. A *migraine* severely affects vision and speech, causes nausea, and produces a pain which is located in one half of the head only. It is pronounced /me-grayne/ in British English and usually /my-grayne/ in American English.

migrant ⇒ **emigrant**

militate ⇒ **mitigate**

million ⇒ **billion**

minimal ⇒ **marginal**

minimum, minute, minuscule

The **minimum** is the the least possible amount or quantity of something. *Minimum* can be used as a noun or as an adjective. Something very small is referred to as **minute**. When something is even smaller still, it can be described as **minuscule**: *Minute bacterial spores and other odd minuscule organic bodies showed up in places.* Note especially that *u* follows *min-* in *minuscule*, that is, it is like *minus*.

minister ⇒ **clergyman**

minor ⇒ **major**

mis-

The prefix **mis-** means that the action of the word to which it is added has been performed badly or wrongly, as in *miscalculate; misdirect; misfire; mishear; misspell*.

mischievous

The pronunciation of **mischievous** is /mis-tche-viss/ with three syllables only. Avoid using the mispronunciation /mis-**tchee**-vee-us/, which is frequently encountered.

misogynist, misanthropist
A **misogynist** expresses an irrational dislike of women, a **misanthropist** expresses an irrational dislike of all human beings. Note that these words are not formed using the *mis-* prefix.

misrelated participle ⇒ **unrelated participle**

mistrust ⇒ **distrust**

mitigate, militate
These words are frequently confused. The word **mitigate** means 'make something less unpleasant than it could be': *I felt these facts might mitigate the pain.* If, in a court of law, something is said *in mitigation* it is given as a reason or an excuse for some act or behaviour.

Mitigate is commonly used where **militate** is meant. **Militate** (often followed by *against* and sometimes by *for*) means 'have an influence or effect on something': *What makes for good leadership in one situation may actually militate against it in another; Any act that militates for peaceful cooperation is to be welcomed.*

Mohammedan ⇒ **Muslim**

molten ⇒ **melted**

momentary, momentarily, momentous
Something **momentary** lasts for a moment only or is temporary: *There was a momentary silence at the other end.* In British English, the adverb **momentarily** has a similar meaning and is used of an action or event that takes place for a very brief time: *He paused momentarily and said, 'I studied some water samples'.* In American English *momentarily* has a different sense. It can be used

of an action or event that is about to happen in a moment. This difference can be the cause of some confusion between British and American speakers.

The word **momentous** is not connected in meaning to those above despite a similarity in spelling. It is a rather formal, literary word that means 'important' or 'crucial' and is used in relation to events and decisions: *I couldn't believe Eugene would have done something so momentous without dropping a hint; Three momentous weeks had passed since that morning.*

money

Money is a singular noun. The plural form *moneys* (or rarely, *monies*) is now used only in legal documents or in a context where different types of money are discussed: *the paper moneys of defunct governments.*

When sums of money are written down it is usual to avoid using figures for round numbers and use words instead, e.g. £234.75 but *two hundred pounds.* When very large sums are involved, a figure can precede the relevant word, e.g. *twenty thousand pounds* or *£20 thousand; one million dollars* or *$1 million.* Do not use both the symbol and the name of the currency. ⇒ **pound**

moonlight

In British English only, **moonlight** is used as a verb meaning 'hold a second job'. This has overtones of disreputable behaviour which is not easily understood in other English-speaking countries where holding two jobs is not seen as unusual: *Some teachers were forced to moonlight as office cleaners.*

moral, morale, morality

The adjective **moral**, and its corresponding noun **morality**, relates to the judgment that society places on the correctness of certain actions. Something *moral* is held to be right or acceptable: *We are driven to believe in an existent moral order.* The noun **moral** means the lesson in behaviour and attitude that an action, a story, or an event can provide: *The moral is: Beware of talking to strange men.*

The spirit of optimism and confidence possessed by an individual or a group, is **morale**: *All around me, I could feel morale disintegrating; Society ought to help to sustain the morale of the aged.*

mores

The word **mores** is a formal term for 'the conventions or customs of a group'. It is used in the social sciences and comes directly from Latin. The pronunciation is either /**maw**-rays/ or /**maw**-reez/.

mortar ⇒ cement

most, mostly

The meanings of **most** and **mostly** should not be confused. In a sentence like **most** was *most affected by the news*, *most* is equivalent to *very*. This use of *most* is common when the judgment involved is subjective, as in *a most interesting choice; a most effective campaign; I had the most appalling depression.* The usage is rather informal, but broadly acceptable. In a sentence like *She was mostly affected by the news*, the implication is that there was something else, in addition to the news, which affected her, although less so.

When used in comparisons, *more* applies to cases involving two people or objects, *most* to cases involving three or more: *John is the more intelligent of the two; He is the most intelligent of the students.*

movable, moveable

Both spellings are used. ⇒ **-able**

Mr, Mrs, Miss, Master, Ms

The abbreviations of these polite titles are normally written without a full stop in British English and with one in American English.

There is no set age or other factor governing the use of **Mr** as the polite title for a man. The use of **Master** as the polite title for a boy is very old-fashioned and formal.

Married women are formally addressed (using their husband's first name before the surname) as, for example, *Mrs Stephen Smith*, unless they divorce. Many women do not favour this form of address because of the way that it conceals their individuality, but only acquaintance gives a guide to the appropriate form to use.

The polite titles for women, **Mrs** and **Miss**, indicate married or unmarried status in a way that *Mr* does not. One response to this in the 1970s was the coining of the neutral form **Ms**. When the form was new it was frequently used, although it has a problematic pronunciation; both /miz/ and /muz/ are difficult. Since then, the term has been used less and is disliked by some women, who feel that the associations with feminism make the term unacceptable to them. In general, if there is no indication of a woman correspondent's status, *Ms* may be appropriate and useful, but do recognize that not all recipients favour its use. ⇒ **Esq.**

multi-

The prefix **multi-** means either 'many', as in *a multiflora rose*, or 'more than one', as in *a multinational company*. The British pronunciation is /**mul**-tea/. American speakers sometimes use the pronunciation /**mul**-tie/.

mumps

Mumps looks plural but is singular and is used with a singular verb: *...ill with the mumps; Mumps is a disease of the saliva glands.*

Muslim, Mohammedan

An adherent of Islam is referred to as a **Muslim**. This is the preferred form that believers use when they refer to themselves. The spelling *Moslem* is old-fashioned. The use of **Mohammedan** (or some variation of this spelling) for *Muslim* has a long history of previous use in English and will be found in older literature. It was never used by Muslims, and should not be used now, as it implies worship of the Prophet, which is forbidden in Islam.

must

The verb **must** may be used informally as a singular noun meaning 'necessity' if it is preceded by *a: Rubber gloves are a must if you have sensitive skin.*

mutual, reciprocal

Older usage books insisted that **mutual** had to be used with the sense of 'acting in both directions', with only two participants or groups involved in the relationship, as in *Occasionally a woman and a man reach a mutual private treaty of equality; ...a bond of mutual dependence and love.* The use of *mutual* to mean 'common' or 'shared', as in *He sent an embassy who was a mutual friend to ask me to reconsider; a world where mutual ignorance ran deep; a mutual acquaintance,* was treated as nonstandard.

Nowadays the use of *mutual* for a relationship involving more than two people with a common interest is tolerated by all but purists. This is not a major change in use; historically, *mutual* had this wider sense which later became restricted. Some of the older uses such as *a mutual child/parent* still seem rather strange. Those who want to avoid any apparent casualness in the use of *mutual* can use the phrase *common*, if no ambiguity is likely, or *in common: We shared a common goal; they had a friend in common.* Because an *agreement* or *cooperation* involves a shared decision, phrases like *mutual cooperation* are strictly tautologous.

The use of **reciprocal** (and the verb *reciprocate*) differs slightly from *mutual.* To begin with, it is a more formal word. Also, a *mutual* situation is viewed from both sides at once, but when something is *reciprocal* one party can initiate an action and the other respond later: *We felt compelled to organize some reciprocal display of strength.*

myself ⇒ **I**

N

naive, naivety, naïveté

The word **naive** means 'innocent' or 'unworldly': *Contemporary thought dismisses as naive or childish many former beliefs.* In art, *naive* is used to mean 'characteristic of the work of an artist who has not had formal art education'.

As the word has been in English for some time, it should normally have the English spelling. The French forms are no longer appropriate. The related noun has several spellings; the most natural to English is **naivety**. If you wish to use the French form, note that it is **naïveté** with both a diaeresis and an accent.

naked, nude

Both words mean 'unclothed' but the normal contexts for each differ. **Naked** is used as the more general term with the fewest overtones: *a naked baby; naked and unprotected*. It is also used in extended comparisons: *naked ambition; a naked blade; the naked sky*.

Nude is used when the unclad figure becomes the subject of aesthetic study or to mark the absence of clothing: *seven nude studies by Coldstream; nude bathing. Nude* is also used as a noun: ... *looking at the nudes on page 3*.

napalm, naphtha

Napalm, an inflammable jelly used in weapons, is pronounced /**nay**-palm/. **Naphtha**, a type of solvent, is pronounced /**naf**-the/.

napkin, serviette

The word **napkin** or *table-napkin* is regarded by many speakers as formal and rather old-fashioned. The alternative word **serviette** is in common use. However, those people who set store on such matters regard *serviette* as a genteelism and avoid using the word. ⇒ **U and non-U**

nappy

The word **nappy** or *nappie* began as an abbreviation of *napkin*, meaning 'a small towel', but is now regarded as a full word. In some English-speaking countries, however, the more formal term a *baby's napkin* is still used. In American English a *nappy* is called a *diaper* /**die**-per/.

Used of a horse, **nappy** means 'stubborn'.

native

A **native** is 'one who was born in a place' or, when used about plants and animals 'indigenous'. It is used in phrases such as *a native of Sussex* or *native plants*. *Native wit* is the intelligence that one is born with.

The word *native* was formerly in common use as a synonym for 'non-white': *The most offensive advertisements like, 'Reliable watchdogs ... Trained to bite Natives', were easy to deal with.* This use would nowadays be regarded as offensive because of the racialist and imperialist overtones of the word.

nature, nurture

These two complementary words are often used in discussions of the factors that influence a child's behaviour or learning. **Nature** includes all the inherited qualities; **nurture** includes the elements that upbringing and teaching contribute: *They talk about the balance of nature and nurture, but when it comes down to it, they're all on the side of nurture because you can interfere with that.*

naught, nought, zero

The spelling **naught** for *nothing* is archaic in current British English but it is found in older literature, as in *all your alarms will avail you naught in that hour...* . In American English, *naught* is current as a spelling for *nought*.

Some British users prefer **nought** instead of /oh/ when dictating telephone numbers; 004 606211 may be given as *nought, nought, four ...* or *double oh four ...* . **Zero** is used instead of either of the above when dictating scientific figures: *zero, zero, four ...* . The use of *ought* for *nought* is not standard English. ⇒ **zero**

nauseous, nauseated, nauseating ⇒ ill

near, nearly

The form **near** is used as an adverb, as a preposition, and as an adjective. It is therefore equally correct to say *I was near dead with fright* or *I was nearly dead with fright*.

When you want to describe something that is almost or *nearly* what it pretends to be, you can use a hyphenated form, such as *near-perfect*, *near-vacuum*, *near-white*, etc. A *near miss* (with no hyphen) is close to being a hit. The *nearside* means 'the side close to the kerb', and *near-sighted* means the same as *short-sighted*.

nearby, near by

Nearby is an adjective. Use it when you want to describe how close something is: *the nearby huts; the nearby seaside towns; a nearby lake; a nearby table*. When you want to say where something took place, use the adverbial form, which can either be two words, **near by**, or one: *They stood near by/nearby; I sat down near by/nearby*. The two-word form is older and some purists prefer it.

née

The word **née** is useful when it is necessary to indicate both a woman's maiden and married surname. As this is not a frequent need, the usage is quite formal. *Née* (or *nee*) is used before the maiden surname only: *Mrs Margaret Jones, née Smith*.

need

There are two important constructions that use *need*.

In the first construction **need** takes an *s* in the third person singular of the Simple Present (the form used with *he/she/it*). Examples are *He needs to go* and *She needs to be an exceptionally well-organized person*. *Need* is followed by the *to* form of another verb. The Simple Past form of *need* (*he needed* etc.) can also be used in this construction, as in *They needed to be near the hospital.* Questions and negatives are formed with *do: Does she need to see me?; Don't they need a hand?* In this construction, *need* resembles *want*.

The second construction is illustrated by: *He need not go* or *Need he go?* **Need** is used without an *s* together with a negative word or in a question. The verb that follows is in the base form, but not by the *to* form of the verb: *Change need not always be so abrupt; Need you stay?* The negative words include those like *barely* or *hardly* that are indirectly negative: *I need hardly tell you what a delight it would be.* The form *(he) needn't* is used as alternative way of expressing the negative: *Change needn't always be so abrupt.* In this construction, *need* resembles *must*.

There are also some special set phrases that use **need**. If you want to make a comment on what someone feels impelled to do you can use *needs must* (or *must needs*): *…the conviction that people needs must love the highest when they see it.* The phrase *(if) need be* is used only in the present or in the future: *It is much easier to part with a machine, or if need be, smash it with a hammer.* Note that this construction does not place an *s* on *need*.

negatives

A **negative** can be direct, using *no*, or indirect, using a **semi-negative** that suggests a negative meaning. Examples of a semi-negative are *hardly, barely,* and *scarcely.* When the abbreviated form of a direct negative combines with certain verbs, the shape and sound of both words alters; *will not* becomes *won't, shall not* becomes *shan't,* etc.

English normally has only one negative relating to the verb in a clause, although there are special cases when more than one negative is used. Many people find that sentences that use more than one negative construction can become difficult to understand; a phrase like *It is not unlikely that…* is not as clear as *It is probable that…* Other types of multiple negative sentences usually benefit from rewriting. ⇒ **double negative** ⇒ **never**

neither…nor

When a sentence has two nouns connected by *neither…nor*, making an alternative subject, the verb should be in the singular if both subjects are in the singular: *Neither Margaret nor John was there.* When one subject is singular and the other is plural, the verb usually agrees with the subject nearest to it: *Neither they nor Jack was able to come.* ⇒ **both**

neologism, archaism, nonce word

The vocabulary of a language is never fixed. When people have new ideas or invent new things, they create new words to discuss them. A **neologism** is a word that has been freshly coined to meet a particular need, or a new meaning given to an established word. A word that is initially regarded as a *neologism* may become accepted by use, in which case it gradually loses the feeling of novelty. Words that are no longer needed fall out of use and become **archaisms**.

An example of a *neologism* is the term *hypermarket*, which has joined the longer-established word *supermarket*. While *supermarket* was once a neologism, it could not now easily be dispensed with and the usefulness of *hypermarket* suggests that it too will remain in permanent use.

Most *slang* words are neologisms but they generally do not last long enough to become part of the regular vocabulary of the language. A word that comes into being for a specific and limited purpose is called a **nonce word**. 'Family words' such as *quoosh* for 'hot-water bottle', are *nonce words*.

nephew

The most common pronunciation of **nephew** is /**nef**-ew/ This has replaced the older pronunciation /**nev**-ew/ as the usual form.

nerve-racking

The established spelling is **nerve-racking**. ⇒ rack

never

In standard British usage, **never** is not used in combination with Simple Past tenses to mean *not: I was asleep at midnight, so I did not see* [not *never saw*] *her go.*

nevertheless, nonetheless

Both **nevertheless** and **nonetheless** are usually spelled as one word although in the past the spelling *none the less* has been used. The meaning of these words is identical, but *nevertheless* is the one more commonly used: *There could, nevertheless, be no compromise on principals.*

news

The word **news** looks plural but is used with a singular verb: *The news is bad.* This differs from *scissors, pliers,* and similar words, which are used with plural verbs. The notion that *news* is an acronym of 'north, east, west, south' is an interesting idea, but quite untrue.

nice

The adjective **nice** is generally regarded as overworked:

Her aim in life is to have a nice time, go to nice places, and meet nice people. There is nothing wrong with using *nice* but, like any word, overuse can reduce its impact. In a phrase like *Have a nice day* or *Have a nice time* it simply indicates general pleasantness. In a sentence like *It was a nice, pleasant, seaside town,* it indicates general approval. The older meaning of *nice,* 'subtle' or 'precise', has almost been lost. It survives in one or two phrases such as: *a nice distinction, a nice point,* and *a nice turn of phrase.*

nite, night

Nite is a fairly standard form for **night** in public notices in American English but it is certainly not acceptable in British English.

no

When **no** is preceded by the verb *be* and followed by a noun or an adjective, it has the same sense as *not a: Harold was no coward; Anna was no fool.*

noisome

The word **noisome** is used to describe offensive smells and other harmful items. It has nothing to do with *noise* but comes from the same stem as *annoy: ...a tube for the discharge of noisome vapours.*

nom de plume, pen name, pseudonym

Like *cul de sac,* **nom de plume** is an example of 'English' French. The French use *nom de guerre* for an adopted name used when writing. The alternative terms **pen name** and **pseudonym** mean the same as *nom de plume* and are preferable.

nomenclature

The **nomenclature** of a field of knowledge is the system

of names used to classify it: *I could not recall the scientific nomenclature.* It is pronounced /no-**men**-cla-ture/. Avoid using it as a synonym for *name*.

nominative

The grammatical term **nominative** is outmoded as a synonym for *subject* in English grammar. It still applies in Latin and other languages with a system of grammatical cases.

non- ⇒ in-

none

None and *no-one* have distinct uses. **None** is a pronoun meaning 'not any' and is often used as a fairly formal replacement for that phrase, as in *Is there any tea? No, there isn't any left,* or *No, there is none left.* When *none* is used in the construction *none of,* it is part of a quantity expression and is normally followed by a noun: *None of my books were to leave my hands,* or a pronoun such as *us* or *them: None of us occupy a place of real safety.*

It is incorrect to suppose that *none* must always be followed by a singular form of the verb, although this was once taught. The verb will be singular or plural depending on the sense of the sentence. If you are asked: *Have any of the guests arrived yet?* the answer, *No, none have arrived,* is certainly correct. The response that old-fashioned grammar expected: *No, none has arrived,* would not be idiomatic, although *Nobody has arrived* would be.

If *none* were combined with a word like *bread* or *sugar,* which cannot be counted, the following verb would have to be singular, as in *None of the bread was left.* Instead of *None of us occupy* (plural) *a place of real safety,* you could just as well say *None of us occupies* (singular) *a place of real safety,* depending whether your meaning is 'not any of us', or 'not a single one among us'. This principle also applies when *none* is not followed by *of*: *Staring into the flames of an open fire, making pictures where none exist.*

⇒ **no-one**

nonsense

Nonsense is normally used as an uncountable noun: *A lot of nonsense is talked about the temperature of wine.* The use of **nonsense** as a singular countable noun is acceptable when it means 'foolish behaviour', as in *Stop this nonsense right away*, and in the idioms *be a nonsense* and *make a nonsense of* something: *It would patently be a nonsense to put him in complete control.*

no-one, nobody

No-one is a pronoun. It may also be written **no one** without a hyphen but should never be written as one word. The equivalent of *no-one* is **nobody**, which is always written as one word. Do not confuse these two uses of the unhyphenated phrase *no one*. They are used in different constructions: *No one was in* (*nobody was in*); *No one rider was good enough to qualify* (*not a single rider was good enough*).

No-one, nobody (and *anybody*) are followed by a singular verb and traditional teaching says that they should also be referred to by a singular pronoun or a singular possessive adjective. This 'rule' is not at all helpful when the reference is to 'people in general'. *Nobody had a torch with them,* is idiomatic, while the clumsy expression: *Nobody had a torch with him or her,* is not: similarly *No-one finished their drink* is more natural than *No-one finished his or her drink.*

nor ⇒ neither

normalcy, normality, norm

The preferred form of the noun related to *normal* is **normality** in British English. The word **normalcy** has some currency in American English but should be avoided.

The noun **norm** has very specialized uses. It is often used to mean 'a required standard' in the context of industry and similar activity: *The worker who exceeded his norm or worked too hard came under threat.* In the social field it means 'the group average': *One-child families became the norm.*

Norm is often used where *normal* or *usual* would be more suitable. *Stone kitchens began to become the norm in the fourteenth century* would be more appropriately expressed as *Stone kitchens became more normal/usual in the fourteenth century.*

no sooner...than

When **no sooner** is used in a sentence it is usually found in conjunction with **than** and forms part of a comparison. The verb and subject that go with *no sooner* are inverted: *No sooner had he begun to draw than he would scratch it out.* The verb and subject that follow *than* are in the normal subject-verb order.

noted, notable, noteworthy

If someone is well known for a particular activity, then an appropriate word to describe them is **noted**: *He translated an essay on relativity by the noted French physicist, Paul Langevin.* If someone or something has attracted exceptional attention, she, he, or it is **notable**: *Other people's wives and servants played a notable part in this celebrated trial; He bought a book on the notable churches of France; There seems to have been a notable lack of campaigning activity. Notable may be used as a noun, but* this usage is rare and rather literary in tone: ...*a dinner for sixty notables.*

The word **noteworthy** has a similar meaning to *notable* but is much less common and has literary overtones. It is used to describe things and events rather than people: *It was noteworthy that the Count was the only person who did not seem to care.* ⇒ **notorious** ⇒ **noticeable**

nothing, nothing but

Nothing is singular and takes a singular verb in normal usage, as in *Nothing was on the shelf.* Sentences that have the correct singular form of the verb can often sound awkward when a plural noun comes between *nothing* and its verb, as in *Nothing but children's voices was heard.* In informal speech, a more natural sounding plural verb is often used in such sentences: *Nothing but books were on the shelf,* but this is not standard English. One solution is to rewrite the sentence, for example: *Nothing was heard but children's voices....*

The set expression **nothing but** means 'nothing other than': *As the end of the month approached, I was eating nothing but Quark; It's nothing but a mockery, you know.*

nothing less than

The set expression **nothing less than** has two possible meanings. One is a form of emphatic statement and is equivalent to *nothing short of*: *The invention of micro-electronics has been nothing less than a technological explosion.* The other sense is more literal and means 'this much and no less' and is equivalent to *no less than*: *The present moment is nothing less than the second great divide in human history.*

nothing like as

The expression **nothing like as** is informal. Use *not near-*

ly in formal contexts: *'Nothing like as bad/Not nearly as bad'*, he said.

noticeable, notable

If something attracts notice, it may be *noticeable* but it may not necessarily be *notable*. Something **noticeable** can be quite unimportant, as in *a noticeable increase in mildew on the walls*. A **notable** event is always one that is beyond our normal expectations. ⇒ **noted**

not only...but also

This construction needs care if it is to mean what is intended. The words **not only** should be followed by the first set of items that you wish to compare, the words **but also** by the second set: *Not only my family but also thousands of other families.* If one verb refers to both parts of the comparison, it is placed outside it: *Not only my family but also thousands of other families were affected by the famine.* If there is a verb within the first part of the comparison, there must be a verb within the second part: *Not only is this happening in the advanced industries but it is also affecting the low technology industries.*

Note carefully the inverted order of the verb and the subject when *not only* begins the sentence: *Not only do insects rob man; Not only had he checked the facts...; Not only can such wonders be brought to reality.*

notorious, notoriety, infamous

A person who is **notorious** or **infamous** is well known for some disgraceful reason. It is generally accepted that the word can only be used of people.

The associated noun is **notoriety**: *These activists acquired notoriety for their approval of bombing as a political weapon.* The noun *infamy* is equivalent to *notoriety*. ⇒ **famous**

not that, not but what

The phrase **not that** is used mostly at the beginning of sentences. It means 'but it is not to be supposed that', as in *It is what I would call a bribe. Not that any real harm can be done*, or in *It was the most impressive event of the festival. Not that they performed in a polished way.* While *not that* is acceptable, the similar phrase **not but what** has fallen out of general use, except in some dialects of English. It is not a new construction, but it now sounds incorrect. The use of the phrase **not but** for *not that* is definitely nonstandard.

not…too

This construction, as in *I'm not feeling too well*, is very informal and is not standard usage, although it usefully allows speakers to understate their feelings. Use *very* instead of *too* for a more formal statement: *I'm not feeling very well* (even more formal usage would omit *very*).

nought ⇒ **naught**

noxious, obnoxious

The word *noxious* is often confused with *obnoxious*. A **noxious** substance is poisonous or otherwise harmful to life: *Butterflies mimic leaves or even noxious creatures to deceive their predators; noxious gases like hydrogen sulphide.* Something, or by extension someone, **obnoxious** is very unpleasant: *The carcasses gave off a most obnoxious smell that could be detected miles away.* The smell in question may be unpleasant, but it is not necessarily harmful. ⇒ **noisome**

nth

The word **nth** is used for an unspecified number, usually the final one of a series. The term comes from mathematics but may be used informally to mean one of a seemingly unending series: *I sat there dutifully clapping the nth boy on his way to the podium to collect his school prize.* The pronunciation is /enth/.

nubile

The basic meaning of **nubile** is 'of marriageable age' but a second meaning 'young and sexually desirable' has now become so common that it is overtaking the first meaning: *He fantasized about happiness with some nubile Hollywood actress.*

number

The word **number** takes a plural verb when it means 'a quantity or group': *A number of units were constructed and marketed; A considerable number were included in the sculpture exhibition.* When it refers to a sum or a figure, as in *a million is a number which gets flung around more and more today,* it takes a singular verb.

In counting or measurement, a *number* is the quantity represented by any combination of the numerals 0 to 9. ⇒ numeral

numeral

A **numeral** is a symbol that can be used to represent a number. The modern world uses the numerals 0 to 9 in everyday activities that involve counting. In Britain, the Roman numerals I, V, X, C, M, etc. are still sometimes found in dates, on the title pages of books and in the credits of films. ⇒ number ⇒ billion

nutritional, nutritive, nutritious

All these words are used in the context of food. The adjectives **nutritional** and **nutritive** are used in scientific contexts. They mean 'relating to the process of nourishment': *nutritional experts; nutritional science; nutritive values; the nutritive qualities of sorghum.* **Nutritional** is the word used most often with this sense.

The adjective **nutritious** is a more informal word meaning 'nourishing' and is used either before the noun it modifies, as in *a nutritious meal*, or after a linking verb: *You will find that these berries are extremely nutritious; Swedes are more nutritious than turnips.*

O

O, oh

The interjection **oh** has an older, literary spelling **O**, which is no longer used.

-o, -oes

Some English words that have an **-o** ending have a plural form in **-os**, others have an **-oes** plural. There are a few words that can be written with either ending. The list includes: *buffalo, cargo, flamingo, fresco, ghetto, innuendo, mango, manifesto, memento, mosquito, motto, salvo, stiletto, tornado, volcano.*

oath

The pronunciation of the plural form of **oath**, *oaths* rhymes with 'clothes' /ohthz/. The pronunciation /ohths/ is sometimes heard but it is not standard.

object, subject

In study and research, the topic of your studies is known as the **subject**. The aim of your study, what you hope that it will prove, is your **object**. These are often confused.

objective, subjective

Subjective and *objective* are both used to describe someone's attitude towards an event or to an aspect of behaviour. If someone is **subjective** they judge the relevance of an event by the effect that it has on their own situation: *...a twilight realm of subjective imaginings. Statements about beauty are merely subjective.* A person who is acting *subjectively* may respond to a situation without reference to any outside considerations. If someone is **objective**, they attempt to stand back and form a judgment without letting their own emotions and interests interfere: *It is not easy to be objective about one's own child.*

oblige, obligate

When you **oblige** someone, you carry out a service that gives them reason to feel gratitude towards you: *You know I would do a great deal to oblige you.* Oblige is also used in a command or as a euphemistic replacement for *force* or *make*: *We must thus oblige you to talk; Don't oblige me to call the usher and lodge a complaint.*

Oblige is frequently used in the passive voice to mean 'have to' with overtones of a duty imposed on one or of unwillingness: *Everyone over twelve was obliged to do two hours of work each week.*

Another way of suggesting that you have a binding duty towards someone is to say that you are **obligated** *to(wards)* them, or *under an obligation. Obliged,* or an expression using the noun *obligation,* can often express the meaning more naturally: *We are under no obligation to give him what he wants; I feel I have an obligation to his father.*

oblivious, oblivion

Oblivious means 'unaware' or 'forgetful'. In standard British English *oblivious* is followed by *of*: *He is oblivious of his surroundings*. The use of *to* after *oblivious* is non-standard but is becoming more frequent.

obnoxious ⇒ noxious

observance, observation

The word **observance** is used for the following or marking of a religious occasion: *Moral values were supposed to be inculcated by religious observances and compulsory games*. It should not be confused with **observation**, which means 'watching' or 'noticing' and comes from a different meaning of the verb *observe*: *...Rothermere's observation of the comet; The drawings contained exquisite details of observation and execution.*

An **observation** is also a comment: *I don't mean this as a criticism, just an observation.*

obsolete, obsolescent

An item that has outlived its usefulness and is no longer capable of efficiently performing the task for which it was designed is **obsolete**.

When an item is in the process of becoming *obsolete*, it is described as **obsolescent**: *Planners must allow for plant which becomes obsolescent, for example by being overtaken by new techniques.*

obviate

If you **obviate** an event, you prevent it happening by anticipating it and taking suitable steps: *A central form of leadership would obviate endless procedural delays. Obviate* is not used with the sense of stopping or finishing an action that has already started.

occasion

When **occasion** means 'reason' or 'motive' it is followed by *to* or *for*: *A month or so later we had occasion to recall our pleasant chat; Summer was an occasion for drifting walks and idle picnics*. When it means 'opportunity', it is followed by *to*: *I would not have thought that he had much occasion to meet brilliant people*. When it is used for 'the time that something happens', it is followed by *of*: *We saw this kind of affection revealed on the occasion of Lumumba's homecoming*. This word is frequently misspelled. Note that it contains *c* twice and *s* once.

occupant, occupier

In British English the words **occupant** and **occupier** are both used for someone who has the legal right to occupy a building or who possesses a piece of land. In American English only the word *occupant* has this legal sense; an *occupier* is merely someone who occupies a place.

occur, happen

In careful English, **occur** and **happen** are not used of prearranged events: *The accident happened* (or *occurred*) *last night*, but: *The wedding took place in the afternoon*.

octopus

The normal English plural of **octopus** is *octopuses*. The form *octopi* is a joke form. The formal scientific plural is *octopodes*.

odd

Odd can be added to a round number to indicate that it is only an approximate number. It is only added to multiples of ten, e.g. *50 odd* but never [*55 odd*]: *It's a long time ago, 40 odd years*. If it forms a compound adjective, *odd* should be linked to the number with a hyphen: *50-odd students*. The usage is informal.

odour, odious, odorous

Something **odious** is detestable. An **odour** is a smell of any kind but not a strong one. The word **odorous** is used to describe the general presence of a smell: *...the sweetly odorous premises of big department stores; ...the daytime air was odorous with petrol fumes.* The American spelling is *odor*.

The familiar set expression *in good/bad odour* makes no allusion to smell and means 'in/out of favour' with someone: *I'm not in very good odour with the chief these days.*

-oe-, -ae-, -e-

Words that in British English are spelled with -oe- and -ae- are increasingly being replaced by -e- especially in American English, e.g. *mediaeval/medieval.* ⇒ **digraph**

of

When two nouns are linked by **of**, it is generally supposed that the connection is one of possession. It is, however, more correct to say that it indicates a close relationship, as in *the mother of the twins*, or a location, as in *the top of the bottle*. (Note that this is not exactly the same thing as a *bottle-top*.) In this construction, if the first noun is indefinite and the second noun is definite and refers to a person, it can have the *'s* possessive form added to it, e.g. *A friend of my sister* can also be written as: *a friend of my sister's*.

If the relationship between a person and a thing is one of possession, then this is normally shown by the use of the *'s* possessive form with the first noun: *the boy's scarf.* This cannot be expressed by using *of*.

off

The preposition **off** is pronounced nowadays with an *o*

sound that rhymes with 'hot'. An older pronunciation that is still used by a number of speakers is /awf/. The latter pronunciation is sometimes regarded as a mark of real or assumed upper-class speech.

In standard usage, *off* is not followed by *from* or *of*: *Debbie got off* [not *off of*] *the bus; It took the pressure off* [not *off of*] *her.*

Careful writers also avoid using *off* in the place of *from*: *They bought some milk from* [rather than *off*] *the farmer.* ⇒ **often** ⇒ **RP**

off-

Words formed by the addition of **off-** as a prefix are normally written with a hyphen, e.g. *off-course; off-air; off-duty.*

officious, efficient

An **officious** person interferes in the usual course of an event in order to impose their own will: *...officious interference by managerial groups; Linda Snell is an officious busybody in a radio serial.* Someone who is **efficient** organizes the running of events in the best manner possible.

often

The modern pronunciation of **often** has a silent *t* and the vowel *o* rhymes with 'hot': /**off**-en/. The pronunciation /**off**-ten/ is heard less commonly, although some speakers use both forms at different times. An older pronunciation that is still used by a number of speakers is /**aw**fen/. ⇒ **off** ⇒ **RP**

olden, olde

Olden is an archaic form of *old* and is only used in certain set phrases, such as *olden days; olden times.*

The spelling **olde** is only found in commercial use where the user is trying to evoke an old-fashioned atmosphere.

older ⇒ **elder**

on, onto, on to

On, as a preposition, and **onto** are largely interchangeable, except that it is possible to use *onto* to convey the sense of movement towards something. *He jumped on the spot* suggests that he was already standing there and jumped up and down, while *He jumped onto the spot* indicates a movement from one point to another.

On to is written as two words when *on* is part of the verb. For example, contrast the construction using *pass on*: *We passed on to a small pantry*, to that with *jump*: *He jumped onto the rear platform of the bus.*

on, upon

The only distinction between **on** and **upon** is one of formality. *Upon* is a more formal and literary term. If you need to state that something is both *up* high and *on* another object, write *up on* as two words.

one

When the pronoun **one** is used as an impersonal or general pronoun, as in *One might think one would be unwise to say that*, the third-person pronoun *he* or *she* should not be substituted for it at a later point, as in *One might think he would be unwise to say that.* This is not unusual in American English, but it is a point of style that is avoided in British English because of possible ambiguity. In the sentence given, the pronoun *he* could refer either to the same person as *one*, or to some other person.

Many British users have a mild prejudice against the use of the pronoun *one* when it is used by a speaker concerning the speaker, as in *One must be careful what one eats with this new diet.* The style is seen as pretentious or as a mark of real or assumed 'upper-class' speech. British English often substitutes an impersonal *you* in situations where *one* could as well be used: *One has to be careful at this crossing/You have to be careful at this crossing.*

ones

Avoid the use of **ones** directly after *these* and *those* or after possessives. An acceptable response to *I see you have new shoes* is *What, these?* It is not necessary to say *these ones* because *these* (or *those*) can stand on its own.

Similarly, instead of saying *my one(s)* or *our one(s)*, the possessive *mine* or *ours* is sufficient: *It wasn't much of a garden. Not like ours* [not *our one*]. In the following sentence, the clumsy expression *the ones* could be replaced by *those*: *I saw them all; the ones* [use *those* instead] *I had really seen and the ones* [use *those* instead] *I had imagined.*

ongoing

The use of **ongoing** as an adjective is regarded by many people as a mark of careless writing. It can always be omitted, or replaced by *developing, continuing,* or *current.*

only

In informal English, **only** is often used as a sentence connector: *It would have been possible, only he was not present at the time.* This use is avoided in formal contexts, where it is preferable to write: *It would have been possible, except that* (or use *but* instead of *except that*) *he was not present at the time.* Another alternative is *It would have been possible had he been present.*

In formal speech and writing, *only* is placed directly before the word or words that it modifies: *She could interview only three applicants in the morning.* In informal contexts, however, it is generally regarded as acceptable to put *only* before the verb: *She could only interview three applicants in the morning.*

Care must be taken not to create ambiguity, especially in written English, in which intonation will not help to show to which item in the sentence *only* applies. Sentences that are capable of two interpretations are better rephrased. A sentence such as: *She can only talk to you this afternoon,* can be rewritten either as: *She can talk to you only in the afternoon* (i.e. at no other time), or as *She can talk to you, and no-one else, this afternoon.*

onward, onwards

Onward can be used as an adjective, as in *the onward march of intellect,* and as an adverb, as in *I must go onward.* The word **onwards** is an alternative form of the adverb only: *He might have gone onwards; We are being carried onwards.*

op. cit.

Op. cit. is an abbreviation for the Latin *opere citato,* meaning 'in the work mentioned'. It is used to refer a reader to the details of a book that has already been quoted: *Greely (p93 op. cit.) has stated that....* This is no longer a common style of reference in modern works.
⇒ **ibid**

operative, operator

The word **operative** is rather formal and, in the context of work, is generally reserved for someone who has a special skill: *The Council's concern is for training operatives, craftsmen, and technicians.* An **operator**, by contrast, is anyone who operates a machine or instrument: *Outside phone calls can be made through the operator.*

A very specialized use of *operative*, as 'spy' or 'secret agent', has become familiar through popular spy stories: *He might have been a KGB operative who went sour on them.*

opposite

When **opposite** is used as an adjective it is followed, when necessary, by the preposition *to*. For example, if a sentence such as *He stood at the opposite end* or *Paul turned and walked in the opposite direction* carries on and provides information about what is opposite, it becomes *He stood at the opposite end to Max* or *Paul turned and walked in the opposite direction to his partner*. Be careful not to confuse this with the noun usage.

When *opposite* is used as a noun, it is followed, when necessary, by the preposition *of*: *This had the effect of bringing about the opposite of what the Prime Minister wanted; …the opposite of the truth; …the opposite of each other.* The accepted pronunciation in British English has the last vowel rhyme with 'sit' not 'sight', /o-po-zit/. ⇒ **contrary**

optician, optometrist, oculist, ophthalmologist

There are a number of highly specialized occupations concerned with the care of eyes. An **ophthalmologist**, formerly called an **oculist**, is a medical practitioner whose speciality is in the diseases and malfunctions of the eye.

The word **optician** is a general term for someone who supplies spectacles and contact lenses. There are two kinds of optician, the **optometrist** or ophthalmic optician, who is qualified to examine the eye and prescribe lenses, and the dispensing optician, who is qualified to supply and fit lenses but not to prescribe them.

opus, opera

Do not use the word *opus* to describe the work of a writer, as in *his recent opus on Shakespeare.* Unless it is meant as a joke, it is pompous. **Opus** (abbreviated to *Op.*) is correctly used when referring to the catalogued works of a musician: *The quiet and profound Haydn of Op. 20 No. 1.* The plural *opuses* is used in this context, because the Latin plural form **opera** means a music drama.

or, nor

If all the items linked by **or** (or **nor**) are singular, the verb that they govern is also singular: *If a rat or fox enters, the alarm will sound.* If all the items linked by *or* are plural, the verb that they govern is also plural: *They try to determine, day by day, what is most important in the world and what decisions or events have the greatest consequence.*

However, if all the items linked by **or** (or **nor**) are a mixture of singular and plural, the verb that they govern usually agrees with the number of the nearest noun just to make it sound more natural, e.g. *If rats or a fox enters, the alarm will sound;* or *If a fox or rats enter, the alarm will sound.* It may be better to rewrite sentences like these, e.g. *If a fox enters, or some rats, the alarm will sound.*

-or, -er

The suffix **-or**, meaning 'one who …', or 'that which …', is found with a number of nouns, but it is not the normal agent suffix, which is **-er**. The *-or* suffix is generally used with words borrowed from foreign languages, e.g. *author, creator.*

Another useful distinction is sometimes made between

-er, used to refer to a person (*conveyer*), and *-or*, used to refer to a thing (*conveyor*).

oral ⇒ **aural**

ordinance, ordnance

An **ordinance** is a rule or regulation set out by an authority, such as the government or the church. **Ordnance** is a collective term for heavy artillery weapons, and also for munitions and other military supplies. The word is most commonly used outside the Army as part of the title of the *Ordnance Survey*, the official UK map-makers.

other than, but

Two constructions that are used to express an exception are commonly confused. One uses *other than*, and the other one uses *but*: *She did not see that it could be other than an embarrassing relationship; She did not see that it could be anything but an embarrassing relationship.* Avoid mixing the two and using *other* with *but*.

otherwise

Use of the phrase *or otherwise* or *and otherwise*, as in *a slow trend to freedom, political and otherwise*, is disliked by some people. They say that since *otherwise* is an adverb it cannot be linked by *and/or* to adjectives or nouns.

On the other hand, examples of good current usage show that *otherwise* is often used to refer to some alternative to the preceding word: *It had no effect on its users, beneficial or otherwise; ...the legitimacy or otherwise of any political authority.* Those who object to this phrase could rewrite the sentence, e.g. *It had no beneficial or other effect on its users; ...the legitimacy of any political authority or its absence.*

ought to

In standard English, **ought to** is not used with *did* or *had* as auxiliary verbs. The use of one of these auxiliaries with *ought to* is the mark of a regional variety of English.

Ought to has no past forms of its own and is mainly used to refer to the present and the future. The standard usage is: *I ought to do it*. This becomes negative with the addition of *not* or *n't*: *I ought not to do it* or *I oughtn't to do it* [not *I didn't ought to do it*].

If you want to express your present regret for something in the past that you have done (or not done), *ought to* comes before the verb form *have* and a past participle: *I ought (not) to have done it* [not *I had(n't) ought to have done it*].

ought to, should

Both **ought to** and **should** are used to suggest that an obligation exists. As a broad guideline, if it is a formal obligation, use *should*: *You really should write to your father. He's been expecting a letter.* If it is more a matter of general advice, use *ought to*: *I think you ought to go to the library and see if there are some books on this.* Neither is as strong as *must*. Some users feel that the use of *ought to* in questions sounds awkward. Such questions can be rephrased using *should* without a loss of meaning: *Ought you to go to the library?* becomes *Should you go to the library?*

-our, -or

The British spelling of words like *colour* that end in -our is replaced in American English by the form -or.

ours

Ours is a possessive pronoun. Like *yours, hers, its,* and *theirs,* it does not have an apostrophe before the *s.*

out-

When **out-** is used as a prefix it can have one of four different meanings. It can mean 'better than in some way': *outclass, outgun, outperform;* 'located away from the centre': *outpatient, outpost, outrider;* 'something that emerges': *outcrop, outgrowth;* or it can indicate the result of an action: *outcome.* In all cases there is no hyphen between the two parts of the word.

outdoor, outdoors

Outdoor is an adjective; it is used together with a noun: *an outdoor lavatory; an outdoor theatre; the outdoor world.*

Outdoors is an adverb. The phrase *out of doors* can be used instead of *outdoors: It is safe to let them go outdoors; Only sporting dogs should be kept out of doors/outdoors in a kennel.* Less often, *outdoors* can be found used as a noun: *I just loved being in the great outdoors.*

outright

Outright is often overused as an adjective. It means 'open' or 'direct' but in many cases it adds no further information to the sentence and can just as well be left out, as in *It was an outright refusal; It was a refusal.* When *outright* is used as an adverb it retains more of its basic meaning, 'completely': *The government has banned it outright.* In the phrase *He was killed outright,* it means the same as *right away.*

outside, inside

The prepositions **outside** and **inside** are not followed by *of* in standard English: *She waited for Lenny outside* [not *outside of*] *the school.* ⇒ **off**

overall

The precise use of **overall** is in describing the measurement between two extremities. In this use *overall* can follow the dimension: *The beast had a length overall* [or *an overall length*] *of 2 metres.* It is considerably overused with the looser sense of *total, complete,* or *general.* It is often advisable to leave it out as it adds no further information to the sentence: *the (overall) effect is the same; higher (overall/total) food production; a 10% (overall) increase in applications.*

overflow

The Simple Past tense and the past participle of **overflow** is *overflowed.* The form *overflown* is no longer used, probably because this form is also used as the past participle of *overfly.*

oversee, overlook, oversight, overview

When someone is asked to **oversee** a project, they are being asked to control and regulate it: *She was supposed to oversee our homework; Phyllis was overseeing the weighing.*

The verb **overlook** has a rather different meaning. It can be used with the sense of *have a view over* something, if the verb has an inanimate subject. For example, *a house* can *overlook the harbour.*

When the subject is human, **overlook** has two conflicting meanings. One is 'deliberately ignore something', as in *I'm constantly trying to overlook her bad behaviour,* the second is 'accidentally fail to notice something': *I noticed something you overlooked.*

A less ambiguous word is the noun **oversight.** An *oversight* is an accidental failure to notice something: *She seemed to realize her oversight at once.*

The noun **overview** is not in common use. It means much the same as a *review* or *survey: A short report giv-*

ing a useful overview of some recent developments. It is not in standard use as a verb.

overtone

In this book we refer to the **overtones** of a word and its meaning. Most words are capable of being interpreted in a way that it is sometimes difficult to be precise about because there are considerations that subtly alter our understanding of them. For example, the words *house* and *home* have a similar meaning, but the *overtones* of the word *home* include thoughts of ownership, family, and privacy that are missing in the word *house*.

owing to

The phrase **owing to** is a two-word (or compound) preposition. Avoid the long-winded expression *owing to the fact that*. It is just a longer way of saying *because*, *since*, or *as*, all of which have more impact. A much discussed usage problem concerns the appropriate uses of *owing to* and the very similar expression *due to*.
⇒ **due to**

Oxbridge, redbrick

The word **Oxbridge** is sometimes used to refer to the Universities of Oxford and Cambridge. It is often used to signify intellectual eminence but also privilege and exclusivity.

A common contrast to Oxbridge is **redbrick**, which is used to describe the later University foundations. The most modern recent universities are sometimes called *plateglass universities*. While the reference is to the building materials, the overtones suggest middle-class or utilitarian values in contrast to the presumed intellectual aristocracy of the older places. It should not be thought that redbrick universities contain no stone, or

Oxbridge no bricks or concrete.

In American English, the term *ivy league* is used to denote the group of older American universities (simply, those with old ivy-clad buildings) which are thought to provide an element of intellectual or social cachet to those who attend them.

P

pace

The word *pace* is the Latin equivalent of the phrase *with all due respect to*. It is usually used before someone's name when you are about to disagree with them, so it shows only mock respect: *They are more successful in an atmosphere of economic expansion than they are (pace Sir Geoffrey Howe) if the economy is squeezed.* The English phrase is preferable. *Pace* is pronounced /**pay**-see/ or less commonly, /**part**-chay/, but it is so formal that it is rarely used outside writing.

pair

Like other collective nouns, **pair** takes a singular verb when it is seen as a unit: *A pair of shoes was gratefully received*, and a plural verb when it is seen as a collection: *That pair* (the two of them) *are on very good terms with each other.* ⇒ **couple**

pale, beyond the pale, pail

A fence has *palings* or *pales*, that is, narrow strips of

wood. Someone to whom the expression *beyond the pale* applies is outside social limits, literally 'outside the barrier'. It has no connection with the adjective **pale** meaning 'a light shade of some specific colour'.

None of these should be confused in their spelling with **pail**, a wooden or metal bucket.

pan-

The prefix **pan-** is added to adjectives, particularly those derived from place names, to form words that have the sense 'comprising all' or 'relating to all': *pandemic, Pan-American*.

panacea

A **panacea** was a supposed cure for all ills: *He reminded them that a multiparty democracy was not a panacea for the state's ills*. It does not mean a cure for an individual problem. Phrases like *a universal panacea* are tautologous. ⇒ **tautology**

pandit, pundit, guru

Pandit and *pundit* are different English spellings of the same Hindi word. In practice, **pandit** is used as a title honouring someone who is learned in some aspect of Hindu religion, law, or philosophy, as in *Pandit Nehru*. The spelling **pundit** has gained mocking overtones in British English and is used for someone who is a self-appointed authority, real or imagined, about any aspect of life. Another Indian word, **guru,** has been adopted into British English for someone who is regarded as a teacher and a respected authority on some subject: *John Orr was our guru at Edinburgh*.

para-

There are two prefixes spelled **para-**. One is used to add the sense 'beyond' or 'outside', as in *paranormal*, *paramedical.* The other is used to add the sense 'a protection against': *parachute* (protection against a fall), *parasol* (protection against the sun).

parable, allegory

Both words mean 'a story that is told to illustrate a moral or ethical point'. A **parable** is such a story told for the purpose of religious teaching; the overtones of the word are strongly Christian. **Allegory** does not have these overtones and can be used for any type of illustrative tale or symbol in which characters take on a wider significance: *Few Spanish paintings present so intricate an allegory, but the majority have hidden meanings.*

paradox, parody

A **paradox** is a situation or a statement that appears to contradict itself, yet is or may be true: *The paradox is that the banned writers did not disappear with their deaths. They are more alive now than many who are living today.* A **parody** is a story, poem, or piece of music that makes fun of an existing more serious work. It is a form of implied criticism, though usually good-humoured: *a careful and loving Raymond Chandler parody.* When *parody* is extended to refer to someone's actions, it often means a cruel copy: *My face twisted into the parody of a smile; a parody of democracy.*

parallel

Parallel is most often used as an adjective, as in *parallel bars, parallel walls,* but it can also be used as a noun. If so, it is frequently used in the plural: *There are curious parallels between medicine and law.* Both the adjective and noun uses are followed by *between, to,* or *with:* ... *despite obvious parallels to his art; There are clear parallels with the birth of the SDP.*

parameter, perimeter
The **parameters** of a situation, in informal usage, are the circumstances that restrict an undertaking: *Two new parameters must enter the design process*. This use is often objected to by purists. In more technical contexts, a *parameter* is a mathematical constant. The **perimeter** in mathematics is the curve or line that encloses a plane area. The word is informally used to mean 'boundary': *Our way was blocked by the perimeter fence*.

paraphrase ⇒ precis

pardon
A number of social issues influence the choice of forms of apology. *Pardon me* is often regarded as a genteelism by numbers of speakers. It is perfectly acceptable to ask: *What did you say?*

parenthesis ⇒ punctuation

parenting
Parenting is a recent term that means 'the bringing up of a child by a parent': *It is an inescapable fact that children need parenting by both men and women*. It is still classed as jargon by some people.

park
Although the use of the noun **park** to mean 'a parking space' has become quite common, it is not standard usage.

part, portion
The word **part** has a very wide range of reference. It is often used to signify a division, section, or constituent element of something without any reference to its size or importance. A **portion** is a part of something but it usually means either 'a selected part': *He tore it in half and*

slid the lower portion across the counter, or '*a measured part*': *She spooned a second portion of potato onto his plate.*

particular, particularly

Particular is often redundant in phrases such as: *our (particular) station; this (particular) situation;* it adds nothing to the meaning. It is useful to reserve *particular* for what is significant or special: *At this time, a mother should take particular care of herself.* The use of *particular* to mean 'fussy' is generally followed by *about: He was very particular about his appearance.* Note that in speech, the adverb **particularly** should be given five syllables; it is pronounced /par-**tic**-u-lar-ly/.

partly, partially, partial

There is considerable overlap between the use of *partly* and *partially*, which both mean 'in part'. A useful difference does exist, however. **Partly** can be used with the sense of 'only in part' while **partially** can be used to mean 'not fully'. It is therefore possible to use *partly* (but not *partially*) in expressions that divide something: *The reason for this effect lies partly in the physiology of the seeds and partly in the circumstances in which they took root.*

The adjective **partial** is used to describe something that is only partly complete, but it has another sense, that of 'taking someone's part'. A *partial judge* is biased in favour of one person. By extension, the informal expression *be partial to,* as in *I'm rather partial to Black Forest gateau,* means 'have a liking for' something. This expression is regarded as a vulgarism by many speakers.

party

The word **party** meaning *person* is found in legal contexts. Its use outside these contexts in expressions like *the party next door* for 'the person next door' is very informal. Many people regard it as a vulgarism.

pass, past, passed

The Simple Past tense and the past participle of **pass** is **passed**: *The vicar passed along the line of communicants; He had passed a telephone box on his way.* Unlike most other past participles, *passed* is not used as an adjective. The adjective form is **past**. It can be used before or immediately after a noun, as in *the past few years; times past,* or after a linking verb like *is/was*: *Those days are past.*

Past is also used as a preposition meaning 'beyond', as in *They walked along the sand past the bathing-pool,* and as an adverb meaning 'by': *Traffic was roaring past.* Past is also used as a noun: *Why study life in the past?*

pass on, pass away, pass over

All three expressions are euphemisms for **die**. *Die* is generally preferable, especially in formal writing.

passerby

The plural of **passerby** is *passersby*. It follows the pattern of *mothers-in-law*, not that of *spoonfuls*, in placing the plural *s*.

passive voice

For some reason American writers on style and grammar tend to discourage the use of the **passive voice** in all types of writing. This is rather curious. The passive has a useful function in expressive writing. Like any other stylistic device, it is only overuse that makes it a fault.

patent

The pronunciation /pat-nt/ is heard in *letters patent* and

Patent Office and is the usual pronunciation in American English for all senses. In British English /**payt**-nt/ is commoner and is regularly used in collocations like *patent leather*.

pathos, bathos

These are both literary terms, although *pathos* is in more common use. **Pathos** (from which comes the adjective *pathetic*) is the power that certain passages of writing or speech have to call forth pity and sympathy. The term **bathos**, and its adjective form *bathetic*, is less common. It involves a fall to the ridiculous in a situation.

patricide, parricide

Patricide is both the act of killing one's father and the term for anyone who kills their father. **Parricide** is the act of killing either one of one's parents or the term for someone who does so.

patriot, patriotic

The first vowel in **patriot** and **patriotic** rhymes with 'fat' in British English and with 'fate' in American English.

patron, patronize, patronage

Patron and words derived from it are ambiguous. A **patron** is someone who supports the arts, either with money or by protecting artistic endeavour: *Leonardo found a patron in Duke Lorenzo, who arranged for him to work in San Marco.* This protective element is present in *patron saint.* In commerce a *patron* is a regular customer: *He apparently knew how much I was spending as a patron.* If you **patronize** someone, you give them your custom. **Patronage** is the support that a patron gives to a client, or the favours handed out by someone who is in an influential position: *For 11 years the Mayor* *has dispensed bread, circuses and other, more modern, forms of patronage to the mainly black population of the nation's capital.*

An alternative sense of *patronize* is 'act in a superior manner' to someone and treat them with condescension: *Her manner, while tailored to the plain man, was never patronizing. Patronage* in this sense is a condescending attitude towards another person.

pay attention, notice

The construction used with **pay** is *pay attention to*, but the construction used with **notice** is *take notice of*. Be careful not to mix these. The expression [*don't pay any notice*] is not idiomatic in standard English.

peaceable, peaceful

A situation can be **peaceful** or **peaceable**. Both words mean 'calm' and 'tranquil'. However, *peaceable* has a further meaning, the sense of 'inclined to peace', 'quietly behaved', which is not used about a situation but about people and behaviour: *I was known to be a peaceable and studious young man.*

pedal, peddle

These spellings can be confused. You **pedal** a cycle. Cheap goods, drugs, and by extension, gossip and propaganda are **peddled**.

pedlar, peddler

These are variant spellings of the same word, but in British English a distinction is often made. A **pedlar** is an itinerant salesman. A **peddler** is someone who has illegal drugs for sale. In American English *peddler* serves for both.

pejorative

The word **pejorative** is used about the overtones of words and means 'having an unfavourable or unpleasant significance': *...a country where hospitality is so rare that 'landlady' is a pejorative word. Pejorative is normally pronounced /pi-**jorr**-it-iv/ but the less standard pronunciation /**pee**-jirr-it-iv/ can also be heard. It is a very formal word.

pence, pennies, p

Since the decimalization of British currency the abbreviation **p**, pronounced /pee/, has replaced **pence** in speech as well as in writing, as in *10p, 85p*, etc. Some speakers dislike this and prefer the full form, *pence*. The full spoken and written form of *1p, 2p*, etc. is, strictly, *one penny, two pence* not /wun pee/, /two pee/. The abbreviated forms common with the old currency *tuppence, tuppenny, threepence, threepenny*, etc. have not been commonly retained. The plural form indicating an indefinite number of coins is *pennies: I put a few pennies in the charity box*.

pendant, pendent

A necklace with a hanging ornament is a **pendant**, as is a hanging light, such as a chandelier. The word **pendent** is rather rare and simply means 'dangling' or 'jutting'.

peninsula, peninsular

The noun is spelled **peninsula**: *...a small peninsula perhaps three hundred yards in length*. **Peninsular** is an adjective: *the Peninsular War*.

people ⇒ person

per, per capita, per se

The Latin preposition **per** originally meant *by* and then *for every/each*. It has a long history of use in commercial

English but is now considered old-fashioned. It is generally used in the same way as *each* or *a*, as in £5 *per week*/£5 *each week*; £2.50 *per head*/ £2.50 *a head*.

The expression **per capita** nowadays means 'for every person' (although *capita* is plural in Latin) and can also be used as a modifier that comes in front of a noun, as in *Per capita incomes have grown*. This is in addition to constructions like *income per capita*.

Per se is a formal way to say *in itself* or *as such*. You can use it to talk about something in the abstract or from a general point of view, without considering how it works in practice, as in *Most people know little about the educational process per se*. You can also use it to discuss the intrinsic value of something: *Anything socially practical is good per se*. In general, avoid using *per se* when you can use the equivalent English expressions. ⇒ **intrinsic**

per cent, percentage, proportion

The abbreviation **per cent** is written as two words in British English and does not need a full stop. Avoid the use of *per cent* in comments where no accuracy is involved; it should always follow a numeral, as in *34 per cent*. The word **percentage** can acceptably be used to mean 'a proportion' but it needs an accompanying quantity word, like *large* or *small*: *A large percentage of his time was taken up in administration*. Similarly, **proportion** should only be used to mean 'a part' with a quantity word, because the word *proportion* implies a comparison of parts. Note, too, that an expression like *a large*/*small percentage of* something can often be more simply expressed as *most* or *a few*.

perceptible, perceptive, percipient

Something that is **perceptible** can be perceived or seen.

It is often used when something is at the limits of what can be seen without any special aids: *There was a barely perceptible flicker of the lights.* The adjective **perceptive** implies a personal quality involving a blend of insight and good judgment: *...a man of the highest culture, a perceptive critic, a charming essayist.* The noun *perceptiveness* means the ability to view situations in a clear manner. The word **percipient** is a very formal literary equivalent of *perceptive.*

percolate, permeate

The term **percolate** is used to describe the way that liquid or something similar passes slowly through porous materials, as in *rock through which water can percolate; coffee was percolating through the filter; mysterious light was percolating through hangings and stained-glass windows.* The term **permeate** is used of something that spreads throughout a location: *The flavour of the vanilla will permeate the sugar; The tip might leak allowing dangerous materials to permeate the soil.* It is often extended and used to describe the spread of opinions or attitudes through a community.

perfect

Writers are often advised to avoid using **perfect** with modifiers like *absolutely* or *most* because perfection is an absolute quality. However, there are many examples from competent writers who ignore this advice. For example, in *It is like having the most perfect apparatus of precision,* the use of *most perfect* emphasizes the extent of the speaker's admiration. It is quite acceptable for something to be described as *almost perfect.* ⇒ **unique**

permissible, permissive

Something **permissible** is 'allowed': *A third examination* *is permissible if the first two reports are in conflict; Part of the discussion turned on the permissible limits of liberty.* If someone's attitude, or that of an institution, is **permissive**, it means that they allow something that someone else might wish to forbid: *The Church ought to take a more permissive attitude; the tolerant and permissive sixties.*

permit, allow

In most respects the meanings of *permit* and *allow* overlap. When you **permit** something you generally give express approval for it to happen: *French law permits the use of a vintage date for Cognac less than five years old.* It can be used when what is permitted is contrary to what might normally happen: *He permitted himself a slight smile.* The expression *permit of* is formal and somewhat old-fashioned. It is only used to mean 'make possible': *These crimes permit of no defence.*

If you **allow** someone to do something, you do not try to stop them, even though you may have the authority to do so. Most sentences that use *allow* can be rewritten using *permit* with no change of meaning. The major exception is *allow* with the sense of 'make possible' or 'enable', as in *The money they have spent on research has allowed the company to run rings around the opposition.* Another exception is the use of *allow* with the sense of 'provide' or 'make available': *Allow two clumps of ferns or plants to each corner of the bed; Allow two months for unknown creditors to make claims.*

permute, permutate

The shorter form **permute** is standard; **permutate** is a back formation from the noun *permutation* and, as it has no special meaning, need not be used.

perpetrate, commit, perform

Perpetrate and **commit** overlap in one area of meaning but while *perpetrate* is limited and highly literary *commit* is a more general word that has a wide range of meanings. In their main meaning, both words suggest very strongly that what has been done is either illegal or wrong: *Were these the actions of a family knowingly perpetrating a forgery?; ...an elaborate fraud perpetrated on the poor; He has committed a criminal offence. Perpetrate* has an agent form **perpetrator**, as in *one of the perpetrators of the crime*, but *commit* has no agent form meaning 'one who commits something'.

A neutral verb that has none of the overtones of either *perpetrate* or *commit* is **perform**. Be careful not to confuse *perpetrate* and *perpetuate*, which means 'allow something to continue': *After her death, he saw no reason to perpetuate the lie.*

per pro ⇒ **p.p.**

person, persons, people

The noun **person** is normally used in the singular only: *He came across as a person with a lot of dignity*, and the noun **people** is normally used to indicate plural number: *These ordinary people have worked hard to make Japan the extraordinary phenomenon it is today. Person* does have a plural form **persons**, but its use is restricted. It is normally found in very formal written commands or instructions such as: *We have the right to exclude unauthorized persons from the site.*

Avoid using *persons* where the word *people* would be more appropriate, e.g. *...actions producing mirth among the people* (not *persons*) *at the table; Young people* (not *persons*) *cannot be allowed to clean these machines.*

The plural form of *people* is equally restricted in its use and means 'people of different races and nationalities', as in *I respect the equal rights of peoples and their right to self-determination*.

In some contexts, *person* or *persons* may have derogatory overtones. If you say, for example *Snubby is one of those persons whom it's better to look back to…*, it suggests by its distant formality someone whom the speaker does not respect.

persona, persona grata

The word **persona** originally meant a mask. Your *persona* is the side of your character that you choose to let people see: *I knew that there must be something more beneath that hard-boiled persona*. When *persona* is used in the formal phrases **persona grata** or **persona non grata** it simply means someone who is officially either welcome, as in *He appeared to be persona grata*, or unwelcome, as in *They made him persona non grata so he had to leave the Embassy*.

personage, personality, personable

The word **personage** is used when the subject is a famous or important person: *The story involved a great occasion and a royal personage; a great personage of the Church*. There is a tendency now to use the word informally with irony, as in *Your expenses will be questioned by some distant personage in the finance department*. A **personality** is equally 'a famous person' but this word is generally used for someone who has become famous through show business, or by frequent appearances in the media: *In the last decade he has become more and more a television personality*. The most frequently used meaning of *personality* is 'a person's character and nature'.

When someone is described as **personable**, it means that they show an attractive mixture of pleasant features and personal charm. It is an old-fashioned word.

personal, personnel
Personal is the adjective used to describe anything that is private to a person. The noun that is used as a synonym for *staff* or *employees* is **personnel**. Note the differences in spelling between the words and note also that *personnel* has stress on the last syllable /per-son-**nel**/. This word began as a piece of military jargon that spread to commerce and industry and has now become well-established in all forms of employment.

perspicuous, conspicuous, perspicacious
The adjective **perspicuous** is used about comments, remarks, and other observations that indicate a clear or penetrating piece of observation or deduction: *He made a most perspicuous speech.* Do not confuse this word with **conspicuous**, which means 'easily noticeable' or 'outstanding': *He was awarded the Military Cross for conspicuous gallantry in combat.*

The adjective **perspicacious** is used rather formally about people who possess a clear-sighted view of a problem. It describes a personal quality: *Even the most perspicacious of students of human nature may fail to notice this trait in his character.*

perspire, perspiration, sweat
The verb **perspire** and the noun **perspiration** are sometimes condemned as genteelisms, and may once have been so, but both are extremely common alternative words for *sweat*. **Sweat** is the preferred scientific term, both as noun and verb. *Perspiration* is often used to indicate a smaller amount of sweat.

pertinent, relevant (to)

The meaning of **pertinent** overlaps with that of **relevant**. Something that is *pertinent* or *relevant* to a discussion adds to the points being made: *It is only his art that is a pertinent subject for discussion; The medical documents were highly pertinent to the discussion*. The opposite sense is expressed by *irrelevant*, but not by *impertinent*, which means 'cheeky' or 'insubordinate'.

pervert, perverted, perverse

To **pervert** something means to alter it for the worse by turning it from its original path: *Their traditional ceremonies were perverted into superstition and mysticism*. The verb is stressed on the final syllable /per-**vert**/. The noun *pervert* means someone who has been corrupted and may corrupt others. The noun is stressed on the first syllable /**per**-vert/.

The past participle **perverted** can be used as an adjective and has the basic sense of the verb, as in *Some of the details were invented by a perverted imagination*.

Although the adjective **perverse** has a similar origin to *pervert*, nowadays it means 'stubbornly difficult', or 'wilful and changeable', as in *To cultivate a pleasure in being wrong sounds perverse; …her perverse refusal to give them a chance in life*. Careful writers and speakers avoid using *perverse* as a euphemism for *perverted* or *deviant*.

phantasy, phantom

The *ph-* spelling is formal. ⇒ **fantasy**

phenomenon

Although it is often treated as if it were singular, *phenomena* is plural. The singular form is **phenomenon**: *That is an interesting phenomenon; Several new phenomena were recorded in his notes*.

physician, doctor, surgeon, physicist

The term **physician** is a rather formal equivalent of **doctor**. It is not greatly used but has the advantage of indicating that the person concerned practises medicine, whereas *doctor* can also mean doctor of science, doctor of letters, etc.

A *doctor* is broadly understood to mean a medically qualified person who treats diseases by medicine. A **surgeon** is a medically qualified person who has specialized in the skills involved in performing operations. *Surgeons* assume the title Mr or Mrs, not Dr. A **physicist** does not practise medicine but studies the science of physics.

pick, choose, choice

The words **pick** and **choose** overlap almost entirely but there is a slight overtone in the verb *choose* of a deliberate and thoughtful act, especially in the way the past participle *chosen* is used adjectivally. The noun from *choose* is **choice**; there is no corresponding noun from *pick*. *Choice* can be used adjectivally to mean 'selected, special', always with the overtone of something especially good: *choice cuts of beef; a dish of choice fruit.*

pidgin, pigeon

The term **pidgin** is used to describe a language based on a reduced form of a parent language and containing a mixture of other tongues. About 50 years ago, *pigeon* was also used with this meaning. Now, it is only used for the bird. ⇒ **creole**

pigeon, dove

There is no difference in kind between a **dove** and a **pigeon**, but the overtones of the word *dove* are more romantic or picturesque.

piteous, pitiable, pitiful

All three words overlap in their basic meaning, which is 'deserving pity': *His mates remained still, hearing the newcomer's piteous sounds of suffering; Both dog and mistress gave him such pitiable looks that he didn't have the heart to insist.* The word *pitiful* can be ambiguous. Like *piteous*, it means 'deserving pity', as in *the protests of a fragile and pitiful old lady*. It is also used with ironic overtones to mean 'deserving scorn', as in *In their creative endeavours, they were pitiful imitators.*

place

Careful writers will avoid the American usages *anyplace*, *everyplace*, and *someplace*. These should be *anywhere*, *everywhere*, and *somewhere*. The expression *going places*, as in *Fred Bloggs is really going places*, is lively and informal but should be avoided in formal contexts, where *succeed* is preferable.

plane, plain

A **plane** is either an aircraft, a flat surface in mathematics or mechanics, or a woodworking tool.

A flat expanse of land is a **plain**. The adjective that means 'simple', 'unadorned', or 'not pretty' is *plain*. If something is *plain sailing* it is straightforward.

plastic

The current British and American pronunciation is /**plass**-tik/. Older speakers of British English, and users of British English outside the UK, often prefer the pronunciation /**plah**-stik/. Other words starting with *plas-* show a similar difference between regional accents of British English, e.g. Northern /**plass**-ter/ and Southern /**plah**-ster/.

plateful ⇒ -ful

playwright ⇒ **-wright**

plc

The abbreviation **plc** stands for *public limited company*. When writing *plc* use lower case letters and no full stop. Companies not quoted on the Stock Exchange retain the acronym *Ltd*.

please

Avoid the cliché, *please, please, please,* used by many correspondents to the popular media when making a request. Once is enough. Also avoid the old-fashioned business idiom, *Please find enclosed…*. It is sufficient to say: *A copy (of our catalogue etc.) is enclosed.*

plus

Plus is formally used to show that one quantity is to be added to another: *The first £55,000 plus any interest.* It has a range of very informal uses, such as substituting for *as well as,* as in *I suppose it's a mixture of pique, plus the fact that we have our own problems.* Many people dislike this particular use of *plus.* It is also very loosely used, especially in advertising, rather like a sentence adverb, to mean 'additionally': *Plus, you could win a home entertainment system.* Careful writers avoid this stylistic device, which has, in any case, become over-used. *Plus, together with,* and *along with* do not create compound subjects in the way that *and* does. The number of the verb depends on that of the original subject: *This task, plus all the others, was* [not *were*] *undertaken by the government; The doctors, along with a nurse, were* [not *was*] *waiting for the patient.*

poetess

This form of reference is often condescending. Use **poet**

instead. The writer's sex is usually not relevant.

poetic, poetical, poetics, poesy

Poetic and **poetical** are both adjectives meaning 'relating to poetry'. Alternatively, either may be used of something that shows depth of feeling and sensitivity: *...a poetic and beautiful picture of the landscape*. **Poetics** is the study of the art of writing poetry. **Poesy** is an archaic, literary word for *poetry*.

point in time

The expression *at this point in time* is a tautology. The meaning can be rendered by *now, today, these days*, and so on.

politic, political, politics

The word **politic** is no longer used to mean 'political'. It can mean 'wise', 'sensible', or 'shrewd', but it can also mean 'unscrupulous'.

Use **politics** with a plural verb when you are talking about political allegiance or political philosophy: *Mrs Thatcher's politics are not those of the man in the street*. When you are talking about the practice of *politics* use a singular verb: *Politics is a very taxing profession*.

pore, pour, poor, paw

The verb **pore** (usually followed by *over*) is used with the sense 'read intently': *He was poring over an old map*. The verb **pour** is used of liquids. When the word *pore* is a noun, it means any small opening in the skin or a similar surface.

In the majority of British accents these words all have the same pronunciation /paw/. Some speakers prefer /puer/ for *poor*, but it is a matter of speech habits, not of correctness.

portentous, pretentious

Something **portentous** has all the outward appearance of a *portent* or omen, perhaps indicating something of future significance: *Its consequences were historically portentous.* It can mean 'serious', suggesting the announcement of unpleasant news, as in *Mary's face became portentous. She said seriously, 'Just listen to this'*, but the word can also have overtones of overinflated importance. In this sense it overlaps with *pretentious: His humility was a little at odds with the portentous way he signed his name.* Note the spelling: the word ends in *-tous*, there is no *i*. The adjective **pretentious** is used for something or someone that makes a claim to be important without convincing you that this is so: *Critics described it as 'gross, pretentious and, in its own way, hideous'; You are not so pretentious as to think you believe in nothing.*

possible, probable

The word **possible** means 'capable of happening'. If something is **probable** it is likely to happen or be true. The accepted construction is: *It is possible/probable that....* In informal usage, a *possible* is a candidate in a competition who has a strong chance of being successful. A *probable* is a candidate who is likely to be selected.

post-

The prefix **post-** is added to words that describe something as taking place after a certain date or following on from a previous event, as in *postoperative; postgraduate; postdate; postimpressionism.*

potato

Note the spelling of the singular form of **potato**. It does not end in *e*. The plural is *potatoes*. ⇒ **-o**

pound

Note that some people make a difference in meaning between: *I can let you have five pound* (the singular form = weight) and *I can let you have five pounds* (the plural form = money).

p.p.

The correct use of the abbreviation **p.p.** is no longer clearly agreed upon. Traditionally, when you write a letter on behalf of someone but want to show that the content has their authority, you sign the letter *p.p.* followed by your own name, then add the name of the person on whose behalf you are writing.

> *p.p. William Blake*
> *Sir Walter Scott (Managing Director)*

This is correct in accordance with the Latin *per procurationem* meaning 'by delegation to'. Alternative abbreviations are *per pro.* or *per proc.* An alternative form has also come into use. It is increasingly common to see the following format: your name is given first, followed by *p.p.* before the name of the person on whose behalf you are writing, as if it meant 'on behalf of'.

practical, practicable

Practical is used of a person who is more concerned with practice than theory: *He is a very practical person.* A practical idea or project is one that is effective: *The idea had no practical application.*

Practicable refers to a project or an idea that is capable of being done or put into effect. A *practicable* solution may not necessarily be an effective one: *The plan was practicable but far too expensive.* A person cannot be *practicable*.

practice, practise
British English makes a distinction between the spelling of the noun **practice** and that of the verb **practise**. American English does not make this distinction. It uses *practise* for both noun and verb. ⇒ **licence**

pre-
The prefix **pre-** is used to form words that describe something that took place before a certain date or event, e.g. *preamplifier; predate; premature*.

precede, proceed
If someone or something **precedes** another, they go before it. Someone can **proceed** *to* or *with* the next stage of a process: *The winners and runners-up in each of those groups would proceed to two further groups of four.* Notice the spelling. Three verbs end in *-ceed: exceed, proceed,* and *succeed.* The others have *-cede: concede, intercede, precede* and so on except *supersede*.

precedence, precedent
Precedence is priority in importance or, especially when referring to ceremonial occasions, the order of rank. *Precedence* is normally used in the phrase *take* or *have precedence over* someone or something. It is possible to use *of* instead of *over* but this is very formal: *On our next meeting I would be able to take precedence of you.* You give *precedence to* someone or something: *He stood to one side, giving precedence to the Bishop.*

A **precedent** is some instance that can be used as the basis for future decisions. The noun *precedent* is often followed by *for*: *This set a precedent for other agreements; There was adequate precedent for this.*

preceding, previous
Preceding is a rather formal word: *Curtis intends to*

explore the events preceding and following the killings as a matter of important public debate. In many cases it can be replaced, for greater informality, by *before (the events before and after the killings)* or *previous: I noticed the slip of my pen in the preceding/previous paragraph.*

precipitate, precipitant, precipitous

The adjective **precipitate** means an over-hasty or rash action: *Everyone understood Mr Gorbachev's position and did not want precipitate action that could wreck everything.* The rather less common adjective **precipitant** has the same meaning.

The adjective **precipitous** is associated with the noun *precipice.* A cliff or any steep slope is *precipitous: There was no foreshore, just the precipitous plunge of the limestone rock faces.* Because these adjectives have so often been confused, *precipitous* has taken on the subsidiary meaning 'hasty', as in *a precipitous and reckless procedure*, but it is preferable to maintain the distinction between *precipitate* and *precipitous.*

precis, résumé

Either **precis** (or *précis*) or **résumé** is used to mean 'the spoken or written summary of a document'. The word *résumé* has the additional sense of 'a brief account of someone's career'. This usage is more common in American English but can now also be found in British job advertisements. The usual British English equivalent is **CV**, standing for *curriculum vitae.* Precis is pronounced /**pray**-see/, *résumé* is pronounced /**rez**-yu-may/.

predecessor

Your **predecessor** is not necessarily dead. He or she is someone who held a post or office before you did: *The* *organization was in financial difficulties, a fact which my predecessor admitted concealing.* Contrast the spelling with that of *decease.*

preface, prelude, postlude, sequel

A **preface** is a short written introduction to a book. It often contains some account of why the book was written and thanks to any people who helped the author. A **prelude** is a musical term for a short composition. It originally preceded the performance of a longer piece of music but then became a self-contained piece.

A **postlude** is a concluding piece of music, usually the final part of a longer composition. It has also been used to mean a concluding passage of writing set a little while after the main action of a novel or a play has ended. A **sequel** is a continuation, and often the conclusion, of a story that was begun in a previous novel: *"The Lord of the Rings" is a sequel to "The Hobbit".* ⇒ **prequel**

prefer, preferable

There is a change of stress between the pronunciation of the verb and the adjective. **Prefer** is pronounced /pre-fer/; **preferable** is pronounced /pre-fer-able/.

prefix, suffix

A **prefix** is a group of letters added to the beginning of a word to form a new meaning. Similarly, a **suffix** is added to the end of a word. The term that means both of these is an *affix.*

prejudge, prejudice

When someone **prejudges** something, they form an opinion before they have all the facts. **Prejudice** is the state of having fixed opinions in the form of an unreasonable dislike for certain people or things: *I stated to* *him our desire to see a racially free South Africa, a society without prejudice.* **Prejudice** is often followed by *towards*, or by *against*, as in *...prejudices towards intellectuality; She had not my prejudices against television; People were prejudiced against her.* Note the difference in spelling between *prejudge* and *prejudice*.

premise, premises, premiss

The normal term for enclosed property, is the plural form **premises**. It is generally used with *on* not *in*: *You may not store inflammable liquids on these premises.*

The word **premise** or **premiss** (the spelling difference is not significant) is also used in law and logic. This has quite a different meaning. A *premise* is something that you presume is true in order to build up an argument or a case: *I'm rather questioning whether the whole premise is correct.*

preposition

There is no adequate reason for condemning the practice of ending a sentence with a preposition, as in *They are the people I hate talking to*, except that it was not possible in the Latin mode of correctness that many past grammarians adopted. The sound and sense of the sentence should govern the positioning of words. What is natural in speech may look clumsy in writing. The sentence *What did you choose that book to be read to out of for?* is a classic example.

prequel

The word **prequel** is a neologism that has been formed from a combination of the words *preface* and *sequel*. It is a film or book about the lives of characters before the events in the original work that made them popular.

prescribe, proscribe

Something **prescribed** has been advised as being a suitable remedy, as in *He prescribed a course of injections*, or laid down as a rule of behaviour: *All was done in the manner that tradition prescribed for honouring a king.* The noun form is *prescription*. To **proscribe** something is to forbid or ban it by a directive: *The state might proscribe private education altogether.* The noun form is *proscription: We could not allow the proscription of whole groups of people.* Do not confuse this word with *conscription*, 'the forced recruitment of men to the army': *He went to Canada in the '60s to avoid conscription.*

presence, prescience

Presence is the state of being in a place; it is often overused in phrases like *a naval/military presence*. The word is used in several common phrases but is frequently misspelled as [*presents*]. If you are *in someone's presence* you are in the same room with them, if you *make your presence felt* you make people pay attention to you. Another common use is in the phrase *presence of mind*, meaning 'resourcefulness and quick thinking': *Richard had the presence of mind to step forward and pick it up.*

Prescience is the sense of foreknowledge of future events and the ability to take suitable action: *The gallery bought a Zurbaran, an act of prescience much criticized at the time.*

presently ⇒ **promptly**

preserve, conserve

There is a considerable overlap in meaning between these two words. *Preserve* has the wider range of applications. **Conserve** and the noun *conservation* have overtones of trying to restrain something from spoiling or wasting: *We turned the bicycle lights off to conserve the batteries.* Besides this sense, **preserve** and the noun *preservation* can imply an element of rescue for something that has already begun to decay: *They argue that they are preserving the prairie in the form of ranches.* *Conservationists* and *preservationists* appear to be identical, but there is no parallel noun from *preserve* to match the noun *conservator*, an official charged with the upkeep of precious objects.

presume ⇒ **assume**

presumptive, presumptuous
Presumptive is an archaic word now used only in set phrases like *the heir presumptive.* Do not use it where **presumptuous**, which means 'bold' or 'overconfident', is intended: *Having in mind the preliminary nature of our research, it would be presumptuous to explore its theoretical implications.* Note the spelling of *presumptuous;* it has a *u* before the *-ous* ending.

pretence, pretensions, pretentious
Pretence (in American spelling, *pretense*) is the act of pretending. It has two senses. The main one is an action or way of behaving that makes people believe something that is not true: *She said that the friendliness on her side was a pretence.* The second sense is now rare. It was used to mean 'laying claim to something without the proper authority', but nowadays we use the word **pretensions** instead, as in the expression *have pretensions to grandeur: He never ceased thundering against the pretensions of science to explain the mysteries of creation.*

Something **pretentious** is 'showily noticeable'. The word has overtones of falsity, and lack of sincerity or depth:

Ned was denying it for the sake of this awful, false, showy, pretentious person.

preventive, preventative

Both words have the same meaning but **preventive** is more commonly used for the adjective form, as in …*the importance of preventive and remedial action; preventive medicine*. **Preventative** is used as an adjective but can also be used as a noun: *Growing garlic or onions in a rose bed is held to be a preventative against insect pests.*

primarily

The pronunciation of **primarily** is not settled. There is one form that places stress on the first syllable, /**pri**-mar-i-ly/, and another that places stress on the second syllable, /pri-**mar**-il-y/. The first form is marginally more common.

primate, prime minister, premier

The title **Primate** is used for the heads of particular Christian Churches in a country, e.g. the Archbishop of Canterbury is the *Primate of All England*. The term **Prime Minister** is used in Britain and some other countries to denote the rank of the chief minister of the government. In British English it is the description of a function, not a title like *Dr* or *Queen*, so the holder does not bear the title *Prime Minister Hacker*, although in conversation he may be addressed or referred to by his rank, without the use of his name, as in *Are you sure, Prime Minister?* Otherwise, he is referred to in the style: *the Prime Minister, the Right Honourable John Hacker M.P.* The term **Premier** is an alternative to *Prime Minister*. It is officially used by some countries but is often used very loosely in broadcasting to refer to any head of state.

⇒ **false titles**

principal, principle

The correct spelling of these two words is a common problem. The head of an establishment, such as a school or some types of business, is a **principal**. The adjective *principal* is used for whatever is first in importance: *Lully was middle-aged before he decided to make music his principal career.*

An ideal that someone hopes to uphold by their actions is a **principle**: *He suffered from a misplaced principle of charity.* A *principle* is also an underlying rule or law on which other elements are built: *The guiding principle of party policy was democratic centralism.*

The phrase *in principle* means 'in theory', 'if nothing indicates otherwise': *The government view is that such a system would in principle be the same as the one operated by the United States.*

probable ⇒ possible

proboscis

The pronunciation /pro-**bo**-sis/ is usual, but /pro-**bos**-kis/ is also acceptable.

procedures, proceedings

Procedures are the formally accepted ways of doing something: *The security procedures failed in his case.* A *procedure* is the step-by-step way that something is done: *A two stage procedure was set up.* **Proceedings** are events that happen in a particular place, for example in a conference. They can also be the published account of what was said and done.

procrastinate, prevaricate

Someone who **procrastinates** keeps putting off tasks that should be undertaken: *He resists by procrastinating* *or being irritating.* If someone **prevaricates** they avoid telling the direct truth or do not act in a straightforward manner. The related noun is *prevarication.*

professor, lecturer

Note the spelling of **professor**; there is one *f* and two *s*. The title is often more freely given to academic staff outside Britain. Many British **lecturers** would be called *professor* or *associate professor* elsewhere. The abbreviation **Prof.** is acceptable when used on letters, but it is not used for direct address.

programme, program

The normal spelling of this word in British English is **programme**. However, the current usage is to choose the American spelling **program** when the reference is to a *computer program.*

progress

The pronunciation changes depending on whether progress is used as a verb /pro-**gress**/ or a noun /**pro**-gress/. Avoid using the word as a jargon term in commerce for *expedite* or *carry out: I will carry out* [not *progress*] *your recent order.*

prohibit

Prohibit is normally used with a direct object followed by *from: The country has a law prohibiting workers from striking.* It is not an acceptable construction to follow *prohibit* with *to.*

proliferation

This is a rather formal word meaning the rapid increase of something. Note that *a nuclear proliferation treaty* is not a treaty *for*, but a treaty *against*, the spread of weapons.

prolix, prolific

A writer who is **prolix** uses more words than is necessary. A **prolific** writer is a very productive one.

promptly, immediately, presently

British English makes a distinction between doing something **promptly**, meaning 'as quickly as possible', or **immediately**, meaning 'right away', and doing something **presently**, meaning 'soon'. Many speakers of British English dislike the use of *presently* with the sense of 'at present' or 'for the present', as in *He is gaining more experience than Mangold is presently doing; Presently the mountain was deserted.* Some speakers of American English extend this use of *presently* to mean 'now' or 'at this very moment', as in *Flight 274 for Los Angeles is presently boarding at Gate Two.* This is also standard in Scots usage. Speakers of Southern British English often find this usage either ambiguous or impossible to understand.

prone to, liable to

Both phrases include the meaning 'have a tendency to'. **Prone to** means 'have a tendency to be afflicted by' something: *The left brain is prone to accidents; Mothers are prone to exaggeration.* Someone repeatedly subject to a misfortune can be described as, for example *headache prone* or *accident prone.* **Liable to** means 'have a strong tendency to happen'. It is used with objects and with people: *Glass is liable to break in transit; Brian is liable to fly into a rage for no reason.* Knowing that something is *liable to* behave in a particular way is a matter of probability based on past experience. It is an informal expression.

When **liable to** is used in the context of legal matters, it has the particular meaning of being in a position where an action can be taken: *Hugh was liable to arrest at any moment; ...legally liable to the loss of the contract.*

pronunciation

This word frequently causes difficulty. It is related to pronounce but has a different spelling and a different pronunciation /pro-**nun**-see-a-tion/.

prophecy, prophesy

The spelling **prophecy**, meaning 'a prediction', and pronounced /**pro**-fe-see/, is used for the noun; the spelling **prophesy**, meaning 'make a prediction', and pronounced /**pro**-fe-sigh/, is used for the verb.

proportional, proportionate

Both **proportional** and **proportionate** mean 'in proportion': *The amount of heat that can be retained is proportional to the temperature.* Both *proportional* and *proportionate* are frequently followed by *to: The agony would be proportionate to the rewards.* ⇒ **per cent**

pro rata

When a price for goods is quoted **pro rata** it means that you can calculate the cost of a smaller or larger order by simple arithmetic based on the price that you have been given: *The unit price is £1.78. Orders up to 100 units pro rata, with a discount for larger quantities.*

proscribe ⇒ prescribe

prostrate, prostate

The adjective **prostrate** means 'lying flat and face down'. It is sometimes used in error for the word **prostate**, which is part of the body: *Male mammals have a prostate gland that surrounds the neck of the bladder.*

protagonist, antagonist

A **protagonist** is someone who takes a leading part in an action. The word originally signified the main character in a Greek play. However, it is now often used as if it were the converse of **antagonist**, an *opponent* or an *adversary*, and meant 'someone who supports a cause'. Careful users may prefer to avoid this misapplication by using *proponent* or *advocate* instead. The misapplication of *protagonist* is clear in phrases such as [*a leading protagonist*]. This is a tautology. An **antagonist** is someone who is hostile to you or to your point of view.

proved, proven

Proved and **proven** are alternative past participle forms of the verb *prove*. *Proved* is also used as the Simple Past form: *Within minutes of the start he proved himself right.* *Proven* is the form of the past participle that is normally used as an adjective, as in *a proven remedy; A spread of businesses in niche areas of industry, coupled with proven management skill, has attractions in these uncertain times.* *Proven* is usually pronounced /**proo**-ven/.

provided that, providing

If you want to establish a condition or reservation at the beginning of a clause, both **providing** and **provided that** are in regular use: *It would be all right living in Glasgow providing you had a nice house; It would work well provided that there was a safeguard.* It is not correct, however, to use [*providing that*].

provident, providential

A **provident** person is one who plans and regulates their expenditure or who plans for the future. When something is **providential**, it happens by good fortune at just the right time, as if *providence* was responsible: *The stumble was providential as it spoilt the aim of the blow.*

prox. ⇒ **inst.**

PS, NB

These abbreviations have distinctive uses although each generally follows a completed passage of writing. **PS** is normally used at the foot of a letter to add an overlooked piece of information. It stands for *post scriptum* and has the sense of 'after writing what is above'. A second *PS* is written *PPS*. **NB** is not an afterthought but a point that you want to be specially noted. It stands for *nota bene* and has the sense of 'note this carefully'.

pseudonym ⇒ **nom de plume**

pt-, pn-, ps-

English words that begin with **pt-, pn-,** or **ps-** are rather rare. These spellings originate in words adopted from Greek. In each case, the *p* is not pronounced.

public

Public is a collective noun. It is equally correct to say *the public is...* or *the public are...* . The choice usually depends on the context of the statement and whether the writer has in mind a group as a unit or the individual members that make up the group.

public, private, state

In England a **public school** is a private fee-paying school; a **state school** is a publicly funded school; a **private school** is a small *public school*, often one for younger children. An illogical use of language, familiar enough to British speakers of English but a conundrum to the remainder of the English-speaking community world-wide. In Scotland the terminology is much clearer. A state-run school is called a *public school*, and a *private school* is the equivalent of an English *public school*.

punctilious, punctual

If you are **punctilious** in your behaviour, you are very attentive to detail. It also suggests that you follow very closely what etiquette suggests. A person who is **punctual** is on time for an appointment: *A punctilious person is always punctual.*

punctuation

Punctuation is a matter of convention, not something fixed by the rules of a language, and as such is open to changes in fashion. *Colons* and *semicolons* have been particularly subject to change in use and neither is used in the way that it was last century. This is a brief guide to a complex area.

Capital letters are not strictly part of punctuation, except when used to mark the beginning of a new sentence. There are a number of conventions about the use of capital letters in English. The first word in a sentence and, usually, the first word in each line of a poem follows the convention of beginning with a capital letter.

The general rule for words is to use capital letters to begin each word in personal names: *Alison Mitchell,* in job titles: *Senior Manager,* in royal, official, and courtesy titles: *Prince, Prime Minister, Mother,* in book or film titles: *Vanity Fair,* in trade names: *Hoover,* in the names of countries: *New Zealand,* in the names of races and their languages: *Italian, Maori,* and for religions, their gods, and their holy books: *Christianity, Jehovah, the Koran,* and in any adjectives that derive from these nouns: *James/Jacobean; England/English.*

Although capitals are used in titles, as in *Prime Minister,* they are not used when the reference is an indirect one to a minor title like *councillor,* e.g. *Councillor Smith said... but the councillor/Prime Minister refused to comment.*

Capitals are sometimes used to mark a word of special importance, but official bodies often overuse them, probably because an item is more significant to them than it would be to an outsider: *There will be an opportunity to join an Employee Profit Sharing Scheme; You may be required to have a Medical Examination or to obtain a Medical Attendant's Report.*

Full stops (called *periods* in American English) have two uses. Firstly, to indicate the end of a sentence. All sentences, other than those ending with a question mark or an exclamation mark, end with a full stop.

Secondly, to mark the ending of certain abbreviations: *Co.; etc.; Cres.* The modern British practice is for the full stop to be left off abbreviations that end with the final letter of the full word: *Dr; Mrs; Rd,* and so on.

A **question mark** is used to end every sentence that expects an answer: *Have you seen my gloves?* An indirect question does not require a question mark: *Cathy asked whether the visit was still on.*

An **exclamation mark** is rarely used in British English. Avoid using an exclamation mark to indicate normal degrees of emphasis, such as in *It was going to be a really fine day.* Reserve its use for emphatic expressions and exclamations: *Help!; Good Heavens!* The use of a question mark followed by an exclamation mark to express astonishment is a device of comic books and not a normal part of punctuation.

A **comma** is used to mark the end of a clause or to separate out a clause within a sentence. It is a short pause before the topic continues.

A non-defining or non-restrictive relative clause is preceded by a comma: *We leave on Friday, which means that we get a clear three days.* A defining or restrictive relative clause is not preceded by a comma: *People who live in glass houses shouldn't throw stones.*

If two clauses are linked by a conjunction, a comma is used if there is a contrast: *It was a sunny day, but there was a chill in the air.*

A comma is used to mark a subordinate clause that comes before its main clause: *If the weather permits, I am going to join a friend for a walking holiday.*

A comma separates a sentence tag from the main part of a sentence, though these are infrequent in written style: *You just wouldn't let it lie, would you?*

A comma may be used after an adverb such as *however, nevertheless, on the other hand, frankly,* when it begins a sentence: *Frankly, I can't stand Strauss,* or to surround it when it is placed within a clause, as in *On Tuesdays, however, they would go to a friend's house.*

A comma separates items in a list: *The shop was overflowing with books, pamphlets, old prints, and vague piles of scruffy papers.*

A comma may optionally be used between similar adjectives: *a nasty, creeping, miserable man.* No comma is needed if the adjectives modify each other, as in *dark blue,* or modify the noun in different ways: *a tall blond Scandinavian cyclist.*

It is easy to overuse commas in an attempt to remedy clumsy sentence structure. There are two major styles of punctuation, close and light, and each style uses commas to a different extent. This book has a fairly close style of punctuation.

The **colon** is the mark **:** which is used within sentences to link two grammatically complete clauses. It is not a frequently used form of punctuation. The two clauses must relate to each other: the colon tells the reader that what follows adds to, or explains the preceding clause. The other uses of the colon are to introduce a list, as in *The contents included: six used felt pens, a small piece of card, an eraser, and a notebook bound in black,* and to introduce a quotation: *What he said was: 'Never again'.*

The **semicolon** is the mark ; that is used within sentences to mark a longer pause than a comma and is followed by a change of direction without a major change of topic. Because a semicolon signals a close relationship between the two elements that it separates, it can be used to join two clauses; no linking word is necessary. Each clause is generally of equal importance in the sentence. This does not, however, mean that they must be of equal length. The semicolon is not used very often in informal styles of writing but is found more often in literary works, and in technical writing, especially in pointed or balanced remarks, like the following from *Punch: Look here, if this is coffee I want tea; if it's tea I want coffee.*

Separate items in a complex list may also be separated by semicolons, especially when the list consists of phrases and a comma could be part of the phrase: *Further examples are: in good odour; in good hands; a good sort; the good old days.*

A **parenthesis** is the technical name for the **bracket** symbol (and) in writing. It is also the name for any explanatory phrase that is inserted into a text (*like this*) – *or like this* – and divided off by a pair of dashes or brackets. A parenthesis indicates that what it contains does not form part of the grammar of the main section of the clause that it is in. Commas can also be used to indicate a parenthetical element: *Ophelia, as you well know, is a character in a play by Shakespeare.*

When you use brackets (plural *parentheses*) to contain a whole sentence, the full stop goes inside the closing bracket. (This is an example.) When it forms only a part of a sentence, the full stop is placed outside the closing bracket (like this).

In writing, as opposed to mathematics, **square brackets** are used to contain notes, corrections within a text by an editor, and any other material which is not a part of the original sentence. They are not very common: *When he [The Chancellor] was asked later that day* ....

Suspension points, also called an **ellipsis**, ... are used to indicate that a quotation has been shortened to make it more convenient in length or to focus the reader's attention. They are placed at the point where the omission occurs: *That was precisely the reaction that countless journalists and intellectuals would have ... as the New Journalism picked up momentum.*

Dashes are a form of parenthesis. Many users regard them as a sign of informal writing. If the dashes are used in pairs to surround a phrase or a clause in the way that brackets do, then they are quite legitimate. When they are simply a sign of a change in topic and a loose substitute for a colon or a comma, they are less formal and should be reserved for informal writing: *– notes – family correspondence – perhaps jottings of some kind.*

An **apostrophe** is used to mark the possessive form: *Maddy's parents; Anna's best friend.* It is also used to mark an omission: *It's; didn't.* This is the cause of frequent errors as plural forms of nouns are often written as if they were possessive forms.

puns

There is a rather silly prejudice concerning **puns** that arises from the comment by Dryden that they are 'the lowest and most grovelling kind of wit'. This is not so. A *pun* is a play on words and some of the richest effects in literary language are due to inventive wordplay. Punning and wordplay can become tedious if used excessively. So can any stylistic device. A good pun, however, should be welcomed.

pupil ⇒ scholar

purport, repute, pretend

Purport and *repute* are usually used in the passive. When something is **purported** to be true it suggests that while it has all the appearances of truth it is, in fact, a fraud. It is a negative statement: …*advertisements for cosmetics purporting to delay the development of wrinkles*. If something is **reputed** to be the case, it is what is generally believed to be true, often without any proof being available. It makes a positive statement: *He was divorced and reputed to be a lady's man*.

Pretend is always used in the active voice. When someone **pretends** that something is true, they are making a false claim: *They only half believe the things they pretend to believe*. The noun related to the verb is *pretension*. It is often used in the phrase have *pretensions to* something: *An insignificant minority with pretensions to speak in the name of China*.

purposely, purposefully

Something done **purposely** is intended: *We purposely made the package as exciting as possible, showing inspectors going down drains to rescue animals*.

If you are *purposeful* or act **purposefully**, you behave in a determined manner: *Tottenham, appreciably quicker, firmer, and more purposeful, would have avoided the scramble for a winner if they had taken their chances.*

pygmy, pigmy

When **pygmy** is used with a capital letter it means one of the African Pygmy people. When it has a lower case letter, it means a very small example of its type, e.g. *a pygmy horse.* Both spellings are used.

Q

quadri-

The prefix **quadri-** is used to indicate the quantity 'four', or 'fourfold'. For example, if someone is *quadriplegic* they are paralyzed in all four limbs. The prefix ends in *-ri* but alternative endings are *-ra, -ro,* and *-ru.* The spelling depends on how it combines with the following word.

qualitative, quantitative

When a distinction is **qualitative** it is based on quality: *There is a qualitative difference between the first three positions and all the others.*

When a distinction is **quantitative** it is based on amount: *Most of the alterations have been quantitative, where there were three servants there are now twelve.* It is usually pronounced with four syllables as /**kwan**-ti-te-tive/. The pronunciation that uses three syllables /**kwan**-ti-tive/ is not liked by a number of speakers.

quantum

In physical science and its associated mathematics, a **quantum** is a significant but minute unit of quantity. A *quantum shift* or *quantum leap* is a sudden significant change of state, not a large change.

In everyday usage, however, the term *a quantum leap* has taken on the meaning of 'a major leap forward'. This use is best avoided; it is now a cliché and annoys those who use the term in its true context.

quash, squash

When something is **squashed** it is physically flattened. If a government or some other form of authority decides to **quash** an action, it uses force or persuasion to stop it happening: *They tried to use the Official Secrets Act to quash a parliamentary question.* If a law or a decision is *quashed*, a court declares that it has further effect: *Their prison sentences were quashed on appeal.*

quasi-

As a prefix, **quasi-** means 'as if' or 'seemingly'. So a *quasi-autonomous body* is an organization that can act as if it were independent of its parent body. The pronunciations /**kwar**-zee/, /**kway**-zee/, or /**kwayz**-eye/ are equally acceptable.

quater-, quarter

The prefix *quater-* is pronounced /**kwat**-ter/. Note that it has no *r* before the *t*. It means 'in a series of four' and should be distinguished from **quarter** which is a division into four.

Quater- is used in *the Quaternary Era* (the fourth great geological era) and *quatercentenary*, (a four hundredth anniversary). ⇒ **quadri-**

Queen's English

This is a somewhat old-fashioned form of reference to a particular standard of English usage. It implies a rather narrow or conventional view of what is acceptable in grammar and pronunciation. It now has overtones of a class-based dialect that is not fully representative of the accepted range of educated usage. It is not synonymous with 'the English used by the royal family'. ⇒ **RP**

query, question

To **query** something means 'raise a doubt about' it, often in the context of a discussion, as in *The clerk queried my telephone charge card.* Careful users avoid using *query* when **question** is intended: '*Did you ask Miss Read about the twins?' questioned* [not *queried*] *her mother.*

The noun **query** means 'an enquiry': *The Senior Tutor is happy to answer queries from schools and individuals.*
⇒ **beg the question**

question mark ⇒ **punctuation**

questionnaire

The anglicized pronunciation /**kwes**-tyuh-nair/ is more common than the form that copies the original French, /**kes**-ti-o-nair/.

quick, quicker

You can use the adjectives **quick** and **quicker** in place of the adverbs *quickly* and *more quickly* when you want to be emphatic or urgent: *Quick, get it right; He slithered out of the tree quicker than he had expected.*

quiet, quite

The meaning of both words is clear, but the two are commonly confused when written down. If you have this problem, look closely at **quiet**, meaning 'still' or 'silent'.

It is pronounced as two syllables, /**qui**-et/, and the spelling should show that there is an *et* sound. **Quite** does not have an *et* sound or spelling.

quit

Quit is used formally in legal jargon, as in *Notice to quit*. The general use of **quit** for 'leave' is usually regarded as very informal, but it is broadly accepted. *Quit* meaning 'stop', as in *Oh, do quit complaining*, is an Americanism.

quite

Quite is an adverbial modifier that can be used in conflicting ways. It can be used to mark emphasis, as in *This is quite remarkable*, where enthusiasm is clearly intended. When this is the intended meaning, other words, such as *really* or *extraordinarily*, can be used instead of *quite* or together with it: *She is really quite remarkable for her age.*

It is also used to mark a reservation, as in *He did quite well*, where only a limited approval is intended. This use is often found in negative sentences: *It wasn't quite big enough; It wasn't quite cooked*. The tone of voice helps to distinguish each meaning in spoken English.

quorum

A **quorum** is the minimum number of members required for an official meeting to be able to conduct its business constitutionally. The plural form is *quorums* but this form is very rarely used. A meeting with insufficient members present to take binding decisions is declared to be *inquorate*.

quota

A **quota** is an allowance or permitted quantity of something: *We established a quota system for the number of books that were to be replaced*. Avoid using the word in the general sense of 'a large amount'. For example, say *It still has a large number of the poor and needy* instead of [*It still has its quota of the poor and needy.*]

quotation marks ⇒ inverted commas

quote, quotation
Quote is the verb form. It means 'to use the exact words of another person'. *Quote* is increasingly found used as a noun, but this usage is best avoided in serious writing where the normal noun form **quotation** is preferable.

In the commercial world, *quote* means 'to provide a projected statement of costs'. The informal noun form is *quote: I'll let you have my quote by tomorrow.* More formally, *quotation* is preferred.

The inverted comma " or ' is frequently called a *quotation mark* in British English or in American English a *quote mark* because it is associated with direct speech.

q.v.
In a reference book, the abbreviation **q.v.** stands for the Latin *quod vide* 'look at this' (i.e. 'look at the entry for whatever has just been mentioned') and is used to direct a reader to a quoted source of information for the purpose of making a cross-reference. It is not used in speech and is usually found only in older books.

R

racialism, racism, racist, racial

The words **racialism** and **racism** mean 'prejudice based on race or colour'. The adjectives from each are *racialist* and *racist*. The shorter forms of both words, **racist** and **racism**, are in more common use. If you need a neutral adjective to describe some aspect of belonging to one race or other, the word **racial** can be used: *...a struggle that transcended racial barriers; An old racial memory was stirred.* ⇒ **sexism**

rack, wrack

One of the meanings of **rack** is 'cause stress and suffering' or 'strain'. Several set phrases use this sense of *rack*. Two of these are *to rack one's brains*, and *to be racked with guilt.* The term *rack-rent* means an exorbitant rent that strains someone's ability to pay.

The same-sounding word **wrack** has two meanings. One is not common. It is a term for seaweed cast up on shore; the other is 'destruction' or 'collapse'. This meaning gives rise to the phrase *going to wrack and ruin*. Because both words sound the same, certain phrases are found where either word has become acceptable, e.g. *rack and ruin; nerve racking* or *nerve wracking.*

racket, racquet

In the context of tennis, both spellings are correct and both are equally used. When the sense is 'a loud noise' or 'an illegal business' the spelling is *racket.*

railway, railroad

Railway is the usual British term and **railroad** is the usual American term.

raise, rear, breed, bring up

Older usage books observed that children are *reared*, and animals *reared* or *raised*. This is not quite true. In British English and American English **raise** is frequently used in the sense of 'bring up a family'. It is rather less acceptable in British English to talk of 'raising a child': *By remaining lovable, we can raise lovable children; You couldn't raise a guinea-pig let alone a child*. The use of *raise* in the passive, as in *He was raised as a ranch kid in Oregon*, is not acceptable in British English.

In British English, the verb **breed** is traditionally associated with animals. It has the special sense of selecting bloodstock and ensuring that animals increase in number: *He went in for pig-breeding in a big way*, but it is also used of any creature: *Mosquitoes breed in stagnant water*. *Breed* is also used as a noun: *a rare breed of snail*. Use of the verb **rear** in connection with animals adds the sense of 'supervising an animal's growth and well-being': *When my wife was young, she won several ribbons for calf-rearing*.

When used in connection with human families, **rear** is a general but rather formal verb; *child rearing* is a term used in text books. When you *rear* a child, you particularly perform the nurturing, clothing, and feeding tasks of parenthood: *…the best modern theories of child rearing; …the bearing and rearing of children; Child rearing is a long hard job*. The verb **bring up** is less formal. It can be used for all aspects of child rearing but particularly for the process of educating and socializing a child. We normally refer to someone's *upbringing* and to *a well-brought-up child*, but not a 'well-reared' one. ⇒ **rise**

Ralph

There are two pronunciations of the first name **Ralph**. The very traditional one is /rafe/; the contemporary pronunciation is /ralf/. Do not confuse either with /raf/, which is the short form of Raphael. ⇒ **golf**

rancour ⇒ **rigour**

rap, wrap, rapt, wrapped

The word that means 'a sharp blow' is spelled **rap**. There are a number of set phrases that use *rap*, such as: *a rap over the knuckles*, 'a reprimand', *take the rap*, an informal equivalent for 'take the blame'. *Rap* is also the name for a monologue with a strong rhythm spoken over a backing of music.

The adjective **rapt** has no connection with the noun *rap*. It means to be totally spellbound by something: *He was watching with rapt attention.*

Wrap means 'parcel up' or 'cover something in paper or cloth'. Both the Simple Past tense and the past participle of the verb *wrap* are spelled **wrapped**. Confusingly, from the point of the sound of the phrase, if someone is deeply involved in work or a relationship, they can be described as being *wrapped up in* a situation (not *rapt*): *His entire life had been wrapped up in his work.*

rare, scarce

The adjectives **rare** and **scarce** are both used to indicate that something is not common. *Scarce* is a general word but something *rare* is either valuable or unusual, either because it exists in small amounts, or because it is not often found. For example, tangerines can be *scarce* in some seasons but they are never *rare*. A disease can be *rare: a rare form of cancer*, but never *scarce*. Diamonds are both *scarce* and *rare*.

rarefy

The spelling of **rarefy** is an exception. Other *-fy* words change the *e* to *i*, e.g. *purify*. Note the *e* in *rarefy* where you would expect *i*.

rather

When it is used in combination with *would* or *had*, **rather** can be used to express a preference in response to a choice: *Shall we go out to dinner or have a take-away? I would rather go out.* In this construction *rather* does not need to have a following *than*. The usage *had rather* is less common and is regarded as slightly old-fashioned.

If you are talking about a hypothetical situation, only *would rather* is acceptable: *I would rather die a hero than live a coward.* In speech *I would/had* is abbreviated to *I'd*.

As a modifier, **rather** is a mild equivalent to *quite*, or *fairly*. Avoid using it with strong adjectives, as such combinations e.g. *rather wonderful*, are usually ineffective.
⇒ **quite**

ravage, ravish

Ravage can be used as a verb or as a noun. The verb means 'cause extensive damage to': *...a raging wolf ravaging helpless flocks.* When it is used as a noun, it is usually plural and means 'destructive actions': *the ravages of war; the ravages of pollution; the ravages of a colony of moths.*

The verb **ravish** is normally used in the passive. The present participle is nowadays used only as an adjective: *a ravishing pair of pink shoes.* The neutral meaning is 'cause great delight', but at one time it was a euphemism for *rape*: *...one of those books where someone is ravished by Satan.*

This sense can become confused with *ravage*, producing a degree of ambiguity, as in *...sank into a down mattress for which geese had been* [*ravished*]*; Give us back our ravished ballroom*. The first example should clearly be *ravaged*, but the second is not clear-cut.

raze, rase, raise

If a town or building is **razed** it is utterly destroyed and levelled. The spelling **rase** is no longer used. The identical pronunciation of *raze* and *raise* can lead to ambiguity: *Many buildings were razed during the brief Crusader occupation of the city.*

Rd

The usual abbreviation for *road* is **Rd** without a full stop. This follows the modern convention of not using stops when the final letter of the word and the abbreviation are identical. ⇒ **punctuation**

re

The preposition **re**, 'with reference to', is common in business or official correspondence in contexts such as *Re your letter, your remarks have been noted*, or *He spoke to me re your complaint.*

In general English *with reference to* is preferable in the former case and *about* or *concerning* in the latter. Even in business correspondence, the use of *re* is often restricted to the letter heading.

re-

The prefix **re-** is long-established and can be found in verbs that come originally from Latin or French. It is possible to distinguish between two uses of **re-** as a prefix. In verbs that are well established (often shown by the absence of a hyphen) it has come to have a meaning that is inseparable from the basic meaning of the verb, which generally indicates a change of state. Examples are: *react, recur, recover, reform, refresh, review.*

The second use is in verbs created for a specialized purpose, e.g. *reformatted*. The prefix **re-** indicates repetition and it is unnecessary to add an adverb such as *back* or *again* to one of these verbs. Further examples are: *reassemble, rebuild, recalculate,* and *redistribute.*

When these overlap with an already existing verb with the same form, *re-* is separated from the body of the verb by a hyphen. While *recover* means 'get something back', *re-cover* has the special meaning 'put a new cover on something'. Other examples are: *re-cede; re-dress; re-fund.* These verbs are often *nonce words*, made up for the need of the moment: *If you've bought one and lost it, you'll just have to re-buy it.* ⇒ **neologism**

-re, -er

British spelling uses **-re** as the normal spelling for words such as *centre, mitre,* and *theatre,* and for decimal units. American English uses the **-er** spelling for all of these.

readable ⇒ illegible

real, really

In phrases like *in real life; She's really nice;* or *It was really good,* **real** and **really** add emphasis but can be overused. Never use *real* with a following adjective; this type of construction intensifies the adjective, which can only be done by an adverb, as in *really good; very good; extremely good* etc.

Note that **real** also has certain specialized uses. In computing *real-time* is a technical term, as are the phrases *real number* (mathematics), *real presence* (theology), and *real estate* (law). In *real tennis, real* is a form of *royal.*

reason

Note the construction *the reason is … that*, as in *The reason is, of course, that people feel safer at night in well-lit areas*. In both speech and writing, careful users of English avoid using the expression *the reason is because* since both *the reason is* and *because* say the same thing. The choice is between *The reason I mention it is that several mothers have raised this point with me* and *I mention it because several mothers have raised this point with me*.

reciprocal ⇒ mutual

reckless ⇒ ruthless

reckon

Some senses of **reckon** are considered informal by many writers and speakers. The usage *I reckon on your support* is avoided in formal contexts, while in a sentence such as *It will snow tonight, I reckon*, the words *believe*, *suppose*, *think*, or *imagine* are preferred to *reckon*. These uses of *reckon* are acceptable in American English.

recollect, recall, remember

Remember is used for most general circumstances. You usually **recall** something in response to an effort of memory: *As far as I could recall everything was as I had left it; Though he had seen both men before, he could not recall their names*. When you **recollect** something, you have made a conscious effort or been prompted by some other stimulus: *I tried to recollect what the letters had said; Now because you heard about this, did you recollect having seen something similar?* **Recall** is more frequently used than *recollect*.

rector ⇒ vicar

redouble, reduplicate

To **redouble** something is to add to it considerably: *To try would have provoked redoubled ferocity.* When someone *redoubles their efforts* they put in an even greater effort although they are already working hard. **Reduplicate**, meaning 'make double' or 'repeat', is used as a technical term. Sounds in language can be reduplicated, e.g. *da* and *pa* in *dada* and *papa*. In botany, leaves with *reduplicated margins* are those that curve outwards.

redundant

In British English, the most common use of **redundant**, meaning 'unnecessary; more than is needed', is in the context of employment. A *redundant* member of staff is one who is not necessary for the operation of a business.

In style, a word is *redundant* if its meaning is already present, or if the sense can be expressed using fewer words, e.g. in *free gift* the word *free* is redundant, and the phrase *at this point in time* is more economically expressed by *now*.

refer

It is redundant to add *back* to **refer** since the meaning 'back' is already contained in *refer: This refers to* [not *back to*] *what has already been said.*

If *refer* were used, it would only be appropriate to say: *He referred the matter back,* in the sense of passing a document or question to the person from whom it was received so that it could have further consideration.

referee ⇒ **umpire**

reference ⇒ **testimonial**

referendum

Referendum follows the preference for established words to have an English plural form. *Referendums* is usual although *referenda* can still be used.

refute, deny

Refute is often used incorrectly as a synonym of **deny**. In careful usage, to *deny* something is to state that it is untrue; to *refute* something is to assemble evidence in order to prove it untrue: *All he could do was deny the allegations since he was unable to refute them.*

regard, consider

Regard, unlike **consider**, needs *as* to complete its meaning: *They considered the term racist; For years, dark-skinned Americans regarded the term as racist.*

regard, regards, regarding, as regards

There are different usages involving **regard**. If the context involves reference to a fresh or relevant topic, the idiom is *with/in regard to* (note that there is no final *s*): *With regard to the payment of fees for services....* ; *My upbringing was fairly strict in regard to truthfulness.* Another possibility in a similar context is to use the idiom **as regards** (*regards* has a final *s*): *As regards the car, I didn't forget to put an advertisement in the paper.* Alternatively use **regarding**: *There will be more said later regarding the curtailment of liberty; Now, regarding the repair of council houses.*

When you ask for polite greetings to be passed on to someone, **regards** may be used; the usual idioms are *with (warm/fond etc.) regards to* or *give (my/our) regards to*: *Give my regards to your daughter, Mrs Donovan.*

regardless

Regardless is normally used together with *of*: *regardless of casualties; regardless of their situation; regardless of race or religion.* As an adverb meaning 'in spite of the consequences' it is informal: *They were doing them up regardless; Mrs Hochstadt walked on regardless, facing the front.*

registrar, register, registry

A **registrar** is an official whose job is to record information and maintain a **register** or record. In medical usage, however, a *registrar* is a middle-ranking hospital specialist.

A **registry** (or *registry office*) is the informal name for a place where you go in order to register births, deaths, and marriages. The formal official title for this is a *register office* or a *registrar's office: The General Register Office at St. Catherine's House.*

regretful, regrettable

If you have performed an action and regret it, or if something that you dislike has taken place, you may be **regretful**: *David, looking immensely regretful, grave and dignified, identified the body; ...the question was followed by a regretful little speech from the Prime Minister.*

An action or a situation can be described as **regrettable** if you feel that it creates an unsatisfactory state of affairs: *They have rejected the safety section; this is regrettable because safety in the building industry is a key issue; It is regrettable, but true.*

relate

There are two basic meanings of **relate**. One is 'tell' or 'narrate' a story etc.: *It relates the story of two women who meet on a golf-course,* the second is 'form the logical associations between things' or 'make connections in one's mind': *I extract a moral value from what I read and* *relate it to my experience.* The use of **relate to** mean 'get on well with someone', as in *They relate to others easily,* is part of the jargon of psychology. This use is becoming a cliché and is best avoided.

relative, relation, relationship

There is no useful distinction to be made between **relative** and **relation** when referring to a member of one's family. When someone is a member of your family, you *are related to* them. The word **relationship** is used for any close bond between people who are not related: *a pupil/tutor relationship; the relationship of patron and client.* However, the expression *have a relationship with* someone, as in *They had been having a relationship for seven years,* usually implies in an informal way that those concerned are lovers.

relevant, relative, relatively

The use of these words overlaps when they mean 'applicable to this case': *This may be subjective but it is also relative to the particular topic under discussion; We would discuss relevant issues amongst ourselves.* **Relevant** is the word used most often for this sense and frequently comes after a modifier: *highly relevant; more relevant; strictly relevant.*

Relative has wider and more general uses, especially with the sense 'not absolute': *...a background of relative permanence; ...relative calm and prosperity.*

The adverb **relatively** is also used informally to modify an adjective. and implies a comparison. If something is *relatively easy, relatively free,* or *relatively large,* it suggests that something less easy, free, or large exists.

remain

The use of the phrase *I remain* before concluding a letter

is usually too formal for most letters nowadays.
⇒ **letter writing**

remit, remittance, remission

The verb **remit** is used for the act of sending payment for goods (especially by post), or for the process whereby a judgment is sent back to a court for further consideration.

The noun **remit** is used in party-political contexts for a proposal that has been debated in a formal meeting and passed to a higher committee for future discussion or action. A **remittance** is a sum of money that has been sent as an allowance or as payment for goods. **Remission** is the term used for the shortening of a period of imprisonment on account of good behaviour or, in medicine, for the temporary respite from the symptoms of a disease: *He experienced several months' remission before the symptoms returned.* ⇒ **revert**

renaissance

This term, meaning literally 'rebirth', is usually applied (when written with an initial capital letter) to the period from the 14th century to the age of Shakespeare, but it can be used of any situation where lost knowledge or skills have re-emerged. The pronunciation is /ree-**nays**-since/.

repair, restore, rehabilitate

A **repair** is any action that is taken to make a damaged article usable. When something is **restored**, an attempt has been made to return it to its original condition: *The stated purpose of the new policy is 'to restore a relationship of trust'; He plans to restore the building using the original colour schemes; They can have their vision restored by surgery.*

Restore is often used as an informal substitute for *return: The lost child is restored and all are going home*, or for *revive: The patient was restored to life*. Careful writers try to avoid this extension of use.

When it is used in a military context, **rehabilitate** generally implies restoring health and physical ability to the injured, otherwise an improvement in social attitudes is implied, with the sense of 'return to a useful place in society': *…women who had not been imprisoned or rehabilitated*. Do not use it about buildings as a synonym for *repair* or *refurbish: There was no money to refurbish* [not *rehabilitate*] *Collindeane Tower*.

replica

A **replica** is 'an exact copy' of something, so do not use the tautologous phrase [*an exact replica*].

repulse, repel

The verbs **repulse** and **repel** share a common meaning of physically driving back or away, but they also have distinctive senses. The usual meaning of *repulse* is 'reject coldly' or 'drive away with discourtesy': *He repulses friendly advances and rejects every suggestion meant to help him.*

A secondary meaning is 'fight off': *Greeks repulse a heavy guerilla attack. Repel* is normally used in the sense 'drive away by arousing disgust': *The sight repelled him and he turned away.* Although the verbs are distinguished in this manner, the related adjectives adjective *repulsive* and *repellent* both mean 'causing feelings of disgust: *In some senses I am myself obscene and repulsive; The sediment of thick slime was so repellent I nearly got out again.*

require, need

The verb **need** is used for demands or desires that originate from within the speaker or writer. **Require** is used when demands are imposed on one person by another or by the situation: *There are one or two local acts which require him to give notice to us; Some organizations require members with special training.*

requirements, requisites, prerequisite

A **requirement** is an essential need or something that you are expected to provide at the request of another person: *The food requirements of these algae are small; As institutions they lay down no formal entry requirements.*

A **prerequisite** is what you need before you can begin to work on some plan or on a course of study: *A GCSE pass in Mathematics at grade C, or its equivalent, is a prerequisite for admission to this course.* The word **requisite** has a similar meaning but is also used as a rather inflated way of referring to 'necessary items': *Take a flannel and other toilet requisites.* The final part of both words rhymes with 'fit', /pre-**rek**-wi- zit/.

resin, rosin

Resin is a gum that exudes from certain trees. One type of *resin* is called **rosin**. In its prepared form, this is used by gymnasts to increase their grip on parallel bars etc., and by musicians for the bows of stringed instruments, to increase friction.

resolution, motion

In formal public meetings, a **motion** is a suggestion for action presented to the meeting for discussion. A **resolution** is a formal decision of the meeting that is based on the discussion of a motion or other business.

resort, recourse, resource

These words are used to express the general idea of

'going to someone for help or using something to solve a problem'. **Resort** and **recourse** both convey the idea of taking up an option.

Resort can be used as a noun: *The people of the ghettos felt they had no resort to official help;* or as a verb: *At meal-times they had to resort to banging knives and forks on empty plates.* If you *resort to* something or use it *as a last resort,* the overtones usually suggest that you have to make use of an unpleasant option: *Some factions resorted to terrorism; Children arrive in care as a last resort.*

Recourse is a noun only. It is either something you turn to because you have to: *He had no option other than to have recourse to violence,* or something helpful that you have a right to use: *Public companies have recourse to the market for new funds; …much greater recourse to work sharing.*

Do not confuse *recourse* with **resource**, which is a 'source of help or information': *Use the teacher as a resource,* or 'what is available to help you to act': *The great spirit had fled leaving me to my own resources.* It often refers to money or aid, as in *resources for books and equipment* but the plural form also means the things a country naturally possesses: *The surplus of energy and resources available.*

respectable, respectful

Respectable means 'deserving respect': *The teacher was a respectable woman who did her best.* **Respectful** means 'showing respect': *He touched his forehead in a gesture that was both dignified and respectful.*

respective, respectively

This pair of words can be used to help distinguish

between several different things that are referred to in a sentence and that would otherwise involve an element of ambiguity. **Respective** is used with the sense of 'related' or 'proper to each person': *They settled back, bracing themselves for their respective tasks in this interchange.* This makes it clear that they each had their own tasks. **Respectively** shows how items in one list refer to those in another: *Harvard University and MIT are respectively the fourth and fifth largest employers in the area.*

respite

A **respite** is a short relief from a difficult situation: The usual pronunciation has a short *i* sound to rhyme with 'pit', /res-pit/.

restaurant, bistro

A **restaurant** prepares meals and serves them at the table; a **bistro** is a small restaurant and bar combined. ⇒ **cafeteria**

restaurant, restaurateur

The proprietor of a **restaurant** is a **restaurateur**, that is, someone who helps restore you. There is no letter *n* in the correct spelling.

restful, restive, restless

A **restful** situation is one in which rest is found. If someone is **restive** they are irritable, impatient of control, and in need of change: *The House of Commons ceased to be merely restive and erupted; Sam was growing restive after the long quarantine.* This sense applies also to **restless**: *I sensed that the restless audience shared my own impatience,* but **restless** more usually means 'taking no rest': *Her mother was a restless human dynamo.*

restore ⇒ repair

retro-

The prefix **retro-** means 'in a backwards direction'. It is used mostly to create new technical terms, e.g. *retrofire; retroflex; retrofit,* although some longer-established words have a more general application, e.g. *retroaction; retrograde; retrospective.*

Reverend

The use of **Reverend** with a surname alone, *Reverend Smith,* or as a term of address, *'Yes, Reverend',* or in the salutation of a letter, *Dear Rev. Mr Smith,* are all generally considered to be poor usage.

reverent, revered

Reverent is used to describe someone who feels humble or respectful in the presence of something sacred or majestic: *We produce conventionally educated students with a sloppily reverent attitude to literature; Mr Gladstone was properly reverent when called to Buckingham Palace.* **Revered** is used of someone who is honoured for a pious or spiritual nature: *He would become a kind of Buddha figure, quoted and revered by everyone,* or for an attitude of deep respect, as in *Seniority is deeply revered in this country.*

revert, reversion, reversal

To **revert** is to turn back to a previous practice or type of behaviour. The verb is normally followed by *to: The overspecialized arable farmers could revert to a more sustainable form of mixed farming.* If the reference is to property, it means 'return to the original owner', as happens when a lease expires. This person then holds the **reversion** of the lease. Because **revert** means 'turn back', it is redundant to write *revert back.*

A **reversal** is any kind of about turn, but often one for the worse: *The war brought about a staggering reversal of values. Cunning, deceit, and lying became the norm.*

review, revue

The word **review** can be used as a verb or a noun. As a verb *review* generally means 'look at again' or 'look back in time'. In a military context it means 'inspect troops', while in a legal context it means 're-examine the decision of a court'. In the arts, *reviewing* involves the writing of a formal criticism of an artistic work.

As a noun, **review** can be used to name any of these activities: *The report recommends a review of policies.* In the arts and in scholarship, a *review* is an article or a collection of articles published in a journal: *The author quotes Ken Tynan's review of her...; I tried to find these results in the Review of Anthropology.* The spelling **revue** is used only for a form of light entertainment on stage or television.

reward ⇒ award

rhetoric, rhetorical question

Rhetoric, the art of using speech to persuade and please, was an important part of general education at one time. The word is now generally used in a negative sense to imply a lack of action and the favouring of empty talk: *A system that was little more than pious rhetoric; ...mere rhetoric cannot win scientific points.*

In American English, the term is still used with the old positive sense and it is the subject of a number of college courses: *This test was sufficient to inform a student that he did not know rhetoric. Rhetoric* is pronounced with a stress on the first syllable, /ret-or-rick/.

A **rhetorical question** is one where no response other than silent agreement or the acceptance of the speaker's viewpoint is expected. It is a device used in persuasion. Rhetorical questions are not normally followed by a question mark: *Who would work for no reward of any kind.*

rhyme, rime

The spelling **rhyme** is the only accepted one nowadays; the spelling *rime* is archaic. There is a different word spelled **rime**, but this means the coating of frost that forms on foliage and other objects.

right, rightly

Avoid using **right** as an emphasizer in formal English. *Right pleased* is an acceptable regional use, but it is nonstandard, as is the expression *I don't rightly know.* The standard expression is, *I (really) don't know.*

rigour, rigor

The spelling of **rigour**, meaning 'strictness' or 'harsh but just action', changes to *rigorous* without *u* when the adjective ending is applied. When the context is a medical one, the word used is **rigor**, meaning 'chilliness' or 'rigidity' as in *rigor mortis*. Note that this is the original Latin form without *u*. American English uses **rigor** for both purposes.

ring, sing

Rang and *sang* are the correct forms of the Simple Past tense of **ring** and **sing**: *He rang the bell.* The past participle forms are *rung* and *sung*: *He has sung before.* Use of *rung* and *sung* instead of the normal Simple Past is informal and non-standard.

riot, rout, routed

A **riot** is a disturbance created when a crowd is out of control. This is similar to one meaning of **rout**, 'a group of people about to commit an illegal act', but, as a *rout* is also 'a complete defeat', there is potential ambiguity in the use of this word. The usual meaning of **routed** is 'thoroughly defeated'. ⇒ **rout**

rise, raise, arise

Both verbs **raise** and **rise** involve movement to a higher point. The general meaning of **rise** is 'move upwards'.

The verb **rise** does not need an object: *…sheer mountainsides rise on either side; Early to bed, early to rise.* The verb **raise** does need an object; you have to *raise* something: *The alternative is to raise taxes; Gregory began to raise his voice in protest.*

The noun *rise* is used in connection with different types of measurement: *…measure a rise of three hundredths of one degree centigrade; The rise in crime.* The noun *rise* is also used in British English for an increase in pay: *Perhaps you'd sooner give me a rise?* American speakers, however, (and a few British speakers) use *raise* in this context: *I'm asking the boss for a raise tomorrow.*

Arise has a more restricted sense. It can mean 'originate', as in *This belief arises from the superstitions of these natives.* It is also used for standing up or getting up, and is usually limited to human actions. The overtones are formal, literary, and archaic: *I will arise and go now.* ⇒ **rouse**

road

The expression *any road*, meaning *anyway*, is not standard usage, though it is common in regional English.

rob, robbery

The technical meaning of **rob** is 'take something from someone by force or violence'. A **robbery** is an act of theft involving violence. *Rob* is widely used, by extension, in the sense of depriving someone of an important possession: *He had been robbed of his childhood.* ⇒ **burglar**

root ⇒ **rout**

rosin ⇒ **resin**

round ⇒ **around**

rouse, arouse

The verb **rouse** means 'wake up': *That brought Minnie to; she roused herself from her daze*, or 'disturb': *He was really roused by something that had displeased him.* The verb **arouse** generally means 'excite' or 'excite sexually'.

rout, route

There is a verb **rout** meaning 'defeat', pronounced /rowt/: *It was he who had conducted the retreat of the routed forces after the battle of Fosombrone.* There is another verb **rout** meaning 'dig' or 'rummage', which is pronounced either /rowt/ or /root/: *Sometimes the boys would rout out the little ground squirrels and chase them.* This verb is also spelled **root**.

A third verb **route** means 'send in a particular direction'. It is always pronounced /root/ in British English but in American English it can be /rowt/: *Departing flights were being routed well around the trouble area.*

It is preferable to retain the *e* in the verb **route** when forming the present participle in order to distinguish *routeing* from *routing*, the present participle of both **rout** verbs: *The dispute was between rich and poor farmers over the routeing of a new road.* The spelling *routing* is, however, sometimes encountered, especially in American English.

Rout meaning 'a defeat' and **route** meaning 'a chosen road' or 'a regular journey' are also nouns. ⇒ **riot**

royal

The use of **royals** as a plural noun to refer collectively to the royal family is very informal but not uncommon in journalistic usage: *This is the jet-set world, where, as with the royals, there is no real power. The royals, incidentally, are having a private rehearsal on Thursday.* It is useful as a shortened form.

RP

The letters **RP** stand for *Received Pronunciation*, the name given to a variety of pronunciation. It originally represented the pronunciation favoured by a small group of speakers belonging to the restricted group of the upper middle-class and living in and around London.

The currently accepted version of *RP* is the speech of an educated person in a fairly formal situation and on his or her 'best behaviour' as a speaker. The accurate description of this pronunciation is *Southern British Standard*. It has no class overtones and is not a dialect. An educated accent in England, Wales, Australia, New Zealand, or South Africa generally varies very little from this standard.

RP is usually presented to foreign students as a model. *BBC English*, meaning the formal English of news presenters, not the informal chatter of disc jockeys, is a form of *RP*. ⇒ **Queen's English**

rural, rustic, rustication

The adjective normally used to distinguish things of the country from things of the town is **rural**: *Mid-Sussex Rural District; Mid-Sussex Urban District.*

The adjective **rustic** is a little archaic. It has overtones of crudeness and lack of finish. A *rustic gate/seat* is rough and made of wood. When *rustic* is used as a noun, there is usually a hint of condescension in its use: *'I'm only here to preside over the rustics having a jolly good game.'*

Rustication has two meanings, neither obviously connected with the words above. It is a technical term in architecture meaning 'bold patterning in stone': *...the division between rustication and smooth exterior....*

It is a term used at the older universities for the disciplining of a student for misbehaviour by sending him or her away from the university for a period (at one time they were sent home or to the country): *Hearst worked energetically during his rustication, to make up for lost time.*

ruthless, reckless

Someone who is **ruthless** is cruel or unremitting in their attitude: *Even the most ruthless state terror could not stop the swelling discontent.*

Someone who is **reckless** is careless to the point of irresponsibility: *The fight against reckless driving has been directed extremely skilfully.*

S

sac, sack

Both words mean a bag or container. The word **sac** is mainly used in biological science for any pouchlike feature in an animal or a plant: *...the nectar that a bee can bring back in its honey sac.*

saint, st, S

The usual abbreviation for **Saint** is **St** but the form **S** (plural **SS**) is common in prayer books.

sake

The noun **sake** is usually used in the phrase *for the sake of*, as in *I agreed for the sake of a little peace and quiet; for the sake of illustration,* or else used with some form of possessive: *for your sake; for their own sake; Art for Society's sake; for Heaven's sake.*

When too many *s* sounds would result, as in a phrase like *for goodness sake*, the possessive **'s** ending is left off the word in front of *sake*. Some writers retain the apostrophe, as in *for goodness' sake*. The use of *sakes* in the plural is a variation on the idiom: *for their own sakes; for Heaven's sakes.* This is less used and may be disliked by some speakers.

salary ⇒ **wage**

saleable

The British spelling is **saleable**. In American English *salable* is preferred.

salon, saloon

The most common use of the word **salon** now, is as the

name of a place where hair is cut and styled. In earlier usage a *salon* was a literary and social gathering, often in the home of a patron of the arts (usually a well-connected woman).

The word **saloon** is historically related but has come to mean a style of car body in British English. A second use of *saloon* in British English is to describe a large public room. This is rather old fashioned. In America drink is served in a *saloon bar*.

salubrious, salutary

A **salubrious** environment or regime is one that is favourable to your health or well-being. Similarly this sort of environment can also be called *salutary*: *There was a romantic notion that it was natural and salutary for people to love each other.*

More often, however, **salutary** describes advice or an experience that is unpleasant but nevertheless beneficial. For example, *a salutary ticking off* would be one that was intended to be good for you by helping you see where you had gone wrong: *The defeat was a deserved punishment but also a salutary shock.*

same

The use of **same** or *the same* to refer to an item already mentioned is common in business and official English, e.g. *If you send us your order for the materials, we will deliver same tomorrow.* In general English this usage should be avoided. Replace *the same* with a suitable pronoun: *May I borrow your book? I'll return it tomorrow.*
⇒ similar

sanctify, sanctity

To **sanctify** something is to make it holy or to reserve it for sacred use. The **sanctity** of something is the condition of holiness or importance that causes it to be respected or honoured: *The sanctity of marriage; the sanctity of human life.*

sanction

The word **sanction** can be used either as a verb or as a noun. Among its several uses are some that seem partly contradictory.

If custom supports and encourages an action, it *sanctions* it: *This ritual has been sanctioned by years of practice.* A *sanction* is the formal authority or approval that allows an action to go forward: *Some months later our squat was given official sanction and a degree of security.* It is whatever formal penalty is prescribed for failing to follow a law: *We must impose the utmost sanction allowed by law.*

When *sanction* is used as a plural noun, it usually refers to the coercion that governments or institutions adopt against one of their group that has infringed some aspect of international law or recognized behaviour: *I called in print for economic sanctions against the Pretoria regime; The Party called for sanctions to be taken against unions who broke the agreement.*

sang ⇒ **ring**

sarcasm, irony, sardonic

Sarcasm is language that is intended to hurt or deflate another person by mocking them: *Humour is an affair of love; sarcasm of hate.* A **sardonic** remark uses mockery, irony, or sarcasm to reveal the speaker's mistrust or dislike of what they are commenting on: *Tim now regarded her with a kind of crazy sardonic joy. 'Yes. And I remember you. Dear girl'.* ⇒ **irony**

satiate, satisfy

When you **satisfy** someone you fulfil their desires or provide what they need: *More frequent feedings will help to satisfy the baby; Does that satisfy your wish?* Satisfy is also used to mean 'convince' or 'assure' someone: *You have to satisfy yourself that things are going well.* The noun from *satisfy* is *satisfaction*.

The verb **satiate** usually refers to physical or sensual needs only. Someone who is *satiated* has had their needs fufilled beyond capacity; they have had more than enough: *There is usually enough fruit on one tree to satiate several of them; The revolutionary urge cannot be satiated.* There are two nouns from this verb, *satiety*, pronounced /se-**tie**-i-ty/, and *satiation*, pronounced /**say**-she-ay-shun/. Both mean 'the state of being satiated'. *Satiate* is pronounced /**say**-she-ate/.

satire, satyr

A **satire** is a piece of writing, originally in the form of a play but now writing of any kind, that mocks the established authorities. The adjective *satirical* relates to *satire*, and there is a less common short form, *satiric*. A **satyr** is a mythological creature, half man, half goat, known for lewd behaviour.

save

The use of **save** as a preposition is largely archaic although it can still be found in literature. It can be replaced by *except: The darkness, save (except) for the useless square of stars, blanketed the village.*

scarce, scarcely

Certain words other than *not* also have a negative element in their meaning. These include *scarcely*, *barely*, and *hardly*. These adverbs can come first in their sentence but the following part of the construction is inverted like a question, with the subject coming after the finite part of the verb, as in *Scarcely had he…*

The regular noun form derived from *scarce* is *scarcity* not *scarceness*. ⇒ **hardly**

scarf

Scarf has two plural forms, *scarfs* or *scarves*. The spelling *scarves* is a little more usual. The identically spelled word **scarf** used in joinery always has the plural *scarfs*.

schedule

The usual pronunciation in British English sounds like 'shed' in its first syllable: /**shed**-yule/. A variation introduced from American English has the initial sound of 'school' /**sked**-yule/. This is now widely used in British English.

scholar, student

The word **scholar** has changed its use over the years. It is no longer the general term for 'someone who studies', but is used mainly to describe an advanced student or a teacher in an academic discipline: *M. Eliade, a scholar of ancient religion; a scholar at the Georgetown Centre…* . The word **student** has the broad meaning of someone who has 'a serious interest in' something: *a student of Islam; a research student.* More particularly, it is used to refer to those who are attending a university, polytechnic, or any other advanced college.

This use is in contrast to *pupil*, which is used for children in the primary and secondary levels of education. However there is a growing tendency to call secondary pupils *students* because of the changing social perceptions of the young, who dislike the overtones of childhood suggested by *pupil*.

school ⇒ **college**

school, shoal

The words **school** and **shoal** are both used to describe a group of fish or sea mammals and are historically related. The use of *shoal* is restricted to smaller fish; nor is it generally used of porpoises, dolphins, and sharks, etc.: *Like the cod, the haddock is very much a shoal fish; a shoal of herring.*

Note that *school* in this sense is not historically related to the other meaning of *school*, 'a place of learning'. The word *shoal*, used for shallow water, similarly has no relation to *shoal* as used above.

scone

The word **scone** has two accepted pronunciations. In the north of England, Scotland, and New Zealand it is pronounced /skon/ rhyming with 'gone'. In the south of England it is pronounced /skoun/ rhyming with 'cone'. The stone on which mediaeval Scottish kings were crowned is called the *Stone of Scone*, pronounced /skoon/.

Scot, Scots, Scottish, Scotch

A native of Scotland is a **Scot** and people native to Scotland are called the **Scots** (outside Scotland they are also known as *the Scottish*, but this is unacceptable usage in Scotland). The element *Scots* is used as a prefix in *Scotsman, Scotswoman*. Do not use *Scotchman* in this sense. The *Scottish* language is called *Scots*.

The normal adjectival form is **Scottish**: *the Scottish education system; a Scottish school of painting; Scottish literature.* *Scots* may also be used as an adjective and is found in certain phrases: *Scots law, the Scots Guards, the Scots Greys.* Several phrases have two possible forms: *a*

Scots/Scotch pine, and *a Scottish/Scotch terrier* (or *Scottie*).

In the north of England and in Scotland, **Scotch** is not used outside fixed expressions such as *Scotch whisky*, *Scotch mist*, and *Scotch egg*. The use of *Scotch* for **Scots** or **Scottish** is otherwise felt to be incorrect, especially when applied to people.

scot-free

The word *scot* in *scot-free* has nothing to do with nationality. In Old English a *scot* was a fee. If you get off *scot-free* from a difficult situation, you avoid having to pay a penalty. ⇒ **welsher**

scream, screech, shriek

These three words overlap considerably in meaning although there are some small differences in use. In all three there is an element of onomatopoeia; that is, the sound of the word imitates the noise it stands for.

A **scream** is usually associated with the human voice: *She vented her feelings in wails and screams of anguish.* A **screech** is often used for harsh or highpitched mechanical noises: *She heard the screech of brakes and she called out 'Don't!'.* A **shriek** is often used for the sounds of nature or for an extremely high-pitched human or animal scream: *She let out a shriek of laughter.* All three words can be used as verbs: *The wind was shrieking in the rigging.*

seasonable, seasonal, seasoned

Seasonable means 'appropriate to the time of year': *This is not seasonable weather.* **Seasonal** means 'depending on the season': *The river was flooded with seasonal rains; Seasonal food shortages are quite common.* **Seasoned**, however, is used for something that has matured: *Lay a* *circle of seasoned wood on the ground...*; or, by extension, of experienced people: *Even seasoned officers did not want to return.* *Seasoned* also means flavoured with herbs or spices known as *seasonings: A delicately seasoned French casserole.*

second

When **second** is a verb that means 'post someone temporarily to undertake different duties', it is pronounced /sec-**cond**/. In other cases the stress is on the first syllable.

seem

When a sentence using **seem** is in the negative, the negative element (*not, barely, un-* etc.) can either go after *seem* or before it in combination with *do*. Instead of, *I seem unable to lift my arm* we can write *I don't seem able to lift my arm.* Similarly, *He seemed not to want my assistance,* can be written *He didn't seem to want my assistance.* The difference is one of formality: *I don't seem able...* is less formal than *I seem unable.*

seize

Note that *ei* is correct in **seize.** It is one of the exceptions to the spelling guideline '*i* comes before *e* except after *c*'.

seldom

Sentences using **seldom** can be inverted: *I have seldom seen a stand-up fight like that./Seldom have I seen a stand-up fight like that.* The inverted form has literary overtones.

Seldom can be used in the construction *seldom if ever. Landy has never been to our house, and you have seldom if ever met him.* The combination *seldom or never* is not standard English.

-self, -selves ⇒ **I**

semi-

The prefix **semi-** is generally used with the sense 'partly or almost in a state or situation' as in *semiliterate; semiconscious; semiautomatic.* Its basic meaning 'half' is found only in some words, e.g. *semiannual* and *semicolon.* The British pronunciation is always /se-mee/ and the usual American pronunciation is /se-my/, to rhyme with 'eye'. An alternative prefix, **hemi-**, can also be used to mean 'half', e.g. *hemisphere.*

semicolon ⇒ **punctuation**

senior, junior

In comparisons, **senior** and **junior** are followed by *to: There are plenty of others senior to me.*

sensibility, sensitivity

The nouns *sensibility* and *sensitivity* are connected in meaning. **Sensibility** is the ability to experience and respond to feelings and emotions. The word is often used in the context of the arts, as in *artistic sensibility; a writer of high sensibility and intelligence.*

Sensitivity is most commonly used to mean the ability to recognize that someone or something needs a thoughtful response: *Much depends on the sensitivity of teachers and other staff. Sensitivity* also means a tendency to be easily hurt or offended by other people's attitudes and actions: *The sensitivity of the poor to injustice. Sensibility* is sometimes used instead with this sense: *...his sensibility to criticism.*

Sensitivity has a much broader range of uses than *sensibility.* In different contexts, *sensitivity* is used to describe the capacity for physical or chemical response, as in

Allergies are occasionally found to be caused by sensitivity to certain foods, and also to describe response to stimuli.

sensible, sensitive

Someone who is **sensible** acts and makes decisions on the basis of reason rather than emotion. A sensible person is generally one who receives praise for their actions.

A **sensitive** person is aware of the feelings and the reactions of others. *Sensitive* followed by *to* is used for a living thing or an apparatus that is equipped to sense activity in its vicinity: *Spiders are sensitive to the vibrations on their web; The receptors are sensitive to infra-red radiation.* Another use of *sensitive*, meaning someone who is too easily upset or worried by the effect events might have on himself or herself, contains an element of implied criticism. When it has these meanings it is usually followed by *over, to,* or *about: You must stop being so sensitive about your looks.*

If *sensitive* is used with a general term such as *issue, matter, topic* or *subject*, it means that reference to what is concerned must be made with care so as not to offend or hurt someone.

sensuous, sensual

A **sensuous** experience is one that pleases the senses or is derived from the senses. The overtones suggest pleasure to the mind or spirit of the person: *Sculpture is a sensuous art.* Something that is **sensual** also gratifies the senses: *The total effect is luxurious, elegant, and often highly sensual.* When the adjective *sensual* is used in a personal description, the overtones suggest that the person described takes pleasure in the gratification that comes through the body, particularly sexual pleasure: *a small, straight nose, a red sensual mouth.*

sentiment, sentimentality

The noun **sentiment** is used for a feeling or an expression of thought: *The sentiments expressed made him smile*. It is a formal, but neutral, word.

The noun **sentimentality** and the related adjective *sentimental* are used to describe excessive indulgence in the emotions, especially in romantic feelings: *His affection contained a thick seam of sentimentality*.

sentinel, sentry, guard

Sentinel and **sentry** are both used in military contexts. Historically, *sentry* is a shortened form of *sentinel*. A **guard** is someone who watches over something or someone in any context: *Passengers must leave the train if asked to do so by the guard*. By extension a *guard* is also any protective device used to keep people from harm: *Machine guards must be in place before switching on*, or any agency that offers protection: *Use an antiseptic cream as a guard against further infection*.

separate

The word **separate** is frequently misspelled. Note that the second syllable is -*par*-. A way to remember this is to associate the spelling of the word with one of its meanings: 'divide into *parts*'.

sergeant

The word **sergeant** is frequently misspelled. A way to remember the correct form is to associate the spelling of the word with the cloth *serge* that is often used for uniforms.

service

The principal use of **service** as a verb is in the context of car and appliance maintenance: *We service any make of washing machine; The car was last serviced in June*. A secondary meaning in British English is 'meet interest on a debt': *Higher mortgage rates have meant that many housebuyers can no longer service their debts.* Avoid using it in the context of services rendered to people where the appropriate verb is *serve*.

serviette, napkin

Both words are in common use to mean a small square of cloth or paper used to protect one's clothes while one is eating. **Napkin** is held by some to be a more 'refined' term. ⇒ napkin ⇒ shibboleth

session, sitting

The meeting of a court or similar body is called a **session**: *The Military Committee was in permanent session.* It is also used for the formal meetings of other groups: *We have a consulting session most evenings.* Session can be used informally to mean any activity that lasts for an indefinite time: *He went into his pub to have a damn good session; He's going to move if he doesn't get promotion this session.* In the context of music, a *session* is time spent in a studio making a recording.

An official body in session is said to be *sitting* and the participle can be used as a noun, as in *...during one sitting of the court...* , but the word has a more general application. It is, for example, the set time for serving meals: *The first sitting is now being served in the dining car,* a period of time spent continually on one task: *I don't expect you to finish this at a sitting,* and the time spent having a portrait painted: *He always spent the first two sittings blocking out the background and putting the sitter at ease.*

set ⇒ lay

sew, sow

The spelling **sew** is used for working with needle and thread. **Sow** is used for planting seeds. ⇒ **so**

sewage, sewerage

Sewage is domestic or industrial waste matter, **sewerage** is the system of drains that carries sewage. Some sewage is treated on *sewage farms*.

sexism, sexist

Sexism means discrimination that arises from perceived or real differences between the sexes: *It is monstrous that sexism should coerce government policy.* **Sexist** is the related adjective: *...a cabaret full of sexist and racist jokes.* It is also found used as a noun: *I became an object of ridicule for small-minded sexists.* This sense is sometimes conveyed by the use of the label *male chauvinist.* *Sexism* usually refers to the attitudes of men towards women; more accurately, *sexism* can also be found in women's language about women.

Sexism in language is in many ways not as blatantly obvious as the linguistic manifestations of racism because distinctions based on sex are part of the structure of many languages. It can therefore be more pervasive while superficially absent or not consciously intended. Sexism is not simply a matter of name calling. It is a product of language's roots in a social structure that incorporates both men and women.

The expectations that are raised by words that describe and name roles are part of unconscious sexism. *Manager, director, pilot,* and *doctor* traditionally suggest male occupations, while *nurse, typist,* and *receptionist* suggest female occupations. That society often places a smaller value on these latter occupations is part of the problem. Similarly, when word pairs exist, as in *author/authoress, actor/actress*, there are sometimes undertones that suggest an inferior ability attached to the word that labels a woman.

Descriptions of typical human responses often display a sexist bias. Women *have a tantrum*, men *fly into a rage*; women *gossip*, men *talk things over*. The list is large.

An interesting area is the changing use of the pronoun *he* throughout documents as a shorthand form of *he or she*. Failing the existence of a neutral pronoun in English, modern practice is to ignore the number difficulties caused and use *they/them* even when the verb remains singular, or when *anyone, someone, no one*, and *anybody*, all traditionally treated as singular, are associated pronouns.

English has a vast range of words and constructions from which to choose. Careful users of English are advised to examine the vocabulary and phrasing of what they write and ask themselves if it is capable of being interpreted as sexist.

shall, will

Shall has come to be largely neglected in favour of **will**, which has become the commoner form for indicating an unconditional element of future time for the first, second, and third persons (*I/we, you, he/she/it/they*). In spoken English, the distinction between the two forms is hidden by the use of *'ll* as the abbreviated form for both.

You may have heard of a complex rule for the use of *shall* and *will* stating that where the meaning indicated simple futurity, *shall* had to be used for the first person of the verb and *will* for the second and third: *I shall drown (please help me)*. Where the meaning involved a command, obligation, or determination, the positions were reversed: *I will drown (and don't stop me)*.

This complex rule was not part of the natural evolution of language but an artificial constraint suggested by an earlier grammarian who was trying to build a future tense for English out of two overlapping verb meanings. Since much of the work of indicating future time is carried out by constructions that use neither of these verbs: *I fly there tomorrow; I am going there on Tuesday; I may help you, if it suits me*, this was not helpful or realistic.

Some may think it advisable to follow the above 'rule' in very formal writing in order to avoid pedantic criticism, but it is not necessary and it is probably a worse mistake to overuse *shall* under the misconception that it is a 'better' word. Note that there is a regional difference in some aspects of usage. The tendency is for questions to be framed using *will* if the speaker is from the North of England and Scotland, and with *shall* in the South. The abbreviated form of *shall not*, *shan't*, is not common in American English. ⇒ **will**

shambles

The noun **shambles** is singular. It used to mean a slaughterhouse but is now used for any situation that has grown out of control: *The Arabian desert was a shambles of burning vehicles; The day ended in a shambles of uncoordinated activity*. The neologism *shambolic* is a very informal adjective.

The verb *shamble*, meaning 'walk in an awkward, unsteady way' is not to be confused with the sense above: *I shambled round, then began to crawl*.

sharp, sharply

Sharp can be used as an adverb in expressions that

involve time and direction: *I'll see you at ten sharp; Turn sharp right just after the pub.* In other contexts use **sharply**: *I'll have to speak sharply to him.*

shew, show

Shew is the old spelling of **show**. It was for a long time found only on maps and charts and is now never used.

shibboleth

A **shibboleth** is a sign by which someone is recognized as belonging to a particular group. In language some items of vocabulary and forms of pronunciation can become a *shibboleth*, indicating to some hearers that the speaker belongs to a particular social class, background, or educational level. Language reflects its speakers. Whether something becomes a *shibboleth* is in the hands of the users. ⇒ **RP** ⇒ **U and Non-U**

shoal ⇒ school

should, would

Should has, as its most common meaning in modern English, the sense 'ought', as in *I should go to the graduation, but I don't see how I can.* It is seen as a polite way of expressing the sense of an obligation to do something.

Would expresses a simple request for a future action: *Would you bring in the clothes?* A less common type of construction is sometimes called 'future in the past'. This odd notion simply means that you are talking now about a past situation during which you expressed some thoughts about the future, as in, for example: *I'll be caught here for hours.* When you tell someone about this later it becomes: *I supposed I would be caught there for hours.* The use of *would* in all these sentences is usual with all but the most formal of speakers, no matter if there is a first-person speaker or a second or third person.

Should is also used after a reporting verb in sentences that express a possible future action: *The report recommends that the Government should set a firm date for the start of funding.* In clauses like this, *should* is often left out. The clause then takes on the form: *The report recommends that the Government set a firm date for the start of funding.* Similarly *should* can be used in clauses starting with *if* that talk about a future possibility: *Would you bring in the clothes if it should rain?* This is more commonly expressed: *Would you bring in the clothes if it rains?*

shriek ⇒ **scream**

sic

The Latin word **sic**, meaning 'just so', is used when an editor wants to point out that an error or some other oddity is as written by the author: *23rd February – Fun-Raising (sic).* As editors usually correct errors silently, the use of *sic* frequently signals amusement or scorn: *It is in the differentiation of classes that the moral (sic) wealth of mankind is exhibited.*

sick ⇒ **ill**

similar, same

Similar is often used inappropriately where the meaning is 'the same' or 'identical'; *similar* means 'alike but not identical'. **Same** takes a definite article, *similar* does not: *He and Tom were the same age; Mike and I have a similar outlook on many things.* *Similar* can be modified by *very* while *same* cannot: *Burmese and Siamese cats are very similar in appearance and size.*

simplistic

The word **simplistic** is well established but is disliked by some people. It does not mean the same as *simple*, as it has overtones of foolishness and unsophisticated or unrealistic reasoning: *Old Stony launched into another of his simplistic sermonettes*, or of superficial and uncritical opinions: *I became tired of facile, simplistic principles that are so cheap to express*. Simplistic has become a vogue word.

simulate, assimilate

When you **simulate** a piece of behaviour or an object, you set out to copy it, often for the purpose of studying it: *The object is to simulate normal working of the muscles; You can use a comb on wet paint to simulate wood-grain.*

To **assimilate** something is to absorb or incorporate it into the main body. It is often used to describe the process of taking in nourishment or knowledge: *Two of the victims assimilated this poison from food; we had no opportunity to assimilate what was going on.* When a person *assimilates* or has been *assimilated*, there has been a steady process of adjustment to a culture so that he or she becomes an integrated part of it: *The debate was whether foreign workers should be assimilated into Swedish culture.*

since ⇒ ago

sing ⇒ ring

sink, sunken

The verb **sink** follows the same pattern as *sing*. The Simple Past is *sank* and the past participle is *sunk*. *Sunk* is acceptable in the informal expression: *Now we're sunk!* meaning 'we have been found out'. **Sunken** is the form used for the adjective, as in *sunken garden*.

sitting ⇒ session

situation

Situation is often used in contexts in which it is redundant or imprecise. Typical examples are: *The company is in a crisis situation* or *...people in a job situation*. In the first example, *situation* does not add to the meaning and should be omitted. In the second example, it would be clearer and more concise to substitute a phrase such as *people at work*.

situation, position, job

There are a number of closely associated words in the set: *situation, posting, post, place, position, job*. The appropriate choice of word reflects the status of the work as it is seen by the employer and the worker. **Situation** covers all types of employment, as seen in the notice *Situations Vacant*. This is a rather genteel term and almost obsolete except in this usage. While **job** has a generalized usage, as in *Job Centre*, it is specifically linked to *work* and is seen as a more forthright term. Manual labour is a *job* not a *situation*.

The words *post, position,* and *place* are used for white-collar and professional work. A Legal Executive or a Dental Nurse would have a **position**. A teacher or lecturer has a **post**, which is usually understood to involve certain defined responsibilities: *The post of Course Leader*. A **place** is often offered within the framework of a *team* as in *a place in our creative team*. A senior executive may have a **posting**, which usually involves the holder working in different branches of the company at different times. ⇒ **wage**

skilful

Note that **skilful** does not retain the second *l* of *skill*.

slander ⇒ libel

slough

The word **slough** when used of a snake shedding its skin is pronounced /sluff/. The archaic word for 'a swampy hollow' is pronounced /slau/ with the same vowel sound as 'loud'.

slow, slowly

The use of **slow** as an adverb (including the comparative form *slower*) is very informal. It is sometimes found on signs: *Drive slow*, and used in requests: *Please talk slower*. The usual form is **slowly/more slowly**. The use of *slow-moving* as a modifier: *We were stuck behind a slow-moving tractor*, and *go-slow* (normally used as a noun) are totally acceptable.

smell, smelled, smelt

When **smell** is used in its neutral sense of emitting an odour, it is followed by an adjective rather than by an adverb: *This fresh bread smells good* rather than *well*. When it means 'emit an unpleasant odour', it can be followed by an adverb or an adjective: *Whatever you are burning smells horrible/horribly*. The usual Simple Past tense and the past participle form of *smell* in British English is **smelt**. American English prefers **smelled**.

Do not confuse this verb with the specialized verb *smelt* that is used in industry and means 'extract a metal from its ore by heating it'. Note also the quite different use of the noun *smelt* to describe a small type of fish.

so

So has many uses, several of which cause problems. Some writers of formal English consider it poor style to use **so** on its own to indicate purpose or reason. However, the usage is well established in informal speech and writing. In more formal use, the construction **so that** is employed before purpose and reason clauses. Purpose: *He took it so (that) he could try it.* Reason: *I was holding her up so (that) she could see better.* The construction *so as to* meaning 'in order to' is an alternative way of expressing reason or purpose: *She screamed loudly so as to wake the neighbours.*

If the linked clause in the sentence expresses a result, *that* is not necessary: *He fell off, so he was disqualified.* However, some writers prefer to use *and so* when *so* means 'therefore', as it does in this example: *He fell off, and so he was disqualified.*

When you make a negative comparison you have a choice between *as… as…* or *so… as…*. For example both of these sentences are acceptable: *It's not nearly so cold as it was yesterday; They're not as nice as the ones I bought in Lindfield.*

so-called

There are two uses for this expression. First, when something is **so-called**, it pretends to be what it is not. This use is usually ironic, as in *Father was in his so-called study; He was peddling a so-called cure for Aids in Rumania.* The second use of *so-called* is as a way of saying, 'This is the name they give it' as in *Their usual unit is a so-called 'brick' of three soldiers.* Although purists object to this usage, it is well-established, especially in scientific and technical writing.

So-called is incorrectly used to imply that someone is ineffective or despicable, as, for example, in the phrase *the jargon of so-called museum curators*, because the people referred to really are *museum curators*, however much the speaker dislikes the way they talk.

sofa, settee

There is really no formal distinction between a **sofa**, a **settee**, and a **couch**. These words all have different origins. Their use is dependent largely on fashion and regional and family preferences, e.g. the poet John Betjeman held that *couch* was a more genteel term.

solecism

A **solecism** is any mistake in the performance of a ritual that sets one apart. A lapse in etiquette can be a *solecism*, as can an error in grammar, as both involve breaking rules of behaviour: *…to commit so gross a solecism. It made him want to hide his face.*

soliloquy

A **soliloquy** is a stage device whereby a character in a play reveals his or her inmost thoughts to the audience, as if confidentially. ⇒ **dialogue**

soluble, solvable

The word **soluble**, meaning 'able to be dissolved', is often misspelled. It is not *solu + able* but *solu + ble*. The opposite is **insoluble**. Something that is *insoluble* will not *dissolve*, while something that is *unsolvable* cannot be *solved*.

These senses are combined in the noun *solution*. Compare: *These are all the pieces of a jigsaw puzzle whose solution you know*, and, *A mild household bleach solution will whiten white nylon.* Therefore, it is not uncommon to hear a puzzle or mystery called *insoluble* instead of the more acceptable *unsolvable*.

somebody, someone

Both these words are singular and traditionally take the

singular form of the verb in formal writing. In informal usage, and increasingly in formal usage, the plural pronoun *they/ their* is used after **somebody** or **someone** to avoid the necessity of writing *he or she/his or her* or being gender-specific in sentences. Compare: *If I annoy someone, he or she will try to embarrass me,* and: *If I annoy someone, they will try to embarrass me.*

sometime

An archaic use of **sometime** can still be found used in certain academic courtesy titles. Somebody addressed as, for example, *Sometime Churchill Professor of Greek,* is a retired or former professor, not an occasional or future professor.

sort

The noun **sort** is singular but it is often found used with a plural determiner when it is followed by a plural noun, as in *There wouldn't have been those sort of opportunities.* This attracts criticism on the grounds that the determiner should modify *sort* not *opportunities* but there are precedents for this construction that go far back. If you feel uncomfortable with the construction, the solution is either to use the plural form *sorts: ...people who have those sorts of possessions* or to invert the sentence, as in *Opportunities of this sort...* ⇒ **kind**

sound

The adverb form *sound* is usually restricted to the set expression *sound asleep.* In other cases use *soundly: Sleep soundly.*

Soviet Union, Russia

In general usage, the labels the **Soviet Union** and **Russia** have been regarded for many years as equivalent. Recent events have clarified and made necessary the distinction

between the *Soviet Union*, a federation of administrative regions, and *Russia*, the largest of these regions.
⇒ **Great Britain**

sow ⇒ **sew**

speciality, specialty
In British English the normal spelling of this word is **speciality**. In American English the spelling **specialty** is common. This form is becoming more common in Britain, especially in restaurants: *Chef's specialty*. It is easier to say and may become the standard, but as yet it is not.

specially ⇒ **especially**

spelled, spelt
The verb *spell* has alternative Simple Past and past participle forms, **spelled** or **spelt**. There is no distinction of meaning or frequency of use. *Spelled* is pronounced either /spelt/ or /speld/. *Spelt* is always pronounced /spelt/. Note that *misspelled* or *misspelt* has a double *s*.

split infinitive
It is supposedly a grammatical error to split an infinitive by writing (to use a well-known example) *to boldly go* rather than *boldly to go* or *to go boldly*. This is no more than a prejudice. The rule against splitting the infinitive came about because of a misconception about the nature of the infinitive in English.

Strictly speaking, English has no infinitive. Some languages, such as French and Latin, have a single word that cannot be 'split'; English normally uses the preposition *to* in front of the base form of a verb in a way that is similar to a Latin infinitive. Some grammarians held that you should not split this *to* infinitive construction by placing an adverb between the two parts.

Although it is true that doing so may result in a clumsy sentence, as in *She decided to firmly and definitively deal with the problem*, this is not enough to justify the absolute condemnation that this practice has attracted from some purists. Indeed, very often the most natural position of the adverb is between *to* and the verb: *He decided to really try next time*. To change it would result in an artificial and awkward construction: *He decided really to try next time*.

Although the *split infinitive* is not a grammatical error, avoid clumsy constructions. Finally, note that writers often decide not to place adverbs between *to* and the base form in formal written English because readers with a more traditional point of view are likely to interpret this type of construction as incorrect.

spoiled, spoilt

The verb *spoil* has alternative Simple Past and past participle forms, **spoiled** or **spoilt**. There is no distinction of meaning or frequency of use. The form *spoilt child* is more common than *spoiled child*. *Spoiled* is pronounced either /spoylt/ or /spoyld/. *Spoilt* is always pronounced /spoylt/.

spoonful

It is usual to treat a **spoonful** as a set quantity, so the plural form is *spoonfuls: three spoonfuls of honey*. An alternative spelling, which some users regard as incorrect, places the *s* before *-ful*. If the expression is thought of as a contraction of three *spoons full* of honey, the origin of the less acceptable plural form, *spoonsful*, can be understood. These remarks also apply to combinations like *tablespoonful* etc. In practice, most of these words are shortened, as in *two teaspoons of sugar; two tablespoons of jam.* ⇒ -ful

squash ⇒ quash

stalk, stem, trunk

The **trunk** is the main support of a large woody plant. A **stem** is the main support of a smaller woody plant or the part of any plant that carries the leaves or flowers: *Make sure you choose carnations with long stems; Occasionally gigantic specimens of kelp are found with stems 20 metres long.* We refer to the *trunk* of a tree but to the *stem* of a rose bush.

Stalk and *stem* overlap in meaning, though **stalk** is usually preferred for the stems of herbaceous plants such as grass: *stalks and seeds of hay; trampling the juicy green stalks.*

Standard English

Because the English language is spoken as a mother tongue by millions of people in a dozen countries, it is not possible to say that any variety of English sets an absolute standard.

However, when we are looking for guidance on grammar, pronunciation, usage, and spelling, it is usual to turn to the variety of English spoken by educated users in Britain and use that as a standard.

In other English-speaking countries, such as America, Australia, and New Zealand, the English used by educated speakers similarly serves as the standard.
⇒ RP ⇒ Queen's English

start ⇒ begin

stationery, stationary

These two words cause a common spelling problem. The

word that means 'not moving' is **stationary** with an *-ary* ending. The word that means 'items for writing with' has an *-ery* ending. Compare this with *baker/bakery*.

staunch, stanch, stem

The word **stanch** or **staunch** is used with reference to bleeding. Although some dictionaries give **staunch** as just a variant spelling, it is now the form more commonly used. It means 'cause to stop flowing', as in *Sophia staunched the blood with a cloth; She wanted affection like a wound wanting to be staunched*. While *stanch/staunch* has a rather specialized application, another word, **stem**, can also be used to mean 'cause to stop flowing'. This is used with any liquid, or as a metaphor: *This failed to stem the speculative tide; …stemming the change of time; This had not stemmed the revolt.*

The expression *stem from* is connected with the other sense of **stem**, that is, a part of a plant. ⇒ **stalk**

stay, stop

Stay is generally used to mean 'live as a guest or visitor', while **stop** is used of a break in a journey: *We had to find somewhere to stop for lunch*. When *stop* is combined with *off* or with *over*, it takes on some of the meaning of *stay*: *On the way home I stopped off in London for a conference; Jem is stopping over in New York for three days before returning home.*

stem ⇒ staunch

still

Care is needed in the placing of the adverb **still** within a clause as it can be ambiguous, meaning either 'without movement' or 'without letting up' according to where it is placed. The first meaning is present in: *In the other* *hand he held his gun still; She could see a figure lying still under the blankets,* the second in: *In the other hand he still held his gun; She could see a figure still lying under the blankets.* Most instances involve the second meaning, with *still* placed before the main verb.

When *still* comes first in a clause, or could be placed first, it means 'nevertheless': *Still, we mustn't get carried away/We still mustn't get carried away.*

stimulant, stimulus, stimulate

When you **stimulate** someone, you rouse them into activity. A **stimulant** is anything that provokes increased activity, usually an artificial substance, as for example a drug: *Cola drinks contain small amounts of caffeine, a stimulant.* A **stimulus** is usually some natural event that spurs someone on: *Increasing size may have been the stimulus that made apes start to swing beneath branches.*

stop ⇒ stay

storey ⇒ first floor

strait, straight

The same-sounding words *strait* and *straight* are used in a number of compounds and phrases and are often confused. A **strait** is a narrow sea channel between two larger areas of sea. The word is sometimes used in the plural: *Cook Strait; The Straits of Magellan.* Because *straits* can be dangerous places, we get the set phrases *dire straits* and *desperate straits.* The meaning 'narrow' or 'constricted' is also found in *straitjacket,* and *strait-laced,* and used in the expression *in straitened circumstances.*

The word **straight** has a basic meaning 'not curved or crooked'. It is used in the expressions *keep on the straight and narrow* and *keep a straight face.* Compounds include *straightedge* and *straightforward.*

strata

Strata should not be treated as a singular noun. It is the plural of *stratum*. The use of 'stratas' as a plural is not acceptable.

strategy ⇒ tactics

stringed, strung

The usual past participle of the verb *string* is **strung**. It is used in the phrase *highly strung* to mean 'tense or nervous by nature'. **Stringed** is used adjectivally in the expression *stringed instruments*. If you are talking about a tennis racquet, you can use either *restrung* or *restringed*.

stupefy

Note the spelling **stupefy**. Unlike *stupid* it does not have an *i*.

subconscious ⇒ unconscious

subjective ⇒ objective

subsequent, consequent

When one thing is **subsequent** *to* another, it follows on in time. When one thing is **consequent** *on* another, it happens as a result of the first event. Note the prepositions that follow each use.

substantive

The word **substantive** is found in older dictionaries and grammars as a term for *noun*. It is no longer used.

such as, like

You can use a construction with *like* if you need to point out some similarity between objects or people: *He eats like a pig; He fights like a tiger*, or draw attention to one particular feature of something: *a small university like*

Sussex; rural towns like Chichester. Like is used as a preposition, so it is followed by a noun phrase or a pronoun. The pronoun should be in the object form: *like him, like me.* Some people prefer to use **such as** instead of *like* in formal contexts if what follows is an example, as in *The control rod is made of a material, such as* [or *like*] *boron, that absorbs neutrons,* and especially if more than one example is given: *They came from traditionally militant areas such as* [or *like*] *Glasgow, Merseyside, and South Wales.* There are no strong reasons for supporting this preference. Both are acceptable.

There is much controversy over using *like* as a conjunction. Most writers on usage agree that, traditionally, *like* should not be followed by a clause. Most also agree that a number of well-known writers have used *like* as a conjunction and that, informally at least, it is acceptable: *It didn't work out quite like I intended it to.* In formal writing use *as* instead: *It didn't work out quite as I intended it to.*

Take care over the use of *as such.* This expression means 'from the point of theory' or 'in itself' and is accurately used in: *He's not terribly interested in politics as such; Their concern is more with manufacturing industries than with technology as such.* It is only being used as a filler in the following example: *Do you have it? Not as such.* Unless the speaker is being deliberately evasive, this is just a long-winded way of saying *No.*

sufficient, enough

In most cases *sufficient* and *enough* have the same meaning. Some users feel that *sufficient* is a genteel substitute for *enough,* but notice that they are used in different constructions. **Enough** may come before or after the noun it modifies: *...enough time to finish; ...time enough to finish.* **Sufficient** must go in front of the noun: *...sufficient time to finish.* *Sufficient* should not be used as a noun, but *enough* can be. Expressions like *Do you have sufficient?* instead of *Do you have enough?* may be regarded as affected and genteel.

suffix

A **suffix** is a group of letters that is added to the end of a word, e.g. *-able; -ize; -less; -ly; -ness*, etc. Suffixes have the effect of changing the meaning or the grammatical class of a word. This is a very common feature of English. ⇒ **prefix**

suite, suit

Both these nouns have the basic sense of 'a group or set'. The word **suite** is used for a set of rooms in a hotel, a set of matching furniture, or a piece of music for several instruments. A **suit** is one of the four types of cards in a pack, and it is used for an outfit of clothes made from the same fabric.

In law, when you bring a case against someone, you *file/ bring a suit* against them. This sense is close to that of the noun *pursuit*.

summary ⇒ **precis**

summon, summons

The verb **summon** means 'call on someone to come': *He summoned the police at his mother's insistence.* The verb **summons** means 'issue an order for someone to appear before a court': *He has been summonsed to appear before the magistrates next week.* A **summons** (noun) is the official document on which the call to court is presented. *Summons* is singular. The plural form is *summonses*.

sunken ⇒ sink

superior, superscript, subscript

A **superior** number is one that is printed above the base-line of the normal printing, as follows: 10^{12}; an *inferior* number is printed below the baseline, as follows: 10_{12}. These can also respectively be called **superscript** and **subscript** numbers.

supper, tea

In British English **supper** is an evening meal, which can also be called **tea**, depending on the social group of the speaker and region in which they live. These two words are not associated with a fixed time or with particular contents of the meal and are used in ways that can be confusing or even socially embarrassing.

Tea can either mean light refreshment, mainly a cup of tea and biscuits or cake, or a substantial meal of hot and cold foods. *Tea* may be taken between four o'clock and eight o'clock depending on the habits of the household and the day of the week. *Supper* can mean a cooked evening meal eaten between six and eight o'clock in the evening, or even later, or a light snack eaten shortly before bedtime. In some social groups the evening meal is always referred to as **dinner**, and the words *supper* and *tea*, if used, mean light refreshments only.

These words are hazardous not only for English speakers from countries outside Britain but also for those who come from different regions of Britain where the usage varies. ⇒ **lunch**

suppose, supposing

If you **suppose** something, you believe it to be true but you have no proof. This basic meaning can be extended. *Suppose* is often used as part of the construction

Suppose we... (do something) or *Let's suppose...* which can either be an informal way of making a suggestion or an informal way of introducing an imagined situation for further discussion: *Suppose we went looking for him; Suppose we did prove Davis to be the culprit; Let us suppose that they believe you.* **Supposing** is a more formal way of introducing imagined situations: *But supposing that something should go wrong?*

surprised

There are several constructions that use **surprised**. The meanings differ. *Surprised at* is used when an action seems out of character: *Nobody could be surprised at anything they did.* *Surprised by* and *surprised to* are used when an event happens without warning or is unforeseen in other ways: *Occasionally he seemed surprised by what he read; I was surprised to find they had such white bodies.*

susceptible

There are two constructions that use **susceptible**. Each has a different meaning. *Susceptible to* means 'easily affected by': *She became susceptible to infections like pleurisy.* *Susceptible of* means 'allows' or 'is capable of': *It is a moral judgment not susceptible of proof or disproof.*

swap, swop

The spelling **swap** is generally used for the verb that means 'exchange one thing for another'. This verb has the alternative spelling **swop**. The custom of slapping hands on a bargain relates this sense to the verb's second meaning, which is 'give something a sharp blow'. Note, for example, that a reaping hook, or a curved blade used for trimming hedges, is called a *swaphook* in some localities. ⇒ **swot**

sweat ⇒ **perspire**

swell

The verb **swell** has a past participle that can be written as either *swelled* or *swollen*. The idiom meaning 'puffed up with pride and self-importance' has several acceptable versions: *swollen-headed* and *swelled-headed* are found in British English, *swell-headed* is also found in American English.

swine

The noun **swine** is a term for a number of pigs. Strictly, then, it is already a plural form, but when you are talking about a person or a group of people whom you despise, *swine* may be used informally as if it were a noun with a singular and plural form: *What a swine; He's an absolute swine; These swines with their big cars.*

swot, swat

A **swot** or a *swotter* is someone who studies harder than his or her fellow students. If you are *swotting* for an examination, you are studying with more concentration than you normally do. *Swot* is usually used as a mildly scornful term.

When you **swat** something you give it a sharp blow with a flat object. This word is similar to *swap/swop* in that it imitates the sound of the action. ⇒ **swap**

syllabus

The plural of **syllabus** is **syllabuses**. The form *syllabi* is only a jocular plural.

sympathy, empathy, sympathetic

Sympathy is the sharing of feeling and emotions, especially in times of stress. The adjective **sympathetic** involves this sense and, by extension, the sense of acting in harmony with something, as happens when the vibration of one string in an instrument causes others to vibrate too.

Empathy is the power of understanding the feelings of others, including creatures, and imaginatively experiencing them: *The tenderness, care, and empathy which we seek from the family; In his writing, he can bridge with empathy the distance between himself and others.* While *sympathy* suggests that someone feels a similar emotion to another being, *empathy* suggests that this emotion is recognized and also experienced.

synergism, synergy

In biology **synergism** or **synergy** is the working together of two entities in such a way that the total effect is greater than the sum of the effects of each separate entity. This word has entered the jargon of business theory where it is loosely used, sometimes as a substitute for 'cooperation', often just as a way of conveying that an enterprise is 'good'. ⇒ **buzz word**

systematic, systemic

Anything **systematic** is marked by planning and order: *a systematic computer analysis; a systematic course of physical training.* The term **systemic** is used in plant biology, and by gardeners, for a substance, such as a fungicide, that enters the *system* of the plant in order to protect it. *Systemic* is also a rarely used synonym for *systematic*.

T

tactics, strategy

The word **tactics** is usually used in the plural. Tactics are the methods that are used to achieve an aim: *Tactics dictate that we move in swiftly; Switches in tactics and doctrine were all made by the British side*. The context is frequently a military one, but its use is extended to business and politics. A **tactic**, in the singular, is one move towards your aim: *War is a tactic for survival*.

A **strategy** is the overall, long-term plan of which your tactics form a part.

tags

Spoken sentences, or clauses within sentences, are frequently completed with a tag. A *tag* is a clause like, *don't you, can't he, will they*.

A *tag* is used for one of two reasons. The first is that the speaker wants to be reassured that the person listening agrees with what is being said: *'Yes, this is very nice, isn't it.'* The second reason is to allow a statement to be turned into a question: *'It's a proper word, isn't it?' asked Celia*.

When you write down a sentence containing a *tag*, which will not be often unless you are writing dialogue, only the second type of *tag* must be followed by a question mark. The first type of tag, the type that checks that the person listening agrees, does not need a question mark if it is within a sentence: *It's strange, isn't it, your being so fond of Sam*. It is optional when it is at the end: *Yes, this is very nice, isn't it (?)*

Listeners usually know what sort of tag is being used because of the speaker's tone of voice, and the context of the sentence.

talent, genius

Talent and genius differ in the extent of the cleverness that is involved. If you have a **talent** *for* something or are **talented** *at* something, you have an inborn ability to do it well: *Creative thinking often requires a talent for expression.* **Genius** is an exceptional amount of talent in some area. In colloquial English, both *talent* and *genius* are used with the sense of 'a special gift': *The British genius for compromise; He has a talent for getting things wrong.* ⇒ **genius**

tall

Tall and **high** are interchangeable in many contexts except when you refer to the height of a person, in which case *tall* must be used: *A tall young man; The uniform tall, white buildings; How high is the Post Office Tower?*

High is also the appropriate adjective when people are commenting on the distance that they find themselves away from ground level: *Look how high up I am.* ⇒ **high**

target

The use of **target** as a verb, as in *We want to target all potential users of the product*, has become a standard term in marketing and sales areas. It is a usage that is disliked by many people. In formal speech and writing the use of an alternative metaphor such as *We want to aim our marketing at…* may be preferable. *Target* does not double the final *t* when forming other verb parts.

taste, tasty, tasteful, tasteless

There are two main senses of **taste**. First, the sense through which flavour is appreciated, secondly, the tact and good judgment of someone in matters of behaviour or aesthetics.

Different words are used in relation to these two areas of meaning. If something is full of flavour it is **tasty**. If behaviour is well judged, or a decoration well chosen, it is **tasteful**: *The decoration of the living room and bedroom was simple but tasteful.* When either flavour or judgment fails, then in both contexts the word **tasteless** is appropriate: *…totally tasteless white bread; A man cracked a few irrelevant and tasteless jokes.*

taut, taught

Taut is used of a rope or something that is stretched out tight: *Blackberries are covered with a shiny, taut skin;…the hiss of a taut sail.* There is a particular nautical phrase, *a taut ship*, which means a well-managed ship. **Taught** is the past form of the verb *teach*.

tautology

Tautology is a relatively common fault in speech and writing. It is the unnecessary repetition of an idea that has already been expressed.

For example, in the sentence: *The car came to a totally complete stop*, the words *totally* and *complete* give the same information, and only *total* or *complete* is necessary, but, going a little further, neither is needed as something that has *stopped* makes no further movement. Tautology can, however, be used for exaggerated effect, as in *It was a tiny little wee thing.*

Other examples of tautology are: *reverse back; absolutely unique; free gift; the unanimous response from everyone.*

tax, toll

Tax is a general term for any money that has to be paid to the state. The word **toll** refers to a set fee, usually one that has to be paid before a river crossing at certain bridges or tunnels, or for the use of some French and Italian motorways.

teaspoonful, tablespoonful, teacupful ⇒ **spoonful**

teem, team

There are two verbs spelled **teem**. If it is pouring with rain, you can say, *It's teeming with rain.* The other verb **teem** means 'be crowded' with the additional sense of restless movement: *This area teems with the young.*

The noun **team** means 'a chosen group acting together', for example: *a hockey team; an editorial team; a team of horses.*

teenager

A **teenager** is anyone between the ages of thirteen and nineteen. The concept of *teenage* (and its short form, *teens*) was originally a creation of the marketing industry. It is not an age group recognized in law as *infant*, *child*, or *adult* is, so that in a Will someone who is a *teenager* will still be referred to as, for example, *the infant Jane* until she is eighteen, when she becomes an *adult*.

teevee, TV, telly

These are the informal spoken forms of words that are occasionally written down. Like *radar* and *laser*, they cannot be regarded as just abbreviations for *television*. Avoid using them in formal writing.

televise

The verb **televise** is a back formation from the noun *television*. It is well established as a word. Note that it cannot be given an *-ize* ending. ⇒ **-ise**

temporal, temporary
The word **temporal** is an opposite of *spiritual*. It means 'to do with the affairs of the world': *The Church then was also a great temporal power; They gave guidance in matters spiritual and temporal.*

There is a rarer adjective **temporal**, formed from *temple* (one of the regions on each side of the head), that is used in medical contexts. These two meanings have no connection.

Temporary means 'not permanent': *Slowly, he approached the temporary barrier that had been thrown across the entrance.* Careful speakers avoid pronouncing *temporary* with three syllables. It should have four syllables: /tem-pe-re-ry/.

tendency, trend
A **tendency** is the strong likelihood of someone or something behaving in a particular way: *On the stage I have always had a tendency to make faces; On the whole, the tendency has been to accept reality.* The use of *tendency* in political contexts is often a synonym for a *faction*, e.g. *He joined the Militant Tendency.*

A **trend** is a gradual, but clear and continued movement towards some change in events or attitudes: *There is a trend towards equal opportunities for men and women.*

tenterhooks
This word occurs only in the phrase **on tenterhooks**, which means 'in a state of excitement and anxiety' about some event, usually one where you have no idea of the outcome: *The courtroom was on tenterhooks.* It should not be spelled or pronounced 'tenderhooks', a common error.

tepid, warm, lukewarm

Tepid is generally used for describing the temperature of water: *She lowered herself into pleasantly tepid water.* Its use with food can indicate an element of disgust on the part of the user: *I resigned myself to drinking tepid coffee.* In this sense, it overlaps with **lukewarm**, which means 'not excessively hot'. The same food or water could be described as **warm** or *tepid* depending on the expectation of the speaker.

When *tepid/lukewarm* and *warm* are used metaphorically, *a tepid/lukewarm welcome* is a grudging one, *a warm welcome* is an enthusiastic one.

terminal, terminus

Terminal or **terminus** can be used for a place where buses start and end journeys. With trains *terminus* is more common, while *terminal* is usually used for planes: *Victoria is the terminus for Brighton and for many lines into Kent; Internal flights leave from Terminal One.*

Only **terminal** is used for the point where an electrical connection is made or for a keyboard connection into a computer system.

terminate

Terminate is a verb of Latin origin meaning 'end'. In certain contexts it is useful in making a statement unambiguous, e.g. *This train terminates here* is clearer than *This train stops here* if the train is at the end of the line. Otherwise, prefer the simpler words *stop* or *end*. *Terminate* is also used euphemistically with the sense of 'kill': *They had him terminated.*

testimonial, reference

When both words are used in the context of job applications, there is a useful distinction in meaning. A

testimonial is a general and open statement of the qualities of the person concerned. It is usually not written for the purpose of a particular job. A **reference** is a confidential statement that is usually not seen by the person to whom it refers.

than

In sentences such as *He does it far better than I*, **than** is usually regarded in careful usage as a conjunction governing an unexpressed verb: *He does it far better than I (do it)*. The case of any following pronoun thus depends on whether it is the subject or the object of that unexpressed verb: *She likes him more than I (like him); She likes him more than (she likes) me*. However, in informal usage, **than** is often treated as a preposition and the following pronoun is used in its objective form. This may result in ambiguity, e.g. *She likes him more than me*.

thank you

People are often confused about how to spell this phrase. It can be seen written as one word, as a hyphenated word, and as two words. When **thank you** is used to express gratitude it should be written as two words: *Thank you very much for the chocolates*. When the word is a modifier it should be hyphenated: *She went home and wrote a thank-you note*. The spelling *thankyou* is less common but is used when the word functions as a noun: *'Thankyous by the yard', she sang out*.

that, which

That has more than one use. First, it can be used to signal a clause that gives specific details about a preceding noun: *I like the coat that you bought yesterday*. The contents of the clause beginning with **that** give the necessary detail for us to identify *the coat* about which the comment is made. When *that* is used in this way it is called a relative pronoun and the clause it begins with is called a defining relative clause.

A different relative pronoun, **which**, may be used instead of *that* in this type of construction, but some users dislike this usage and reserve *which* for nondefining relative clauses, where the clause is separated from the noun phrase by a comma, such as *Programmed textbooks, which guide a pupil through their pages, were much simpler.* Nondefining relative clauses do not add essential details.

In informal or colloquial usage, **that** and **which** (or *who*) are often used interchangeably in defining clauses, but the more formal the level of language, the more advisable it is to preserve the distinction between these two relative pronouns.

Secondly, **that** is used in reported speech as the linking element between the reporting clause and the item that is reported. In a clause of this kind *that* can be left out after most common reporting verbs: *I thought (that) she was still away.* If the verb is a formal one such as *divulge, object,* or *reply,* it cannot be left out: *The woman divulged that her name was Mrs Musprat.* A number of adjectives relate to thought and emotions. These are used in a similar way, and **that** can be left out: *I was glad/sorry/relieved (that) she told you.*

Thirdly, **that** can be used as a demonstrative (i.e. 'pointing out' someone or something, as in *That old woman saved my life*). If greater than normal stress is placed on *that,* it creates overtones suggesting that the person or thing being pointed out is notorious or very well known, e.g. *I can't stand that Amanda* or *Oh, you mean it was **that** man again.*

the, a

The definite article **the** (one of the determiners) is used to specify a particular item, while the indefinite article **a** makes a more general reference. *I met the girl next door* is a more specific reference to a particular girl than *I met a girl next door*.

The is normally pronounced /thuh/ without any stress, unless the word begins with a vowel, in which case the pronunciation /thee/ is used: *the old man; the elephant*. When *the* is given stress where you might not expect it, it is being used for special emphasis: *You're not the Paul McCartney, are you?*

their, there

The use of this pair of words is frequently confused. **Their** is used for possession or close association: *Their hi-fi cost almost £900; I've just seen their new baby*. **There** is an adverb of place: *I'm not going there again*. Users who confuse the spelling of this pair of words may find it useful to make a mental link between *there* and its converse *here* to remind themselves of the spelling pattern: *Come here; I'm not going there. The hens scattered here and there*.

Careful writers and speakers ensure that the verb agrees with the number of the subject, so we say *There is a man waiting* and *There are several people waiting*. When the sentence has a compound subject, it is generally accepted that the number of the first element of the subject governs the agreement: *There is a pen and a book on the table; There are two pens and a book on the table*.
⇒ **they're**

their, they, them

It is increasingly common to find the plural forms **their**,

they, and **them** used to refer to singular entities. The use of *their* etc. in this way is sometimes regarded as unacceptable in formal contexts, though it has existed in the language for at least five centuries: *If a person is born of a gloomy temperament they cannot help it.* (*Lord Chesterfield*). It is especially common in informal contexts after *anyone, everyone, someone,* and *no one,* and after noun phrases that include *each, every,* and *no.*

The reason for this usage is the clumsiness of the alternative *his or her* when you want to refer to both sexes. This awkwardness can be avoided in some cases by using a plural noun, so that instead of writing: *Each student should meet his or her personal tutor* you can write *All students should meet their personal tutors.*

them ⇒ **those**

thesis, dissertation
The word **thesis** (the plural form is *theses*) is equivalent in meaning to **dissertation**, a long written account of some original thinking: *Postgraduate students often spend several years working on their dissertation/thesis.* A *thesis* is also an unproved statement which becomes the subject of a discussion: *My thesis is that secrecy is the greatest enemy of democracy.*

they're
The short form **they're** is often misspelled *their* or *there,* perhaps because it is more common as a spoken form than a written form. It can help if the writer remembers that it is an abbreviation for *they are.*

those, them
A very common error and a mark of nonstandard English usage is the use of **them** where **those** is normally used. Sentences like, *She liked those flowers* and *Give me those*

books are correct. If *them* was used instead of *those*, the sentences would be understandable but would not be standard English.

thou, thy, thee, thine

These words are obsolete in standard English and will usually only be found in literature and especially in the Bible and prayerbooks. As they are sometimes revived in 'period pieces' it can be useful to know that **thou** is a second person singular subject form (compare *I*); **thy** and **thine** are possessive forms (compare *my* and *mine*); and **thee** the object form (compare *me*).

though ⇒ although

thrash, thresh

Both **thrash** and **thresh** mean 'beat' but only *thresh* is used for the process of separating grain from its husks and straw.

thrice, twice

Thrice, meaning 'three times', is now an obsolete word and is only found in older literature but **twice** meaning 'two times', remains part of current usage along with *once*. ⇒ treble

through, thru

The use of **through** in an expression like *Monday through Friday* is not generally understood in British English. In American English it means 'Monday to Friday inclusive'.

The American commercial abbreviation **thru** should be avoided.

thus

Thus is a rather formal adverb. One of its uses is to refer to something already described: *Her eyelids closed with* *weariness. It was thus that Robert Ford saw her.* The meaning 'to this extent but no further' is much more formal. As a sentence connector, *thus* means much the same as *therefore*. The form *thusly* is a jocular invention and has no accepted status.

tie

The present participle form is *tying*, the past tense and participle forms are *tied*.

tight, tightly

Tight can be used as an adverb as well as **tightly**: *I held her tight; They pack themselves in tightly.*

Tightly is usually found in front of a past participle, except in an established phrase like *tight-lipped* or *tight-jawed*: *His lips were tightly compressed; …his tightly buttoned collar.*

till, until

Till is a variant of *until* that is acceptable at all levels of language. **Until** is, however, often preferred at the beginning of a sentence in formal writing: *Until his behaviour improves, he cannot become a member.*

time

Time is usually expressed in British English using a twelve-hour clock except in rail, bus, and plane time-tables.

If the time is given as hours and fractions, use words: *A quarter to six; A quarter past seven; Half past five; Eight o'clock.* The omission of *past*, as in *It's half seven*, is regarded as an Americanism.

The expression *o'clock* is only used with whole hours, not with fractions. When the time is given as hours and minutes, use figures: *5.45; 7.15; 5.30; 8 a.m.*

It is incorrect to combine the abbreviations *a.m.* or *p.m.* with *in the morning* or *in the afternoon* as they give the same information. Similarly, *o'clock* is not used with *a.m.* or *p.m.* Write either *6 o'clock* or *6 p.m.* ⇒ **a.m.**

time, tense

When we describe events we usually give some information about the time when they took place. We can talk about **time** as past, present, or future. In grammar there are a number of ways of making our references to time clear to our listeners. One of these is **tense** but *tense* and *time* are not the same.

English has two *tenses*, the Simple Present and the Simple Past, but they are not just used to refer to present and past *time*. For example, the Present *tense* can also be used with an adverbial phrase to refer to future time: *I fly to New York next Monday.* All our time references have to be made by combining other constructions with tenses. More detail is given in the *Gem English Grammar*.

times

Avoid using expressions that combine **times** with *less*, e.g. *They give you ten times less than the thing is worth.* *Times* implies multiplication, and so the sentence above would be better phrased: *They give you a tenth of what the thing is worth.*

-tion

The **-tion** suffix is used to create nouns. The nouns formed indicate state, condition, action, process, or result.

tire ⇒ tyre

titbit, tidbit

A **titbit** is a small scrap of either food or information. In

American English the spelling is **tidbit**, an older form of the British word.

titillate, titivate

To **titillate** someone is to cause them to experience pleasant excitement: *I can't stand food inexpertly cooked with no sauces to titillate the palate*. To **titivate** oneself is to spend time in rearranging one's dress or one's appearance: *Surely you're ready! You can't go on titivating yourself all night*.

titles

The British system of titles is complex and involves major difficulties of usage. There are four contexts in which it may be necessary to employ someone's formal title: making reference, addressing an envelope, beginning a letter, talking to the person directly. The notes that follow concentrate on points of frequent difficulty.

The title of a clergyman in the Churches of England and Scotland is given in the form *The Reverend John Smith*, not [*reverent*]. When talking to him, John Smith should be addressed as *Mr Smith* or *Dr Smith* according to his qualifications. The same form is used for the Ministers of Nonconformist churches. If he is a Catholic priest, he is referred to as *The Reverend John Smith* but when you talk to him, use *Father Smith*. Some Anglican clergy also prefer *Father*; only knowledge of the individual clergyman can give an accurate indication. A nun is addressed as *The Reverend Sister (Mary Martha)*. In personal conversation, the usage is generally *Sister* or, more formally, *Sister Mary Martha*.

Mrs Smith can choose to be known as *Mrs John Smith* or *Mrs Nancy Smith*. The practice of only using the latter form when divorced has fallen into disuse. If *Mr Smith* is addressed on an envelope as *Esq.*, the *Mr* is dropped, i.e. he is *John Smith Esq.*

If *Dr Smith* becomes a surgeon he or she drops the use of *Dr* and uses *Mr, Miss,* or *Mrs Smith.* A dental surgeon in Britain does not use *Dr*, but one in the USA might do so.

When plain *John Smith* gains a knighthood for his services he is called *Sir John* and addressed on letters as *Sir John Smith.* His wife becomes *Lady Smith.* He is never called [*Sir Smith*]. When *Jane Smith* is knighted, she becomes *Dame Jane Smith.* If she gains a life peerage she will take a title from a place that she is associated with, and become, for example, *Baroness Hove* (but will be called *Lady Hove*). Her husband, however, will in both cases remain plain *Mr Smith.*

If *John Smith* becomes a life peer he will take a title from a place that he is associated with and could similarly be called *Lord Hove* but never [*Lord John*] or [*Lord John Hove*]. His wife is called *Lady Hove.* They would be addressed on an envelope as *The Lord/ The Lady Hove.*

If *John* or *Jane Smith* enters politics and becomes an MP, he or she gains no special title, except the right to add *MP* to their name. In formal Parliamentary reference he or she is known as *The Honourable Member for Hove* until gaining official office, when *Right Honourable* is used. He or she is never [*the Honourable Smith*].

The full titles of the hereditary nobility are not covered here. One point to note is that the Christian names of titled people precede their titles, e.g. *George Gordon 6th Lord Byron,* unless they are younger sons and daughters, in which case their courtesy titles include a Christian name, e.g. *Lord Alfred Douglas; Lord Peter Wimsey; Lady Mary Wortley Montague.*

to ⇒ try

together with

When you join several nouns with *and* they form a compound subject and the following verb should be plural: *Alan Jones and the board of Beaver Properties have taken hefty salary cuts.*

When you use **together with** (or its equivalents *plus*, and *along with*) a compound subject is not formed. The verb is singular if the first noun is singular: *Alan Jones together with the board of Beaver Properties has taken a hefty salary cut.* The phrase that follows *together with* is not part of the subject but is dependent on it, so it has no effect on the agreement of the verb. Some writers show this by separating the clause from the subject by commas: *NASA, together with the Department of Defence, urgently reviewed the launch schedules.*

toilet, lavatory, toilette

Personal hygiene and money are two taboo areas in British society; consequently there are many words and expressions that are used to sidestep direct mention of some aspects of these areas.

A **toilet** is one of many names for a room containing a *lavatory.* A recent writer on usage said that the use of *toilet* for **lavatory** was as much a euphemism as *loo* or *cloakroom*, or the American *bathroom* or *washroom.* Much the same was said about the word *toilet-paper*, and *lavatory paper* was offered as the preferred term. Others, however, feel that *lavatory* is a taboo word. The word *lavatory* is generally used in public situations and the word *toilet* in domestic ones. A plumber is more likely to call the pan a *lavatory pan* than a *toilet pan.*

Loo is a common informal alternative word for a *lavato-*

ry (or toilet). None of these terms is more socially acceptable than the other. Many British speakers prefer to use the word *toilet*. Readers must follow their own preferences in this matter.

In older, very formal, usage your **toilette** or **toilet** meant the whole process of dressing and making ready for the day, thus the term *toilet-water*. Because *toilet* is nowadays associated with defecation, this usage has become obsolete.

toll ⇒ **tax**

ton, tonne, tun
Since metrication and the wider use of international units of measurement, the use of *ton* has been to some degree superseded by the use of *lbs* or *kg* to state overall weight. In the English measure a **ton** is 2240lbs (the *long ton*). In America there is a *short ton* that is equal to 2000lbs. The metric system uses **tonne** or *metric ton* for a unit that contains 1000kg. The use of the term *metric tonne* is not generally approved. Other types of *ton* also exist. Informally, a *ton* is a slang term for 100, as in *He did a ton on the motorway*.

A **tun** is a very large wooden cask. A standard *tun* holds 252 wine gallons. It is rarely used as a measure.

tongs
Tongs is one of the small group of words including *trousers*, *pliers*, and *scissors* that are always used as plurals. You have to use the phrase *a pair of tongs* to refer to one item.

tonight, tonite
Avoid at all times the use of the abbreviation **tonite** found in commercial varieties of American English.

too, so

In British usage a response to a statement is often followed by **so** to avoid repeating the topic: *You haven't cleared your room. I have so.* A strong stress on *so* makes the response very emphatic. A very informal equivalent in some varieties of English uses **too** instead of *so*: *You haven't cleared your room. I have too.*

too, to, two

Although the use and meaning of these three words is clear to all English speakers, the appropriate spelling form is often a problem.

The form **two** is always and only a number. The form **too** is an adverb, and used as a modifier of adjectives: *too hot; too many people.* It is used after verbs to mean 'also' or 'as well': *Can I come too?; It was a pretty play, and very sad too.* The word **to** is usually the form that is needed for all other uses.

torpid, torrid

If something is slow, lethargic, and sluggish it can be described as **torpid**. *Torpid* can also mean having a greatly reduced ability to respond, such as is found in a hibernating animal: *When he was awake he was too torpid to realize what was going on around him.* The noun is *torpor*: *He was sunk in a dismal torpor.*

The adjective **torrid** is used about scorchingly hot weather: *I felt faint and helpless in this land where the sun is so torrid and there are so few shadows.* By extension, emotional encounters are sometimes described as *torrid.* ⇒ **tepid**

tortuous, torturous

Care is needed to distinguish these two words of similar spelling whose uses are quite different. The adjective

tortuous means 'twisting' or 'winding' or, if used about a person, 'cunning and devious': *A tall, Gothic tracery window, rich with a tortuous pattern of huge yellow flowers; …a man of tortuous mind.*

Torturous is an adjective derived from *torture*. It is not common but means 'causing pain and anguish': *The man inside was dying in torturous pain.*

towards, toward

Both prepositions have the same meaning. The spelling **towards** is more usual in British English but is not used in American English.

trade names

Trade names or trademarks are the property of the makers of the goods that bear their label. In some cases the trade names of a product become so popular that they are substituted as generic names or as verbs for various activities. When this happens they can pass into widespread use but are often written without a capital letter.

The owners of *trade names* are usually unhappy about this as they fear that their ownership of the name will suffer. This is particularly the case in the USA. Those who are writing for publication should be sure to acknowledge trade names and give them a capital letter.

Examples of this form of generalization are well known, though they vary from country to country. A popular brand of shoe polish in New Zealand is called Nugget™ and there it became common to *nugget* one's shoes instead of *polish* them. On the other hand, the common British use of *Hoover* to mean *vacuum clean* is not generally used in New Zealand.

trade union

A **trade union** can also be called a *trades union*, but it is always *trade unions* when the term is used in the plural.

tragedy

In drama, a **tragedy** is a type of play that involves the fall from power and the death of an important character. The fall is usually brought about by a flaw in the nature of the character concerned.

In journalese and in informal conversation, *tragedy* and the adjective *tragic* are used to refer to any incident that involves an accidental or unexpected loss of life. Some purists object to this use.

Beware a common misspelling. There is no *d* in the middle; the consonant is just *g*: *tragedy.* ⇒ **trauma**

trait

A **trait** is a characteristic feature of someone's behaviour or personality. It is pronounced /tray/: *The ability to solve problems has always been an inherent and desirable trait throughout human history.*

tramp

In British English a **tramp** is a vagrant; the equivalent in American English is *bum* or *hobo.* American English uses *tramp* as a colloquial term meaning a young woman of casual sexual behaviour.

transient, transitory, transitional

All three words are connected with change or lack of permanence. The adjective **transient** is used to describe something temporary: *Their power was only local and their glory transient.* As a technical noun, it refers to a brief change of physical state: *These signals are characterized by lots of high frequency transients.*

Something **transitory** lasts for a short time only: ...*a transitory enchanted moment*. This word is often used in the context of regret for the passing of time.

If something is **transitional** it is in a temporary state before the development of a more permanent one: ...*dictatorship was only a transitional phase*.

transitive

The term **transitive** is used in grammar to describe verbs that are normally followed by a direct object, e.g. *bring, find, see, visit*. For further details consult the *Gem English Grammar*.

transpire

It is often maintained that **transpire** should not be used to mean 'happen' or 'occur', as in *The event transpired late in the evening*, and that the word is properly used to mean 'become known', as in *It transpired later that the thief had been caught*. The word is, however, widely used in the former sense, especially in spoken English.

In scientific contexts, *transpire* is used of plants and means 'give off water vapour from the leaves'.

transport, transportation

In British English **transport** means both the moving of goods or people by vehicle from one place to another and the means, or the system, by which this is done, e.g. by train, bus, or car. In American English both these meanings are represented by the word **transportation**.

trash

Trash is the usual American word for what is called *rubbish* in British English. Thus the receptacle for rubbish in American English is a *trashcan* and the lorry that takes it away is a *trashcart*.

In modern British English, *trash* is seen as an Americanism but it is a well-established word. It is used about anything that the speaker strongly disapproves of: *The trouble is all that damn trash in the newspapers.* If it is used to refer to people, it is an extremely critical term implying utter worthlessness: *The assorted trendy trash who fill the wine bars.* ⇒ **garbage**

trauma

Trauma has a precise technical meaning in psychiatry and medicine. In psychiatry it is an emotional shock that has long-term effects. In surgery, a *trauma* is any bodily injury: *...evidence of internal and external trauma such as lacerations.*

Trauma is often used very informally, in conversation, to mean 'an upsetting experience' and the adjective *traumatic* is used for 'upsetting' or 'shocking'. Some purists object to the informal usage, but it is well established. The plural *traumata* is rare and associated with the technical sense. The usual plural form is *traumas*. The pronunciation is either /traw-ma/ or /trow-ma/ (to rhyme with 'brown'). ⇒ **tragedy**

travel

The British spelling of words derived from the base form of **travel** i.e. *traveller, travelling, travelled* uses a double *l* but American usage has a single *l* only.

traverse

The pronunciation /**tra**-verse/ is used for the noun, while /tra-**verse**/ is usual for the verb.

treason, treachery

An offence against the safety of the state is called **treason** and is punishable by law. The word **treachery** is used when the act of betrayal is personal or when you wish to talk about the wider implications of the deed: *...treachery that ruins friendships; ...the treachery of his own emotions.*

treble, triple

When the context relates to number or quantity, **treble** and **triple** have the same meaning: *...treble/triple chance; He poured himself a triple whisky; He ordered a treble brandy.*

In a musical context they have different meanings. *Treble* is used to describe the upper register of notes as opposed to *bass*. *Triple* is used to describe a rhythm of three beats to the bar: *in triple time.* ⇒ **thrice**

trend ⇒ tendency

trillion

Because of a change of use, **trillion** cannot be regarded as a meaningfully exact number. Its meaning is ambiguous depending on who is using it and when. A *billion* in British English used to be one million times one million, i.e. a million millions, and a *trillion* was a million times a billion, i.e. a million million millions.

This neat usage has been disrupted by the modern convention that adopted the American usage of a *billion* as a unit meaning a thousand millions and the consequent use of *trillion* to mean what billion used to mean, i.e. a million millions. If the context is recent, the meaning will be reasonably clear, but older books, and older users, may still intend the traditional meanings.

triple ⇒ treble

triumphant, triumphal

Triumphant is the general word for 'victorious' or 'having a feeling of triumph' and describes someone who has a victory to celebrate: *He darted one cold, triumphant look at Fanny, who could only gasp.* **Triumphal** is used to describe the means by which a triumph is celebrated, such as a procession: *He made a triumphal return, cheered by his tenants; They erected a triumphal arch in the capital.*

troupe, troop

Both these words come from the same base but they are now separated in use. A **troupe** is a group of actors, and a **troop** is any other sort of regular group, especially soldiers, and also monkeys: *She was a member of a mime troupe; Once the barrage ends, troop movements can begin; … a troop of chimpanzees.*

Troop can be used as a verb and then conveys the sense of a rather disorganized movement of people: *…the crowds troop along raggedly; …they would troop about blowing bamboo flutes and ringing bells.*

truck, lorry

In British English a **truck** is a railway wagon for carrying loads. In other parts of the English-speaking world it is a road vehicle, in British English called a **lorry**. The influence of American English has made the noun *trucker* for 'long-distance lorry driver' increasingly common in British English.

truculent

Truculent means 'sullenly aggressive': *He glanced at his father with a determined, almost truculent expression on his face.* The pronunciation is /**truck**-u-lent/.

truly

If you want to end a letter in a very formal manner, you can use *Yours truly.* The most appropriate context would be a letter to or from a Government Department, but this phrase has become rare compared to *Yours faithfully* or *Yours sincerely*.

try

The choice of the appropriate construction when **try** is followed by another verb causes some confusion. The construction *try to* is the recognized standard: *Try to start the car again while I'm ringing the AA*. This construction can be used in all circumstances.

An alternative, which is disliked by purists, is *try and*. However, although *try and* is informal, it is not incorrect. It has a long history of use (since 1685 at least) and in some circumstances it has a specialized meaning. The construction *try and* places more emphasis on the second verb than it does on *try*. For example, while *Try to stop me* means 'See if you can do it', *Try and stop me* means 'Just you dare try that, then you'll see what happens!' It is best to treat *try and* as a spoken idiom.

tummy, stomach

The word **tummy** originates as a child's attempt at saying **stomach** (*an upset tummy*) but is frequently used nowadays as an informal synonym for the more technical word *abdomen*: *...tense your tummy muscles*. As it is often used by doctors in talking to patients, it has won a certain validity. Avoid using it in formal contexts.

turbid, turbulent, turgid, tumid

If something is **turbid**, it is cloudy, or opaque because of suspended mud, as is often the case in a river: *...a quarter-mile stretch of shallow, turbid water, studded with sandbanks*. Something **turbulent** is in a state of confused, agitated movement: *There was nothing in the sight of that turbulent, brown flood to remind him of the placid river that it had been yesterday*.

Turgid is used to mean swollen. It is frequently used to describe a pompous manner of speech or writing: *He specialized in the composition of somewhat turgid religious verse.* **Tumid** is a rarer, technical word that also means swollen or distended. It usually describes a part of the body. The adjective *tumescent* has the same meaning and is more literary.

turf
The plural of **turf** is *turfs* or *turves*. The latter form is always used for 'blocks of peat for burning'.

twopence, threepence
The changeover to decimal coinage brought with it some changes in the common names of different amounts of money. In the old coinage, the sum of *2p* (ignoring the change in value) was called **twopence** (written *2d*) but was usually pronounced, and often spelled, *tuppence*. **Threepence** (*3d*) was pronounced /thruppence/. The adjectival forms were /tuppenny/ and /thruppenny/. The /u/ sound rhymes with 'but' or 'put'. ⇒ **pence, p**

tycoon, magnate
Both words have a similar meaning, 'a businessman of great wealth or power'. **Magnate** is a neutral word but **tycoon** conveys a suggestion of disapproval or dislike: *...pop stars waving from aeroplanes, squat tycoons loud with diamonds.*

type
In formal writing **type**, like *kind* and *sort*, should be treated as a singular noun: *...machines of this type* [not *these types*].

tyrannize
The construction **tyrannize** *over* was once the accepted

form but the use of *over* with this verb is now less common. Both constructions are accepted: *They were tyrannized by a bloody mob; No animal must tyrannize over his own kind.*

tyre, tire
British English uses the spelling **tyre** in *car tyre, bicycle tyre*, etc. American English uses the spelling **tire**. In British English **tire** is used for the verb meaning 'become weary': *He tires easily.*

U

U and non-U
In an article written in 1954, Professor Alan Ross reported on some differences between the speech habits of 'the county set' and other English speakers. The article, when reprinted in a book called *Noblesse Oblige*, stirred up a response in those who were unnerved by the suggestion that their language might betray their class origins, and it gave currency to the terms **U**, meaning 'Upper-class speech habits', and **non-U**, meaning 'the speech habits of everyone else'. As these differences are of small importance, except to the very class-conscious, only passing reference to them is made in this book.

UK
The abbreviated form of *United Kingdom* is generally written **UK** without full-stops. The full title is the *United*

Kingdom of Great Britain and Northern Ireland.
⇒ **Great Britain**

ult. ⇒ inst.

ultimatum

An **ultimatum** is a final communication in the course of a negotiation, setting out a condition or conditions and usually containing a threat. The usual plural form is *ultimatums,* but *ultimata* is still found in very formal writing.

ultra-

The prefix **ultra-** combines with an adjective or a noun to add the meaning 'a quality going beyond what is normal', or 'extreme': *ultraviolet, ultrasound, ultraconservative.* The compounds are usually not hyphenated.

umpire, referee

Whether the term **umpire** or **referee** is used in a particular sport is usually a matter of tradition. However, *umpire* is a much narrower term than *referee,* which can also be used for any situation where an impartial person is asked to make a decision: *A third certificate will be signed by the medical referee at the crematorium.*

un-

The prefix **un-** is one of the group (including *in-, ir-, il-*) that makes a negative from the base to which it is added.

There is some ambiguity in the meaning of *un-.* When it is added to a main verb it usually means 'reverse the process', e.g. *wind/unwind,* but when *un-* is added to a past participle that is used as an adjective it means 'not', e.g. *finished / unfinished.* Consequently, a word like *unwrapped* can mean either 'reversed the process of wrapping': *Ruth unwrapped her present very slowly,* or 'not

wrapped': *She gave him the package unwrapped.*

Un- in its negative sense and *non-* are sometimes used in contrast. A compound with *un-* may mean 'definitely not' as in *unscientific*, while the same base with *non-* may mean 'not connected with' as in *nonscientific*, but this is not always the case, e.g. *unhygienic* and *nonhygienic* are identical in meaning. ⇒ **in-**

unanimous, nem. con.

A **unanimous** decision is one that is made with the agreement of everyone: *The first vote went as predicted and it was unanimous.* Expressions such as *the unanimous decision of all* are tautologous.

If a decision is passed **nem. con.** it means that, though some participants may have abstained from voting, they did not vote against it.

unashamed, unashamedly

The pronunciation differs slightly. **Unashamed** is /un-a-shaymd/. **Unashamedly** adds a vowel sound before the *d* /un-a-**shay**-mid-ly/.

unaware, unawares

Careful users of English distinguish between the adjective **unaware** which means 'ignorant of' and is usually followed by *of* or *that*: *They were unaware of the danger*, and the adverb **unawares** 'by surprise': *The danger caught them unawares.*

unbeknown, unbeknownst

Both **unbeknown** and **unbeknownst** mean 'without someone's knowledge'. While they are in reasonably common use, they are rather literary in their overtones: *At that very moment, unbeknown to him, the amazed Francis was looking down on the hill; Then, unbeknownst to him, Mr Hoskins sent out invitations.*

unconscious, subconscious

Unconscious is one of several technical terms based on the psychological view of the mind. These are the *conscious, preconscious, subconscious,* and *unconscious* mind. While *unconscious* thoughts and feelings may be repressed, **subconscious** ones are at the borders of consciousness. However, in general usage there is no real difference between the way the two words are employed.

unconsolable

Although this word is often heard it is not in any dictionary. All give **inconsolable** for 'not able to be consoled'. The use of this *un-* form is an example of an increasing tendency to make *un-* the main prefix for the sense 'not'.

under, underneath, below

The difference in the use of these words is not great, but it is worth noting. **Under** is the converse of *over;* it is a close synonym of *below.* When we say that one thing is *under* another, we not only state the position that it is in, we also have in mind the movement needed to get there: *When I returned she had crept under a chair; A coin slipped out of my pocket and rolled under the chair.*

When we use **underneath**, we are making a statement about the immediate physical position of one thing in relation to another. It has overtones of being covered over: *Several pairs of dirty knickers lay on the floor underneath the bed.* Except when *underneath* is an adverb, *under* can be used instead.

Underneath and *beneath* once had very similar meanings, but *beneath* is now rarely used except in set phrases such as *beneath contempt; beneath consideration,* where it means 'too low for…'. **Under** also implies movement that takes something below and through another object, so that a train or a stream can be said to *run under a bridge*.

Below is the converse of *above*. It is used to state that one object is situated at a lower position than another: *Thus, you don't want a hedge below a sloping orchard*.

When *under* is used in the context of work, it has the sense 'supervised by': *Mark worked under Martin for several years before gaining promotion*. When *below* is used in a similar context it means 'inferior in status to': *A salesman is as far below a director as the office junior is to the salesman*. ⇒ **below**

under-

Under- is a productive prefix with two possible meanings: 'beneath', as in *undermine, undercut*, and 'insufficient', as in *underprovide, underestimate*.

If *under-* is added to a word that starts with a capital letter, use a hyphen, e.g. *Under-Secretary*.

underlie, underlay

The verbs *lay* and *lie* form the basis of these two words. The main parts of **underlie** are, Simple Past *underlay*, present participle *underlying* (often used as an adjective: *…the underlying problem*), past participle *underlain*.

If one thing **underlies** another, either it lies underneath it: *Much of the state is underlain by old hard rocks that contain valuable ores*, or is its cause or foundation: *It was this democratic spirit that underlay the Declaration of Independence; The view of human nature that underlies present-day economic theory*.

What causes confusion is that the past form of *underlie* is spelled the same as the base form of **underlay**. The Simple Past and past participle of *underlay* is spelled *underlaid*.

Underlay is not a commonly used verb. It literally means 'lay one thing under another'. The word *underlay* is more common as a noun, for example in *carpet underlay*.

undertone

An **undertone** is an underlying suggestion that resides in words or actions: *His measured behaviour contained an undertone of menace.* An *overtone* suggests a meaning that goes beyond the words actually used. In this figurative sense the two words overlap. An *undertone* is also a hushed tone of voice. ⇒ **overtones**

underwhelm

This is not a serious English word. It is a jocular formation derived from *overwhelm*.

uneatable, inedible

A useful distinction can be made between *uneatable* and *inedible*, even though the former is not recorded in some dictionaries. An **uneatable** substance is one that cannot be pleasurably eaten by a human being: *Just as raw flour, barley, and oatmeal are uneatable...; She used to make that uneatable gingerbread.*

An **inedible** substance is one that is not safe to be eaten although it can be eaten: *...inedible, poisonous plants like the turpentine bush.* Inedible, being the more established word, also contains the meaning of *uneatable*.

unexceptional, unexceptionable

If something is **unexceptional** it is no better than you would expect. If a statement or someone's behaviour is **unexceptionable** there is no possible objection that can be raised about it. It is beyond criticism: *He read the letter carefully. It was official, dry, unexceptionable.*

uninterested ⇒ **disinterested**

unique

The traditional view of words such as *unique, perfect,* and *simultaneous,* is that they describe absolute states, that is to say, states that cannot be further modified. Something is either *unique* or it is *not unique,* but it cannot be, for example, *rather unique.* Those who dislike the use of comparatives or intensifiers where absolute states are concerned would prefer: *That is very exceptional* [not *very unique*]. Others point out that it is possible for something to aspire to perfection and almost reach it, so that *almost perfect* is justifiable. Similar arguments can be made in favour of modifying other 'absolute words' and for the use of emphatic modifiers like *totally* with *unique* etc. Note that *unique* is preceded by *a* not *an.*

university

The usual written abbreviation of *university* is *Univ.* In informal British speech someone who is at a **university** may refer to it as the *uni.* The older short form was *varsity* and generally referred mainly to Oxford and Cambridge. *Uni* probably originated with Australian speakers; New Zealand and South African usage is *varsity* for any university. The American use of the expression *at school* to mean *at university* is puzzling to British speakers, who associate *school* with the earlier stages of education. ⇒ **college**

unlawful ⇒ **illegal**

unloose

Unloose has the alternative form **unloosen**. Both words have slightly archaic overtones: *The cords around her box were unloosed; He unloosened his broad, multiflow-*

ered tie. Suitable alternative words are *undo, untie,* or *loosen.*

unpractical ⇒ **impractical**

unreadable ⇒ **illegible**

unrelated participle

An **unrelated participle** is a small point in the grammar of sentences whose importance is often exaggerated, though it can result in some unintentional humour or ambiguity.

A participle relates to a possible subject. If the subject is not clear, the relationship is made with the nearest suitable noun or pronoun.

In the sentence, *Whistling happily, he went off down the road,* the participle *whistling* relates to the pronoun *he* as a subject. In the sentence, *Rounding the corner, the house came into view,* the participle *rounding* relates to the noun *house* as a possible subject. As the sentence suggests that the *house* was rounding a corner, which is unlikely, the participle is said to be **unrelated**. This is also called a *dangling* participle or a *misrelated* participle.

unstable, unsteady

If someone does not have full control over their voice, hands, or feet, these can be described as **unsteady**: *Stephen poured three brandies with an unsteady hand; My heavy breathing and unsteady legs forced me to rest.* An object that is not firmly placed is *unsteady: She balanced three boxes in an unsteady pile against her cardigan.* An object that is not secured firmly can be described as **unstable**: *...the unstable guttering on the houses opposite.*

It is also used for something that does not maintain a

steady state (for example, a chemical compound): *The dynamite was sweating and in a dangerously unstable state*, or for someone whose mental or emotional state is likely to change suddenly: *The drug made Harold emotionally unstable and subject to sudden swings of mood.* By extension, this can apply to a rapidly changing commercial situation: *Unstable oil prices made the cost of petrol fluctuate.*

unthinkable

On the surface it seems an absurdity to say that *such and such is unthinkable* when you have clearly just thought it. **Unthinkable** does not mean that it is impossible to think of some particular thing but that the thing concerned is so horrible or terrible that you do not want to think about it: *The idea of stripping Beauty's hide was unthinkable; The animal images would be unthinkable in Moslem worship.*

until ⇒ till

unwonted, unwanted

Something **unwonted** is unusual and out of the ordinary: *The unwonted luxury of a week in bed did Fanny much good.* It is not a commonly used adjective. The pronunciation has the same sound as *don't*, not *unwanted*. An **unwanted** action or item is not desired by its recipient: *He showered her with unwanted gifts and unwelcome attention.*

up-

The prefix **up-** can be readily used for word formation with the sense of 'upwards' (*uprate*) or 'higher up' (*up-river*).

upon, on

The only difference between the use of **upon** and **on** as prepositions is found in certain set phrases, e.g. *once upon a time; Newcastle Upon Tyne; row upon row; mile upon mile; thousands upon thousands.* There is no connection between *upon* and *on* when it used as an adverb: *Get on with it.*

upstage

The **upstage** area is the rear of the stage. When an actor *upstages* another he moves to the back of the stage, forcing the upstaged actor to turn away from the audience. The verb *upstage* has become a synonym for treating someone in a supercilious manner. As an adjective it means 'haughty', 'aloof': *It's not a bit of use your being upstage about the domestic arrangements.* Both uses are informal.

uptight

The word **uptight**, meaning 'tense and irritable', is still regarded as informal. Avoid using it in formal contexts.

up-to-date

When **up-to-date** is used as a compound adjective meaning 'modern' or 'current', it is optionally hyphenated: *Their teaching should be based on an up-to-date appreciation of the real issues.* Hyphens are not used in a sentence such as *Bring the files up to date.*

urbane, urban

Someone who has suave manners and an easy, cultivated personality could be described as **urbane**: *He was composed, urbane, and affable.* Urbane can still be used in its original sense of 'fitted to the nature of a town': *the urbane stateliness of the pale façade of a Wren church.*

Urban is an adjective that means 'to do with the town rather than the country': *Urban clearance schemes were popular in the sixties.*

us, we

Be careful when using *us* or *we* together with a noun. If the noun is plural and part of the subject, it is used with **we**: *'We nations have organized ourselves,'* began the speaker. If the noun is part of the object of a verb (or a preposition), **us** is used: *They took it out on us men; She played with all of us children.*

US, USA

The abbreviation **USA** for *United States of America* is sometimes abbreviated further to **US**. Both forms are usually written without full stops. The phrase *United States of America* is usually treated as a singular and followed by *is*, although the use of a plural would not be incorrect. In general usage, the USA is more frequently called *America*. While this is potentially misleading, it creates few misunderstandings in practice. ⇒ **America**

usage, use

In general contexts the term **usage** means 'habitual or customary use': *Airline pilots were conditioned, by training and usage, to swift, sure reflexes.*

When we describe language, *usage* is the name we give to the finer distinctions between words and points of grammar that might be concealed by a general discussion; it is the way that language is used rather than just the fact of its use: *There are occasions on which the usages of ordinary language cannot help us.*

Avoid using *usage* to replace *use*: *What's the main stumbling block in the use* [not *usage*] *of fuel cells?; ...his nitrogen use* [not *usage*].

use, useful

Notice the range of acceptable constructions that are possible with **use**. *It was no use; It was of no/some use;*

Was it (of) any use?; *Was it of some use?* Although *use* cannot occur on its own, when the word chosen is **useful**, we can say: *It was (not) useful; Was it useful?*

used to, use to

Used to is an unusual verb. It is similar to verbs like *shall* and *may* because it does not normally change its form and is always followed by the base form of another verb. The verb includes the particle *to*, and in rapid speech both parts run together and sound like /useta/. The verb **used to** always takes the past form, with one exception. When it is used with *did* in negatives or questions, (the past form of the auxiliary verb **do**), it normally changes to **use to**.

If we take a sentence like: *I used to go out with her,* and turn it into a question we can have: *Did you use to go out with her too?* or *Used you to go out with her too?* The first construction is the more common, the second is the more formal, and rather old-fashioned. Some writers retain the form *used* when *did* occurs. This is not standard.

In a negative sentence we can say: *He didn't use to go out with her,* or *He used not to go out with her.* Again the first construction is usual, the second is more formal. You can also abbreviate the formal version to: *He usedn't to go out with her.* Although this is formally correct many people find it very odd-looking, and instead write: *He usen't to go out with her,* with **use** instead of **used**. All the constructions above are really quite acceptable, but some are disliked by purists. The one that is not standard is: [*He didn't used to go out with her*].

Note that if *used to* means 'accustomed to' it is not the same as the verb above. Here we have **used** (adjective) **to** (preposition) followed by a noun, a verbal noun, or a pronoun: *I grew used to despair; I became used to her calling on me with the latest piece of gossip; There was no getting used to it.*

utilize, use

When you **utilize** something, you use it in a practical or worthwhile way. This is a rather formal word: *Carbohydrate from the potatoes helps the body to utilize all the protein from the fish; If this land were fully utilized it could produce 12 million tons of grain.*

The verb **use** is a more general term. Note that the verb is pronounced /yuze/ but the noun is pronounced /yoos/.

V

v.

The written abbreviation **v.** standing for *versus* should be pronounced in full when team lists are read aloud. Some BBC sports commentators do not do this, however.

vacant, empty, vacuous

While **vacant** and **empty** overlap in part of their meanings, *vacant* has a number of special meanings. A house without its occupants can be described as *an empty house* but it only becomes *vacant* when it has no owners or tenants, as in *vacant possession*. A similar use of *vacant* applies to unoccupied hotel rooms and to unfilled jobs.

An extended meaning of *vacant* is 'lacking expression or apparent awareness': *She gazed around her with the vacant stare of someone who is waiting for a friend to turn up.*

If someone appears **vacuous** they show no clear sign of intelligence. A more formal word than *vacant*, it suggests a basic lack of intelligence rather than a brief failure of concentration: *...beamed with a sort of self-conscious, vacuous, all-embracing benignity.*

vacation, holiday

Vacation and *holiday* have overlapping meanings. **Holiday** is a very general word, used for *public holidays, holiday pay, package holidays*, etc. In British English **vacation** is generally restricted to use in universities and some professions: *It was vacation and the students went home.* It is a more common term in American English, where it can also be used as a verb: *...the penchant of Mexico's middle class to vacation in the United States.* The informal abbreviation *vac* is sometimes used in universities: *What are you doing in the long vac?*

vaccinate, inoculate

When someone is **inoculated**, they have the virus causing a disease introduced into their body in small quantities, to which their body responds by forming a resistance. When someone is **vaccinated** they have a disease-resisting preparation introduced into their body. In general terms the words are regarded as equivalent in meaning.

vacillate

To **vacillate** means to be undecided and to waver in one's choice. It is pronounced /va-sill-ate/.

vacuum cleaner

The use of *Hoover* as a noun and a verb instead of **vacuum clean(er)** exists only in Britain. Note that Hoover™ is a trade name. ⇒ **trade names**

vale, valley

The word **vale** is a poetic equivalent for **valley**.

valet

Valet can be used as a noun or a verb. When it is a verb it keeps a single *t*: *Car valeting services available.* The pronunciation of the noun is either /va-lit/ or /va-lay/ but when it is used as a verb, the *t* is always pronounced.

valid

Valid is a technical term in logic, but in everyday contexts it is used of any soundly based behaviour, irrespective of logic. It means 'recognized as relevant or sound': *a valid reason; a valid question; a perfectly valid technique.* It is also used for documents that are current, meaning 'in force or in effect': *His visa had been issued in December but it was still valid.*

value, worth

As a singular noun, **value** is equivalent to *cost*, *worth*, or *use* but each is used in different constructions. Something can *be of (some/no) value/use: His opinion was of no value; This information was of some use in establishing who was responsible.* The noun *cost* is not used with *some/no in* this way while an equivalent construction with *worth* is, *of little worth.* We can ask, *Is it value for money?* but none of the others fit this construction. In the plural, *values* changes meaning to 'standards': *I cannot accept his values.* ⇒ **worth**

valueless, priceless

If an action or an object is **valueless** it has no use or

effect: *They received hundreds of messages, most quite valueless.* A **priceless** object is worth so much that it is beyond the ability of anyone to suggest how much it is worth: *Thank you for the priceless gift of your music.*

vane, vain, vein

The noun **vane** means a fin or a projection on something that is designed to catch the wind: *The tail vane can be hinged to turn the rotor.* **Vain** is an adjective meaning 'excessively pleased with oneself'. The most common related noun form is *vanity*, but *vainness* is sometimes heard. The noun **vein** means a blood-vessel that carries blood to the heart (the converse of *artery*); *vein* is also used for a seam of mineral running through rock.

vantage

There are two main contexts where **vantage** is used. One is in phrases like *a vantage point*, where it means 'a commanding or superior position', especially one that provides a view: *A chairlift takes visitors to a fine vantage point high above the valley.* The second is in the context of tennis, where *vantage* means 'an advantage over an opponent' in terms of the score: *Vantage, Mandlikova.*
⇒ advantage

variance

Variance is always followed by *with* and is frequently used in the phrase *at variance with*. Someone who is *at variance with* you holds different and often irreconcilable views from yours: *He expresses views totally at variance with the contemporary climate.*

vein ⇒ vane

venal, venial

A **venal** act is one that is done for the sake of money. Someone with a venal nature is easily corrupted:

…accommodating accountants, who can be as venal as the next lot. A **venial** sin is one that is not seriously condemned: *'Curiosity and vanity; venial sins'*, said the monk, *'and yet they may lead to more serious ones.'*

venue

A **venue** is a meeting place: *…the venue; in or near Committee Room 14, House of Commons.* There is a tendency to use the word to mean any *location*, *place*, or *setting*. In the following examples, one of those words would be better: *The house chosen as the venue/setting for the final encounter…*; *from both venues/locations the fish will be finicky.*

verbal, oral

The word **verbal** is often loosely used as a contrast to *written*, as in phrases like: *verbal statements, verbal questioning, verbal language difficulties;* or *…an immediate verbal denial.* Although this use of *verbal* is widely used, it can be ambiguous because *verbal* more properly means 'to do with words', as in *…verbal and nonverbal reasoning tests; …a verbal picture of a visual subject.*

The better contrast to *written* is **oral**, meaning 'to do with the mouth' or 'using spoken words'. Alternatively, use *spoken*, as in *spoken statements, oral questioning, spoken/ oral language difficulties.*

verify ⇒ corroborate

veritable ⇒ virtual

vermin

Vermin is a collective noun and is used as if it were plural: *It is a pity that so many animals should be considered vermin because they are a nuisance to man.*

vernacular, demotic

Both these words can be used when talking about language. A **vernacular** is the everyday language of a country with all its abbreviations, colloquialisms, and slang: *'I'm on the loo', he said, recollecting the English vernacular.* The word can be used as a noun or as an adjective. The *vernacular* language can be contrasted with the more specialized or formal uses of language in literature, or for ceremonial or ecclesiastical purposes.

Vernacular has further uses. When used to describe architecture, it means 'in a style that is typically used for local domestic buildings': *...ordinary, everyday, vernacular buildings.*

The term **demotic** is also used for the language of ordinary people. The word is derived from Greek. It is a less common term than *vernacular* but in one instance it must be used, as modern spoken Greek is called *Demotic Greek* (in contrast to classical Greek or modern literary Greek). *Demotic* can be used of things other than language that are part of popular culture: *Television, that most demotic of the arts.*

very, much

In strict usage, adverbs of degree such as *very, too, quite, really,* and *extremely* are used only to modify adjectives: *He is very happy; She is too eager.*

By this rule, these words should not be used to modify past participles that follow the verb *be,* since they would then technically be modifying verbs, which should be modified by adverbs such as *much, greatly, seriously,* or *excessively: He has been greatly [not really] inconvenienced; She was much [not very] abused by her contemporaries.*

The rule is difficult to apply since so many participles, such as *broken, tired, disappointed,* and *hidden* can also be used as adjectives or have a distinct adjectival meaning. This has blurred the distinction stated above. In cases of doubt, remember that *much* has a greater degree of formality and adapt your usage to the context.

vest

In British English a **vest** is a sleeveless garment worn beneath a shirt. In other English-speaking countries this is called a *singlet*. In these countries a *vest* is the sleeveless buttoned garment that British people call a *waistcoat*.

vestige, trace

Both words overlap in part of their meaning, 'a small amount' but **vestige** refers both to something that there ought to be more of, as well as to something that used to be there in larger quantities. *Vestige* is a very formal word. Because of what it implies, *vestige* is used in the context of things that have diminished to the smallest possible amount: *I exercised the last vestiges of my free will; There were still vestiges of judicial law surviving,* or of something that does not exist even to the smallest degree: *Carling had no vestige of charm; Winds swept the plain denuding it of every vestige of vegetation.* In many contexts, the less formal word **trace** is to be preferred, especially when the context involves a positive amount, as in *I usually put a trace of curry powder in this soup.*

veterinary

This full form of the word **veterinary** is a frequent cause of problems in spelling and pronunciation; as a result, the short form **vet** is in common use. Note that the central section is *-erin-* and the end *-ary*. The accepted pronunciation is /vet-er-in-a-ry/ but this proves such a tongue twister for many speakers that variants like /vet-in-ree/ and /vet-rin-ree/ are commonly heard.

via

This word is from Latin. It means 'by way of' and is common in transport timetables to indicate the route that will be taken. The pronunciation of *via* can be either /vee-uh/ or /vye-uh/. Do not use it for the means of transport; you may go *via Reading* but avoid [*via the train*].

viable

Purists would like to restrict the meaning of **viable** to 'capable of independent life', as in *Some bacteria stay viable right up to just below the boiling point of water*. However, the main use of *viable*, as shown by the number of times that it occurs in the corpus, is as a synonym for 'feasible' or 'workable': *It might not be commercially viable; We must also find viable ways of sharing our wealth; …a viable alternative*.

vicar, rector, priest, minister

In the Church of England, **vicar** and **rector** are both titles for a clergyman in charge of a parish. A historical difference, now ignored, is that whereas the *rector* received all the benefits of the parish, including tithes, a *vicar* was only paid a stipend or salary. Both are **priests**, but in Britain this term is frequently restricted to the Roman Catholic church. An Anglican clergyman may be called a *priest*, a nonconformist clergyman is generally not. Nonconformist clergy are usually called **ministers**.

vicious, viscous

The adjective **vicious** is used of someone who is cruel and violent. This sense is not connected with the use of the word in **a vicious circle**, which is a situation in which, to solve one problem, we find ourselves creating another problem that in turn brings us back to the original difficulty. Do not confuse this word with **viscous**, meaning 'sticky'.

vide

This is a Latin word that is used as a direction to the reader to look in the book or at the work of the person that is named: *vide Burgin, Kelly, etc.* It is little used now; modern writers prefer *see Burgin, Kelly, etc.* It is pronounced /**vee**-day/ or /**vi**-day/.

viewpoint, point of view

Careful users restrict the use of **viewpoint** or **point of view** to situations where the writer provides a second set of opinions or options: *…but from the players' viewpoint I can see only drawbacks.*

Avoid using either of these expressions when *opinion* or *attitude* could as well be used. For example, *attitude* or *outlook* would be a better choice in: *Provincialism is taken to indicate narrowness of viewpoint.*

vigour, vigorous

Note the way that the spelling changes between the noun, **vigour**, and the adjective, **vigorous**, shifting the position of -*ou*- to the end.

A small group of words behaves similarly: *dolour, dolorous; glamour, glamorous; humour, humorous; labour, laborious; odour, odorous; rancour, rancorous; rigour, rigorous; splendour, splend(o)rous; valour, valorous; vapour, vaporous.*

Note the difference in spelling beteen the noun *ardour*, and the adjective *arduous*.

villain, villein

The spelling **villain** is used for someone of criminal behaviour or, in literature and film, for the character who is seen to hinder the fortunes of the hero or heroine: *The judge expressed his relief that such a villain was caught at last; …manly encounters with the hero and the villain taking turns to knock each other down. Villain* is sometimes used with teasing affection, much like the word *rascal: She hugged David. 'You little villain.'*

A **villein** was a feudal tenant personally subject to his lord. Both words have the same pronunciation.

vindicate, vindictive

If you **vindicate** someone's behaviour, you provide an explanation and justification for it, especially when they have been believed to be wrong: *It was our 'thankyou' to a group of kids who had vindicated our trust in them; Events in China vindicated White's judgment.*

When someone is **vindictive** they want to exact a full revenge for a real or imagined offence: *She was petty, vindictive, resentful; …a vindictive and violent man.*

violoncello, cello

Although **violoncello** is the full name (note, it is *violon* not *violin*), the word **cello** does not start with an apostrophe.

virtual, veritable

Virtual is often used as if it meant *veritable*. The adjective **virtual** has two senses. In its technical sense it means having the appearance of something or simulating its function. It is the opposite of *actual* or *real: The virtual image produced by a biconcave lens is erect and diminished; …computer-generated virtual realities.* The more common use of *virtual* is 'true in effect but not admitted to be so': *He ended up as the virtual leader of the conspirators; the virtual absence of lectures as a teaching mode.* It is this meaning that is confused with **veritable**, which is used when you want to say that although a description may seem exaggerated it is indeed appropriate: *His hands perform a veritable ballet of airborne movements; By comparison, Lee was a veritable tape recorder.*

virtuoso

In common with most well-established foreign borrowings, **virtuoso**, 'a master of technique', offers a choice of plural forms, either the original Italian *virtuosi* or the English-based *virtuosos*. The corpus shows a preference in modern English usage for the latter.

vis-à-vis

Vis-à-vis is an example of 'English French' where a word has a different meaning in English from the one it has in its parent language. In French **vis-à-vis** means 'face-to-face' or 'opposite'; in English it means 'in relation to': *His rights vis-à-vis his wife gave him legal status as master; This underlines the independent traditions of the City vis-à-vis the Crown.* It is pronounced /veez-ah-**vee**/.
⇒ nom de plume

viscous, viscid

The adjective **viscous** is usually associated with thick liquids and means 'sticky' and 'slow flowing': *A viscometer is used to test the viscous properties of oil.* The adjective **viscid** also means 'sticky' but is usually applied to coatings on surfaces. We generally use *viscous* to describe one characteristic of oil or treacle and *viscid* to describe something that binds or holds an object that comes into contact with it: *He realized that some viscid substance* *was coating his soles causing small objects to adhere to them.*

visible, visual

Each of these adjectives refers to different aspects of sight. What is **visible** can be seen: *The brilliant flash that accompanied the detonation was visible in London.* Avoid the overuse of *visible* as a synonym for *clear* or *evident* or *obvious* when one of these words could be used, as in *The Belgian's relief was visible; The results are visible in the growth of the Communist vote; McGovern was the only visible candidate.*

The word **visual** means 'relating to sight' and is used when you want to contrast the sense of sight with the other senses: *Television should increase visual awareness; The monorail system intrudes only minimally upon the physical and visual environment.*

visit, visitation

The verb **visit** is used with the general sense of making a journey to see someone or something. A *visit* is usually dependent on an invitation. The American idiom *visit with* someone is not acceptable in British English.

An archaic and literary use of *visit* means 'afflict', particularly when the subject is illness, punishment, or disease. The verb is usually followed by *(up)on* or *by*, as in, *visit the sins of the fathers upon the children* meaning that the children will suffer. It is sometimes used of memories, ghosts, or visions coming into someone's mind: *She was visited by a precious memory of his face.*

A **visitation** is a noun meaning a formal or official visit. In this case, the visitor usually invites himself or herself. It carries with it the overtones of possible stress: *We have until tomorrow to structure our approach to the visita-*

tion committee. It may also involve unexpectedness, such as with a supernatural event: *The visitation began in a dream...*, or some kind of unpleasantness: *In past centuries this had made the Plague a yearly visitation; ...the visitation of vengeance upon a scapegoat.*

vitamin

The older, and more logical, pronunciation of **vitamin** as /vyt-a-min/ has given way, at least in British English, to /vitt-a-min/. This has the unfortunate effect of blurring the connection between the other *vit-* words with the same base meaning. For example, *vital, vitality,* and *revitalize* all relate, as does *vitamin*, to the meaning 'life', but have a different sound. Logic is never a strong element in linguistic behaviour. American English and some other forms of English retain the pronunciation /vy-ta-min/.

vitiate

Vitiate, meaning debase, corrupt, or destroy the efficacy of something, is pronounced /vish-i-iate/: *The force and singleness of his purpose was vitiated and destroyed by professional politicians.*

viz.

An abbreviation for the Latin *videlicit*, **viz.** means 'namely'. It is sometimes used to begin a list, as in, *...The Managing Agency Houses of Calcutta, viz. Messrs. Andrew Yule, Baird, Shaw Wallace....* It is not in frequent use; most writers prefer to use *i.e.* or *namely.*

vocal cords

When vowel sounds are produced, the passage of air from the lungs sets up a rapid vibration in the lip-like folds that form part of the larynx. These are called *vocal folds* or **vocal cords**. The false belief that the name is connected with music results in the common mistake of using the spelling *vocal* [*chords*].

vogue words

There are fashions in words as in most other things and some words become overused as a result of temporarily finding favour with the press or by suiting the trend of the moment. As with most fashions, the use of these words is dependent on whim, so some stay in vogue for much longer than others. Examples of recent **vogue words** and phrases include the terms *wet* and *dry* in politics, and the use in general commentary of *ongoing* for *continuing* and *at this point in time* for *now*. In self-contained groups of users, some *vogue words* become *buzz words* that often have little meaning outside the group.

By the very nature of their use, *vogue words* do not stay in vogue for long. Overuse of any word can lead to its meaning being devalued so that it loses impact and has to be replaced. In this, they are like slang. ⇒ **buzz word**

volcano ⇒ **-o**

vulgarism

A **vulgarism** is any element of speaking or writing that encourages the hearer to perceive the speaker as vulgar. What is perceived as vulgar will differ according to the context and to the sensibilities of the listener or reader.

It is broadly agreed that obscene words and lavatorial humour constitute *vulgarisms*. Some people may extend vulgarism to include slang and a range of words, often of considerable antiquity, that are on the border between slang and obscenity, such as *prat*, *berk*, *slag*, and so on.

Speakers and writers should be aware of the likely effect of their use of vulgarisms while recognizing that there are often contexts where they are appropriate.

vulgarity, profanity
The definition of a *vulgarism*, given above, sets a wide range of possible applications. The same can be said of **vulgarity**, which can include vulgar speech and vulgar behaviour in the broader sense. **Profanity** differs from vulgarity in that, while *vulgarity* may shock, *profanity* can offend the listener or reader. *Profanity* extends to the use of language in ways that offend religious belief and practice, such as *blasphemy*.

W

wage, wages, salary, remuneration, pay
The distinctions in use between these words often reflect the status of different kinds of work in Britain. A **wage** or, more often, the plural form **wages**, is payment made in return for labour. These terms are usually associated with hourly- or weekly-paid manual work.

A **salary** is also money paid in return for labour, but is associated with an annual rate of pay that is paid out monthly. A person receiving a salary is usually a white-collar worker or a member of a profession.

When, as in some professions, there is no regular payment of salary, and the reward is based on fees or commission, the word **remuneration** is often used. The term *emolument* is often used for money paid for unspecified services, e.g. a nonexecutive directorship. **Pay** is a common neutral term. ⇒ **job**

wagon, waggon

Both spellings are used. The more common spelling is **wagon**.

waistcoat

At one time the word **waistcoat** was pronounced /wes-kit/. This pronunciation is regarded as odd today and the usual pronunciation is /wais-coat/.
⇒ forehead

wait, await

Await is rather archaic and literary in its overtones. It means *wait for* and must always have an object: *I await your answer with impatience*. The word **wait** does not need an object: *The Doctor will see you soon. Please sit down and wait*.

waive, wave

When you agree to give up something that could be yours, you **waive** your rights: *I shall be able to persuade them to waive all death duties; For the benefit of other harassed authors, I waive all copyright*. Be careful not to confuse this with **wave**. There is no connection other than the pronunciation.

wake, awake

When the sentence contains an object and the sense is the literal one of ceasing to be asleep, the common form is **wake up** (the particle *up* can be left off) or, alternatively, **waken**: *I woke him (up); I wakened him*. Both verbs are also commonly used without an object: *I woke up; Babies often wake and cry*. A following adverb or adverb phrase is common: *I tend to wake up early; He did not wake up until dawn*. **Awake** and *awaken* are preferred to other forms of *wake* when the sense is a figurative one: *He awoke to the danger*.

want, need

Something that you **want** is usually not a necessity but a desire. If you **need** something, the notion of necessity is strong. At certain points, however, the meanings of *want* and *need* overlap.

Want followed by the *to* infinitive is normally used to mean 'desire or wish', as in *I don't really want to start a new career; Do you want to ride now?* When *want* is followed by an object, it usually means 'require', or, loosely, 'would like', as in *If you want socks, I've got stacks.* If the desire is urgent, the alternative use of *need* becomes more probable: *They want teachers of German* is close to *They need teachers of German*, but there is still a difference in meaning between *He wants your help* and *He needs your help.*

Less frequently, *want* followed by an object means 'lack': *There are times that I think he wants commonsense.* This sense of *want* is sometimes followed by *for: She certainly doesn't want for money.* Alternatively, the construction *wanting in* is used to mean 'lack': *Don't you feel that is really wanting in charity?*

Want followed by a present participle meaning 'have need of' is a common, but nonstandard, regional usage in British English: *Her coat wants cleaning.* The construction *want to be*, followed by a past participle, can be used to express the same meaning, and is another regional idiom: *The car wants to be cleaned before we go on holiday.* Although there is no difference for some between *need* and *want* in these constructions, the standard usage prefers *need* and others either dislike, or do not understand, the usage.

Want meaning 'ought', as in *You want to get that cough seen to quickly*, is informal. ⇒ **want for**

want for

A usage that is particular to American English is **want for** followed by the *to* infinitive of the verb in order to express a wish: *I want for John to meet him.* The construction is labelled non-standard in several American books on usage, which prefer the form used in British English: *I want John to meet him.*

In British English, the phrase *want for* means 'be in need of', as in *Her husband makes sure that she wants for nothing,* but this use is somewhat dated. ⇒ **want**

want in, want out, want off

The phrases **want in**, **want out**, and **want off**, as in *I want in on this deal* or *I want out,* meaning *I want to get in* or *be let in/out/off* are not common even in informal usage in British English. Although the construction is regarded as an Americanism, American writers on English usage are divided on its acceptability. In Scottish English it is well established. ⇒ **require**

want that

The use of **want** followed by a **that** clause to express a wish, as in *Do you want that I should ask him for you?* is an Americanism. In British English *want* with a direct object follows a similar construction to the one used with *like*: *Would you like me to ask him?*; *Do you want me to ask him?* ⇒ **want for**

-ward, -wards

These suffixes are found with a number of words and mean 'direction towards', so *home+ward* becomes *homeward,* 'towards home'. In British English the -**ward** suffix usually indicates that the word is an adjective, e.g. *a backward glance; a forward engagement.* The -**wards** suffix always indicates that the word is used as an adverb: *move forwards; lying upwards on the grass.*

In American English, the use of *-ward* without the *s* is common as an adverb-forming suffix. Some dialects of British English also use this form as an adverb.

was, were

The constructions *if (I/he) was* and *if (I/he) were* can be used with the same meaning. The difference is between a modern form, **if I was**, that can be used formally or informally in speaking and writing, and a very traditional formal construction, **if I were**, that is usually restricted to writing. The verb form *were* is part of the subjunctive mood which may be used when speaking about unlikely or hypothetical situations that express a possible future: *If he were to die, she would inherit everything;* suppositions contrary to fact: *If I were you, I would be careful;* and also to express desire: *I wish he were here now.* The subjunctive is used much less often than formerly and the normal past forms of *be* are used in its place. Both *was* and *were* forms are equally acceptable in this type of expression.

waste, wastage

Waste and *wastage* are not identical in meaning. **Waste** is the careless use of resources, as in *What a waste of opportunity,* or what is left over after a product has been used: *The kitchen waste is collected and fed to pigs.* Waste can mean 'a useless by-product'. The plural form is common with this meaning: *Propylene was a waste material from the oil industry that no one could find a use for; Acid tars are unpleasant wastes produced when oil is recycled.*

Wastage is a loss that is brought about by natural causes or by wear and destruction: *Because of present depletion, and the current level of wastage, the UK will have to start importing oil again.*

In recent usage *wastage* is also used for the steady decline of a workforce or similar group through resignations or retirement rather than through dismissals: *British Universities could take the most able students, lose a few of them through wastage, and send a large proportion of them on to post-graduate studies.*

A quite different use of the plural **wastes** has the sense 'a barren or deserted landscape': *Unchartable wastes of water; the rocky wastes of Western Alaska.*

way

The use of **the way** as a conjunction with a meaning similar to *like* or *as* is well established: *Nothing has quite turned out the way Mrs Thatcher hoped and confidently expected.*

The expression **no way**, meaning 'under no circumstances', is very informal.

way, weigh

When a ship is in motion it is *under way.* Through confusion with the phrase *weigh anchor,* (meaning 'raise the anchor'), the alternative spelling *under weigh* has come about. ⇒ **weight**

we ⇒ editorial we

weal, wheal

There are two words with the spelling *weal.* A **weal** is the raised red mark left after a blow, usually from a stick, a belt, or some thin instrument. It is also called a *welt: His back was streaked with crimson, and from weal to weal, ran thin trickles of blood.* A spelling variant of this word, *wheal,* is sometimes found.

The second word **weal** is an old form of the modern word *wealth.* It is only found in set phrases such as *the com-*

mon weal and *the public weal* meaning 'benefit'.

The word **wheal** is Cornish and means 'a mine': *Wheal Jane*.

weave

There are alternative Simple Past tense forms for **weave**. The usual form is **wove**, which is used when the action described is to do with weaving or is similar to weaving: *The road hugged the shore and wove in and out of the hills.*

If you mean that someone makes a path by winding around obstructions or moves in an indirect line, you normally use the form **weaved**: *They weaved back and forth so that their paths intertwined; A stout woman with blue hair weaved her way along the edge of the pool.*

The usual past participle (frequently used as an adjective) is **woven**: *…an endless woven carpet; …the creepers had woven a great mat.*

wed, marry

Books on usage used to suggest that **wed** should not be used as a verb and that **marry** should be used instead, but *wed* has become more common. Although it was once felt to be a rather formal or literary word, it now has journalistic rather than formal overtones.

The Simple Past of **wed** is *wed*: *The two wed or lived together and were indulged by the community.* The ceremony can be referred to as either a *wedding* or a *marriage*. The most common meaning of the past participle *wedded* is 'attached to' or 'committed to' rather than 'married': *This school of thought is firmly wedded to a class analysis of society; …coolness was wedded to discomfort.*

weight, height

English makes nouns from *long* and *broad* with the help of the suffix *-th*; *long/length*; *broad/breadth*. Some people seem to become confused by this and try to turn all words that indicate physical features into nouns of this type. As a result, the noun **height** formed from *high*, and **weight**, which is already a noun, are sometimes incorrectly spelled with a *th* ending.

well, ill, good, bad

Well and **ill** are frequently combined with participles. When the combination is used as an adjective premodifying a noun, as in *well-established pasture; well-fed child; well-fitting jacket; well-mannered; ill-favoured brat; ill-bred lad*, they are generally linked with a hyphen to show that *well* or *ill* modifies the participle, not the noun. It is important to note that the hyphen is used only when the combined form is a premodifier.

Though there are fewer expressions involved, a similar reason explains the hyphen in some compounds using **good** and **bad**, as in *a good-looking girl; a good-natured person, a bad-tempered tyrant*. An important difference between the two pairs is that *well* and *ill* are adverbs and cannot modify nouns on their own whereas *good* and *bad* are adjectives and can do so.

When the combination using *well* or *ill* follows a verb, no hyphen is used because *ill* or *well* now modifies the verb of which the participle is a part: *Stuart had been well fed and well looked after generally*. This becomes clear if the words are rearranged: *Stuart had been fed well*.

When you want to put these expressions in the comparative or superlative you have to change **well** to *better* or *best* and **ill** to *worse* or *worst*: *a better-fitting jacket; the* *best-fed child; a worse-behaved child; man is the worst-behaved species.* ⇒ **well, unwell**

well, unwell

Well may be used as adjective when it means 'in good health' and is the opposite of **unwell**, **ill**, or **sick**. It has become particularly current in one set phrase, *a well-woman clinic*. In British English [*He is a well man*] is not standard usage and *He is well* is preferred. The normal position of the adjective *well* is after the verb: *She looked quite well, considering.* If the sentence is negative, *well* is sometimes used in front of the noun: *He is not a well man.*

Note the use of *well* as a part of a compound noun in *wellbeing,* and *well-wisher.* These are different from the uses of *well* as an adverb.

well-nigh

In strict usage, **well-nigh** is an adverb meaning 'nearly' or 'almost' and not a preposition meaning 'near'. It can be used with a verb: *He well-nigh cried,* or with an adjective. So we must either say: *He was near* [not *well-nigh*] *death,* or *He was well-nigh dead.* This expression has become a cliché and, generally, is best avoided.

Welsh, Welch, Wales

Welsh can be used an adjective meaning 'relating to Wales': *the Welsh side of Offa's dyke,* or 'native to Wales': *the former Welsh rugby player.*

When *Welsh* means 'a native of Wales' it can be used as a collective noun: *I think that on the whole the Welsh are more honest, more sincere… ; You cannot lump the English, the Welsh, the Scots, and the Irish together and call them British.* It is also used as a noun meaning 'the language of Wales': *…people spoke little or no Welsh.*

The spelling *Welsh* has an earlier form, **Welch**. The singular noun meaning 'a native of Wales' is **Welshman** or **Welshwoman**: *...the charm and eloquence of the Welshman and his passion for social reform; This costume sits better on waitresses and folk dancers than on an ordinary Welshwoman.* The plural form is *Welshmen/women.* In many parts of Wales, Celtic rather than Saxon names are now preferred for the country and its inhabitants, e.g. *Cymry* instead of Wales. ⇒ **Scotch**

welsher, welcher

A **welsher** or **welcher** was originally a racecourse pest who ran off without paying debts. The word began as a spoken form so that the spelling is only an attempt at the sound. The verb *welsh/welch*, as in *welch on a debt* came after. There is no connection with Welsh, apart from a similar sound.

Welsh rabbit, Bombay duck

Welsh rabbit is neither Welsh nor rabbit but grilled or melted cheese on a toast base (trimmings to suit). Rabbit was the poor countryman's cheap food; *Welsh rabbit* is for those too poor even for rabbit. This familiar snack has also gained the name **Welsh rarebit** as a result of attempts to rationalize the derivation. It is not alone in not being what it seems. The once familiar **Bombay duck** is a type of dried fish.

were ⇒ was

wh-

There is a small difference between the sound of *wh* and the sound of a *w* on its own, in some people's pronunciation. This makes *whether* sound a little different from *weather*. This difference is not meaningful.

wharf

Like many words that end in *f,* **wharf** has two accepted plural forms; *wharfs* and *wharves.* The latter form is more usual.

what

What can be used with either singular or plural reference. It can mean either 'that which': *He only believes what pleases him,* and in this case has a singular verb, or 'those which': *We are rationalizing all our books. What we don't keep are to be auctioned off.* Accordingly, the verb used with it must change from singular to plural.

Avoid the use of the nonstandard phrase *like what* in a construction such as: [*Do it like what I do*]. Either use *Do it like me* or, more formally: *Do as I do.* ⇒ **like**

when, where

When and **where** are commonly used in informal language to introduce definitions, as in *Famine is when food runs dangerously low causing malnutrition and death.*

Purists object to this usage and only allow *when* and *where* as substitutes for *in which* if they refer explicitly to time or place, as in *The year when this took place.* Otherwise, formal definitions either use *in which,* as in *Paralysis is a condition in which parts of the body cannot be moved,* or use a direct paraphrase: *Remorse is a strong feeling of guilt.*

whence, whither

Careful users of English avoid the expression *from whence,* since **whence** already means 'from which place': *…the tradition whence* [not *from whence*] *such ideas flow.* Both *whence* (from which place) and its converse *whither* (to which place) are no longer in general use.

where

Where includes the notion of *to* and *at*, so write *Where is she going?* [not *Where is she going to*]; *Where was it?* [not *Where was it at*]. ⇒ **when**

where-, whereas, whereby

The majority of words with a **where-** prefix should be treated as either very formal or as normally to be used only in literary contexts. Many are moving out of current use. Those to use cautiously are: *whereafter, whereat, where'er, wherefrom, whereunto, whereof, whereon, whereto.*

The words with a **where-** prefix that are still in common use are: *whereas, whereby, wherein, whereupon,* and *wherever.*

whereabouts

Whereabouts can be used as a noun, meaning 'the place where someone/something can be found': *Nothing was known of her whereabouts.* It must be written with an *s* ending, but it may be used with either a singular or a plural verb: *He may have surreptitiously made an extra copy; if so, its whereabouts remain/remains unknown.*

wherefore

This word is generally only found used as a plural in the set phrase **the whys and wherefores.**

wherewithal

This word, meaning 'whatever is necessary', or 'funds' is always written as one word. It has only a single *l* at the end. It must be used with a preceding *the: Western banks have loaned to Argentina the wherewithal to buy expensive weapons; From the increased product comes the wherewithal to buy the fertilizer.*

whet, wet

The words **wet** and **whet** often become confused in two common idiomatic phrases. Because it is hard to whistle with a dry mouth, when someone offers you a drink, it serves to *wet your whistle*, but something served as an appetizer before a meal will sharpen or *whet your appetite*.

whether, weather, wether

Whether is a conjunction that introduces a choice; **weather** has to do with the state of the atmosphere; a **wether** is a male sheep castrated when a few weeks old. All three words have the same pronunciation in most British accents.

which ⇒ **that**

while, whilst

The main sense of **while** is 'during the time that'. However, many users of English accept the use of *while* to mean *although* as established: *While he disliked working, he was obliged to do so.* In careful usage, *while* is not used to mean *whereas: He thought that they were in Paris, whereas* [not *while*] *they had gone on to Rome.*

Careful writers try to avoid any ambiguity that may result from conflicting interpretations of *while*. For example: *While his brother worked in the park, he refused to do any gardening at home* may mean either *Although his brother worked in the park...* or *During the time that his brother worked in the park....* It is therefore preferable to substitute one of these items for *while*. **Whilst** is archaic. Avoid using it. ⇒ **wile**

whisky, whiskey

The usual spelling is Scotch **whisky**, but Irish **whiskey** and Bourbon **whiskey** are spelled with an *e*, as shown.

who, whom

In formal and especially in written English, careful writers always use **whom** when the object form of **who** is required. In informal contexts, however, many educated speakers consider *whom* to be unnatural, especially near the beginning of a sentence: *Who were you looking for?* is preferable in these contexts to the very formal: *For whom were you looking?*

While it is quite correct to use *whom* where it closely follows a preposition, as in *To whom did you give it?* it is not good usage, in any context, to use *whom* where the preposition is separated from the pronoun, as in [*Whom did you give it to?*]

A further problem arises when the sentence has a deceptive relationship between one of its verbs and the relative pronoun *who(m)*, as in *...two men whom he declared were spies of his rival...* . This sentence looks superficially correct, but *whom* should be *who*. The clause *he declared* is a reporting verb that is outside what was actually said: '*...two men, who are spies of my rival'*.

whoever, whosoever

Whoever means 'anyone who' or 'it doesn't matter who': *Whoever debases others is debased himself; Whoever it was, he was past caring.*

When you start a question with *who ever*, and you are asking 'who possibly?' or 'who in the world?', you should write it as two words: *Who ever returned to tell us?; Who ever would have thought that?*

The word **whosoever** is an archaic form of *whoever* and should not normally be used.

whole new, best ever

These phrases involve elements of tautology and irritate

many hearers. It is advisable not to use them in formal contexts.

who's, whose

The distinction between **who's** and **whose** causes frequent problems when one of these words has to be written down. The problem is partly caused by their similar sound when spoken.

Who's is an abbreviation of either *who is* or *who has: Who's coming tonight?* (Who is coming tonight?) *Who's got my rubber?* (Who has got my rubber?) As with all the abbreviated forms, the apostrophe shows where the shortening has taken place.

Whose is used to indicate possession, either when a question is being asked: *Whose little boy is this?* or when something is being described: *I've no idea whose it is; Would the person whose car is blocking the forecourt, please move it?* ⇒ **their, there** ⇒ **they're**

whose, of which

Whose is the possessive form of *who* and used both for people, as in *I know a famous writer whose family live entirely on her earnings*, and for things: *He found the trousers from an old suit whose jacket had worn through at the sleeves.* The last sentence can also be rephrased as *...the jacket **of which** had worn through at the sleeves.* The choice is a matter of style, not one of correct usage.

why

If **why** is made plural and preceded by *the* it can be used as a noun in informal contexts. This is true for a number of simple adverbs, e.g. *the hows; the wherefores; Even the whys no longer seem to matter, only the how-longs.*

wide ⇒ broad

wile, guile

Wiles (usually used in the plural) are cunning tricks: *He confused them with his wiles, he fooled them with false promises*. They often involve a sort of half-serious artfulness: *You seem familiar with the wiles of children*. Someone who is clever in a sly way is *wily*, pronounced /**wai**-lee/, and knows how to be cunning to get what they want: *a wily and politically lethal opponent*.

Guile (nowadays only used as a singular noun) is the quality that wily people have: *Empire building is not done by war but by guile and long-term pressure*. Someone who does not use *guile* is *guileless: …such clear, blue, guileless eyes*. The opposite term, *guileful*, is now found only in older literature.

will, shall

The old formal rule was that when expressing the future, **shall** should be used with *I* and *we*, and that **will** should be used with *you* and the third person subject pronouns, *he, she, it* and *they*.

When determination or compulsion was intended, together with all other shades of meaning that expressed the imposition of will rather than future time, the system was reversed and *shall* was used with *you, he, they* etc., while *will* was used with *I* and *we*. Not only was this complex, but it was, in fact, not a rule of English. It represented a tidying up of these verbs by a grammarian. Modern usage is more relaxed about these 'differences'.

In formal speech and writing outside England, most speakers of English use *shall* with any of the subject pronouns in order to express different shades of determination. *Will* is used to express future time with any of the subject pronouns and it is gradually becoming the accepted form to use for all purposes. In informal speech, since all we hear is *I'll*, *we'll*, *you'll*, *he'll* or *she'll*, there is no way of telling which modal verb is intended.

Speakers of Southern and Northern British English, usually make a distinction between the use of *will* and *shall* in different types of question. The following meanings are usual. *Will* raises the matter of need or likelihood. *Will I need a cardigan?* means 'Is it going to be necessary?' *Will you meet him off the plane?* asks about your intentions. *Shall I call a doctor?* means 'Would you like a doctor?' and *Shall we eat out tonight?* or *Shall I help you?* makes a proposal or an offer. In Scottish English the use of *shall* in questions is regarded as an affectation and *will* is used throughout. ⇒ **should**

wind, wound

One of the characteristics of English is that its varied history has produced a number words that look alike but sound different. The Simple Past tense and past participle forms of the verb **wind**, meaning 'twist' or 'turn', are both *wound*, pronounced /wownd/: *He has wound both clocks.* The Simple Present tense of the verb **wound** meaning 'injure' is pronounced /woond/.

-wise, -ways

The suffix **-wise** is used in two different ways. It is used as an adjectival ending meaning 'in this direction': *The M25 is completely blocked by an accident at exit 17 in the clockwise direction.* Less commonly, *-wise* has an adjectival meaning 'wise to the ways of something': *If the bard was weather-wise, who made the grand old ballad…*; *Bill is streetwise.*

When you want to add the meaning 'in this direction', or 'in this manner', you can use either *-wise* or the variant form *-ways* as an adverbial ending: *He scuttled sideways from the room; It had been folded once lengthwise.*

The addition of **-wise** to a noun as a replacement for a lengthier phrase, e.g. *such as, as far as something is concerned*, while becoming increasingly common, is considered unacceptable by most careful speakers and writers: *It's been a lovely day as far as the weather's concerned* is preferable to *It's been a lovely day weatherwise*. Other examples of similar compounds using *-wise* that should be avoided include *moneywise, travelwise, investmentwise*, and *safetywise*.

wish, want

Avoid using **wish** when **want** is intended. The use of *wish* with this meaning has become a feature of the excessively polite style known as genteelism. It makes the speaker sound servile without impressing anyone: *The Party would not want* [not *wish*] *us to place a premium on an unorthodox style; I want* [not *wish*] *to introduce George Burton*.

with-

When **with-** is used as a prefix the resulting words are written without a hyphen, e.g. *withstand, withhold,* (note that *withhold* has a double *h*).

without

The most common use of **without** is as a preposition meaning 'not having': *I can only speak as a married man without children*. Another use is to show that an action is 'not accompanied' by a following action: *He said he would take me for a ride without being asked; He turned on the lamp so that he could find his way without bumping into anything*. When a sentence has this meaning, the second clause usually contains a present participle

(*…without being asked; …without bumping into….*)

The use of **without** to mean 'on the outside of' as in, *…without the city walls,* is not part of standard usage in British English, but *without* can be used as a very formal adverb meaning 'outside': *He is standing without.* It is much less used than *within,* which itself is quite formal. Scots has the related preposition *outwith* meaning 'outside'.

When *without* is used to replace *unless* it is nonstandard: *I won't do it unless* [not *without*] *you tell me to.*

woman ⇒ **lady**

wonder

The adjective form *wondrous,* derived from **wonder,** does not keep the *e.*

won't, wont

The abbreviation for *will not* is **won't.** The spelling **wont** belongs to a very literary and little used adjective (and noun) meaning 'accustomed'. The adjective always follows the verb *be: He was wont to take immediate and drastic action; I was talking to them as I was wont.* When *wont* is a noun it cannot be modified by an adjective: *She is, as is the wont of dedicated people, self-willed.*

wool

Wool has two adjective forms; each has a different meaning. *Woolly* means 'like wool'; *woollen* means 'made of wool'. The British spellings have a double *l.* In American English both words have a single *l.*

work ⇒ **wrought**

worse, worsen

The word **worse** is the comparative of **bad,** which gives us the sequence *bad, worse, (the) worst.*

There is an archaic word *worser* but this form is not part of modern English usage. If we want to say that something is *growing worse* we can use the verb **worsen**: *The weather steadily worsened.*

worth, worthwhile

If **worth** is followed by a present participle it is not used with -*while*: *worth repeating; worth saying; worth spending.* Traditionally, when **worthwhile** is used as an adjective in front of a noun, it is written as a single word: *...a very worthwhile contribution; ...a worthwhile precaution.* Other uses were then written as two words: *It has proved worth while; It has all been worth while.* This is no longer a strictly followed rule, so you can write: *It had been worthwhile to come here,* but you may wish to observe the older rule in formal writing.

There is a rather formal expression that places a possessive pronoun between *worth* and *while*: *It will be well worth your while to track down these treasures.* ⇒ **value**

would ⇒ will ⇒ should

wouldn't, I wouldn't know

I wouldn't know as a replacement for *I don't know*, always sounds rather arrogant. The overtones of this phrase come from the use of *would*, which suggests that the speaker wishes to place at a distance his or her connection with the situation.

wrapped ⇒ rap

-wright

The spelling of the suffix **-wright** is often confused with -*write* in *playwright*. This ending is used because we treat the writer as a special sort of craftsman, for instance, like a *wheelwright* or a *shipwright*.

wring, ring

The verb **wring** is used for the action of squeezing or twisting something. The verb **ring** is used when you make a bell or a similar item give out a sound.

The past forms of these two verbs are often confused.

The verb **wring** has a Simple Past tense and a past participle that are both spelled *wrung*: *I thanked him for his kindness and wrung his hand; I would have wrung his fat neck there and then.* For **ring** we should write and say: *He rang the bell* in the Simple Past and *He has rung the bell* when we are using the past participle, but sometimes you will hear *rung* used for both of them. This is probably because the user is being confused by the pronunciation of the past forms of *wring*.

write

In British English we use **write** followed directly by the object if it is something like a letter that we are writing: *He could never write plays; I never write letters.*

When we have the person receiving it in mind, we can either use the construction: *I will write Howard a note* or *I will write to Howard* or, using *to* after the object of the verb **write**, *I don't have time to write a note to Howard.*

In American English it is possible to use *write* without *to* in the second of these cases, as in, *I will write Phil.* This would not be acceptable in British English.

wrought, worked

The usual Simple Past tense and past participle form of the verb **work** is **worked**. **Wrought** is an archaic past form of the same verb and as such will often be found in older literature. It is preserved in expressions like *wrought iron* and *wrought up* (this has its equivalent in *worked up*), but otherwise, avoid using it.

X Y Z

-x

There are a few English words that end in **-x** in the singular. The plural form of each word depends on the origin and history of the word. *Ox* has the Old English **-en** plural form, while *fox* and *box* have an **-es** plural. A word derived from Latin may have both a Latin-based plural and an ordinary plural, e.g. *index* has *indices* or *indexes*.

The word *prix*, from French, has no special plural ending in that language, i.e. the French plural of *Grand Prix* is *Grands Prix*. It is the same in English if the French model for the plural is followed, but if an English model has been used, it can be seen written *Grand Prixs* .

Because of the number of variations, it is always advisable to check in a dictionary for the appropriate plural form.

Xerox™

Xerox is one of a small group of trade names strongly associated with a process or an activity. It is common to read or hear a phrase like: *I enclose a Xerox of the records* when the user simply means 'copy'.

Frequently the word is used without a capital letter: *He looked at xerox copies from the Berlin document centre.* The name Xerox is copyright and should therefore be used with a capital letter.

In a critical context, if the machine used was not an actual Xerox, it is advisable to substitute *copy* or *photocopy.*

⇒ **trade names**

Xmas

Xmas is a very common abbreviation for *Christmas*. It is usually associated with the commercial aspects of the season and not with the religious festival. Some Christians dislike the abbreviation and it should not be used in personal messages on cards etc. The pronunciation /**eks**-mas/ is only used jocularly.

yank, yankee

The word **yank** (or **yankee**) is the slang term for any American and belongs with *limey, frog, wop, kraut*, etc. in a group of nationality terms that are used to indicate general antipathy. In America, *yankee* is an old Civil War term meaning 'an inhabitant of the Northern states' and it is sometimes still used with this particular sense.

ye

The use of **ye** in 'old-fashioned' shop names such as *Ye Olde Tea Shoppe* is a harmless eccentricity. The form *ye* is, historically, one form of *you*. Its use in place of *the* results from an even older confusion between the letter *y* and an obsolete letter (called *thorn*) that looked like *y* when it was written hastily, but was in fact the equivalent of *th*.

yeah

This is an informal form of *yes*. It is fundamentally the *yes* form without the final consonant, that is, it is an unfinished form. Its use is often regarded as sloppy or vulgar but its function is the same as the drawled pronunciation of *yes*: it is used when a speaker is reflecting on a reply or offering a tentative agreement.

year

In writing spans of years, it is important to choose a style that avoids ambiguity. The practice adopted in *Collins*

English Dictionary is, in four-figure dates, to specify only the last two digits of the second date if it falls within the same century as the first: *1801–08; 1850–51.* Otherwise give both dates in full: *1899– 1901.* In writing three-figure BC dates, it is advisable to give both dates in full: *159–156 BC.* It is also advisable to specify BC or AD in years under 1000 unless the context makes this clear.

yoghurt, yogurt, yoghourt
This word is a relatively recent introduction. It has a number of acceptable spelling forms based on the original pronunciation. **Yoghurt** is the most common.

you know
The phrase *You know* is a filler. It is often overused and becomes a mark of sloppy or ill thought-out speech. Users should check that it has not become an unconscious habit. ⇒ **in fact**

your, you're
When these words are written down, they constitute a frequent problem for many users because they sound the same. The form **your** is used as the possessive determiner, 'belonging to you': *Is this your towel?* The form **you're** is not one word but two. It is the contracted form of *you are* and is the usual spoken form: *I can't believe you're serious.*

yours
Yours is the possessive pronoun form of the second person. It does not have an apostrophe in front of the *s*: *Am I supposed to believe that this drawing is yours?*

Yours sincerely, Yours faithfully ⇒ letter writing

youse, you-all

The use of **youse** is not part of standard English. It is, however, well established in some Northern dialects of English and serves the very useful function of distinguishing between singular and plural forms of the pronoun *you*: *Listen youse. I want to talk seriously.*

You-all is a Southern American form similar to *youse* in British English and fills the same gap in standard usage. It is used when referring to more than one person: *I'm returning my speaker's fee to the society, with the hope that you-all can make better use of it.* The use of *youse* is seen by purist British speakers as a mark of uneducated speech (although it is not) but *you-all* is more widely acceptable in American English.

z

The British English pronunciation for the letter *z* is /zed/. This spoils some puns and rhymes found in American English, where the letter is called /zee/, e.g. *An EZ Rider.*

zealous, devout

The adjective **zealous** is used to describe an excessive and fanatical devotion. By extension it refers to any sort of thorough attention to the letter of duty: *'Let us begin at the beginning,' said the D.H.C. and the more zealous students recorded this intention in their notebooks.* Someone who is **devout** has a sincere, heartfelt religious belief.

zebra

The pronunciation normally used in British English has an *e* sound that rhymes with *web*. The American pronunciation favours an *e* sound that rhymes with *sea*. The plural can be *zebra* or *zebras*.

zero, nought, O

The name **zero** for the symbol 0 is usually found in a scientific context. The plural can be *zero* or *zeroes*. When counting or numbering, **nought** is more usual: *There should be another nought in that figure.* When giving a telephone number in British English, it is common to use the name of the letter **O** /oh/ instead of *nought* or *zero*.

zillion

A **zillion** is not a real number but an expression meaning 'an uncountably large number'. ⇒ **trillion**

Zimmer™

A **Zimmer** is the more usual name for a *walking frame* as used by elderly people.

zoology

The pronunciation of **zoology** has been steadily changing from /zo-**ol**-og-y/, rhyming with *so*, to /zoo-**ol**-og-y/ as in *zoo*. Purists object to the latter pronunciation but it is now the normal form and is not susceptible to challenge.

zucchini, courgette

These words are interchangeable; they refer to the same vegetable. In Britain, *courgette* is the more common term; *zucchini* is standard in American English.